WOMEN'S
ACTION
ALMANAC

WOMEN'S ACTION ALMANAC

A COMPLETE RESOURCE GUIDE

By the WOMEN'S ACTION ALLIANCE
Edited by JANE WILLIAMSON,
DIANE WINSTON *and*
WANDA WOOTEN

WILLIAM MORROW AND COMPANY, INC.
NEW YORK 1979

Library of Congress Cataloging in Publication Data

Women's Action Alliance.
  Women's action almanac.

  Includes bibliographies and index.
  1. Women—United States—Dictionaries. 2. Women—United States—Societies and clubs. 3. Women—Information services—United States. 4. Reference books—Women—Bibliography. I. Williamson, Jane. II. Winston, Diane. III. Wooten, Wanda. IV. Title.
HQ1115.W64   1980   362.8   79-16326
ISBN 0-688-03525-6
ISBN 0-688-08525-3 pbk.

Book Design by Carl Weiss
Picture Research by Flavia Rando, PICTUREBOOK PHOTORESEARCH

Printed in the United States of America

First Edition
1 2 3 4 5 6 7 8 9 10

Grateful acknowledgment is made for permission to reprint:

"Abortion: Questions and Answers." Reprinted by permission of National Abortion Rights Action League, 825 15th St. N.W., Washington, D.C. 20005.

"Women's Bookstores." Reprinted by permission of Womanbooks, 201 West 92nd St., New York, N.Y. 10025.

"How to Examine Your Breasts." Reprinted by permission of the American Cancer Society, 777 Third Ave., New York, N.Y. 10017.

"National Network of Local Resource Centers." Reprinted by permission of Catalyst, 14 East 60th St., New York, N.Y. 10022.

"Roster of Commissions for Women." Reprinted by permission of the National Association of Commissions for Women, 926 J St., Sacramento, Calif. 95814.

"Feminist Federal Credit Unions," from *Directory of Financial Aids for Women.* Reprinted by permission of Reference Service Press, 9023 Alcott St., Los Angeles, Calif. 90035.

"What Creditors May Ask," from *New Credit Rights for Women.* Reprinted by permission of Consumer Credit Project, 261 Kimberley, Barrington, Ill. 60010.

"What You Can Do to Help Women Offenders," from *From Convict to Citizen.* Reprinted by permission of District of Columbia Commission on the Status of Women, #204 District Bldg., Washington, D.C. 20004.

"How Will the ERA affect . . ." Reprinted by permission of Common Cause, 2030 M St. N.W., Washington, D.C. 20036.

"Vitamin Therapy for Menopausal Symptoms," from *Women and the Crisis in Sex Hormones* by Barbara Seaman. Reprinted by permission of Rawson, Wade Publishers, 630 Third Ave., New York, N.Y. 10017.

"Your Rights as a Patient," from *Women's Health Care* by Belita Cowan. Reprinted by permission of Anshen Publishing, 556 2nd Ave., Ann Arbor, MI 48103.

"Help Wanted: Homemakers," from the July 1972 issue of *Ms.* magazine. Reprinted by permission of *Ms.* magazine.

"Facilities with Incest Treatment Programs," from *Kiss Daddy Goodnight* by Louise Armstrong. Reprinted by permission of Hawthorn Books. Copyright 1978 by Louise Armstrong.

"Types of Insurance and How They Discriminate Against Women," from *Sex Discrimination in Insurance: A Guide for Women* by Ruth Brannon, Naomi Naierman and Beverly Wahl. Reprinted by permission of Women's Equity Action League, 805 15th St. N.W., Washington, D.C. 20009.

"Chronology: Female Participation in the American Trade Union Movement," from *Workers and Allies.* Reprinted by permission of the Smithsonian Institution Press, 1000 Jefferson Dr. S.W., Washington, D.C.

"How to Avoid Sexism," from *How to Avoid Sexism* by Merriellyn Kett and Virginia Underwood. Reprinted by permission of Lawrence Ragan Communications, 407 S. Dearborn, Chicago, Ill. 60605.

"Overlap of Employment Coverage in Federal Laws and Regulations Concerning Sex Discrimination in Educational Institutions." Reprinted by permission of Women's Equity Action League, 805 15th St. N.W., Washington, D.C. 20005.

"Gay Rights Protection in the U.S." Reprinted by permission of National Gay Task Force, 80 Fifth Ave., New York, N.Y. 10011.

"The American Family," from the August 1978 issue of *Ms.* magazine. Reprinted by permission of *Ms.* magazine.

"Materials Questionnaire." Reprinted by permission of the Superintendent of Public Instruction, Old Capitol Bldg., Olympia, Wash. 98504.

"Denominations Ordaining Women to the Full Ministry," from *Women Ministers in 1977* by Constant Jacquet. Reprinted by permission of National Council of the Churches of Christ, 475 Riverside Dr., New York, N.Y. 10027.

"How to Move Women into Appointive Office." Reprinted by permission of Women's Education Resources, University of Wisconsin/Extension, 610 Langdon St., Madison, Wis. 43706.

"The Gurus of the New Right Maintain a Tight Web of Relationships," reprinted from the second quarter 1978 issue of *Viewpoint*. Reprinted by permission of the Industrial Union Dept., AFL-CIO, 815 16th St. N.W., Washington, D.C. 20006.

"Rural Women in Profile," from *Educational Needs of Rural Women and Girls*. Reprinted by permission of National Advisory Council on Women's Educational Programs, 1832 M St. N.W., Washington, D.C. 20036.

"Physiological Differences Between the Sexes," from *What Constitutes Equality for Women in Sports*. Reprinted by permission of Project on the Status and Education of Women, Association of American Colleges, 1818 R St. N.W., Washington, D.C. 20009.

"Sterilization Abuse: The Law," from *Sterilization: What You Need to Know Before Making a Decision*. Reprinted by permission of Committee to End Sterilization Abuse, P.O. Box A244, Cooper Sta., New York, N.Y. 10003.

"Anyone's Guide to Filing a Title IX Complaint." Reprinted by permission of Project on Equal Education Rights, 1029 Vermont Ave. N.W., Washington, D.C. 20005.

"Title IX Enforcement Record," from *Stalled at the Start: Government Action on Sex Bias in the Schools*. Reprinted by permission of Project on Equal Education Rights, 1029 Vermont Ave. N.W., Washington, D.C. 20005.

"Veteran's Preference." Reprinted by permission of Federally Employed Women, 481 National Press Bldg., Washington, D.C. 20045.

"Glossary of Substitute Terminology." Reprinted by permission of Task Force on Equality of Women in Judaism, New York Federation of Reform Synagogues, Union of American Hebrew Congregations, 838 Fifth Ave., New York, N.Y. 10021.

"Attitudes Toward Women and the ERA," from *ERA Campaign Paying Off* by Louis Harris. Reprinted by permission of Louis Harris and Associates, 630 Fifth Ave., New York, N.Y. 10020.

ACKNOWLEDGMENTS

We were privileged to work on this project with many talented and generous people. First, we would like to thank our agent, Frances Goldin, for helping us to make this a "real" book. Claudette Kulkarni's skilled design of the organization questionnaire made compiling the directory information possible. Betty Rosen was indispensable at the rewrite stage of the directory compilation. Maryann Turner not only took over information services at the Alliance, freeing our time for the book, but also helped compile the women's centers list. Without the hard work and talent of picture researcher Flavia Rando, the book would lack the life given it by the excellent photographs. Our editor, Julie Weiner, has been wonderful. She has been enthusiastic from the beginning, and has provided sisterly criticism and support. We are grateful to typists Marion Shore and Marcelle West. Finally, a number of friends pitched in at the eleventh hour; for this we would like to thank Larayne Ewald, Robert Oppedisano, Lauren Rosenbloom, Gloria Slaughter and the research staff of *Ms.* magazine.

In particular, we would like to thank the Merit Gasoline Foundation for their generous contribution which helped to finance the research from the early stages; we are very grateful to them.

CONTENTS

INTRODUCTION

The Women's Action Alliance was founded in 1971 as a national center for information on women's issues and programs. Since then, we have received tens of thousands of requests: What is the text of the ERA? How many women work? Whom do I call to make a Title IX complaint? Is there a women's organization working on sexual harassment on the job? My husband isn't keeping up with child support payments, what can I do? Can you recommend a women's newspaper for our public library?

The requests that come in every day cover a wide range of issues and come from many different constituencies with different needs. We get calls from women's organizations seeking information on current issues, addresses and phone numbers for sister organizations or help in finding research materials. We have been asked to supply background information on the ERA for an editorial in a national magazine, to prepare a list of minority women's groups for a corporate foundation, to provide the names of experts on women's issues for government hearings. And we have made countless service referrals to individual women all across the country. Despite the differing constituencies and needs, however, all these requests have one thing in common: they are all answered in the pages of this book.

Publishing a directory of national women's organizations has been part of the Alliance's information services since its founding. With this edition, we have done something new. *Women's Action Almanac* is designed to do, in print and in one place, what we do every day: provide answers to questions on women's issues and programs. The *Almanac* is in two parts. First are subject entries on 84 issues and topics of concern to women. In compiling these entries, we kept our information service experience strongly in mind, and developed a unique format that responds to the needs of *all* our constituencies. In every case we have tried to summarize the prevailing feminist perspective. Each entry includes background information, historical context, current status, and up-to-date statistics. A list of pertinent national women's organizations (and in some cases local women's organizations) follows each entry. A selection of print resources, including those we found most useful in compiling the text, concludes each entry. Anyone searching for more information on a topic will find it in the sources listed. Frequently, we have also provided charts, tables, graphs, how-to guides or other aids for action.

The second half of the book is a directory of national women's organizations and women's caucuses or divisions of national organizations. Here you will find full information for all the national groups in the subject entries. The goals of each organization are set forth, often in its own words, as is a description of its programs and activities.

We hope this book finds its way onto your desk—no matter what your work or concerns—for we know it will be helpful. If by chance we've missed you, your organization or an issue close to your heart, please let us know; we are always anxious to learn more. With your help, the next edition of *Women's Action Almanac* will be that much better.

SUBJECT
ENTRIES

ABORTION

ABORTION IS A COMPLICATED, MULTI-FACETED ISSUE THAT HAS BEEN THE focus of more controversy than perhaps any other issue. It has medical, legal, and philosophical implications. Like birth control, it is a fundamental demand of the women's movement; control over one's body and reproductive life is essential to all other freedoms.

Laws controlling access to abortion were not enacted in the United States until the late nineteenth century. Until then, abortions had been fairly common, terminating approximately one out of five pregnancies. The laws were enacted to protect the life and health of the woman. Medical science was not advanced and primitive abortion procedures were quite dangerous.

In the late 1960's, sentiment against these laws began to develop. Women's groups built an uneasy alliance, maintained to this day, with population control groups to demand the repeal of abortion laws. Although their motives were different—indeed, contradictory—they sought the same ends.

New York State was the first. In 1969, the state legislature liberalized the law and hundreds of thousands of women traveled to New York each year to use the services of abortion clinics. The new vacuum aspiration method made abortion one of the easiest—and safest—of medical procedures. Many of the clinics provided counseling and psychological support for their clients. Others were motivated more by profit than anything else.

Women in other states began to organize class-action suits attempting to have state laws prohibiting abortion struck down. A national organization—the Women's National Abortion Action Coalition—was founded in 1971 and soon had chapters all across the country. Then, two of the state class-action suits made it to the Supreme Court—those launched in Texas and Georgia—and in January of 1973 the Court declared the anti-abortion laws unconstitutional. The decision said that during the first trimester, the state cannot bar any woman from obtaining an abortion from a licensed physician; in the second trimester, the state can regulate the abortion procedure only if such regulations relate to the preservation and protection of the woman's health; in the third trimester, the state can regulate or even prohibit all abortions except those necessary to save the woman's life or protect her health.

It is estimated that in the first year after the Supreme Court decision, 700,000 legal abortions were performed. An additional 300,000 to 700,000 *illegal* abortions were also performed due to ignorance of the law or lack of medical services.

But the work on behalf of free choice did not go unopposed. As early as 1971, anti-abortion forces began stirring up opposition. In 1976 alone, more than a hundred dioceses of the Roman Catholic Church contributed nearly $500,000 to the National Committee for a Human Life Amendment. Believing that abortion is murder and attempting to impose that definition on everyone, anti-abortionists have been ruthless. In the early days, their tactics were merely tasteless and sensational—for example, displaying gigantic, full-color photos of aborted fetuses. Today, they are better organized, well financed and relentless. They have harassed the staff of abortion clinics and threatened the patients. They are responsible for more than a dozen fire bombings of abortion clinics across the

A demonstration in New York City for abortion rights. Catholic women are highly visible among organizers and supporters of abortion rights at the same time the Church finances the anti-abortion movement. © *Suzanne Williamson*

country. And they have developed tremendous political clout on all levels—local, state and national.

In 1977 they succeeded in getting the Hyde Amendment to the HEW/Labor appropriations bill through Congress. The amendment prohibits the use of federal funds for Medicaid abortions. Unfortunately, the constitutionality of this regulation has been upheld. And, it passed the Congress again in 1978 with little trouble. The intent of the antichoice forces is not to discriminate against poor women, but to deny all women the right to abortion. The compulsory pregnancy advocates view the Hyde Amendment as merely the first step.

Women's groups have reorganized all across the country and are now working on many fronts to restore Medicaid funding and insure the right to legal abortion for all. Meanwhile, the so-called "right to life" groups are attempting to call a constitutional convention for the purpose of passing an anti-abortion amendment. So far, fourteen out of the required thirty-five state legislatures have called for such a measure. This is especially dangerous in light of the recent growth of the far right and the confusion over what a constitutional convention can do.

Before the Supreme Court decision, more than 1,000,000 illegal abortions were performed each year. Many of the women who sought those abortions died or suffered permanent physical damage. That is an era to which we must not return. The issue of abortion is one of the greatest challenges facing the women's movement today.

See also: Birth Control
Legal Status
Right-wing Attacks
Sterilization Abuse

Organizations:

American Civil Liberties Union
Reproductive Freedom Project
22 East 40th Street
New York, NY 10016

Catholics for a Free Choice
201 Massachusetts Avenue N.E.
Washington, DC 20002

Center for Constitutional Rights
Women's Rights Project
853 Broadway
New York, NY 10003

Ms. Foundation
Pro-Choice Project for Reproductive
Freedom
370 Lexington Avenue
New York, NY 10017

National Abortion Federation
110 East 59th Street
New York, NY 10022

National Abortion Rights Action League
825 15th Street N.W.
Washington, DC 20005

Planned Parenthood Federation of
America
810 Seventh Avenue
New York, NY 10019

Religious Coalition for Abortion Rights
100 Maryland Avenue N.E.
Washington, DC 20002

Rosie Jimenez Fund
711 San Antonio Street
Austin, TX 78701

Resources

Abortion and Alternatives, by Marjory Skowronski. Millbrae: Les Femmes, 1977.
Order from: Les Femmes Publishing, 231 Adrian Road, Millbrae, CA 94030.
A thoughtful discussion of abortion, this book includes a realistic look at
alternatives and an important chapter on being "Young, Pregnant and Scared."

Abortion in America, by James C. Mohr. New York: Oxford University Press,
1978.
A history of abortion policy and laws in America from 1800 to the present, the
book concentrates on the development of state laws against abortion, enumerates
the reasons for changes in social policy and state laws affecting abortion rights,
and identifies the leading organizers of the anti-abortion movement at the turn of
the century.

*Provisional Estimates of Abortion Need and Services in the Year Following the
Supreme Court Decision,* prepared by Alan Guttmacher Institute. New York,
1975. Order from: The Alan Guttmacher Institute, Planned Parenthood
Federation of America, 515 Madison Avenue, New York, NY 10022.
This booklet provides a statistical analysis of abortion needs and services for
each state and metropolitan area in the United States.

♀ ABORTION: QUESTIONS AND ANSWERS ♀

What are the health benefits of legal abortion?   By eliminating the horror of
criminal, back-alley abortion and the brutality of self-induced abortion, legalized abortion has saved countless women from injury and death.

Abortion-related deaths drop dramatically. It is impossible to know how
many deaths due to abortion occurred prior to legalization, as the cause of death
was not always accurately reported. Since the Department of Health, Education
and Welfare has been collecting data, the number of deaths due to illegal

procedures has dropped markedly as fewer are performed, while deaths from legal abortion are rare in spite of the fact that more legal abortions are performed each year.

An abortion at eight weeks or less is 25 times safer (maternal mortality) than childbirth. 87.9 percent of all abortions are performed at 12 weeks or less, when the risk is also far less than continuing pregnancy. The 1975 mortality rate for legal curettage abortion at 12 weeks or less was 1.7 per 100,000 abortions, compared to 12.0 deaths per 100,000 live births for 1975. The total mortality rate for legal abortions is 3.2 per 100,000. Only 0.4 percent of all abortions are performed involving major surgery. These late abortions are associated with the highest death rate (42.6 deaths per 100,000 late abortions, 1972–1975) because major surgery is necessary. *But all other curettage abortions are 5 to 8 times safer than carrying a pregnancy to term.*

The National Academy of Sciences, in *Legalized Abortion and the Public Health* (1975), states, "The frequency of medical complications due to illegal abortions cannot be calculated precisely, but the trend in these complications can be estimated from the number of hospital admissions due to septic and incomplete abortion . . . The number of such admissions in New York City's municipal hospitals declined from 6,524 in 1969 to 3,253 in 1973; most restrictions on legal abortion in New York City were lifted in July of 1970. In Los Angeles, the number of reported hospital admissions for septic abortions declined from 559 in 1969 to 119 in 1971."

Very young women and poor women are apt to have less prenatal care and therefore are at greater risk for premature delivery. They and others with medical problems *also* stand the greatest risk of having unhealthy infants. Where these women have had the option of legal abortion, there has been a decline in the infant mortality rate. For example, in New York City in 1969, before abortion was legal the infant mortality rate was 24.4 per 1,000 live births, compared with 19.9 in 1973 and 19.6 in 1975.

What are the psychological effects of legal abortion? Although it may be a stressful experience, there is no indication that abortion leads to any detectable increase in the incidence of mental illness. Any depression or guilt feelings associated with legal abortion are described as mild. One study shows an incidence of post-abortion psychosis ranging from only 0.2 to 0.4 per 1,000 legal abortions as compared to a rate for postpartum psychosis of 1 to 2 per 1,000 deliveries. Another study states: "Recent experience in the U. S. indicates clearly that well motivated women with no previous history of psychiatric disorder will emerge from a legal abortion performed under medical conditions with no psychiatric sequelae. On the contrary, most women report only a feeling of unalloyed relief."

If contraception is available, why is abortion necessary? Unfortunately, there is no foolproof method of preventing conception, and not all women have access to contraceptive drugs, devices and information. At least 3.5 million low-income women do not have access to family planning assistance. One out of three married couples *practicing birth control* over a five year period have unwanted pregnancies. To prevent the tragedies caused by the birth of unwanted children, abortion is needed as a backup when contraception fails or is not used.

How are abortions performed? SUCTION CURETTAGE—the cervix, the opening of the womb, is dilated; a small tube is inserted through the cervix and by suction, the uterus is gently emptied. 82.6 percent of all abortions are performed using this technique. SHARP CURETTAGE (D & C)—the cervix is dilated and the uterus is cleaned by gentle scraping with a spoon-shaped instrument, the curette. 8.4 percent of all abortions are done by this technique. DILATION AND EVACUATION (D & E)—this is a combination technique of both suction and D & C techniques. There is a growing acceptance of this technique after the first 12 weeks in reaction to evidence that it is safer for the woman than intrauterine instillation. This and other combination techniques comprise 2.4 percent of all abortions. INTRAUTERINE SALINE or PROSTAGLANDIN INJECTION or INSTILLATION—amniotic fluid is withdrawn from the uterus and replaced by salt or prostaglandin solution, which induces a miscarriage, usually within 12–24 hours. 6.2 percent of all abortions are done by this technique, used for later abortions. HYSTEROTOMY/HYSTERECTOMY—hysterotomy is a miniature Cesarean section by abdominal incision. Hysterectomy is removal of the uterus. Both are late abortion techniques, and comprise 0.4 percent of all abortions.

Who has abortions? In the U.S., in 1975:

Age	Percentage of legal abortions
under 15	1.5%
15–19	31.2%
20–24	31.6%
over 24	34.5%
unknown	1.2%

- 65.3% of the women were white and 31.0% nonwhite, with 3.7% unknown. The percentage of minority women seeking legal abortions has increased each year since 1971.
- 25.6% of women who had abortions were married.
- Despite the fact that the hierarchy of the Catholic Church is highly critical of legal abortion, evidence from several states indicates that Catholics are obtaining abortions in excess of their proportional representation in those states:

Estimates of the number of illegal abortions performed in the United States prior to legalization vary from a few hundred thousand to two million each year. Dr. Christopher Tietze of The Population Council estimates that at least one million abortions per year were performed in the 1960's.

The Alan Guttmacher Institute estimates that 900,000 legal abortions were performed in the United States in 1974 and that over one million were

Area	Percentage of abortion patients reported as Catholics	Percentage of Catholics in the population
Maryland	17.6	11.2
Colorado (Denver Hospital)	20.7	13.2
New York City (Elmhurst Hospital)	33.3	30.7
Connecticut (Yale-New Haven Hospital)	41.7	30.4
Hawaii	29.0	26.2
California (San Diego Planned Parenthood)	32.0	20.0

performed in 1975, yet 40 to 60 percent of women in need could not obtain abortions.

Don't Most People Support Legal Abortion?   All major national opinion polls demonstrate that most Americans think abortion is a personal decision to be made by a woman and her doctor.

• A *New York Times*/CBS News poll in February 1976 found 67% of Americans agree that "the right of a woman to have an abortion should be left entirely up to the woman and her doctor."
• A Knight-Ridder Newspaper survey in January 1976 found 81% of Americans agree "if a woman wants to have an abortion, that is a matter for her and her doctor to decide and the government should have nothing to do with it." [sic]
• A DeVries & Associates poll in December 1974, commissioned by the National Conference of Catholic Bishops, found disagreement from all religious groups with the statement "abortion should not be allowed under any circumstances":

	Total	Catholic	Protestant	Jewish
Strongly agree	15.8%	22.3%	14.6%	2.6%
Mildly agree	7.8%	9.0%	7.9%	3.6%
Mildly disagree	21.7%	22.7%	23.2%	4.5%
Strongly disagree	50.5%	42.0%	49.5%	86.9%
Not sure	4.2%	4.0%	4.8%	2.4%

What is the Religious View on Abortion?   Almost all major Protestant and Jewish groups have position statements in support of legalized abortion and view efforts to outlaw abortion as direct infringement of the First Amendment right to religious freedom. Many belong to the Religious Coalition for Abortion Rights. The hierarchy of the Roman Catholic Church actively works against abortion through its lobbying arm, the National Committee for a Human Life

Amendment, Inc., in spite of several national polls documenting support from a majority of Catholics for the right to choose abortion. A few small Protestant denominations and Orthodox Judaism join the Catholic Church in opposing abortion in certain circumstances.

Excerpted from "Abortion: Questions and Answers," a brochure prepared by National Abortion Rights Action League.

AFFIRMATIVE ACTION

AFFIRMATIVE ACTION. THOSE ARE TWO OF THE MOST LOADED WORDS TO COME out of the movement for equal opportunity in education and employment. It has been difficult for many people to understand just what affirmative action is, what it means, what it does. Unfortunately, it has become a catchall term for so many different activities that it is difficult to know what is meant by anyone who uses it.

Specifically, the laws on affirmative action apply in two areas: employment (recruitment, hiring, promotion) and admissions to institutions of higher education. Affirmative action as it relates to employment was set forth in Executive Order 11246/11375 and covers any federal contractor or subcontractor receiving monies in excess of $10,000. Several laws regulate college and university admissions. Title IX of the Education Amendments of 1972 is the most comprehensive; it states simply: "No person . . . shall, on the basis of sex, be excluded from participation in, be denied the benefits of, or be subjected to discrimination under any education program or activity receiving Federal financial assistance." The Executive Order is enforced by the Office of Federal Contract Compliance. Title IX's enforcement body is the Office for Civil Rights in the Department of Health, Education and Welfare.

Affirmative action is complicated and confusing because it goes beyond simple nondiscrimination. It's not sufficient for employers and educational institutions to cease discriminatory practices: they must go beyond that neutral stance and take positive steps to redress past discrimination. They must actively recruit, employ, and promote members of "affected classes"—minorities and women. The written affirmative action plans required of federal contractors must include, when appropriate, "specific goals and timetables for the prompt achievement of full and equal employment opportunity."

How does an employer know if he or she is meeting affirmative action guidelines? There is a simple formula to follow. Let's say an employer is hiring economists. The number of women economists employed by the institution should be consistent with their availability in the population. Recent statistics indicate that 13.1% of economists are women, so if there are substantially fewer than that on the employer's staff, affirmative action is needed. The employer must develop a plan with goals and timetables to bring the percentage of women economists employed by the firm up to 13.1%.

It is over the question of how to increase the employment opportunities of women and minorities—the issue of instituting and meeting goals—that the major problems and disagreements arise. Some people believe affirmative action requires preference in hiring or school admissions, others believe it forbids it.

What if "goals" are not met? Are "quotas"—a prescribed number of reserved places—allowable or illegal? In a tight job market such problems intensify, and there has been a hue and cry from white males—charges of "reverse discrimination." Suits are now being brought claiming that the use of goals and quotas denies equal access to education and jobs.

The conflict raised by so-called "reverse discrimination" suits is between Executive Order 11246 and Title VII, between efforts to redress discrimination against groups and efforts to protect individuals. The Order requires employers to take positive steps to alleviate the effects of past discrimination and Title VII prohibits discrimination in employment on account of sex, race, color, religion or national origin. If a white male loses a job to a minority male or a woman because of a sex- and/or race-conscious affirmative action plan, isn't he entitled to sue under Title VII?

The well-known Bakke case is an example of a "reverse discrimination" case related to education. As part of a voluntary affirmative action plan, the University of California medical school reserved sixteen places for minorities in the entering class. When Allan Bakke, a white male, was denied admission, he sued the University for race discrimination. The lower courts decided in favor of the University, but Bakke appealed to the Supreme Court. In a highly divided decision, the Court contributed little to clear the air. While they ordered the University of California to admit Bakke, they also ruled in favor of race as a factor in admissions programs. They did say that strict numerical quotas were illegal.

A related case, this one concerning employment opportunities, is *Weber* v. *Kaiser Aluminum and United Steelworkers*. That suit is before the Supreme Court as of this writing. Because of requirements that skilled workers have previous experience, blacks and women had been effectively cut out of jobs in Kaiser plants. In 1974, the United Steelworkers had negotiated a plan requiring that half of all trainee positions be held for minorities and women until certain modest goals were met. Brian Weber, a white male, charged Kaiser with reverse discrimination. If his case succeeds, this would threaten the right of unions to negotiate affirmative action plans for workers.

In December of 1978, the Equal Employment Opportunity Commission issued guidelines which attempt to deal with these conflicts. The guidelines assert that it is "fundamentally unfair" to require affirmative action plans on the one hand, while leaving the employer open to suit under Title VII on the other. The Commission has attempted to save employers from the untenable "damned if you do, damned if you don't" position, *and* reaffirm the commitment to equal employment opportunity. The Commission wishes to discharge its duty of enforcing Title VII without obliterating the affirmative action requirements of Executive Order 11246.

First of all, the Commission stated flatly that "there is no separate concept under Title VII of 'reverse discrimination.'" Secondly, any suit brought against an affirmative action plan that complies with EEOC guidelines will not receive a "reasonable cause" ruling. That is, it will not be found to violate Title VII. This supplies employers and unions with the protection they need to proceed with affirmative action plans. To help clarify the situation, a new section was added; it is reprinted below with a summary of the guidelines.

While the legal situation is currently confused, where the discrimination lies is not. A look at the statistics in the education and employment sections of this book should put to rest any fears of massive discrimination against white males. But the argument has not—and probably will not—end there. The EEOC guidelines are crucial, and the Supreme Court's decision in the Weber case will further clarify the parameters. But the struggle over equality in employment will not be ended quickly or easily.

See also: Earnings Gap
             Executive Order 11246/11375
             Title IX
             Title VII

Organizations:

American Association for Affirmative
  Action
c/o Betty Newcomb
Ball State University
Muncie, IN 47306

Equal Employment Opportunity
  Commission
2401 E Street N.W.
Washington, DC 20506

Office for Civil Rights
Department of Health, Education and
  Welfare

Washington, DC 20201
(for regional offices see Title IX)

Office of Federal Contract Compliance
Employment Standards Administration
Washington, DC 20210
(for regional offices see Executive Order
  11246/11375)

Women's Equity Action League
805 15th Street N.W.
Washington, DC 20005

Resources:

Academic Women, Sex Discrimination and the Law. New York: Commission on the Status of Women, Modern Language Association. Order from: MLA, 62 Fifth Avenue, New York, NY 10011.
This is a useful, brief guide to employment rights for the woman faculty member.

Affirmative Action and Equal Employment: A Guidebook for Employers. Washington: Equal Employment Opportunity Commission, 1974. This two-volume guide is no longer available. However, it and the *Resources for Affirmative Recruitment* listed below are being revised and will be issued in one volume. For information, write to the Equal Employment Opportunity Commission at the address above.

Affirmative Action: A Selected Bibliography, ed. by Catherine J. Matthews and Marnie Shea. Toronto: Research Library, Ontario Ministry of Labour, 1975. Order from: Research Library, Ontario Ministry of Labour, 400 University Avenue, Toronto, Ontario, Canada.

Affirmative Action Register. Order from: AAR, 8356 Olive Boulevard, St. Louis, MO 63132.
A monthly newsletter listing professional, managerial and administrative positions designed to inform potential candidates and assist employers.

Affirmative Action Resources. Washington: College and University Personnel

Association, 1976. Order from: CUPA, 11 Dupont Circle, Washington, DC 20036.

This pamphlet, in addition to listing sources of information for affirmative action, provides a general outline and guide to required procedures.

Equal Employment Opportunity: Recommended Publications and Information, ed. by G. R. Bruning. San Francisco: Fair Employment Practices Commission, 1974. Order from: Division of Fair Employment Practices, 455 Golden Ave., San Francisco, CA 94101.

Although it is somewhat dated, this pamphlet bibliography provides a good listing of key resources on equal employment opportunity.

Higher Education Guidelines: Executive Order 11246. Washington: Office for Civil Rights, Department of Health, Education and Welfare, 1972. Order from: OCR, Department of Health, Education and Welfare, Washington, DC 20201.

Although now somewhat out of date, this volume offers valuable assistance in understanding the basic precepts and requirements of affirmative action. For the college and university administrator.

Resources for Affirmative Recruitment. Washington: Equal Employment Opportunity Commission, 1975.

This guide to recruitment aids is being revised and will appear in one volume with *Affirmative Action and Equal Employment.* For information, write to the Equal Employment Opportunity Commission at the address above.

A Working Woman's Guide to Her Job Rights. Washington: Women's Bureau, Employment Standards Administration, Department of Labor, Washington, DC 20210.

This pamphlet includes information on a working woman's rights under several federal laws relevant to such issues as equal pay, retirement benefits, unemployment insurance, and others.

♀ AFFIRMATIVE ACTION GUIDELINES ♀

STATEMENT OF PURPOSE

Need for Guidelines. Since the passage of Title VII in 1964, many employers, labor organizations, and other persons subject to Title VII have changed their employment practices and systems to improve employment opportunities for minorities and women, and this must continue. These changes have been undertaken either on the initiative of the employer, labor organization, or other person subject to Title VII, or as a result of conciliation efforts under Title VII, action under Executive Order No. 11246, as amended, or under other Federal, state or local laws, or litigation. Many decisions taken pursuant to affirmative action plans or programs have been race, sex, or national origin conscious in order to achieve the Congressional purpose of providing equal employment opportunity. Occasionally, these actions have been challenged as inconsistent with Title VII, because they took into account race, sex, or national origin. This is the so-called "reverse discrimination" claim. In such a situation, both the affirmative action undertaken to improve the conditions of minorities and women, and the objection to that action, are based upon the principles of Title VII. Any uncertainty as to the meaning and application of Title VII in such situations threatens the accomplishment of the clear Congressional intent to encourage voluntary affirmative action. The Commission believes that by the enactment of Title VII Congress did not intend to expose those who comply with the Act to charges that they are violating the very statute they are seeking to implement. Such a result would immobilize or reduce the efforts of many who would otherwise take action to improve the opportunities of minorities and women without litigation, thus frustrating the Congressional intent to encourage voluntary action and increasing the prospect of Title VII litigation. The Commission believes that it is now necessary to clarify and harmonize the principles of Title VII in order to achieve these Congressional objectives and protect those employers, labor organizations, and other persons who comply with the principles of Title VII.

Purposes of Title VII. Congress enacted Title VII in order to improve the economic and social conditions of minorities and women by providing equality of opportunity in the work place. These conditions were part of a larger pattern of restriction, exclusion, discrimination, segregation, and inferior treatment of minorities and women in many areas of life.[1] The Legislative Histories of Title VII, the Equal Pay Act, and the Equal Employment Opportunity Act of 1972 contain extensive analyses of the higher unemployment rate, the lesser occupational status, and the consequent lower income levels of minorities and women.[2] The purpose of Executive Order No. 11246, as amended, is similar to the purpose of Title VII.

In response to these economic and social conditions, Congress, by passage of Title VII, established a national policy against discrimination in employment on grounds of race, color, religion, sex and national origin. In addition, Congress strongly encouraged employers, labor organizations, and other persons subject to Title VII (hereinafter referred to as "persons," see section 701(a) of the Act) to act on a voluntary basis to modify employment practices and systems which constituted barriers to equal employment opportunity, without awaiting litigation or formal government action. Conference, conciliation, and persuasion were the primary processes adopted by Congress in 1964, and reaffirmed in 1972, to achieve these objectives, with enforcement action through the courts or agencies as a supporting procedure where voluntary action did not take place and conciliation failed.

[1] Congress has also addressed these conditions in other laws, including the Equal Pay Act of 1963, P.L. 88-38, 77 Stat. 56 (1963), as amended; the other Titles of the Civil Rights Act of 1964, P.L. 88-352, 78 Stat. 241 (1964), as amended; the Voting Rights Act of 1965, P.L. 89-110, 79 Stat. 437 (1965), as amended; the Fair Housing Act of 1968, P.L. 90-284, Title VII, 82 Stat. 73, 81 (1968), as amended; the Educational Opportunity Act (Title IX), P.L. 92-318, 86 Stat. 373 (1972), as amended; and the Equal Employment Opportunity Act of 1972, P.L. 92-261, 86 Stat. 103 (1972), as amended.
[2] Equal Pay Act of 1963: S. Rep. No. 176, 88th Cong., 1st Sess., 1–2 (1963). Civil Rights Act of 1964: H.R. Rep. No. 914, pt. 2, 88th Cong., 1st Sess. (1971). Equal Employment Opportunity Act of 1972: H.R. Rep No. 92-238, 92nd Cong., 1st Sess. (1971); S. Rep. No. 92-415, 92nd Cong., 1st Sess. (1971). See also, Equal Employment Opportunity Commission, *Equal Employment Opportunity Report—1975, Job Patterns for Women in Private Industry (1977);* Equal Employment Opportunity Commission, *Minorities and Women in State and Local Government—1975*; United States Commission on Civil Rights, *Social Indicators of Equality for Minorities and Women* (1978).

Interpretation in Furtherance of Legislative Purpose. The principle of non-discrimination in employment because of race, color, religion, sex, or national origin, and the principle that each person subject to Title VII should take voluntary action to correct the effects of past discrimination and to prevent present and future discrimination without awaiting litigation, are mutually consistent and interdependent methods of addressing social and economic conditions which precipitated the enactment of Title VII. Voluntary affirmative action to improve opportunities for minorities and women must be encouraged and protected in order to carry out the Congressional intent embodied in Title VII.[3] Affirmative action under these principles means those actions appropriate to overcome the effects of past or present practices, policies, or other barriers to equal employment opportunity. Such voluntary affirmative action cannot be measured by the standard of whether it would have been required had there been litigation, for this standard would undermine the legislative purpose of first encouraging voluntary action without litigation. Rather persons subject to Title VII must be allowed flexibility in modifying employment systems and practices to comport with the purpose of Title VII. Correspondingly, Title VII must be construed to permit such voluntary action, and those taking such action should be afforded the protection against Title VII liability which the Commission is authorized to provide under section 713(b) (1).

Guidelines Interpret Title VII and Authorize Use of Section 713(b) (1). These Guidelines describe the circumstances in which persons subject to Title VII may take or agree upon action to improve employment opportunities of minorities and women, and describe the kinds of actions they may take which are consistent with Title VII. These Guidelines constitute the Commission's interpretation of Title VII and will be applied on the procession of claims of discrimination which involve voluntary affirmative action plans and programs. In addition, these Guidelines state the circumstances under which the Commission will recognize that a person subject to Title VII is entitled to assert that actions were taken "in good faith, in conformity with, and in reliance upon a written interpretation or opinion of the Commission," including reliance upon the interpretation and opinion contained in these Guidelines, and thereby invoke the protection of section 713(b) (1) of Title VII.

Review of Existing Plans Recommended. Only affirmative action plans or programs adopted in good faith, in conformity with, and in reliance upon these Guidelines can receive the full protection of these Guidelines, including the section 713(b) (1) defense. Therefore, persons subject to Title VII who have existing affirmative action plans, programs, or agreements are encouraged to review them in light of these Guidelines, to modify them to the extent necessary to comply with these Guidelines, and to readopt or reaffirm them.

The major elements in the Guidelines are:

1. Employers and others covered by the law are obligated and encouraged to

---

[3] Affirmative action often improves opportunities for all members of the workforce, as where affirmative action includes the posting of notices of job vacancies. Similarly, the integration of previously segregated jobs means that all workers will be provided opportunities to enter jobs previously restricted. See, e.g., *EEOC* v. *AT&T,* 419 F. Supp. 1022 (E.D. Pa. 1976), *aff'd* 556 F. 2d 167 (3rd cir. 1977) *cert. denied,* 98 S.Ct. 3145 (1978).

eliminate barriers to equal employment opportunity without awaiting the action of any governmental agency or private party.

2. There is no violation of Title VII if:
   — an employer conducts a self-analysis of his employment system;
   — has a reasonable basis for concluding that affirmative action is appropriate; and
   — takes voluntary affirmative action that is reasonable in relation to the problems disclosed.

3. If EEOC receives a charge alleging discrimination and the employer asserts that the action complained of was taken pursuant to a voluntary plan or program meeting the standards of these Guidelines, the Commission will conduct an investigation and if it finds that the employer took the action in good faith, in conformity with and in reliance upon these Guidelines, the Commission will make a finding of no reasonable cause. Further, the Commission will state that such a finding is specifically made pursuant to Section 713 of Title VII so that the employer may rely upon it in dealing with allegations of so-called "reverse discrimination."

4. Illustrative of the type of affirmative action covered by these standards would be an affirmative action compliance program adopted by a government contractor subject to the Executive Order 11246. We specifically state that an employer who has adopted an affirmative action program to bring himself into compliance with the Executive Order may rely on that program in order to demonstrate that it meets the standards of these Guidelines.

5. The lawfulness of affirmative action does not depend upon an admission or proof that there was an actual violation of the law. The focus is on a reasonable basis for concluding that action is appropriate.

6. The affirmative action programs may be race, color, sex, and national origin-conscious and may include goals and timetables. Such goals and timetables must be reasonable under the facts and circumstances of each case which would include the problems identified in the self-analysis, the need for prompt elimination of those problems, availability of qualified applicants and the number of employment opportunities expected to be available.

7. The Guidelines apply to both private employers and government employers.

BATTERED WOMEN

"A WOMAN, A SPANIEL, A HICKORY TREE; THE MORE YOU BEAT 'EM THE BETTER they be." So goes the old adage. Unfortunately, it describes more than just folk wisdom, it describes centuries of common practice. "Rule of thumb," another old saying, comes from English Common Law. The rule in question regulated the size of stick a husband could use to beat his wife. If it were the width of his thumb or smaller, he was within his rights in using it on her. The rule of thumb may have passed out of the law, but wife-beating continues.

There are no adequate national statistics on the extent of wife-beating. It is, like rape, a severely underreported crime. It is also almost completely ignored by our legal system. However, the smattering of localized figures available suggest the national proportions. A 1970 study in Oakland, California, discovered that police responded to more than 16,000 so-called family disturbance calls within six months. In Kansas City, Missouri, domestic-related calls accounted for 82 percent of all disturbance calls in 1972. Wife-assault complaints totaled nearly 5000 in Detroit in 1972. Boston City Hospital reported that approximately 70 percent of emergency-room assault victims are women who have been attacked at home. New York City's Family Court handled 14,167 cases of wife abuse in 1972–73. The FBI suggests multiplying reported rapes by 10 to get an accurate total picture. Since wife abuse is reported even less frequently, the factor of 10 produces a low estimate. Yet at that conservative rate, there were more than 140,000 cases in one year in New York City alone. Nationally, the number of abused women figures in the millions.

Such staggering numbers are difficult to comprehend. One is left asking: How? Why? Maria Roy, founder of Abused Women's Aid in Crisis, answers the questions this way: "Why do women stay in these violent marriages? Because they have no place to go. Why do men beat their wives? Because nobody stops them."

At first, many battered women are too ashamed and frightened to ask for help. But research shows that if the woman takes no action after the first beating there are likely to be others. Battered women themselves may have a strong belief in marriage; they have a lot invested in their marriages and don't want them to fail. Because they are economically dependent on their husbands, battered wives have little or no available money. If they have children, their mobility is restricted even further. Until the opening of shelters in the last few years, they literally had *no* place to go. Now there is some relief, but shelters are full to overflowing and many have no accommodations for children.

And what are the prospects for the woman who does leave her marriage? She may have little education, no job skills or work experience. How will she support herself—and her children? Where will they live? And, finally, what is there to prevent an abusive husband from coming after her?

The central issue in wife abuse is the total lack of response from the legal system. Feminists believe that wife abuse is a crime just like any other assault. No state denies legal protection to citizens who are victims of assault and battery. In most states the crime is a misdemeanor. "Aggravated assault" carries a heftier punishment and is considered a felony. Husbands break both of these laws repeatedly by beating their wives, yet only 2 percent are ever prosecuted.

The first legal authorities a battered woman contacts are the police. In cities all across the country, their instructions are to mediate, not arrest. Often they give the woman incorrect or misleading information about what her legal rights and options are. The overall effect is to discourage her from exercising her rights and to leave her unprotected. The following guidelines from the Michigan Police Training Academy illustrate this point:

    a. Avoid arrest if possible. Appeal to their vanity.
    b. Explain the procedure for obtaining a warrant.
        1. Complainant must sign complaint.

2. Must appear in court.
3. Consider loss of time.
4. Cost of court.
c. State that your only interest is to prevent a breach of the peace.
d. Explain that attitudes usually change by court time.
e. Recommend a postponement.
  1. Court not in session.
  2. No judge available.
f. *Don't* be too harsh or critical.

It is indeed incongruous for the police to worry about a woman's loss of time in filing a complaint when she may be worrying about the loss of her life.

Should a battered woman persevere, she will continue to face discouragement and delays. Although assault is a crime, she will find, for the most part, that her only relief comes from the civil court. She may get a restraining order or peace bond requiring her husband to stop beating her. Unfortunately, such orders are easily broken and poorly enforced. Public prosecutors and judges, like the police, show more interest in reconciliation than in enforcing the law. In one particularly brutal case in New York City, a battered woman went to court five times in a year and a half. Each time the judge released her husband with a warning. As a result of the third beating, she lost an eye. Such cases leave one wondering if it is reconciliation our legal system believes in, or a husband's right to beat his wife.

The first major legal victory for battered women came in New York City. Fifty-nine women filed a class action suit against the police and Family Court which was settled out of court. New York City police are now required to arrest the husband/assailant; they are also required to locate him if he has left the scene as they would in any other case. Lawyers for the women have already received many requests from attorneys across the country seeking advice in launching similar class actions.

Legal experts and activists disagree about whether or not additional legislation is needed to protect battered women. Some feel enforcement of current laws is sufficient. The New York experience should be helpful in settling this debate. Either way, however, battered women must and will have legal protection.

See also: Legal Status
        Rape
        Self-Defense

Organizations:

Abused Women's Aid in Crisis
G.P.O. Box 1699
New York, NY 10001

Center for Women Policy Studies
2000 P Street N.W.
Washington, DC 20036

National Communications Network for the
  Elimination of Violence Against Women
4520 44th Avenue South
Minneapolis, MN 55406

National Coalition Against Domestic
  Violence
c/o Cynthia Dames
Battered Women's Project
P.O. Box 1501
Santa Fe, NM 87501

Women's Resource Network
4025 Chestnut Street
Philadelphia, PA 19104

Resources:

Annotated Bibliography on Woman Battering, ed. by Claudette McShane. Milwaukee: University of Wisconsin, School of Social Welfare, Midwest Parent-Child Welfare Resource Center, 1977. Order from: Midwest Parent-Child Welfare Resource Center, School of Social Welfare, University of Wisconsin, Milwaukee, WI 53201.

The bibliography lists both psychological and sociological research studies and more activist-oriented writings from the feminist antiviolence movement.

Battered Wives, by Del Martin. San Francisco: Glide Publications, 1976.

Martin's book was the first full-length treatment of wife abuse to appear and remains the best. The text above draws heavily on it.

Household Violence Against Women: The Social Construction of a Private Event. New York: Health Movement Organization, 1978. Order HMO Packet #3 from: Health Movement Organization c/o Health/PAC, 17 Murray Street, New York, NY 10007.

Based on sociological study of women served by Yale Medical School's emergency room, this shocking but well-documented paper shows the ways in which medical and social "institutions respond to incidents of violence against women in ways that actually reinforce the likelihood that they will be victimized again and repeatedly" by returning women to situations in which they are in danger, redefining their problems as "the family in crisis."

Resource Kit on Battered Women. Washington: Women's Bureau, Department of Labor, 1977. Order from: Women's Bureau, Office of the Secretary, Department of Labor, Washington, DC 20210.

This packet includes an overview article, a rundown of the legislative issues, a program and resource directory. There are also guides to funding sources. An excellent collection.

Wife-Beating: A Selected Annotated Bibliography, ed. by Pamela F. Howard. San Diego: Current Bibliography Series, 1978. Order from: Current Bibliography Series, P.O. Box 2709, San Diego, CA 92112.

Although compiled for the layperson, this bibliography lists a variety of types of materials and would probably be of interest to the researcher or social worker as well.

Working on Wife Abuse, ed. by Betsy Warrior. Cambridge, 1976. Order from: Betsy Warrior, 46 Pleasant Street, Cambridge, MA 02139.

The personal project of Ms. Warrior through seven editions, *Working on Wife Abuse* is the most comprehensive directory of shelters, research projects, and activists available.

BIRTH CONTROL

IN THE LAST DECADE THE SCIENTIFIC COMMUNITY, SUPPORTED BY THE UNITED States government, has made significant progress in cloning, creating test-tube babies, and synthesizing hormones. However, little time, energy, and money have been devoted to the development of safe, effective, and easy-to-use birth control methods. Although ten million women take oral contraceptives and another four million use intrauterine devices (IUDs), no one knows how safe these methods are. In 1960, the Food and Drug Administration (FDA) approved Searle Laboratory's oral contraceptive although the pill, Enovid, had only been tested for one year on 132 women. During the next few years critics who suggested that there might be a link between the pill and thromboembolic disorders (blood clotting) were ignored. Others—aware that estrogens speed up cancerous growths—feared that the pill would prove to be carcinogenic and were likewise ignored. Not until 1975 did the FDA acknowledge that the pill was linked to heart disease, liver disorders, and birth defects. The FDA was also slow to insure that informational inserts about the dangers of the pill made their way into the package.

The FDA's track record on the IUD is not much better. For several years IUDs were not subject to FDA premarketing testing guidelines since they were neither food nor drugs. During that period the Dalkon Shield was linked to more than ten deaths caused by spontaneous septic abortion and the Majzlin Spring proved so difficult to remove that surgeons, in several cases, had to take out the entire uterus.

In short, many of today's birth control methods are as much a curse as they are a boon to women. After losing ground to the pill, the diaphragm is now being rediscovered by many women interested in safe birth control. In 1961, Planned Parenthood dispensed diaphragms to 64 percent of their clients; by 1971 only 4 percent were choosing this method, while 77.4 percent opted for the pill. What had happened? The pill and the IUD were being touted by the medical industry as safer, more reliable and easier to use than the diaphragm. However, diaphragms, when correctly fitted and worn, are more reliable than most IUDs and safer than the pill. Since the nadir of its popularity in the early 1970's, the diaphragm has enjoyed a comeback. Recent studies at the Margaret Sanger Research Bureau show that it is 99 percent effective if used correctly. According to Planned Parenthood's statistics, 11.6 percent of their 1977 clients chose this method of birth control.

There is nothing new about the desirability of safe and effective contraception. Vaginal suppositories have been used for thousands of years. Women in some cultures (ancient India and Egypt) used animal dung, others tried inventive mixtures (one Greek preparation combined oxgall, serpent fat, verdigris and honey), and still others employed whatever natural resources were at hand. Chinese women made discs of silk paper, Asian women concocted feather fans.

The barrier technique—blocking the entrance to the cervical canal—is not only effective and time-tested, it is also economical and easy to use. The cervical cap, or pessary, is shaped like a thimble, fits over the cervix, uses suction to stay in place and is made of Lucite, rubber, or polyethylene. The cap, available in Europe, satisfies its users because it can stay in place between menstrual periods, lasts for several years and does not require spermicides. Why aren't these cervical caps available in the United States? In *Women and the Crisis in Sex Hormones,* Barbara Seaman speculates that the pharmaceutical companies don't want to produce them. If one cap works for several years and needs no jellies or spermicides, how will a profit be made?

Instead of experimenting with barrier birth control, the drug industry and the

Margaret Sanger dares to tell the truth about Birth Control

FOR centuries the world has played a game of "hush" about the one most important fact of marriage. Even to-day tens of thousands of women are doomed to a life of hopeless, helpless drudgery—and their children are doomed to privation and neglect because the mother simply cannot give so many of them the proper care or support.

Words alone cannot tell the terrible sacrifice in wasted bodies and blasted lives that has been exacted from women every year. Words alone cannot express the untold suffering of thousands of women—and children—must endure every year. That is why Margaret Sanger, herself a mother, and President of the American Birth Control League, dares to tell the truth about this important subject.

Will You Ever Write a Letter Like This?

Only these agony-laden letters can tell the story of woman's sacrifice in all its anguish. These are but a few of thousands sent every day to Margaret Sanger by unhappy mothers who have turned to her for help in their greatest need, revealing to her the nameless fears and terrors that clutch at their hearts. Read these letters, and know for yourself what women still suffer.

"It is terrible to think of bringing these little bodies and souls into the world without means or strength to care for them. I know that this must be the last one, for it would be better for me to go than to bring more neglected babies into the world."

"My baby is only 10 months old, and the oldest of my four children is 7. I am so discouraged I want to die. Ignorance on this all-important subject has put me where I am."

Is the Husband or Wife to Blame?

Whose is the blame for the tragedy of too many children—husband or wife?

Margaret Sanger, the great Birth Control advocate, comes with a message vital to every married man and woman.

"Why is it," Mrs. Sanger asks, "that the women of Australia, New Zealand, Holland, France, and many other nations are permitted to know the truths that can save them from this terrible suffering while the women of America must still endure the agonies to which they are needlessly condemned?" Margaret Sanger considers it a slur upon the intelligence of American womankind to deny to them the knowledge which has brought freedom, health, happiness, and life itself to the women of other nations. That is why she has braved the storms of denunciation, why she has fought through every court in the land for her right to arouse womankind.

Woman and the New Race

Margaret Sanger's startling new book points the way to women's freedom

In her revolutionary book, Margaret Sanger, internationally famous for her ceaseless activities in behalf of women and hailed as the liberator of her sex, shows the way out for tired, struggling womankind. With utter frankness she tears down the veil of silence that has always surrounded the subject of birth control. It is a startling revelation of a new truth that will open the eyes of women everywhere.

In her wonderful book Mrs. Sanger shows how women can and will rise above the forces that have ruined their beauty—that drag them down—that wreck their mental and physical strength—that make them an easy prey to death—that disqualify them for society, for self-improvement—that finally shut them out from the thing they cherish most, their husbands' love.

In blazing this revolutionary trail to the new freedom of women, this daring and heroic author points out that women who cannot afford to have more than one or two children, should not do so. It is a crime to herself, a crime to her children, a crime to society.

A Priceless Possession

Now Margaret Sanger's message to all women, contained in "Woman and the New Race," is made available to the public. A special edition of this vital book has been published in response to the overwhelming demand. Order your copy of this wonderful book at once, at the special edition price of only $2. Then if after reading it you do not treasure it as a priceless possession return it to us and your money will be refunded.

It is not even necessary to send a penny now. Just the coupon will bring your copy of "Woman and the New Race." It is bound in handsome, durable gray cloth, printed in clear readable type on good quality book paper and contains 286 pages, sent to you in a plain wrapper.

When the book is delivered at your home, pay the postman the special low price of $2 plus the few cents postage. But mail the coupon at once. Tear it off before you turn this page.

Truth Publishing Company
Dept. TA-144, 1658 Broadway
New York City

Partial List of Contents
*Woman's Error and Her Debt
Cries of Despair
*When Should a Woman Avoid Having Children
Two Classes of Women
Birth Control—a Parent's Problem or Woman's
*Continence — Is it Practical or Desirable
Women and the New Morality
*Are Preventive Means Certain
Legislating Women's Morals
*Contraceptives or Abortion
Progress We Have Made
*Any one of these chapters is alone worth many times the price of the book.

A 1923 advertisement for Margaret Sanger's book, *Woman and the New Race*. Sanger, who coined the term birth control, fought the Church, the law and the government to bring contraceptive information to poor and working women. She opened the first birth control clinic in the U.S. in 1916 and later imported the first diaphragms from Japan. *Culver Pictures*

medical establishment prefer more exotic and expensive solutions. In November 1978, the Ford Foundation handed out grants totaling $1.5 million for projects "aimed at furthering the development of new contraceptives." One grant will help to support the testing of new contraceptives, such as a small silicone capsule implanted under the skin of a woman's forearm. It releases a hormone-like chemical which prevents conception by suppressing ovulation. Another new device is an intravaginal ring containing spermicidal chemicals. An antipregnancy vaccine which stimulates production of antibodies to neutralize hormones and prevent pregnancy is also being tested.

There is one new contraceptive, however, which does seem to have the potential for being safe and effective. A *Medical World News* article (reported in the Winter 1978 issue of *Healthright*) describes "a vaginal inserted cylindrical collagen sponge treated with zinc." The report goes on to say "though studies are still being performed to determine effectiveness, an interesting side effect of this sponge had been identified; apparently it can be used to effectively treat and prevent herpes simplex II."

Birth control is an issue involving more than just technology. The right to reproductive freedom is a cornerstone demand of women's liberation. Because of woman's biological role as childbearer, the availability of birth control has sweeping implications for all areas of her life. And because patriarchal society has seen woman only in this aspect of her biological role—and has attempted to limit her to it—safe, effective birth control is crucial for her emancipation.

See also: Abortion
DES
Legal Status
Sterilization Abuse

Organizations:

Association for Voluntary Sterilization
803 Third Avenue
New York, NY 10017

Planned Parenthood Federation of America
810 Seventh Avenue
New York, NY 10019

Resources:

The Birth Control Book, by Howard Shapiro. New York: St. Martin's Press, 1977.
   Wonderfully informative and enjoyable to read; written by a gynecologist who insists (and proves) that he wants to do right by women.

Woman's Body, Woman's Right, by Linda Gordon. New York: Grossman, 1976.
   A social history of birth control in America; discusses the politics of reproduction, moving toward womanpower, the move from women's rights to family planning.

Women and the Crisis in Sex Hormones, by Barbara Seaman. New York: Rawson, 1977.

BREAST CANCER

SEVEN PERCENT OF AMERICAN WOMEN CAN EXPECT TO DEVELOP BREAST cancer. By publicizing their stories, women like Betty Ford, Shirley Temple Black, and Betty Rollin have increased the public's awareness of procedures and precautions. All women should examine their own breasts between visits to the gynecologist (see diagram). It is best to do this at the same time every month, preferably after menstruation, when the breasts are at minimum fullness. Nine times out of ten a lump on the breast is benign, but if one is discovered, see a doctor immediately.

A frequent form of surgical abuse is the surgeon's refusal to perform a biopsy unless the patient gives prior consent to remove the breast immediately if cancer is found. Even though a cursory diagnosis can be made at once, a thorough examination requires several days. If cancer is discovered, a woman should be aware of all her options. A second opinion is, of course, wise. Many American surgeons are still inclined to perform a radical mastectomy because it is the traditional approach. Doctors in Scandinavia and England doubt whether this surgery is necessary; many consider it outmoded and barbarous.

In early 1979, after studying the results of follow-up studies in the United States, Britain, and Denmark, Dr. Maurice Fox of Massachusetts Institute of Technology concluded that radical mastectomies are "no more effective than more conservative, less mutilating treatment." Dr. Bernard Fisher of the University of Pittsburgh reports that after following the five-year progress of 1,680 women who had been treated for breast cancer there was no difference in survival rates between those who underwent radical surgery and those treated alternatively. Possible operations for breast cancer patients include:

— super radical mastectomy: removes the breast, armpit glands, underlying nodes of chest wall, and nodes under sternum
— radical mastectomy: removes breast, pectoral muscles, armpit nodes
— simple mastectomy: removes breast only
— partial mastectomy: removes lump and surrounding tissues
— subcutaneous mastectomy: removes the inner breast but leaves the outer skin and nipple

Conservative surgery is often supplemented by radiation therapy and chemotherapy (use of anti-tumor drugs). Some doctors use these alternatives by themselves. Dr. Fox, noting the rise in reported cases of breast cancer among American women—in 1955 55 cases per 100,000 were diagnosed, today 90 to 95 per 100,000 are diagnosed—has suggested that today's intensive screening procedures may mistake benign lumps for ones which are malignant.

See also: Health Care

Organizations:

American Cancer Society
Reach to Recovery
777 Third Avenue
New York, NY 10017

ENCORE
YWCA National Board
600 Lexington Avenue
New York, NY 10022

How to examine your breasts

This simple 3-step procedure could save your life by finding breast cancer early when it is most curable

In the shower:

Examine your breasts during bath or shower; hands glide easier over wet skin. Fingers flat, move gently over every part of each breast. Use right hand to examine left breast, left hand for right breast. Check for any lump, hard knot or thickening.

Before a mirror:

Inspect your breasts with arms at your sides. Next, raise your arms high overhead. Look for any changes in contour of each breast, 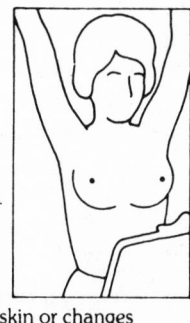 a swelling, dimpling of skin or changes in the nipple.

Then, rest palms on hips and press down firmly to flex your chest muscles. Left and right breast will not exactly match—few women's breasts do.

Regular inspection shows what is normal for you and will give you confidence in your examination.

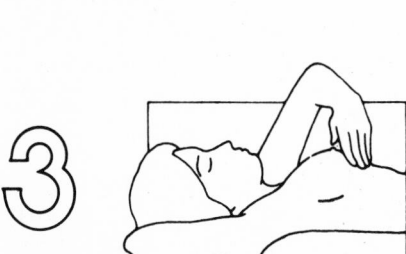

Lying down:

To examine your right breast, put a pillow or folded towel under your right shoulder. Place right hand behind your head—this distributes breast tissue more evenly on the chest. With left hand, fingers flat, press gently in small circular motions around an imaginary clock face. Begin at outermost top of your right breast for 12 o'clock, then move to 1 o'clock, and so on around the circle back to 12. A ridge of firm tissue in the lower curve of each breast is normal. Then move in an inch, toward the

nipple, keep circling to examine *every part of your breast*, including nipple. This requires at least three more circles. Now slowly repeat procedure on your left breast with a pillow under your left shoulder and left hand behind head. Notice how your breast structure feels.

Finally, squeeze the nipple of each breast gently between thumb and index finger. Any discharge, clear or bloody, should be reported to your doctor immediately.

WHY YOU SHOULD EXAMINE YOUR BREASTS MONTHLY

Most breast cancers are first discovered by women themselves. Since breast cancers found early and treated promptly have excellent chances for cure, learning how to examine your breasts properly can help save your life. Use the simple 3-step breast self-examination (BSE) procedure shown here.

FOR THE BEST TIME TO EXAMINE YOUR BREASTS:

Follow the same procedure once a month about a week after your period, when breasts are usually not tender or swollen. After menopause, check breasts on the first day of each month. After hysterectomy, check your doctor or clinic for an appropriate time of the month. Doing BSE will give you monthly peace of mind and seeing your doctor once a year will reassure you there is nothing wrong.

WHAT YOU SHOULD DO IF YOU FIND A LUMP OR THICKENING

If a lump or dimple or discharge is discovered during BSE, it is important to see your doctor as soon as possible. Don't be frightened. Most breast lumps or changes are not cancer, but only your doctor can make the diagnosis.

Know Cancer's Warning Signals!

Change in bowel or bladder habits
A sore that does not heal
Unusual bleeding or discharge
Thickening or lump in breast or elsewhere
Indigestion or difficulty in swallowing
Obvious change in wart or mole
Nagging cough or hoarseness

If you have a warning signal, see your doctor.

Resources:

First You Cry, by Betty Rollin. Philadelphia: Lippincott, 1976.

Down to earth, very human and entertaining (!) story of a news correspondent's bout with breast cancer. Made into TV movie, fall 1978.

Our Bodies, Ourselves, by the Boston Women's Health Book Collective. New York: Simon and Schuster, 1976.

Section on breast problems. Explains how to perform a self-examination, types of cancer, treatments, resources.

Why Me? What Every Woman Should Know About Breast Cancer to Save Her Life, by Rose Kushner. New York: Signet, 1977.

A well-written account of Ms. Kushner's struggles with breast cancer. Thorough discussion of breast-cancer surgeries, treatments, controversies.

Women's Health Care: Resources, Writings, Bibliographies, by Belita Cowan. Ann Arbor: Anshen Publishing, 1977. Order from: Belita Cowan, 3821 T Street N.W., Washington, DC 20007.

Section includes Dr. Oliver Cope's "A Physician's Comments about Breast Cancer," and other resources for understanding the nature of breast cancer and its treatment.

CAREER DEVELOPMENT

BUILDING A CAREER—SOMETHING MOST MEN ARE SOCIALIZED TO DO FROM childhood—is an endeavor many women must make special efforts even to begin. Women have been blocked by a combination of sex-role stereotyping, socialization, and discrimination from other than low-paying and dead-end positions. While individually women can take only limited steps against discriminatory practices, there are many things they can do to prepare themselves for careers.

Career development provides skills and strategies which help women take their working lives into their own hands to move up and out of dead-end jobs. Whether through self-education or as part of a professional guidance program, career development usually involves (1) self-assessment to determine individual interests, needs and skills; (2) research to identify potential career areas and pinpoint occupational trends; (3) evaluation of education and training required for both current and future career interests; (4) assertiveness training to improve skills in communicating opinions, feelings and needs; (5) résumé writing and interviewing techniques for an effective presentation of personal capabilities. Finally, career development in any form should provide a network of personal and professional supports—friends, co-workers and, when needed, trained professionals able to provide encouragement and advice.

There are several excellent books available to help in planning career and job-hunting strategies. Also, you can contact the Catalyst Resource Center nearest you (see list below).

See also: Earnings Gap
Higher Education
Nontraditional Occupations
Vocational Education

Organizations:

Business and Professional Women's
    Foundation
2012 Massachusetts Avenue N.W.
Washington, DC 20036

Catalyst
14 East 60th Street
New York, NY 10022

Minority Women Employment Program
40 Marietta Street West
Atlanta, GA 30303

National Council of Career Women
818 National Press Building
Washington, DC 20045

Resources:

Career Opportunity Series. New York: Catalyst, various dates. Order from: Catalyst, address above.

A series of 27 booklets on various fields such as accounting, environmental affairs, publishing, retailing and fashion, including information on the status of women, successful women, and opportunities in each field.

Directory of Career Counseling Services. Washington: International Association of Counseling Services, 1978. Order from: International Association of Counseling Services, 1607 New Hampshire Avenue N.W., Washington, DC 20009.

An annotated listing of accredited, member career counseling groups, including private and college-affiliated centers.

Directory of Special Programs for Minority Group Members: Career Information Services, Employment Skills Banks, Financial Aid Sources, ed. by Willis L. Johnson. Garrett Park: The Garrett Park Press, 1975.

A comprehensive resource section on programs specifically for women is included in addition to detailed sections on general programs, federal programs, and college and university awards for minorities.

Guidelines for Preparing Resumes. Washington: Women's Equity Action League, 1978. Order from: WEAL, 805 15th Street N.W., Washington, DC 20005.

A basic guide including sample résumé formats.

A Resource List on Aspects of Women and Employment. Washington: Women's Equity Action League, 1977. Order from: WEAL, 805 15th Street N.W., Washington, DC 20005.

An information packet providing resource groups and bibliographies on job hunting, career opportunities, alternative employment opportunities, and additional bibliographies.

Self-guided Career Counseling, by Kathleen Hart Broad. Amherst: Everywoman's Center, 1976. Order from: Everywoman's Center, University of Massachusetts, Amherst, MA 01002.

An excellent guide containing sections on self-help career counseling, the job search, and occupational information on various fields such as banking, health, public relations and skilled crafts.

Women's Work. Order from: Women's Work, 1302 18th Street N.W., Washington, DC 20036.

A bimonthly covering such areas as assessing your career potential, changing career directions, two-career couples, and a Market Hotline.

♀ CATALYST NATIONAL NETWORK OF LOCAL RESOURCE CENTERS ♀

Alabama
Enterprise State Junior College
Women's Center, Career Development
  Center
Highway 84 East
Enterprise, AL 36330

University of Alabama
Career Planning and Placement
1300 8th Avenue South
Building 5, Room 110
Birmingham, AL 35294

Alaska
University of Alaska
Anchorage Educational Opportunity
  Center
2533 Providence Avenue   K-101
Anchorage, AL 99504.

Arizona
University of Arizona
Student Counseling Service
Old Main
Tucson, AZ 85721

California
Advocates for Women
256 Sutter, 6th Floor
San Francisco, CA 94108

American River College
College Opportunity Center
4700 College Oak Drive
Sacramento, CA 95841

California State University
Sacramento
Career Development & Placement Center
6000 J Street
Sacramento, CA 95819

Center for New Directions
7112 Owensmouth Ave.
Canoga Park, CA 91303

Crossroads Institute for Career
  Development
2288 Fulton Street
Berkeley, CA 94704

Cypress College
Career Planning Center
9200 Valley View Street
Cypress, CA 90630

Foothill College
Continuing Education for Women
12345 El Monte
Los Altos Hills, CA 94002

Anita Goldfarb
19434 Londelius Street
Northridge, CA 91324

Susan W. Miller
1710 Durango Avenue
Los Angeles, CA 90035

New Ways to Work
149 Ninth Street
San Francisco, CA 94103

Resource Center for Women
445 Sherman Avenue
Palo Alto, CA 94306

San Jose State University
Re-Entry Advisory Program
Old Cafeteria Building
San Jose, CA 95192

University of California, Berkeley
Women's Center
T-9 Building
Berkeley, CA 94720

University of California,
Irvine Extension
The Women's Opportunities Center
148C Administration Building
Irvine, CA 92717

Woman's Way
710 C Street
San Rafael, CA 94901

Colorado
Women Enterprises
158 Fillmore Street   #307
Denver, CO 80206

Women's Resource Agency
25 North Spruce Street, Suite 309
Colorado Springs, CO 80905

Connecticut
Albertus Magnus College
Life Career Development Center
700 Prospect Street
New Haven, CT 06511

Information and Counseling Service for
  Women
301 Crown Street, P.O. Box 5557
New Haven, CT 06520

Career and Educational Counseling Center
  of the Stamford YWCA
422 Summer Street
Stamford, CT 06901

Fairfield University
Women's Bureau
North Benson Road
Fairfield, CT 06430

Norwalk Community College
Counseling Center
333 Wilson Aveue
Norwalk, CT 06854

District of Columbia
George Washington University
Continuing Education for Women
Suite 621–624
2130 H Street, N.W.
Washington, DC 20052

Florida
Face Learning Center
12945 Seminole Boulevard
Building 2, Suite 8
Largo, FL 33540

Stetson University
Counseling Center
North Woodland Boulevard
Deland, FL 32720

Valencia Community College
Center for Continuing Education for
   Women
P.O. Box 3028
Orlando, FL 32802

Illinois
Applied Potential
Box 19
Highland Park, IL 60035

Flexible Careers
Suite 703
37 South Wabash Avenue
Chicago IL 60603

Kishwaukee College
Career Guidance Center for DeKalb and
   Kane Counties
Malta, IL 60150

Moraine Valley Community College
Adult Career Resource Center
10900 South 88th Avenue
Palos Hills, IL 60465

Oakton Community College
Adult Career Resource Center
7900 N. Nagle
Morton Grove, IL 60053

Southern Illinois University at
   Edwardsville
General Studies Division

Campus Box 44
Edwardsville, IL 62026

Thornton Community College
Counseling Center
15800 S. State Street
South Holland, IL 60473

Women's Inc.
15 Spinning Wheel Road, Suite 14
Hinsdale, IL 60521

Indiana
Ball State University
Student Services
Office of Admissions
Muncie, IN 47306

Indiana University
Continuing Education for Women
Owen Hall
Bloomington, IN 47401

Indiana University/Purdue University
Counseling and Academic Development
   Division
Student Union, Room 113
2101 Coliseum Boulevard East
Fort Wayne, IN 46805

Indiana University/Purdue University at
   Indianapolis
Continuing Education Center for Women
1301 East 38th Street
Indianapolis, IN 46205

Purdue University
University Center for Women
2101 Colieseum Boulevard East
Fort Wayne, IN 46805

Woman Alive
YWCA
229 Ogden Street
P.O. Box 1121
Hammond, IN 46325

Women's Career Center
YWCA
802 N. Lafayette Boulevard
South Bend, IN 46601

Iowa
Drake University
Community Career Planning Center for
   Women
1158 27th Street
Des Moines, IA 50311

Women's Work/Work Associates
820 First National Building
Davenport, IA 52801

Kansas
University of Kansas
Adult Life Resource Center
Division of Continuing Education
1246 Mississippi Street, Annex A
Lawrence, KS 66045

Maryland
Baltimore New Directions for Women
2517 N. Charles Street
Baltimore, MD 21218

Binder/Elster Associates
7837 Aberdeen Road
Bethesda, MD 20014

Massachusetts
Civic Center and Clearing House
14 Beacon Street
Boston, MA 02108

Continuum
785 Centre Street
Newton, MA 02158

Middlesex Community College
Widening Opportunity Research Center
Division of Continuing Education
P.O. Box T
Bedford, MA 01730

Resource Center for Educational
  Opportunities
19 Fort Hill Street
Hingham, MA 02043

Smith College
Career Development Office
Pierce Hall
Northampton, MA 01060

Why Not? Program
YWCA
2 Washington Street
Worcester, MA 01608

Women's Educational & Industrial Union
Career Services
356 Boylston Street
Boston, MA 02116

Michigan
Every Woman's Place
23 Strong Avenue
Muskegon, MI 49441

Macomb County Community College
Community Resource Center
14500 Twelve Mile Road, K-332
Warren, MI 48093

Michigan Technological University
Center for Continuing Education

Room 301A, Administration Building
Houghton, MI 49931

Montcalm Community College
Career Information Center
Sidney, MI 48885

C. S. Mott Community College
Guidance Services and Counseling Division
1401 East Court Street
Flint, MI 48503

Northern Michigan University
Women's Center for Continuing Education
Marquette, MI 49855

Oakland University
Continuum Center for Adult Counseling
  and Leadership Training
Rochester, MI 48063

Western Michigan University
Center for Women's Services
A-331 Ellsworth Hall
Kalamazoo, MI 49008

Women's Resource Center
226 Bostwick N.E.
Grand Rapids, MI 49503

Minnesota
Southwest State University
Personal Development Center
268 CAB
Marshall, MN 56258

Working Opportunities for Women
65 East Kellogg Boulevard, Room 437
St. Paul, MN 55101

Mississippi
Mississippi State University
Placement and Career Information Center
Drawer P
Mississippi State, MS 39762

Missouri
University of Missouri, Kansas City
The Women's Resource Service
5325 Rockhill Road
Kansas City, MO 64110

University of Missouri, St. Louis
Extension Division—Women's Programs
8001 Natural Bridge Road
349 Education Office Building
St. Louis, MO 63121

Washington University
Continuing Education for Women
Box 1099
St. Louis, MO 63130

Montana
Montana State University
Focus on Women
9 Hamilton Hall
Bozeman, MT 59717

Nebraska
University of Nebraska at Omaha
Women's Support Programs
Box 688, Downtown Station
Omaha, NE 68101

New Jersey
Adult Service Center
112 Main Road
Montville, NJ 07045

Bergen Community College
Division of Community Services
295 Main Street
Hackensack, NJ 07652

Caldwell College
Career Planning and Placement
Caldwell, NJ 07006

College Counseling and Education Center
369 Forest Avenue
Paramus, NJ 07652

Douglass College
Douglass Advisory Services for Women
Rutgers Women's Center
132 George Street
New Brunswick, NJ 08903

Fairleigh Dickinson University
Center for Women
Madison Avenue
Madison, NJ 07940

Jersey City State College
The Women's Center
70 Audubon
Jersey City, NJ 07305

Jewish Vocational Service
454 William Street
East Orange, NJ 07017

Kean College of New Jersey
Eve
Administration Building
Union, NJ 07083

Middlesex County College
Women's Career Information Center
Woodbridge Avenue, West Hall Annex
Edison, NJ 08817

Montclair State College
Women's Center

Valley Road
Upper Montclair, NJ 07405

New Careers
Box C-26
706 Meadowview Drive
Cinnaminson, NJ 08077

The Professional Roster
5 Ivy Lane
Princeton, NJ 08540

Reach, Inc.
Box 33
Convent Station, NJ 07961

Union County Technical Institute
Women's Center for Career Planning
1776 Raritan Road
Scotch Plains, NJ 07076

New York
Academic Advisory Center for Adults
Turf Avenue
Rye, NY 10580

Barbara Holt Associates
527 Madison Avenue
New York, NY 10022

Columbia University
Womanspace
School of General Studies
306 Lewisohn Hall
Broadway and 116th Street
New York, NY 10027

Counseling Women
14 East 60th Street
New York, NY 10022

Hilda Lee Dail
140 East 56th Street, Suite 10F
New York, NY 10022

Hofstra University
Counseling Center
240 Student Center
Hempstead, NY 11550

Kingsborough Community College
Office of Career Counseling and Placement
2001 Oriental Boulevard, Room C102
Brooklyn, NY 11235

Janice LaRouche Assoc.
Workshops for Women
333 Central Park West
New York, NY 10025

Mercy College
Career Counseling and Placement Office
555 Broadway
Dobbs Ferry, NY 10522

More For Women Inc.
52 Gramercy Park North
New York, NY 10010

New Options
26 West 56th Street
New York, NY 10019

New School for Social Research
Human Relations Center
66 West 12th Street
New York, NY 10011

NYCTI's Educational and Career
  Headquarters
225 Park Avenue South, Suite 505
New York, NY 10003

Orange County Community College
Office of Community Services
115 South Street
Middletown, NY 10940

Placement 500
A Womanschool Affiliate
424 Madison Ave.
New York, NY 10017

Personnel Sciences Center
341 Madison Avenue
New York, NY 10017

Potential Unlimited
241 East 49th Street
New York, NY 10017

Regional Learning Service of Central New
  York
405 Oak Street
Syracuse, NY 13203

Ruth Shapiro Associates
Career Development and Self-Marketing
  Workshops
200 East 30th Street
New York, NY 10016

SUNY at Buffalo
University Placement and Career Guidance
14 Capen Hall
Buffalo, NY 14260

SUNY at Stony Brook
Mid-Career Counseling Center, Room
  N235
Sociology and Behavioral Science Building
Stony Brook, NY 11794

Vistas for Women
YWCA
515 North Street
White Plains, NY 10605

Women's Career Center
121 North Fitzhugh Street
Rochester, NY 14614

Wonderwomen Employment
3 Johnson Park
Buffalo, NY 14201

North Carolina
Duke University
Office of Continuing Education
107 Bivins
Durham, NC 27708

Fayetteville Family Life Center
North Carolina Baptist Hospital
Bordeaux Shopping Center
Fayetteville, NC 28304

Salem College
Lifespan Center, Lehman Hall
Box 10548, Salem Station
Winston-Salem, NC 27108

Ohio
Baldwin-Wallace College
Experience CUE
Counseling and Advising Center
Administration Building   #118
Berea, OH 44017

Bowling Green State University
Center for Continued Learning
194 S. Main Street
Bowling Green, OH 43402

Cleveland Jewish Vocational Service
13878 Cedar Road
University Heights, OH 44118

Cuyahoga Community College
Lifelong Learning/Women's Programs
2900 Community College Avenue
Cleveland, OH 44115

Ohio State University
Women's Program
Continuing Education
1800 Cannon Drive
Columbus, OH 43227

Pyramid
1642 Cleveland Avenue N.W.
Canton, OH 44703

University of Akron
Adult Resource Center
Akron, OH 44325

Wright State University
Women's Career Development Center
140 East Monument Avenue
Dayton, OH 45402

Oklahoma
Women's Resource Center
207½ East Gray
P.O. Box 474
Norman, OK 73070

Pennsylvania
Institute of Awareness
YM-YWHA
401 South Broad Street
Philadelphia, PA 19147

Job Advisory Service
Chatham College
Beatty Hall, Woodland Road
Pittsburgh, PA 15232

Options for Women
8419 Germantown Avenue
Philadelphia, PA 19118

Swarthmore College
Office of Career Counseling and Placement
Swarthmore, PA 19081

Temple University
Career Services
Mitten Hall
Philadelphia, PA 19122

University of Pennsylvania
Resources for Women
Houston Hall
Philadelphia, PA 19104

Villa Maria College
Counseling Services for Women
2551 West Lake Road
Erie, PA 16505

Wilson College
Office of Career Planning and Placement
Chambersburg, PA 17201

South Carolina
Converse College
Women's Center
Spartanburg, SC 29301

Greenville Technical College
Center for Continuing Education for
  Women
Greenville, SC 29606

Tennessee
Scarrit College
Center of Women's Studies
1008 19th Avenue South
Nashville, TN 37203

YWCA of Nashville
Career/Life Planning Center
1608 Woodmont Boulevard
Nashville, TN 37215

Texas
Amarillo College
Women's Programs
P.O. Box 447
Amarillo, TX 79178

Brookhaven College
Brookhaven College Counseling Center
3939 Valley View Lane
Farmers Branch, TX 75234

The University of Texas at Austin
Services for Returning Students
Office of the Dean of Students
Students Services Building, Room 10-E
Austin, TX 78712

Vocational Guidance Service, Inc.
2525 San Jacinto
Houston, TX 77002

Women's Center of Dallas
3107 Routh Street
Dallas, TX 75201

Utah
The Phoenix Institute
989 East 900 South
Salt Lake City, UT 84105

Virginia
Hollins College
Career Counseling Center
Administration Building
Hollins College, VA 24020

University of Richmond
Women's Resources Center
University College, VA 23173

Virginia Commonwealth University
Evening College
901 West Franklin Street
Richmond, VA 23284

Washington
Individual Development Center
Career and Life Planning
1020 East John Street
Seattle, WA 98102

University of Washington
Career and Life Planning
1209 N.E. 41st Street
Seattle, WA 98105

Wisconsin
Alverno College
Research Center on Women/Community
  Services
3401 S. 39th
Milwaukee, WI 53215

Skilled Jobs for Women
111 South Hamilton Street
Madison, WI 53703

CHILDBIRTH

HOME BIRTH AND OTHER ALTERNATIVES TO HOSPITAL DELIVERY HAVE BECOME increasingly popular among American women. The self-help health movement has encouraged women to view their reproductive functions as natural and normal, and to question medical procedures which feel alienating and seem unnecessary. Childbirth is generally under the control of doctors and hospital administrators who use procedures convenient to themselves, convincing women that giving birth at home or in the hands of a midwife is too dangerous. But childbirth has been reappropriated by many women as an experience too important to leave in the hands of someone else. Procedures which had been taken for granted—preparation (shaving the pubic hair, enemas), inducing labor by bursting the bag of waters or by drugs, forcing a woman to lie down during birth, anesthesia, forceps, episiotomy, separating the mother and child after birth—all have been called into question. Some doctors have responded by re-evaluating what they do; others have refused.

Today there are alternatives to medical practitioners who won't change with the times. Prepared childbirth, often referred to inaccurately as natural childbirth, was developed by Dr. Lamaze, a French obstetrician. Introduced into the United States after World War II, it has become increasingly popular and has gained

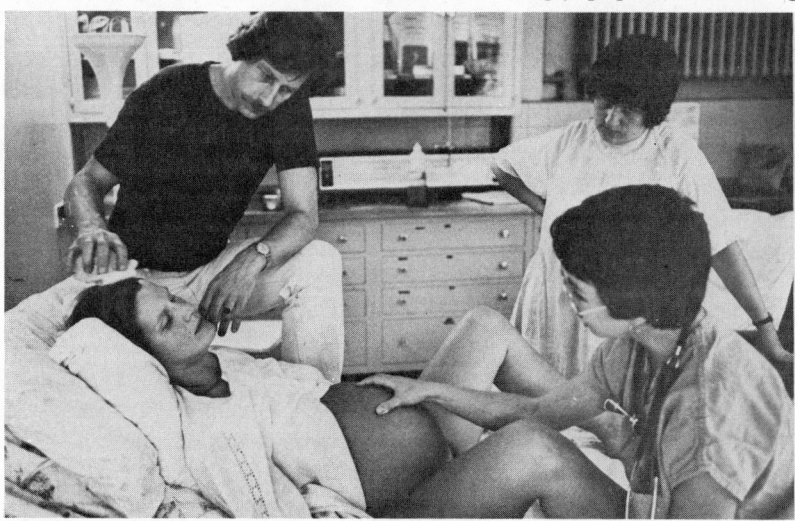

Giving birth at the Maternity Center Association, New York City. For parents-to-be who want to avoid the impersonal experience of a hospital delivery but feel uncomfortable about home birth, the Maternity Center provides a unique alternative. Its Childbearing Center seeks to provide a homelike setting with the security of attending midwives and obstetricians. © *Mariette Pathy Allen*

acceptance in many hospitals. The couple works as a team; the woman learns a series of breathing exercises to keep control of the contractions and the man serves as combination coach and cheerleader. There are now many variations of the basic Lamaze method.

Another French doctor, Frederic Leboyer, has developed new procedures which show concern for the newborn. Deliveries take place in dimly lit rooms and, instead of being spanked on arrival, the baby is placed in a basin of warm water and gently massaged. Mother and child are *not* separated. Everything is done to ease the transition from womb to world.

Medical institutions are changing too, and in some cases being dispensed with altogether. Some hospitals use obstetrical teams of doctors and nurse-midwives, registered nurses who have studied management and care of mothers and infants throughout the maternity cycle. Maternity care centers, staffed by obstetricians and nurse-midwives, provide the safety of a hospital with the warmth of the home; home birth is assisted by lay midwives who have learned their craft through apprenticeship and study.

Mary Bafs, *Midwife*,

From BOSTON,

BEGS Leave to inform the Ladies in this Place and in the Vicinity, that having been inftructed and recommended by the firft Practitioners in Midwifery, in Bofton ; in Compliance with the Requeft of feveral Ladies, fhe has removed to Salem, where fhe intends to purfue the Bufinefs of Midwifery.-- Any Lady who may favour her with her Commands, may depend upon her earlieft and beft Attendance. Enquire at the Houfe of Mr. OSGOOD, the Corner of Prifon-Lane.

Midwives have attended pregnant women for thousands of years and in every culture. Even today 80 percent of the world's babies are delivered by midwives. In colonial America midwives attended all births. But after the introduction of obstetrical forceps in 1750, physicians were able to claim that only they were qualified to deliver babies. This idea was challenged by the Popular Health Movement of the 1830's, which counseled "every man (woman) his (her) own physician." Ladies Physiological Societies caught on in the Mid-Atlantic and New England states. The nineteenth-century crusade for women's health rights was linked to the burgeoning feminist movement, as is today's. Midwifery was advocated as a way for women to serve other women and to have control over their own bodies.

Hard hit at first, the medical profession regrouped in the latter half of the nineteenth century and organized the American Medical Association (AMA) to protect its interests. The AMA looked disparagingly upon "unclean" midwives. Women doctors, in order to protect their shaky position, also attacked midwives as ignorant and unclean. In 1910, 50 percent of births were attended by midwives; this number dropped sharply as the United States became the first and only country ever to outlaw midwifery. As a consequence, the infant mortality rate rose; poor, immigrant, and rural women suffered the most.

Realizing that they were not reaching these women, obstetricians gave tacit consent to midwives serving these populations. Soon schools of midwifery opened.

Based on a model brought to the United States by Mary Breckenridge, an English public health nurse, the schools offered a nursing degree along with midwifery training. But these midwives did not make a dent in the booming obstetrics business. Only within the past fifteen years has there been a resurgence of support for midwifery along with the renewed interest in home birth among educated, urban, middle- and upper-class women.

Even so, lay midwives tend to serve in rural poverty areas like Appalachia, in poor urban centers with high concentrations of immigrant populations, and in pockets along the Northwest Coast. Since they are harassed for practicing medicine without a license, they work quietly and do not seek publicity. Nurse-midwives, on the other hand, practice freely as long as they work with doctors as part of an obstetrical team. Currently there are 2,000 certified nurse-midwives practicing in the United States, and estimates suggest that each new graduate may have up to ten job offers awaiting her in hospitals nationwide.

Childbirth practices range far and wide, from Lamaze to Leboyer and from spiritual midwifery to filming the birth for posterity. Many national organizations have sprung up to keep prospective parents informed about all their options. Women who have had distressing and alienating hospital experiences are particularly appreciative of the alternatives available for future births and for the chance to reclaim the experience of motherhood.

See also: Health care

Organizations:

American College of Nurse-Midwives
1012 14th Street N.W.
Washington, DC 20005

International Childbirth Education
 Association
P.O. Box 20852
Milwaukee, WI 53220

La Leche League International
9616 Minneapolis Avenue
Franklin Park, IL 60131

Maternity Center Association
48 East 92nd Street
New York, NY 10028

National Association for Parents and
 Professionals for Safe Alternatives in
 Childbirth
Marble Hill, MO 63764

National Midwives Association
P.O. Box 163
Princeton, NJ 08540

Resources:

Birth Book, by Raven Lang. Ben Lomond: Genesis Press, 1972. Order from:
 Genesis Press, P.O. Box 877, Ben Lomond, CA 95005
 One of the earliest books on home birth, *Birth Book* tends to be pointedly counter-cultural in language and style, but it is nonetheless interesting to read and is informative.

The Complete Book of Nurse Midwifery, by Barbara Brennan and Jean Rattner
 Heilman. New York: Dutton, 1977.
 Brennan, one of the first nurse-midwives, makes a strong case for midwifery in the hospital, using statistics which underscore her points.

Homebirth, by Alice Gilgoff. New York: Coward, McCann, and Geoghegan,
 1978.
 A wonderfully well-written book on alternatives to hospital birth. Gilgoff uses

her own experiences as a starting point and then cogently persuades the reader that hospitals, far from helping, often hinder mothers-to-be.

Immaculate Deception, by Suzanne Arms. Boston: Houghton Mifflin, 1975.

Thought by many to be the finest book on home birth and lay midwifery, Arms' well stated argument helped to convince many parents and professionals that proponents of alternative birth-care mean serious business.

Of Woman Born: Motherhood as Experience and Institution, by Adrienne Rich. New York: Norton, 1976.

In one of the most thought-provoking feminist books, Rich describes the history of childbirth, the institution of motherhood, and her personal experiences with both.

Women and Men Midwives: Medicine, Morality and Misogyny in Early America, by Jane Donegan. Westport: Greenwood Press, 1978.

Donegan makes use of primary source materials to relate the status of early American midwives and the transition from midwife to male doctor. Excellent bibliography.

CHILD CARE

TODAY, OF THE MORE THAN TWENTY-EIGHT MILLION CHILDREN UNDER SIX, almost six million have mothers working outside the home, and more than one million are in single-parent homes. While women traditionally have been the main providers of full-time child care, almost half of all mothers now hold full-time jobs. Quality child care, then, is an absolute necessity, yet a 1972 study by the National Council of Jewish Women found that only 1 percent of the private, profit-making child-care centers sampled provided high-quality care. Unfortunately, these findings are not obsolete.

In 1975, there were places in day-care centers for only one million children. Parents unable to secure one of these spaces for their children most often turn to family members and baby-sitters, or to family day-care arrangements, i.e. individuals caring for small groups of children in their own homes. It is estimated that almost two million children, ages seven to thirteen, are unsupervised during after-school hours.

Federal legislation supporting child-care services has been minimal. To date, legislation providing for comprehensive child-care services has been defeated in Congress. The Child Day Care Services Act under Title XX of the Social Services Act provides the bulk of federal funding for child-care services. Head Start, the Child Care Food Program, and several other related federal programs provide some additional funds, but primarily serve low-income families and those receiving public assistance. The Tax Reform Act of 1976 provides some tax relief for those using private group-care facilities in the form of credits for child-care expenses. But even when all patched together, these miscellaneous efforts do not create an effective whole.

The only time substantial federal funding has ever been provided for day care was during World War II, when large numbers of women entered the work force under emergency conditions. The Lanham Act funded 2,800 child-care programs

© Chuck Ford

in the defense industries from 1943 to 1946. One of the largest industry-sponsored day-care programs during the war was begun by the Kaiser Shipbuilding Corporation. Peace brought an end to most of these programs. When women workers were no longer needed they were sent back to the home, and child-care services were cut.

Private industries as well as unions continue on a very limited scale to provide group child-care facilities for employees and union members. But the frustrations of finding low-cost, high-quality child care have led parents to turn increasingly to alternative solutions. Cooperative group-care centers formed and controlled by parents have been developed, varying from small groups with parents contributing scheduled amounts of space and time, to larger groups with established facilities, programs and trained staff. Another more "radical" alternative proposed by child-care advocates calls for fathers to share—and be able to share—in child-care responsibilities. Proposals call for paternity leave for new fathers, equal time off for both parents, job sharing, and flexible work schedules. In some countries, like Norway and Sweden, flexible work structures have been instituted to complement comprehensive child-care programs. Overall, the United States has a poor rating on child-care-related programs and services when compared with other industrialized nations.

See also: Child Support
Homemakers
Marriage and Family

Organizations:

Black Child Development Institute
1463 Rhode Island Avenue N.W.
Washington, DC 20005

Coalition for Children and Youth
815 15th Street N.W.
Washington, DC 20005

Day Care and Child Development Council
of America
805 15th Street N.W.
Washington, DC 20005

Day Care Services Division
Office of Child Development
P.O. Box 1182
Washington, DC 20013

Resources:

Child Care: A Workshop Guide. Washington: National Commission on the Observance of International Women's Year, n.d. Order from: Superintendent of Documents, Government Printing Office, Washington, DC 20402.
A very useful guide including a resource section listing speakers, organizations, films and comprehensive bibliographies.

Choosing Child Care: A Guide for Parents, by Stevanne Auerbach and Linda Freedman. San Francisco: Parents and Child Care Resources, 1976. Order from: Parents and Child Care Resources, 1855 Folsom Street, San Francisco, CA 94103.
A thoughtful resource to assist parents in selecting quality day-care services.

A Commitment to Children, by Ruth Jordan. New York: Coalition of Labor Union Women, 1977. Order from: CLUW, 15 Union Square, New York, NY 10003.
A report on the CLUW Child Care Seminar, which visited day-care programs in Sweden, Israel and France.

The New Extended Family: Day Care that Works, By Ellen Galinsky and William H. Hooks. Boston: Houghton Mifflin, 1977.
A detailed sampling of fourteen different kinds of child care, how and why they work, funding, and the problem of each.

Windows on Day Care, by Mary Dublin Keyserling. New York: National Council of Jewish Women, 1972. Order from: NCJW, 15 East 26th Street, New York, NY 10010.
An essential national study of day-care needs, and how they are—and are not—being met.

CHILD SUPPORT

FOR THE WOMAN WITH YOUNG CHILDREN, DIVORCE CAN MEAN SERIOUS economic problems. She is almost certain to have responsibility for the children— the mother is given custody in nine out of ten cases. Unfortunately, she is equally as likely to receive little or no child support from her ex-husband.

Statistics on child support are difficult to find. The miscellaneous information that is available suggests two facts: child support awards are too small and payment is erratic to nonexistent. A 1971 California study found that the average award in that state was $75 per month per child. Contrast that with the $150 per month per child (exclusive of medical expenses) paid to foster parents, and the magnitude of the inadequacy is revealed.

The record of payment is equally dismal. A recent study of women receiving Aid to Families with Dependent Children (AFDC) showed that over a four-year period the rate of payment dropped from 28.7 percent to 17.4 percent. In the third year, not one of the families received more than one-third of its income from child-support payments. About 85 percent of the 900,000 children on AFDC in California receive no support from their fathers.

What does the divorced mother of young children do? The lack of high quality, inexpensive day care, coupled with the low wages she is likely to command, leaves more and more of these women with one alternative—welfare. The number of female-headed families receiving AFDC tripled from 1960 to 1973. During this same period, divorce rates skyrocketed. Conservative estimates suggest that 42 percent of AFDC children are from divorced homes. According to the Department of Health, Education and Welfare, the AFDC program serves 700,000 families which receive no support from the father and former husband. The amount owed totals nearly $8 million annually.

Certainly, many fathers default for economic reasons. Yet recent research suggests increasing willful nonsupport on the part of able-to-pay fathers. The study of AFDC mothers cited above found that about equal numbers of them came from affluent marriages as poor ones.

Some help is now available to these women. The Federal Parent Locator Service makes government records available to track down missing fathers. But the effectiveness of redress through the courts remains very erratic. A better solution may be divorce insurance, an idea advocated by some as the way to bolster the economic situation of single mothers. Clearly, some solution other than AFDC must be provided.

See also: Displaced Homemakers
Divorce
Homemakers

Organizations:

National Organization to Insure Support
Enforcement
12 West 72nd Street
New York, NY 10023

Federal Parent Locator Service
Office of Child Support Enforcement
Department of Health, Education and
Welfare
Washington, DC 20201

Resources:

Nonsupport of Legitimate Children by Affluent Fathers as a Cause of Poverty and Welfare Dependence, by Marian P. Winston and Trude Forsher. Santa Monica: The Rand Corporation, 1971.
This report provided the basis for much of the text above. Based on research done in California, it provides excellent insights into the child-support problem.

"Use of AFDC by Previously High-and-Low-Income Households," by Nancy R. Mudrick. *Social Service Review* 52(1):107–115, March 1978.
This interesting study provided much of the information in the text above.

♀ OFFICE OF CHILD SUPPORT ENFORCEMENT OFFICES ♀

REGION I: Connecticut, Maine, Massachusetts, New Hampshire, Rhode Island, Vermont

Mr. Thomas W. Hughes
Regional Representative, OCSE
John F. Kennedy Federal Building
Government Center
Boston, MA 02203

REGION II: New York, New Jersey, Puerto Rico, Virgin Islands

Mr. Joseph E. Steigman
Regional Representative, OCSE
Federal Building—Room 4016
26 Federal Plaza
New York, NY 10007

REGION III: Delaware, Maryland, Pennsylvania, Virginia, West Virginia, and District of Columbia

Mr. Daniel Fascione
Regional Representative, OCSE
3535 Market Street
Philadelphia, PA 19101

REGION IV: Alabama, Florida, Georgia, Kentucky, Mississippi, North Carolina, South Carolina, Tennessee

Mr. Charles Post
Acting Regional Representative, OCSE
101 Marrietta Tower, Suite 1801
Atlanta, GA 30323

REGION V: Illinois, Indiana, Michigan, Minnesota, Ohio, Wisconsin

Mr. William Kelsay
Regional Representative, OCSE
300 South Wacker Drive, 18th Floor
Chicago, IL 60606

REGION VI: Arkansas, Louisiana, New Mexico, Oklahoma, Texas

Mr. Arlus Johnston
Regional Representative, OCSE
Office of Child Support Enforcement
Main Tower Building—Suite 1345
Dallas, TX 75202

REGION VII: Iowa, Kansas, Missouri, Nebraska

Mr. Harvey Leroux
Regional Representative, OCSE
601 East 12th Street—Room 1759
Kansas City, MO 64106

REGION VIII: Colorado, Montana, North Dakota, South Dakota, Utah and Wyoming

Mr. Garth Youngberg
Regional Representative, OCSE
Room 11037, Federal Office Building
19th and Stout Streets
Denver, CO 80202

REGION IX: Arizona, California, Hawaii, Nevada, Guam

Mr. Richard Lewis
Regional Representative, OCSE
50 United Nations Plaza
Federal Office Building—Room 270
San Francisco, CA 94102

REGION X: Alaska, Idaho, Oregon, Washington

Mrs. Barbara Henderson
Regional Representative, OCSE
Arcade Plaza Building
1321 Second Avenue
Seattle, WA 98101

COMMISSIONS ON THE STATUS OF WOMEN

THE FIRST NATIONAL-LEVEL COMMISSION ON THE STATUS OF WOMEN WAS established by President Kennedy in 1961. Its 1963 report, *American Women,* recommended the establishment of state level commissions. In response to this report and to pressure exerted by women's groups, state and local level commissions were established. As of 1971 there were 137 officially appointed commissions representing forty-five states, the District of Columbia, and Puerto Rico, as well as forty-five county and forty-three municipal and two regional commissions.

Commissions are usually appointed either by legislative or executive authority and vary in capabilities and programs depending on the level of support in each state. Those appointed by executive authority are the most vulnerable to a changing climate of support with each new incumbent in the executive office.

In 1970 the Interstate Association of Commissions on the Status of Women formed to provide a national coordinating organization and communications network for the commissions. The group's name was officially changed to the National Association of Commissions for Women in 1975; the Association includes both local and state commissions.

See below for a listing of member Commissions.

Organizations:

National Association of Commissions for
  Women
c/o Patricia Hill Burnett, President
Michigan Women's Commission
18261 Hamilton Road
Detroit, MI 48203

Resources:

Breakthrough. Order from: National Association of Commissions for Women, address above.
  A monthly newsletter of the National Association of Commissions for Women.

Catalogue of Publications of the Commissions for Women. Washington: National Association of Commissions for Women, forthcoming. Order from: National Association of Commissions for Women, address above.

Commissions for Women: Participation of Racial and Ethnic Minority Women in Membership and Program Activities. Washington: Women's Bureau, Department of Labor, 1977. Order from: Women's Bureau, Office of the Secretary, Department of Labor, Washington, DC 20210.

♀ COMMISSIONS ON THE STATUS OF WOMEN ♀

Alabama
Women's Commission
No. 9 Office Park Circle, Room 106
Birmingham, AL 35223

Arizona
Women's Commission
1624 West Adams Street, Room 305
Phoenix, AZ 85007

Phoenix Commission on the Status of
  Women
5101 North 35th Avenue
Phoenix, AZ 85108

Tucson Women's Commission
1515 East Broadway
Tucson, AZ 85719

Arkansas
Governor's Commission on the Status of
  Women
State Capitol, Room 101
Little Rock, AR 72201

California
Commission on the Status of Women
926 J Street, Room 103
Sacramento, CA 95814

Alameda County Commission on the
  Status of Women
1730 Franklin, Suite 200
Oakland, CA 94612

El Dorado County Commission on the
  Status of Women
P.O. Box 383
South Lake Tahoe, CA 95705

Fresno County Commission on the Status
  of Women
Fresno City Hall
Fresno, CA 93721

Humboldt County Advisory Committee on
  the Status of Women
3855 Newell Lane
Eureka, CA 95501

Kern County Commission on the Status of
  Women
1111 18th Avenue
Delano, CA 93215

Los Angeles County Commission on the
  Status of Women
383 Hall of Administration
500 West Temple Street
Los Angeles, CA 90012

Marin County Commission on the Status of
  Women
Marin Civic Center, Room 276
San Rafael, CA 94903

Merced County Commission on the Status
  of Women
2941 June Court
Merced, CA 95340

Monterey County Commission on the
  Status of Women
P.O. Box 180
Salinas, CA 93901

Napa County Commission on the Status of
  Women
8th and River Streets
Napa, CA 94558

Orange County Commission on the Status
  of Women
801-C North Broadway
Santa Ana, CA 92701

Placer County Council on the Status of
  Women
11481 B Avenue, Suite 6
Auburn, CA 95603

Riverside Advisory Committee on Women
c/o Administration
4080 Lemon Street, 12th Floor
Riverside, CA 92501

San Bernardino County Commission on
  the Status of Women
San Bernardino County Human Resources
  Agency
602 South Tippecanoe Avenue, Room 1110
San Bernardino, CA 92415

San Diego County Commission on the
  Status of Women
1375 Pacific Highway, Mail St. D-13
San Diego, CA 92114

San Francisco Commission on the Status of
  Women (Joint City/County)
50 Fell Street
San Francisco, CA 94102

San Luis Obispo Commission on the Status
  of Women
310 Cerro Ramauldo
San Luis Obispo, CA 93401

Santa Barbara County Commission on the
  Status of Women
105 East Anapamu Street
Santa Barbara, CA 93104

Santa Clara County Commission on the
  Status of Women
70 West Hedding, East Wing
San Jose, CA 95110

Santa Cruz County Commission on the
  Status of Women
701 Ocean Street
Santa Cruz, CA 95606

Sonoma County Commission on the Status
  of Women
2403 Professional Drive   #101
Santa Rosa, CA 95401

Tehama County Commission on the Status
  of Women
Route 1-A, 101 Faye Street
Red Bluff, CA 96080

Tulare County Commission on the Status
of Women
1620 West Mineral King, Suite D
Visalia, CA 93277

Chico Area Commission for Women
P.O. Box 245
Chico, CA 95927

Compton Commission on the Status of
Women
205 South Willowbrook Avenue
Compton, CA 90220

Concord Status of Women Committee
c/o City of Concord, City Manager
1950 Parkside Drive
Concord, CA 94519

Los Angeles Human Relations Committee
Status of Women Subcommittee
111 City Hall, 200 North Spring Street
Los Angeles, CA 90012

Los Angeles City Commission on the
Status of Women
1701 City Hall, 200 North Spring Street
Los Angeles, CA 90012

Community Roundtable of Greater Los
Angeles
10548 Eastborne Avenue
Los Angeles, CA 90024

Pasadena City Commission on the Status
of Women
732 Rosemont
Pasadena, CA 91103

Sacramento Community Commission for
Women
2015 J Street, Suite 33
Sacramento, CA 95814

City of San Diego Advisory Board on
Women
City Administration Building
202 C Street
San Diego, CA 92101

San Joaquin Community Women's Council
215 West Stadium Drive
Stockton, CA 95204

Colorado
Commission on Women
State Service Building, Room 600-C
Denver, CO 80203

Connecticut
Permanent Commission on the Status of
Women
6 Grand Street
Hartford, CT 06115

Delaware
Delaware Council for Women
Department of Consumer Affairs &
Economic Development
630 State College Road
Dover, DE 19901

District of Columbia
Commission on the Status of Women
14th & E Streets, N.W.
District Building, Room 204
Washington, DC 20005

Florida
Governor's Commission on the Status of
Women
Office of the Governor
The Capitol
Tallahassee, FL 32304

Central Florida Commission on the Status
of Women
1011 Wymore Road, Suite 105
Winter Park, FL 32789

Dade County Commission on the Status of
Women
Dade County Courthouse, Room 2004
73 West Flagler Street
Miami, FL 33120

Monroe County Commission on the Status
of Women
P.O. Box 1293
Key West, FL 33040

Palm Beach County Commission on the
Status of Women
205 Datura Street, Suite 306
P.O. Box 1989
West Palm Beach, FL 33401

Jacksonville Mayor's Advisory Commission
on the Status of Women
330 East Bay Street
Jacksonville, FL 32202

Miami City Commission on the Status of
Women
c/o Transition, Inc.
1150 S.W. 22nd Street
Miami, FL 33129

Miami Beach City Commission on the
Status of Women
505 17th Street
Miami Beach, FL 33139

Georgia
Commission on the Status of Women
4713 Mark Court
Lilburn, GA 30247

Columbus Mayor's Commission on the
  Status of Women
P.O. Box 7171
Columbus, GA 31907

Hawaii
Commission on the Status of Women
250 South King Street, Room 500
P.O. Box 150
Honolulu, HI 96813

Hawaii County Commission on the Status
  of Women
c/o LEAA
34 Rainbow Drive
Hilo, HI 96720

Kaui County Commission on the Status of
  Women
4396 Rice Street
Lihue, HI 96766

Maui County Commission on the Status of
  Women
c/o Box F, Office of the Mayor
County of Maui
Wailuku, HI 96793

Honolulu Mayor's Committee on the
  Status of Women
Office of the Corporation Counsel
City & County of Honolulu
Honolulu, HI 96813

Idaho
Commission on Women's Programs
State House
Boise, ID 83720

Illinois
Commission on the Status of Women
1166 Debbie Lane
Macomb, IL 61455

Indiana
Lafayette/West Lafayette/Tippecanoe
  County Mayor's Task Force on the
  Status of Women
112 Knox Drive
West Lafayette, IN 47906

Columbus Mayor's Task Force on the
  Status of Women
2075 Lincoln Park Drive
Columbus, IN 47201

Crawfordsville Commission on the Status
  of Women
c/o Mayor's Office, City Building
Crawfordsville, IN 47933

Fort Wayne Women's Bureau
P.O. Box 554
Fort Wayne, IN 46801

Gary Commission on the Status of Women
475 Broadway, Suite 508
Gary, IN 46402

South Bend Commission on the Status of
  Women
P.O. Box 525
South Bend, IN 46617

Iowa
Commission on the Status of Women
Farm Bureau Building
507 10th Street
Des Moines, IA 50309

Kentucky
Commission on the Status of Women
2908 Lima Kiln Lane
Louisville, KY 40222

Louisiana
Commission on the Status of Women
2609 Leaf Lane
Shreveport, LA 71109

Baton Rouge Commission on the Needs of
  Women
1050 South Foster Drive
Baton Rouge, LA 70806

Alexandria Commission on Women
1406 Texas Street
Alexandria, LA 71301

Lafayette Mayor's Commission on the
  Needs of Women
P.O. Box 4017-C
Lafayette, LA 70502

Maine
Commission for Women
State House
Augusta, ME 04333

Maryland
Commission for Women
1100 North Eutaw Street
Baltimore, MD 20201

Anne Arundel County Commission for
  Women
Arundel Center
P.O. Box 1831
Annapolis, MD 21404

Charles County Commission for Women
149-D Jenkins Lane
Indian Head, MD 20640

Howard County Task Force on Women
5030 Eliots Oaks Road
Columbia, MD 21044

Montgomery County Commission for
Women
150 Maryland Avenue
Rockville, MD 20850

Prince George's County Commission for
Women
County Administration Building, Room
1091
14741 Governor Oden Bowie Drive
Upper Marlboro, MD 20870

Massachusetts
Governor's Commission on the Status of
Women
State Office Building, Room 1105
100 Cambridge Street
Boston, MA 02202

Boston Mayor's Commission on the Status
of Women
City Hall, Room 603
Boston, MA 02201

Quincy Mayor's Commission on the Status
of Women
City Hall, 1305 Hancock Street
Quincy, MA 02169

Michigan
Women's Commission
18261 Hamilton Road
Detroit, MI 48203

Washtenaw County Advisory Committee
on the Status of Women
Washtenaw County Building
P.O. Box 645
Ann Arbor, MI 48104

Minnesota
Council for the Economic Status of
Women
State Office Building, Room 400SW
St. Paul, MN 55155

Mississippi
Commission on the Status of Women
4361 Willawood Boulevard
Jackson, MS 39212

Hattiesburg Mayor's Committee on the
Status of Women
214 35th Avenue
Hattiesburg, MS 39401

Missouri
Commission on the Status of Women
720 Winston Place
Offallon, MO 63366

Montana
Status of Women Advisory Council
Box 202, Capitol Station
35 South Last Chance Gulch
Helena, MT 59601

Nebraska
Commission on the Status of Women
P.O. Box 94985
301 Centennial Mall South
Lincoln, NE 68509

Columbus Mayor's Commission on the
Status of Women
P.O. Box 385
Columbus, NE 68601

Omaha Mayor's Commission on the Status
of Women
Room 501, Omaha/Douglas Civic Center
1819 Farnam
Omaha, NE 68102

Lincoln/Lancaster Commission on the
Status of Women
Mayor's Office, City/County Building
Lincoln, NE 68508

Nevada
Governor's Commission on the Status of
Women
6669 Happy Circle
Las Vegas, NV 89120

Reno Commission on the Status of Women
523 Smithridge Park
Reno, NV 89502

New Hampshire
Governor's Commission on the Status of
Women
301 Capitol Street, Suite 301
Concord, NH 03301

New Jersey
Advisory Commission on the Status of
Women
Division of Community Relations, ILGWU
#3 Williams Street
Newark, NJ 07102

Bergen County Commission on the Status
of Women
170 State Street
Hackensack, NJ 07601

Union County Advisory Board on the
Status of Women
Courthouse
Elizabeth, NJ 07207

New Mexico
Commission on the Status of Women
Suite 811, Plaza del Sol
600 2nd, N.W.
Albuquerque, NM 87102

New York
State Women's Division
Office of the Governor
1350 Avenue of the Americas
New York, NY 10019

New York City Commission on the Status
of Women
250 Broadway, Room 1412
New York, NY 10007

North Carolina
Council on the Status of Women
526 North Wilmington Street
Raleigh, NC 27604

Greensboro Commission on the Status of
Women
City of Greensboro, Drawer W-2
Greensboro, NC 27402

North Dakota
Commission on the Status of Women
Governor's Council on Human Resources
State Capitol Building
Bismarck, ND 58505

Ohio
Women's Division Advisory Council
Ohio Bureau of Employment Services
145 South Front Street
Columbus, OH 43216

Oklahoma
Governor's Advisory Commission on the
Status of Women
212 State Capitol
Oklahoma City, OK 73105

Oregon
Governor's Commission on the Status of
Women
307 State Library Building
Salem, OR 97310

Pennsylvania
Commission for Women
512 Finance Building
Harrisburg, PA 17120

Puerto Rico
Commission for the Department of
Women's Rights
P.O. Box 11382
Fernandez, Juneso Station
Santurce, PR 00910

Rhode Island
Advisory Commission on Women
235 Promenade Street
Providence, RI 02908

Warwick Commission on Women
Mayor's Office, City Hall
Warwick, RI 02887

South Carolina
Commission on the Status of Women
360 Betsy Road
Charleston, SC 29407

South Dakota
Commission on the Status of Women
State Office Building
Illinois Street
Pierre, SD 57501

Tennessee
Commission on the Status of Women
100 Andrew Jackson Building
Nashville, TN 37219

Texas
Cameron County Commission on the
Status of Women
343 East Adams
Brownsville, TX 78520

Austin Commission on the Status of
Women
Travis Building
Austin, TX 78701

Dallas Commission on the Status of
Women
City Hall
Dallas, TX 75201

Fort Worth Mayor's Committee on the
Status of Women
2555 Greene Avenue
Fort Worth, TX 76109

San Angelo Commission on the Status of
Women
34 West Harris, P.O Box 5111
San Angelo, TX 76901

San Antonio Mayor's Commission on the
Status of Women
235 Yolanda Drive
San Antonio, TX 78228

Wichita Falls Mayor's Commission on the
Status of Women
4207 University
Wichita Falls, TX 76308

Utah
Governor's Commission on the Status of
Women
118 State Capitol
Salt Lake City, UT 84114

Vermont
Governor's Commission on the Status of
Women
Pavilion Office Building
Montpelier, VT 05602

Virginia
Commission on the Status of Women
P.O. Box 26
Waynesboro, VA 22980

Arlington Committee on Women
County Manager's Office
Court House, Room 204
Arlington, VA 22201

Fairfax County Commission for Women
8800 Mansion Farm Place
Alexandria, VA 22309

Alexandria Commission for Women
City Hall
Alexandria, VA 22313

Falls Church Commission for Women
217 Lee Street
Falls Church, VA 22046

Washington
State Women's Commission
15th and Columbia
Duplex Building
Olympia, WA 98504

Seattle Women's Commission
1923 Smith Tower Building
506 Second Avenue
Seattle, WA 98104

West Virginia
Women's Commission
P.O. Box 446
Institute, WV 25116

Beckley Mayor's Commission on the Status
of Women
P.O. Box 1028
Beckley, WV 25801

Wisconsin
Governor's Commission on the Status of
Women
30 West Mifflin, Room 210
Madison, WI 53703

Beaver Dam Commission on the Status of
Women
218 Front Street
Beaver Dam, WI 53916

Merrill Commission on the Status of
Women
1008 Monroe Street
Monroe, WI 54452

Wausau Mayor's Commission on the Status
of Women
3434 Riverview Court
Wausau, WI 54401

Wyoming
Commission for Women
Office of the Labor Commissioner
Barrett Building
Cheyenne, WY 82002

CONTINUING EDUCATION FOR WOMEN

THE CONCEPT OF CONTINUING EDUCATION *FOR WOMEN* WAS PIONEERED IN 1960 at the University of Minnesota. That program was developed to serve women in their middle years who had interrupted their education and work lives to marry and raise families. With their children grown, these women faced a tight job market armed only with rusty skills, outmoded credentials and little or no marketable work experience. This "retooling"-oriented program represented a shift away from the noncredit, leisure time continuing-education offerings of the pre-1960 period. The new programs of continuing education for women are essentially remedial; they attempt to redress women's discontinuous education and work patterns which result from family role expectations, and poor, inadequate, unrealistic or simply nonexistent career counseling in the undergraduate years. During the years from 1960 to 1972, the number of women twenty-five to thirty-four years old returning to school tripled. From 1963 to 1973, the number of programs increased from twenty to five hundred; today there are nearly a thousand.

The emergence of these programs raises many questions about the relative patterns of men's and women's education and career lives, and points up the need for adequate child care and for paternity leaves to make possible equal sharing of home and child-rearing responsibilities. While remedial programs are necessary now, they do nothing to eliminate the original problem—the interruption of women's education during the years their children are young. Perhaps continuing education for women should be seen as a *transitional* program, bridging the gap until both men and women have a full range of options: until women are free to continue their education and careers because adequate day care is available; until men are free to interrupt their work lives to raise children; until both parents have the option of part-time work and shared child-rearing responsibilities.

See also: Displaced Homemakers
Financial Aid for Education
Older Women

Organizations:

Continuing Education for Women Section
Adult Education Association
810 18th Street N.W.
Washington, DC 20006

Continuing Education for Women Section
National University Extension Association
One Dupont Circle N.W., #360
Washington, DC 20036

Resources:

Continuing Education: A Guide to Career Development Programs. Syracuse: Gaylord Professional Publications, 1977.

A major compilation of continuing education programs, this volume is organized by state and includes an annotated bibliography.

"Continuing Education for Women, 1960–1975: A Critical Appraisal," by Joy K. Rice. *Educational Record* 56 (4):240–249.

An excellent article discussing the history of and changes in continuing education for women. It provided the basis for the text above.

Continuing Education for Women: Current Development. Washington: Women's Bureau, Department of Labor, 1974. Order from: Women's Bureau, Office of the Secretary, Department of Labor, Washington, DC 20210.

A description of the overall situation for women's continuing education programs with statistics on growth up to 1972.

Continuing Education: Reentry and the Mature Woman: Annotated Selected References, ed. by Rita Costick. San Francisco: Women's Educational Equity Communications Network, 1977. Order from: WEECN, Far West Laboratory, 1855 Folsom Street, San Francisco, CA 94103.

A good source of information on the mature woman student, counseling for her, and continuing-education program development.

Get Credit for What You Know. Washington: Women's Bureau, Department of

Labor, 1974. Order from: Women's Bureau, Office of the Secretary, Department of Labor, Washington, DC 20210.

For the returning student who can't attend classes and wants to know how to get high school or college credit by examination.

CREDIT

"WOMEN CONTROL THE WEALTH IN THIS COUNTRY" IS AN OFTEN RECITED myth. Many women do *manage* the household expenses, but that does not constitute wealth nor even control over the average household budget. Until 1974 married women could not even get credit in their own names, and single women were frequently denied credit because they were deemed unstable, even though studies have shown women to be better credit risks than men. Discrimination against women credit seekers is not uncommon, even though it is now illegal. The Equal Credit Opportunity Act (ECOA) of 1974 prohibits discrimination in the extension of credit based on sex or marital status and, as amended in 1976, also prohibits discrimination based on race, color, religion, age, national origin, and receipt of public assistance. Although there are twelve separate federal agencies responsible for enforcement of the Act, women as well as creditors are often uninformed and uneducated about the importance of credit rights.

In order to borrow money you must establish credit worthiness based on *your* ability to pay and *your* past credit history. Under the ECOA, wives can have joint credit accounts reported in their own names instead of solely in the husband's name (e.g., Ms. Mary Doe rather than Mrs. John Doe). This is especially helpful to homemakers, who have the most difficult time of all establishing credit and are the most financially vulnerable in cases of divorce or widowhood. However, little has actually changed since the ECOA went into effect. According to research by the Consumer Counseling Corporation, only 9 percent of the women queried nationwide responded to an offer by financial institutions to list the wife's name as well as the husband's on credit accounts.

There are many ways to establish a credit history: open a checking and savings account in your own name, and then apply for a loan against your savings account; apply for a local department store charge account; have a phone and utilities listed in your name. Once you have established a good payment record, usually after one year, you should have an adequate credit history, and depending on income and job stability, should be able to obtain credit. If you are denied credit you have a right to know the reason in writing. If you have difficulty getting a reasonable answer and suspect discrimination you can do something about it. For specific information on credit rights in your state, contact the state Commission on the Status of Women (see listing on page 55) or the local chapter of the National Organization for Women.

Organizations:

Consumer Credit Project
261 Kimberley Road
Barrington, IL 60010

Resources:

Credit: A Workshop Guide. Washington: National Commission on the Observance of International Women's Year, n.d. Order from: Superintendent of Documents, Government Printing Office, Washington, DC 20402.
This guide includes in its resource section a glossary of terms, speakers, local NOW Credit Task Force Coordinators, and bibliography.

Everywoman's Guide to Financial Independence, by Mavis Arthur Groza. Millbrae: Les Femmes, 1976. Order from: Les Femmes, 231 Adrian Road, Millbrae, CA 94030.
A comprehensive resource covering budgeting, credit (how to get it and your rights), money management, and a helpful chapter on financing a divorce.

Let's Talk About Money. New York: Consumer and Community Services, Institute of Life Insurance, 1976. Order from: Consumer and Community Services, Institute of Life Insurance, 277 Park Avenue, New York, NY 10017.
A pamphlet covering the basics of money management.

New Credit Rights for Women, by Sara Lyn Smith. Barrington: Consumer Credit Project, 1978. Order from Consumer Credit Project, 261 Kimberley Road, Barrington, IL 60610.
A comprehensive guide to credit rights and remedies for women.

Women: To Your Credit. Baltimore: Commercial Credit Corporation, 1977. Order from: Public Relations Commercial Corporation, 300 St. Paul Place, Baltimore, MD 21202.
This free booklet outlines your credit rights and includes a state-by-state list of Commissions on the Status of Women for further information.

♀ WHAT CREDITORS MAY ASK ♀

The ECOA does not *guarantee* anyone an automatic right to credit. It does, however, require the creditor to apply the same criteria of credit worthiness to all applicants. The creditor has the right to be assured that you are willing and able to repay your debts. To determine your credit worthiness *the creditor may request information about and consider the following:*

GENERAL

— Your name
— Your age (provided the creditor uses a valid credit scoring system)
— The source of the income upon which you are relying for credit
— The number of children (dependents) you have, their ages, and any financial obligations you may have related to them
— Any obligations you have to pay: alimony, child support, or separate maintenance payments
— Your permanent residence and immigration status
— A list of all of your assets and the name of anyone who owns them jointly with you
— The amount of your income
— The place of your employment

— The length of time you have worked at your place of employment
— Any outstanding debts that you have
— Whether you have a telephone in your home
— Whether your own or rent your home
— The length of time at your present residence
— The savings and checking accounts in your name

MARITAL STATUS

The creditor may ask about your marital status only if:
— You are making a joint application with your spouse
— Your spouse will be an authorized user of the account
— You reside in a community property state
— You list assets which are located in a community property state
— If, and only if, one of these exceptions applies, the creditor may only ask whether you are "married," "unmarried" or "separated."

INFORMATION ABOUT YOUR SPOUSE

The creditor may ask you for information about your spouse *only if:*
— Your spouse will be a joint holder of the account or an authorized user or contractually liable for it
— You are relying on your spouse's income to repay your debts
— You are living in or relying upon assets that are located in a community property state
— You are relying on alimony, child support or separate maintenance payments from a spouse or former spouse as a basis for your repayment ability.

ALIMONY, CHILD SUPPORT, AND SEPARATE MAINTENANCE

— If you are relying on these sources of funds to establish your ability to meet your financial obligations, the creditor may ask whether there is a court order that requires the payments, and may also consider the length of time and regularity of the payments and your ex-spouse's credit history.

PART-TIME WORK

— Though creditors may not discount your income because it is from part-time work, they may consider the regularity and probable continuity of such income (for example, they may consider whether it is temporary or a regular part-time job).

WHERE TO SEND YOUR COMPLAINT

Lending Institution   *Regulatory Agencies*

National Banks   Comptroller of the Currency
                                  Consumer Affairs Division
                                  Washington, DC 20219

State Member Banks	Federal Reserve Bank serving the area in which the state member bank is located
Non-Member Insured Banks	Federal Deposit Insurance Corporation Regional Director for the region in which the non-member insured bank is located
Savings Institutions Insured by the FSLIC and members of the FHLB System (except for Savings Banks insured by FDIC)	The Federal Home Loan Bank Supervisory Agent in the district in which the institution is located
Federal Credit Unions	Regional Office of the National Credit Union Administration serving the area in which the federal credit union is located
Creditors Subject to Civil Aeronautics Board	Director, Bureau of Enforcement Civil Aeronautics Board 1825 Connecticut Avenue N.W. Washington, DC 20428
Creditors Subject to Interstate Commerce Commission	Office of Proceedings Interstate Commerce Commission Washington, DC 20523
Creditors Subject to Packers and Stockyards Act	Nearest Packers and Stockyards Administration area supervisor
Small Business Investment Companies	U.S. Small Business Administration 1441 L Street N.W. Washington, DC 20416
Brokers and Dealers	Securities and Exchange Commission Washington, DC 20549
Federal Land Banks Federal Land Bank Association Federal Intermediate Credit Banks Production Credit Associations	Farm Credit Administration 490 L'Enfant Plaza S.W. Washington, DC 20578
Retail Department Stores Consumer Finance Companies All Other Creditors All Nonbank Credit Card Issuers	Federal Trade Commission Equal Credit Opportunity Washington, DC 20580

(Lenders operating on a local or regional basis should use the address of the FTC Regional Office in which they operate.)

Bank Cards issued by national banks (the word "national" appears in the bank's name)	Comptroller of the Currency Consumer Affairs Division Washington, DC 20219

Bank Cards issued by state banks   Contact the Federal Reserve Bank
serving the area in which the state
member bank is located.

Excerpted from *New Credit Rights for Women* (Consumer Credit Project, Inc., 1978).

♀ DIRECTORY OF FEMINIST FEDERAL CREDIT UNIONS ♀

Alaska Feminist Federal Credit Union
621 West 5th Avenue
Anchorage, AK 99501
   (907) 276-3261

Bay Area Feminist Federal Credit Union
944 Market Street, #617
San Francisco, CA 94101
   (415) 391-3003

California Feminist Federal Credit Union
   Main Office
   P.O. Box 2329
   920 F Street
   San Diego, CA 92112
      (714) 238-1922

   L.A. Service Center
   P.O. Box 19176
   1112 South Crenshaw
   Los Angeles, CA 90019
      (213) 936-0950

Chicagoland Women's Federal Credit
Union
P.O. Box 163
Chicago, IL 60659
   (312) 674-5650

Colorado Feminist Federal Credit Union
1458 Pennsylvania Street
Denver, CO 80203
   (303) 837-0622

Connecticut Feminist Federal Credit Union
170 York Street
New Haven, CT 06510
   (203) 777-6330 or 777-6329

Feminist Federal Credit Union
   Main Branch
   P.O. Box 20008
   Detroit, MI 48220
      (313) 892-7190

   Ann Arbor Branch
   500 East William
   Ann Arbor, MI 48104
      (313) 662-5400

   Lansing Branch
   217 Townsend Street
   Lansing, MI 48933
      (313) 489-4521

First Pennsylvania Feminist Credit Union
4th and Market Streets
Harrisburg, PA 17101
   (717) 761-1836

Florida Feminist Credit Union
5900 S.W. 73rd Street, Room 102
South Miami, FL 33143
   (305) 665-7611

Freedom Feminist Federal Credit Union
P.O. Box 8123
Pittsburgh, PA 15217
   (412) 521-5183

Houston Area Feminist Federal Credit
Union
2418 Travis
Houston, TX 77006
   (713) 527-9108

Los Angeles Feminist Federal Credit
Union
1516 Westwood Boulevard, Suite 204
Los Angeles, CA 90024
   (213) 475-3889

Massachusetts Feminist Federal Credit
Union
186½ Hampshire Street
Cambridge, MA 02139
   (617) 661-0450

Metro Toronto Women's Credit Union
15 Birch Avenue
Toronto, Ontario, Canada
   (416) 960-0322

New York Feminist Federal Credit Union
   Main Branch
   23 Cornelia Street
   New York, NY 10014
      (212) 255-4664

Brooklyn Branch
c/o National Congress of
 Neighborhood Women
11-29 Catherine Street
Brooklyn, NY 11211
 (212) 388-6666

Washington Area Feminist Federal Credit
 Union
1424 16th Street N.W., Room 104
Washington, DC 20036
 (202) 322-1132

Washington State Feminist Federal Credit
 Union
P.O. Box 22382
Seattle, WA 98122
 (206) 325-7162

Westchester Women's Federal Credit
 Union
100 Mamaroneck Avenue, Room 4
White Plains, NY 10601
 (914) 948-5532

Women's Southwest Federal Credit Union
P.O. Box 431
Dallas, TX 75221
 (214) 522-3560

CRIMINAL JUSTICE

UNTIL RECENTLY FEMALE OFFENDERS WERE INVISIBLE AS A GROUP. LITTLE HAD been written about them, few statistics had been collected, and even fewer projects had been developed or initiated specifically for them. Nearly all of the penal reform introduced in the last fifty years has benefited men only. And most new programs allowed women to participate only as an afterthought.

The picture is changing—but very slowly. One reason is that the women's movement has called attention to discrimination against all women, pointing out that the woman offender automatically has two strikes against her—as an offender and as a woman. Also, there has been a dramatic increase in the number of women who are arrested and who go to jail and prison. From 1960 to 1972, female arrests for serious crimes increased three times faster than the rate for males. In 1970, 50 percent more women were admitted to state and federal prisons than in 1960.

If you are concerned about the status of the woman offender, it is important to know what the facts are—and how they have been distorted. Some popular articles have made the following *false* claims:

— Violent crimes committed by women are increasing rapidly.
— The rise in crimes committed by women is due to the women's movement encouraging female crime.
— Prostitutes account for the majority of women offenders, and since prostitutes enjoy their work, they can't be rehabilitated.

The truth is:

— Women offenders account for only 10 percent of violent crimes, and this figure has remained constant for the past twenty years.
— The average woman in prison has little of the consciousness associated with the women's movement. She is typically poor, has little education and few marketable skills—and this often desperate economic reality has made her turn to crime.
— Only 3.4 percent of women arrested in 1973 were charged with prostitution.

Although arrest rates of women have increased, women still commit fewer crimes than men. Women represent one of every five persons arrested, one of every ten persons in jail, one of every sixteen persons on parole, and 26 percent of cases heard in juvenile court. Property crimes—specifically larceny—account for 24 percent of all female arrests. The next largest percentage is for disorderly conduct and running away. Homicides account for less than 1 percent of arrests. The most dramatic increases in arrests have involved such property crimes as larceny, embezzlement, forgery and fraud.

More than anything else, female offenders need help finding jobs. Lack of job skills is the most important problem they report. The second is a lack of education, and the third is difficulty in arranging for child care, readjusting to family life and coping with prejudice. Most want clerical, professional or semiprofessional jobs.

The typical prison industrial program puts women to work at dead-end jobs sewing prison clothes or making flags or mops. An Oklahoma study of 101 women showed that 25 percent wanted to learn business-related skills, 25 percent wanted medical skills. Eight women wanted technical trade skills such as welding, meat cutting and barbering.

Despite their special and very pressing needs, women offenders often receive inadequate services and inferior treatment. In the areas of training, facilities, provision for child care, health services, and sentencing, women offenders are not being treated equally.

Many communities and at least four states and the District of Columbia do not have institutional facilities for women. Women offenders are either sent to other towns or states, or kept in segregated sections of existing male facilities. This means, in some cases, separation by hundreds of miles from their families. Women in male prisons do not have equal access to special education and job programs. Finally, because facilities are so limited, first-time offenders, girls, and hard-core repeaters are often housed together—more so than happens with men.

Men's prisons have an average of ten vocational training programs per institution compared with 2.7 in women's prisons. Men's programs include such high-paying skills as electronics, printing, plumbing, data processing—while women's focus on housekeeping, cosmetology, food services and the like.

Few programs are sensitive to the needs of offenders as mothers. Their special problems include loss of contact with their children, and loss of custody for mothers who are sole supporters, with the possibility that their children will be placed in foster homes or referred to adoption agencies. A 1974 survey of eighty-one federal and state prisons by the Junior League of New York revealed that thirty-nine did not have any programs for inmates' children, and of the rest, only three had actual nurseries. Even under supervision in their communities, offenders face similar problems to those in prison. Probation and parole conditions often require them to find and keep jobs. But most training and education programs do not provide for child care.

Women's prisons are less likely than men's to have a full-time medical staff or hospital facilities. In Texas, no regular Pap tests are given and no gynecologist is available to serve 650 female inmates. Most prisons have no health-care facilities for either mothers or their newborn children. In Pennsylvania and Connecticut, studies showed that women were pressured to give their babies up for adoption. In some prisons, women are denied abortions.

Certain state statutes dictate that women, but not men, be given indeterminate sentences, which means that their sentences are potentially longer than men's for the same violations. Prior to trial, young, nonviolent first offenders are often given the option to participate in a supervised program that may lead to dismissal of pending charges. In most communities that have such programs and that allow women to participate, women have second-class status, their special needs and problems are not acknowledged and the staff is primarily male. Most programs still exclude women charged with prostitution and, in some cases, shoplifting.

Health, counseling, libraries, religious and recreational services are less available to women than to men. In all-female institutions, such services are more likely to be lacking entirely.

Teenage female offenders face an even greater level of discrimination. Most juvenile girls in custodial institutions are there because of "status offenses" such as truancy, running away and incorrigibility—offenses for which adults could not be confined. Most boys are there because they are "delinquent"—i.e., have committed offenses that would be criminal if committed by an adult. Only girls are confined for promiscuity, which can include anything from prostitution to having sex before a parent thinks she is ready. Girls are also confined for longer periods of time than boys.

♀ WHO *IS* THE WOMAN OFFENDER? ♀

Age: Two-thirds of women behind bars are under thirty years old.

Ethnic background: Fifty percent are black.

Education: Forty-five percent have not finished high school.

Marital status: At the time of incarceration, 27 percent were single, and only 10 percent had been living with spouses.

Children: Seventy-three percent have children. Fifty-six percent had dependent children living at home when they went to jail or prison.

Welfare: Fifty-six percent received welfare as adults.

Childhood: Half came from two-parent homes; 31 percent lived with the mother only.

Work: Almost all have worked at some time in their lives. Most want to continue working.

Vocational training: Most often in clerical skills, cosmetology, nursing or paramedical services.

Reprinted from the May 1977 issue of *Women's Agenda* and based on two publications of the Female Offender Resource Center (now defunct): *Female Offenders: Problems and Programs* and *Female Offender Workshop Guide* (see Resources).

See also: Prostitution

Organizations:

Center for Women Policy Studies
2000 P Street N.W.
Washington, DC, 20036

Girls Clubs of America
205 Lexington Avenue
New York, NY 10016

National Association of Women in
  Criminal Justice
906 Fifth Avenue
Pittsburgh, PA 15219

New Directions for Women
346 South Scott
Tucson, AZ 85701

Women's Prison Association
110 Second Avenue
New York, NY 10003

Resources:

The Female Offender, by Laura Crites. Lexington: Lexington Books, 1976.
An anthology covering areas such as the history of female offenders, laws and the courts, incarceration and prostitution.

Female Offenders. Madison: Women's Education Resources, University of Wisconsin Extension, 1977. Order from: Communications Program, University of Wisconsin Extension, 217 Lowell Hall, 610 Langdon Street, Madison, WI 53706.
An information packet containing a fact sheet, articles, a list of services, research findings and a bibliography.

Female Offender Workshop Guide. Washington: Commission on the Observance of International Women's Year, 1977. Order from: Superintendent of Documents, Government Printing Office, Washington, DC 20402.
Includes an extensive resource list of organizations and government agencies. The text above is based partially on the *Guide.*

Little Sisters and the Law. Washington: Female Offender Resource Center, National Offender Services Coordination Program, American Bar Association, 1977. Order from: National Criminal Justice Reference Service, P.O. Box 600, Rockville, MD 20580.
Looks at the criminal justice system as it affects young women, discusses what can be done and includes resources.

Symposium on Status Offenders, Proceedings. New York: National Council of Jewish Women, 1976. Order from: NCJW, 15 East 26th Street, New York, NY 10010.
Proceedings of the conference, including recommendations and a participants list.

♀ WHAT YOU CAN DO TO HELP WOMEN OFFENDERS ♀

You or your group may want to help women offenders but you may not know where to start or how to put your energies to the best use. The following recommendations may suggest some projects:

1. *Read.* Begin with materials listed here and go on from there. Bibliographies on women offenders are now becoming available.

2. *Study your community's criminal justice system.* Find out where women in your community go when they are arrested, are sentenced and return to community life. Attend a trial. Ride in a police car. Visit the jail. Find out who controls funds for prisoners in your state and community. How interested are these people in helping women offenders? How can citizens' groups make sure the problems of women offenders are not dismissed as insignificant?

3. *Compile facts and figures* on women offenders in your community. How many are arrested? Convicted? How many have private lawyers, and how many have court-appointed lawyers? What sentences are the women getting? How

many get probation? How many have children for whom they are responsible? How many have a history of drug addiction? You need facts and figures to plan programs, and to obtain funding to establish programs. (High school and college students might be willing to help gather this information for school projects.)

4. *Find out what community resources exist* for offenders. One way to do this is to prepare a directory of prisoner assistance programs in your area. Such a directory could list all the groups that serve offenders or ex-offenders, their activities, criteria for eligibility for the services they offer, and names and addresses of contacts at the organization. In the course of this investigation, your group could also identify organizations that refuse to help offenders.

5. *Keep your local newspaper informed* of conditions of prisoners and ex-prisoners, of correctional programs and budgetary allocations. Bring to the public more information about women prisoners. Don't let them be ignored because of their numerical minority in the system.

6. *Meet officials* in the criminal justice system. Find out what they are doing, are planning, or would like to do for women offenders. Discuss your group's interest in helping women offenders. Identify people in the system who will support your efforts. Invite them to talk to your group.

7. *Talk to women offenders* to determine what kinds of programs they believe would be most useful.

8. *Learn about the problems of juvenile offenders.* Who are the girls who get into trouble with the law in your community? What are their needs? What kinds of personal counseling, help with independent living and with education, vocational training and employment are they getting?

9. *Develop tentative plans* for a few programs. Discuss these with officials and try to obtain their support.

Different groups have different strengths. Groups with connections in the state legislature, for example, might consider undertaking a project to reduce legally sanctioned restrictions on employment of ex-offenders, particularly in occupations with high concentrations of female employees.

Groups with strong community ties might undertake projects aimed at easing the reintegration of women offenders after incarceration, or projects to build support for community residential programs.

Other groups might concentrate on heightening public awareness of offenders' problems—particularly those of women offenders—and ascertaining the views of public officials and candidates for elective office on the proper treatment of women offenders.

Still other groups could teach women prisoners and youthful offenders their legal rights. Students in a course on women and the law might assist in such efforts.

Reprinted from the May 1977 issue of *Women's Agenda,* and excerpted from *From Convict to Citizen* by Virginia A. McArthur. Washington: District of Columbia Commission on the Status of Women, 1974.

DES

DES STANDS FOR DIETHYLSTILBESTROL, A SYNTHETIC ESTROGEN THAT WAS given to millions of women from the 1940's through the 1960's for certain pregnancy complications. Now, research has revealed that female children born to these women may develop an abnormal growth of the genital tract called adenosis as well as a rare form of vaginal cancer. It is estimated that there are up to three million DES daughters, as they are called, and so far, three hundred cases of cancer have been reported. Fifty percent to 85 percent of DES daughters can expect to develop adenosis. If you're under thirty-five, ask your mother if she was given DES and if she was, see a doctor.

Organizations:

Coalition for Medical Rights for Women
4079A 24th Street
San Francisco, CA 94114

DES Action National
Long Island Jewish-Hillside Medical
 Center
New Hyde Park, NY 11040

Resources:

The Facts on DES Action. Plainview, 1977. Order from: DES Action, P.O. Box 1977, Plainview, NY 11803.

This pamphlet explains to both mother and daughter the facts about DES and how to cope with it.

DISABLED WOMEN

WHILE DISABLED WOMEN FACE ALL THE SAME BARRIERS TO FULL PARTICIPA-tion in society that handicapped men do, they often find themselves at a double disadvantage. Some have made the case that it is easier for women to adjust to disability because dependence is accepted as part of the female sex role. But because less is expected of them, disabled women may find themselves left out of vocational training programs or other special services for the handicapped. Now, just as other women have demanded access to a full range of options, so have disabled women.

Because the census has not fully recorded information on handicapped persons, statistics are hard to find. Estimates place the number of disabled women at five million. Several laws have been passed in recent years, addressing the problems of public transportation, education, employment and vocational training, and health care. But enforcement has not been good. There are not adequate complaint procedures and redress is slow to come, where it is available at all.

Disabled women demonstrated their strength as a significant force within the women's movement at the International Women's Year conference in Houston in 1977. Organized into a caucus, they completely rewrote the original, inadequate plank of the National Plan of Action concerned with disabled women. They took the floor, presented the new motion, and saw it passed amid cheers of support. Continuing activity from this spirited group may be expected in the years to come.

See also: International Women's Year
            (National Plan of Action)

Organizations:

Disability Rights Center
1346 Connecticut Avenue N.W.
Washington, DC 20036

National Center for Law and the
  Handicapped
1235 North Eddy Street
South Bend, IN 46617

Office for Handicapped Individuals
Department of Health, Education and
  Welfare
Washington, DC 20201

Resources:

*Ready Reference Guide: Resources for Disabled People.*Washington: Rehabilitation Services Administration, Department of Health, Education and Welfare, 1977. Order from: Superintendent of Documents, Government Printing Office, Washington, DC 20402.

An extensive guide to government agencies and private organizations which provide services of all types for the handicapped.

Toward Intimacy: Family Planning and Sexuality Concerns of Physically Disabled Women, by the Task Force on Concerns of Physically Disabled Women. New York: Human Sciences Press, 1978.

Written for the physically disabled woman, this pamphlet helps her understand and deal with her feelings about her body, her partner, and her sexual needs. Includes excellent concrete advice and information on birth control.

Within Reach: Providing Family Planning Services to Physically Disabled Women, by the Task Force on Concerns of Physically Disabled Women. New York: Human Sciences Press, 1978.

A companion volume to *Toward Intimacy,* this pamphlet provides information for health-care facilities on how to serve disabled clients. Both are recommended.

Laws Prohibiting Discrimination Against the Handicapped

Civil Service Act: amended in 1948 to prohibit discrimination in federal employment.

Architectural Barriers Act: passed in 1968; requires that accommodations and facilities be accessible to the handicapped; this may include the installation of ramps where there are stairs or elevators where there are escalators.

The Rehabilitation Act: passed in 1973, this is probably the most comprehensive legislation; it requires, among other things, affirmative action in employment, placement and advancement of handicapped persons, prohibits discrimination by federal contractors and establishes a compliance board for the enforcement of the Architectural Barriers Act.

The Urban Mass Transit Act: amended in 1970 to require access for the elderly and handicapped.

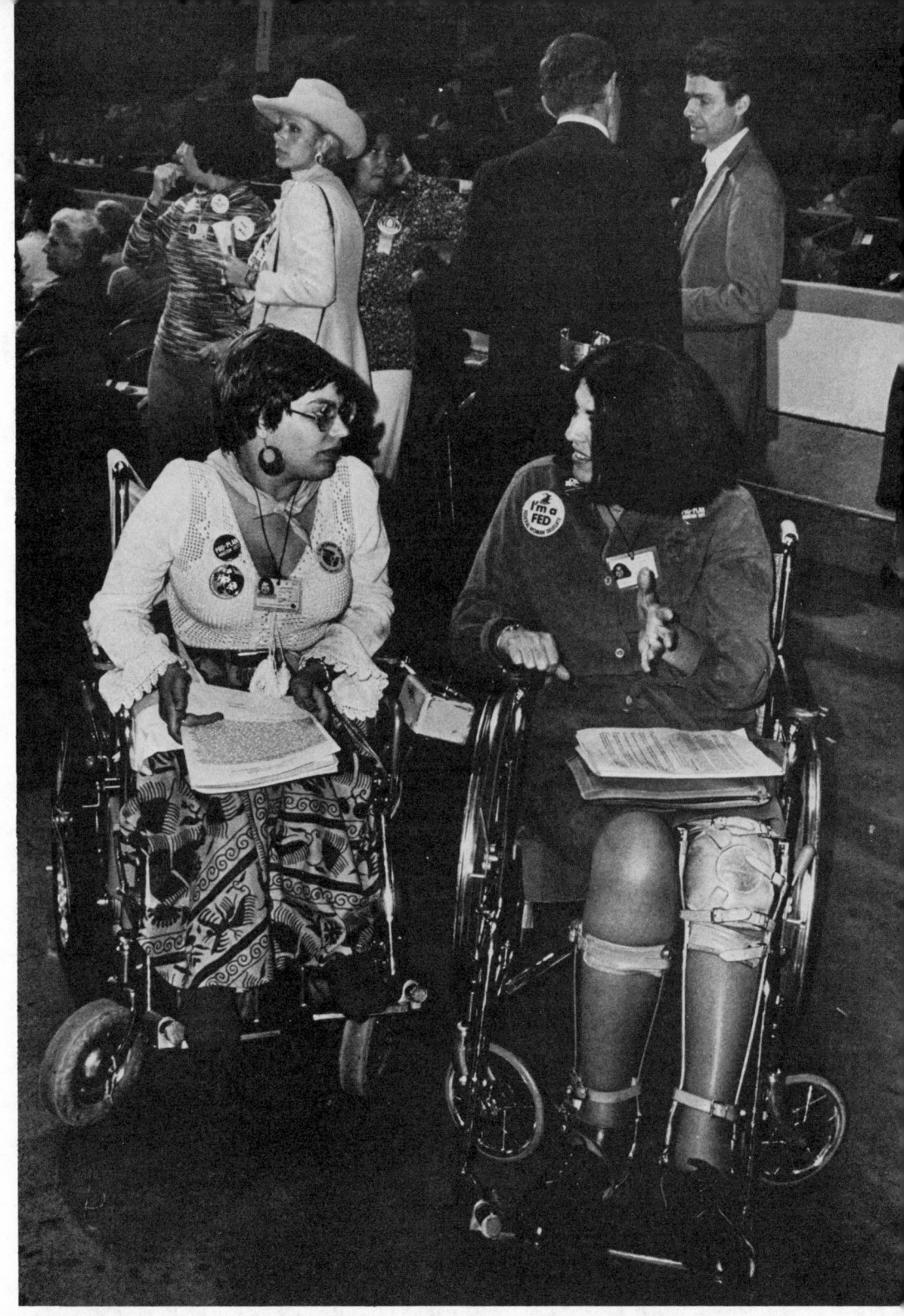

Two members of the disabled women's caucus at the National Women's Conference in Houston, November 1977. © *Diana Mara Henry, 1978*

DISPLACED HOMEMAKERS

A DISPLACED HOMEMAKER IS AN INDIVIDUAL WHO HAS BEEN DOING UNPAID labor in the home, who is not gainfully employed, who has had or would have difficulty in securing employment, and who has been dependent on the no-longer-available income of another family member. Most often, a displaced homemaker is a woman in her middle years who has devoted her life to raising children and keeping house, and who is "displaced" through divorce or widowhood. These women, if widowed, are not eligible for Social Security because they are under the age limit (sixty years) and, until 1979, could not qualify if their marriages did not last the required twenty years. Due to the efforts of displaced-homemaker activists, the length-of-marriage requirement was dropped to ten years. Divorced women have an equally rough time; only 14 percent are awarded alimony and only about half of those collect regularly. There are an estimated 3.3 million displaced homemakers nationwide.

Legislation which would create multiservice centers for displaced homemakers in each of the fifty states was first introduced into the Congress in 1975. In 1978, it was passed in a different form as part of the Comprehensive Employment and Training Act. Title III of the Act states that the Secretary of Labor "shall make available financial assistance to conduct programs to provide employment opportunities and appropriate training and support services to displaced homemakers." These women desperately need the job counseling, vocational training, and education this legislation provides.

See also: Divorce
            Homemakers
            Legal Status
            Marriage and Family

Organizations:

Displaced Homemakers Network
c/o Business and Professional Women's Foundation
2012 Massachusetts Avenue N.W.
Washington, DC 20036

Resources:

The Displaced Homemaker. Madison: Women's Education Resources, University of Wisconsin Extension, n.d. Order from: Communications Program, University of Wisconsin Extension, 217 Lowell Hall, 610 Langdon Street, Madison, WI 53706.
While this packet of reprints includes some material that is specific to Wisconsin, it also covers the national scene and provides a needed resource in this area.

The Legal Status of Homemakers. Washington: Homemakers Committee, National Commission on the Observance of International Women's Year, 1977. Order from Superintendent of Documents, Government Printing Office, Washington, DC 20402.
This state-by-state series of fifty pamphlets provides an excellent background on the homemaker before she is displaced, and sheds light on how she becomes a displaced homemaker. Specify the state(s) desired when ordering.

DIVORCE

OVER THE PAST TWENTY-FIVE TO THIRTY YEARS, DIVORCE HAS BECOME increasingly socially acceptable—certainly it is much more common. In fact, one-third of first marriages taking place today will probably end in divorce. Add to that the number of remarriages that fail and the rate rises: approximately 40 percent of all marriages end in divorce. Another factor contributing to the higher divorce statistics is the recent reform of divorce law which has made getting a divorce much easier. So-called no-fault divorce laws are now in effect in almost every state.

The basic change instituted by no-fault divorce laws is the removal of the concept of guilt from the divorce proceedings. Previously, one member of the marriage sued the other for divorce and had to prove guilt according to certain criteria. Acceptable grounds for divorce varied from state to state and included such things as desertion, adultery and mental cruelty. No-fault divorce is pretty universally considered an improvement; it eliminates the emotional scars of long court battles, makes divorce cheaper, and simply makes more sense. It is more in line with today's "equal partnership" concept of marriage.

The no-fault divorce laws are fine as far as they go. Unfortunately, they don't go far enough. Marriage law is still based on an old set of assumptions, while divorce law has had partial reform based on new ones. The woman who held up her end of a traditional marriage now finds herself unprepared to face a modern divorce. The final result for many women is economic hardship.

One of the crucial factors in divorce is the division of property. State laws vary widely, making any generalizations difficult to draw. Basically, state laws are of two types—common law and community property—with individual variations of each. But the tremendous discretionary power of judges tends to blur even this basic difference in many cases. If considerable common property has accumulated over the years, and the woman has contributed to the marriage through working in the home, she may find herself in unfortunate financial circumstances. The homemaker's contribution to the support of the family is ignored in all but a handful of cases. A woman may have put her husband through professional or graduate school, kept house, raised the children, and provided all the support necessary to a successful and prosperous career. But at the time of divorce, the courts may simply award all property to her husband as titleholder.

Alimony presents another problem. There is an unfortunate but popular stereotype of the divorced woman living in the lap of luxury while the ex-husband toils endlessly to keep up with huge alimony payments. Recent research has shown just how false this picture is. Some states never award alimony and others disallow it—by law or by custom—in the case of a wife's adultery. A 1975 survey found that only 14 percent of divorced women are awarded alimony in the first place, and fewer than half of those collect regularly; many do not collect at all. Divorced women also lose such benefits as health insurance and social security.

Finally, there is the relative earning power of the parties at the end of a marriage. Property settlements and alimony awards are often made as if the two parties were economically equal. In fact, they are not equal at all. A basic function of the traditional marriage is to enhance the husband's career and his earning power. This is done at the expense of the wife's economic independence. Instead of preparing herself for employment and building her own career, she stays home and provides all the necessary support for her husband's success. When divorced, she has rusty skills, if any, and little or no job experience. She is in no condition to support herself, yet may get only a small settlement or alimony award. A study from the University of Michigan states flatly, "The economic status of former husbands improves while that of former wives deteriorates."

There is little doubt that extensive reform of the law is necessary. The National Conference of Commissioners on Uniform State Laws has drafted a piece of model legislation called the Uniform Marriage and Divorce Act. It has been approved by the American Bar Association, but has been adopted in full by only eight states (Arizona, Colorado, Georgia, Kentucky, Minnesota, Montana, New Jersey, and Washington). Many states have adopted the first, no-fault part of the divorce section which states that "the legal dissolution of a marriage should be based solely on a finding that factually the marriage is irretrievably broken." But adoption of the second part is crucial to equitable divorce settlements: "Distribution of property upon the termination of a marriage should be treated, as nearly as possible, like the distribution of assets incident to the dissolution of a partnership." This method of property distribution would disallow the automatic transfer of all property to the husband and would encourage careful consideration of the wife's contribution to the marriage, in whatever form.

See also: Child Support
            Displaced Homemakers
            Marriage and Family

Organizations:

Children's Rights
3443 17th Street N.W.
Washington, DC 20010

National Association for Divorced Women
200 Park Avenue
New York, NY 10017

Organization of Women for Legal
  Awareness
94 Claremont Avenue
Maplewood, NJ 07040

Resources:

Issues in Marital Property Reform. Madison: Women's Education Resources, University of Wisconsin Extension, n.d. Order from: Communications Program, 217 Lowell Hall, University of Wisconsin Extension, 610 Langdon Street, Madison, WI 53706.

This packet on marital property reform includes several important articles on women's contributions to marriage and how common property is—or should be—divided in divorce.

The Legal Status of Homemakers. Washington: Homemakers Committee, National Commission on the Observance of International Women's Year, 1977. Crder from: Superintendent of Documents, Government Printing Office, Washington, DC 20402.

This series of pamphlets, one for each state, describes the divorce law of the state and the implications for the divorced woman. Specify state(s) desired when ordering.

Marriage and Divorce Today: The Professionals' Newsletter. Order from: Marriage and Divorce Today, 2315 Broadway, New York, NY 10024.

Uniform Marriage and Divorce Act. Chicago: National Conference of Commissioners on Uniform State Laws, 1970. Order from: National Conference of Commissioners, 645 North Michigan Avenue, Chicago, IL 60611.

EARNINGS GAP

THE EARNINGS GAP IS THE DIFFERENCE IN AVERAGE WAGES RECEIVED BY women as compared to men. Women who worked at full-time jobs in 1976 earned only fifty-eight cents for every dollar earned by men. This means a woman would have to work nearly nine days to receive the same earnings gained by a man in five days. Unfortunately, over the past twenty years, the earnings gap has widened instead of closing. In 1955, women's median earnings were 63.9 percent of men's; by 1976, the percentage had dropped to 58 percent. This trend is due largely to the combination of women's increased labor-force participation with their concentration in low-paying jobs, as well as to violations of equal-pay provisions.

See also: Equal Pay for Equal Work
          Labor Union Women
          Sex-Typing of Occupations

Resources:

The Earnings Gap Between Men and Women. Washington: Women's Bureau, Department of Labor, 1976. Order from: Women's Bureau, Office of the Secretary, Department of Labor, Washington, DC 20210.

This excellent pamphlet gives full statistical information on the earnings gap, including factors of race, education, occupation, and amount of overtime worked, as well as analysis of the causes.

Fully Employed Women Continue To Earn Less Than Fully Employed Men of Either White or Minority* Races

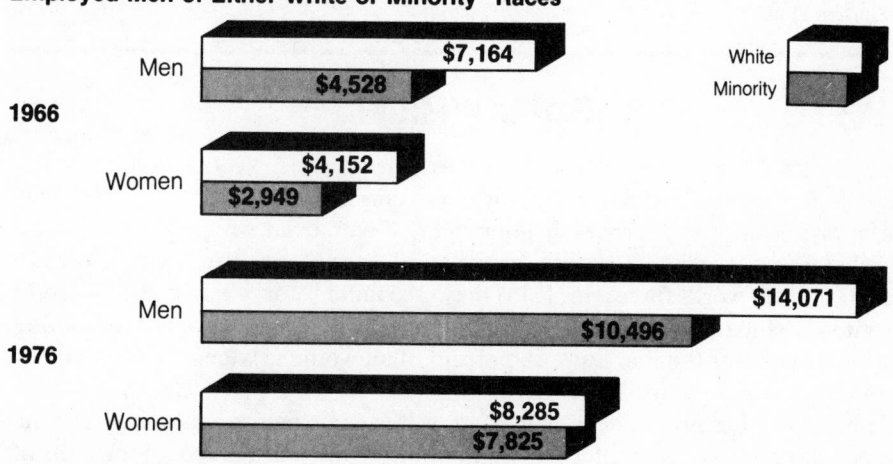

*Includes all races other than white.

Source: Prepared by the Women's Bureau, Office of the Secretary, U.S. Department of Labor, from data published by the Bureau of the Census, U.S. Department of Commerce.

USUAL WEEKLY EARNINGS OF EMPLOYED FULL-TIME WAGE AND SALARY WORKERS, BY OCCUPATION AND SEX, UNION *VS.* NONUNION

	Average Weekly Earnings		Union Members
	Union	Nonunion	Advantage
All Occupations (both sexes)	$262	$221	19%
All White Collar Occupations	270	255	6%
Clerical and Kindred Workers	223	172	29%
Blue Collar Workers	266	194	37%
Male			
Clerical and Kindred Workers	263	235	12%
Blue Collar Workers	280	210	33%
Female			
Clerical and Kindred Workers	192	159	21%
Blue Collar Workers	176	133	32%
Sex Comparison	*Male*	*Female*	*Male Advantage*
Clerical and Kindred Workers			
Union	$263	$192	37%
Nonunion	235	159	48%

Source: U.S. Department of Labor, Bureau of Labor Statistics. Unpublished Tabulations from the May 1977 Current Population Survey.

EMPLOYMENT

WOMEN HAVE ALWAYS WORKED. ALTHOUGH THEIR WORK EXPERIENCE—occupation, wages, duration of employment—has changed over the years, they have always been wage-earners. The number of employed women in the United States has increased steadily during the twentieth century. In 1920, women were 20 percent of the work force; in 1978 they accounted for 42 percent. Current projections estimate that nine out of ten women will work at some time during their lives. And, for the first time, 50 percent of all women sixteen years and older were in the work force in 1978.

Women work because of economic need, as the chart below indicates. Even the presence of children does not keep women out of the work force: 39 percent of women workers have children under the age of six, and 55 percent have school-age children.

Although more and more women have moved into the labor force, their status

Women Are Underrepresented as Managers and Skilled Craft Workers

Percent of Total Workers

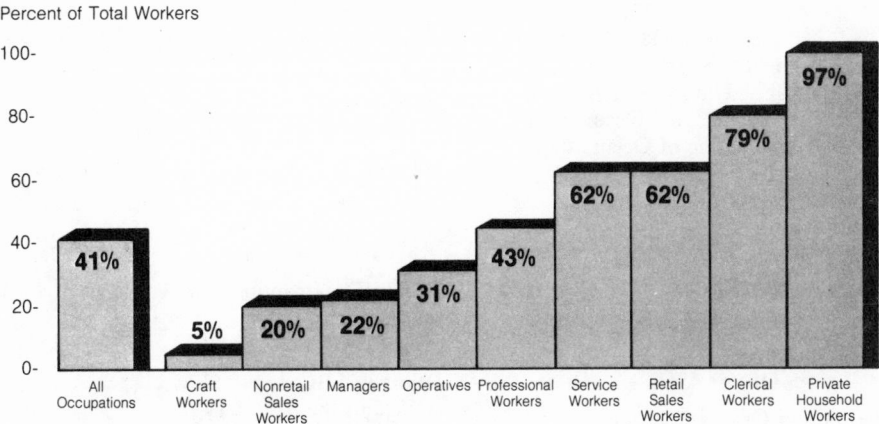

All Occupations	41%
Craft Workers	5%
Nonretail Sales Workers	20%
Managers	22%
Operatives	31%
Professional Workers	43%
Service Workers	62%
Retail Sales Workers	62%
Clerical Workers	79%
Private Household Workers	97%

Most Women Work Because of Economic Need
(Women in the Labor Force, by Marital Status, March 1977)

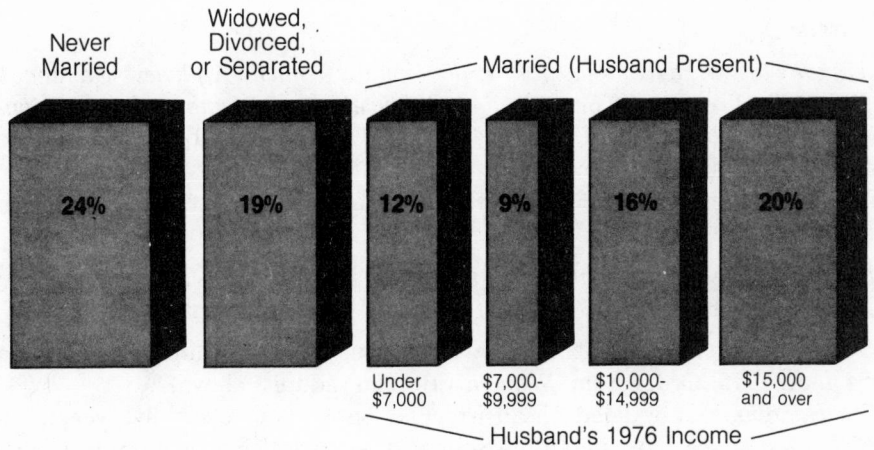

Never Married — 24%
Widowed, Divorced, or Separated — 19%
Married (Husband Present)
Husband's 1976 Income:
Under $7,000 — 12%
$7,000–$9,999 — 9%
$10,000–$14,999 — 16%
$15,000 and over — 20%

as workers has not improved much, at least not in comparison to men. The average annual wage of women is still only 58 percent of that for men. And women are still concentrated in low-paying jobs. The majority of women who work are in sex-typed occupations such as clerical work, nursing, teaching, and sales.

Piecing together the statistics to create a composite—the typical woman worker—produces the following: She is a married woman, the mother of school-age children. She is between the ages of twenty-five and thirty-four, and has a high-school diploma. She works full time in a clerical job which pays between $8,000 and $9,000 per year.

See also: Affirmative Action
Career Development
Earnings Gap
Equal Pay for Equal Work
Executive Order 11246/11375
Flexible Work Schedules
Labor Union Women
Nontraditional Occupations
Sex-Typing of Occupations
Sexual Harassment on the Job
Social Security
Title VII
Women Business Owners

Organizations:

Federally Employed Women
481 National Press Building
Washington, DC 20045

Federation of Organizations for
 Professional Women
2000 P Street N.W.
Washington, DC 20036

National Commission on Working Women
Center for Women and Work
1211 Connecticut Avenue N.W.
Washington, DC 20036

Wider Opportunities for Women
1649 K Street N.W.
Washington, DC 20006

Women's Bureau
Office of the Secretary
Department of Labor
Washington, DC 20210

Resources:

Federation of Organizations for Professional Women Affiliates Handbook: 1977–1978 Directory of Services and Publications of Member Organizations. Washington: Federation of Organizations for Professional Women, 1977. Order from: FOPW (address above).

The most comprehensive directory of professional women's organizations available.

National Directory of Women's Employment Programs. Washington: Wider Opportunities for Women, 1978. Order from: WOW (address above).

1975 Handbook on Women Workers. Washington: Women's Bureau, Department of Labor, 1975. Order from: Women's Bureau (address above).

The *Handbook* is updated on an irregular basis about every five years, and serves as the single most important source of statistical information on women workers.

U.S. Working Women: A Databook. Washington: Bureau of Labor Statistics, Department of Labor, 1977. Order from: BLS, Department of Labor, Washington, DC 20212.

A book of charts and tables updating information on women's labor-force participation and unemployment rates, marital and family status, education and earnings, employment of minority women, and projections for the future.

Women and Work. Washington: Employment and Training Administration, 1977. Order from: Superintendent of Documents, Government Printing Office, Washington, DC 20402.

This pamphlet reports on recent research on women workers and gives a good general overview of current status and trends.

Women Workers Today. Washington: Women's Bureau, Department of Labor, 1976. Order from: Women's Bureau (address above).

This brief pamphlet updates some of the basic information in the *Handbook.*

♀ TWENTY FACTS ON WOMEN WORKERS ♀

1. A majority of women work because of economic need. Nearly two-thirds of all women in the labor force in 1977 were single, widowed, divorced, or separated, or had husbands whose earnings were less than $10,000 (in 1976).
2. About 40 million women were in the labor force in 1977; they constituted more than two-fifths of all workers.
3. Fifty-seven percent of all women 18 to 64—the usual working ages—were workers in 1977, compared with 88 percent of men. More than 48 percent of all women 16 and over were workers. Labor force participation was highest among women 20 to 24.
4. The median age of women workers is 35 years.
5. Fifty-one percent of all women of minority races[1] were in the labor force in 1977 (5.3 million); they accounted for nearly half of all minority workers.
6. Forty-four percent of Spanish-origin women were in the labor force in 1977 (1.6 million); they accounted for 39 percent of all Spanish-origin workers.
7. Women accounted for nearly three-fifths of the increase in the civilian labor force in the last decade—12 million women compared with 8 million men.
8. More than one-fourth of all women workers held part-time jobs in 1977.
9. The average worklife expectancy of women has increased by more than one-half over the two decades since 1950. In 1970 the average woman could expect to spend 22.9 years of her life in the work force.
10. The more education a woman has, the greater the likelihood she will seek paid employment. Among women with 4 or more years of college, about 3 out of 5 were in the labor force in 1977.
11. The average woman worker is as well educated as the average man worker; both have completed a median of 12.6 years of schooling.
12. The number of working mothers has increased more than tenfold since the period immediately preceding World War II, while the number of working women doubled. Fifty-one percent of all mothers with children under 18 years (15.5 million) were in the labor force in 1977.
13. The 5.3 million working mothers with preschool children in 1977 had 6.4 million children under 6. Only 149,000 children 3 to 5 years old were enrolled in licensed day care centers in 1975.[2]

---

[1]"Minority races" refers to all races other than white. Blacks constitute about 90 percent of persons other than white in the United States. Spanish-origin persons are generally included in the white population; about 93 percent of the Spanish-origin population is white.
[2]The latest data available on licensed day-care centers are for 1975.

14. The unemployment rate was lowest for white adult men (20 and over) and highest for minority young women (16 to 19) in 1977.

	Percent
White adult men	4.6
White adult women	6.2
Minority adult men	10.0
Minority adult women	11.7
White teenage men	15.0
White teenage women	15.9
Minority teenage men	37.0
Minority teenage women	39.9

15. Women workers are concentrated in low-paying, dead-end jobs. As a result, the average woman worker earns only about three-fifths of what a man does, even when both work full time year round. The median wage or salary income of year-round full-time workers in 1976 was lowest for minority women.

White men	$14,071
Minority men	10,496
White men	8,285
Minority women	7,825

The median earnings of full-time year-round women private household workers were only $2,570.

16. Fully employed women high school graduates (with no college) had less income on the average than fully employed men who had not completed elementary school—$8,377 and $8,991, respectively, in 1976.

17. Among all families, nearly 1 out of 7 was headed by a woman in 1977 compared with about 1 out of 10 in 1967; 37 percent of black families were headed by women. Of all women workers, about 1 out of 10 was a family head; about 1 out of 5 minority women workers was a family head.

18. Among all poor families, nearly half (48 percent) were headed by women in 1977; about 2 out of 3 poor black families were headed by women. In 1967 about two-fifths (43 percent) of all poor families were headed by women and 57 percent of poor minority[3] families had female heads.

19. It is frequently the wife's earnings which raise a family out of poverty. In husband-wife families in 1977, 10.4 percent were poor if the wife did not work; 5.2 percent if she was in the labor force.

[3]. Data on black families are not available for 1967.

Source: U.S. Department of Commerce, Bureau of the Census; U.S. Department of Health, Education and Welfare, National Center for Social Statistics; U.S. Department of Labor, Bureau of Labor Statistics and Wage and Hour Division, Employment Standards Administration (August 1978).

20. Women were 79 percent of all clerical workers in 1977 but only 5 percent of all craft workers; 62 percent of service workers but only 43 percent of professional and technical workers; and 62 percent of retail sales workers but only 22 percent of nonfarm managers and administrators.

EQUAL PAY FOR EQUAL WORK

FOR MANY PEOPLE, EQUAL PAY FOR EQUAL WORK HAS BEEN THE BOTTOM LINE among demands for women's rights. As a simple concept of basic fairness, it has wide appeal. "I believe in equal pay, but I'm not a women's libber," has become a common refrain.

Equal pay for equal work is also required by law. The Equal Pay Act of 1963 amended the Fair Labor Standards Act to require that men and women performing equal work receive equal pay. "Equal work" refers to jobs which require equal skill, effort, responsibility, and that are performed under similar working conditions. The Act specifically prohibits an employer from reducing the wage of any male employee to equalize rates between the sexes. As of April 1978, the Department of Labor reported 261,155 equal pay complaints, with a total of $156,102,782 claimed by these workers. The Act is enforced by the Equal Employment Opportunity Commission.

See also: Affirmative Action
Title VII

Organizations:

Equal Employment Opportunity Commission
2401 E Street N.W.
Washington, DC 20506

Resources:

Equal Pay for Equal Work under the Fair Labor Standards Act: Interpretive Bulletin 800. Washington: Wage and Hour Division, 1971. Order from: Wage and Hour Division, Department of Labor, Washington, DC 20210.

Equal Pay under the Fair Labor Standards Act. Washington: Wage and Hour Division, 1973. Order from: Wage and Hour Division, Department of Labor, Washington, DC 20210.

Equal Pay for Work of Equal Value: A Selected Bibliography, ed. by Dianne Haist. Toronto: Research Library, Ontario Ministry of Labour, 1976. Order from: Research Library, Ontario Ministry of Labour, 400 University Avenue, Toronto, Ontario, Canada.

EQUAL RIGHTS AMENDMENT

TWO HUNDRED YEARS AFTER THE FOUNDING OF THE REPUBLIC, AMERICAN women still do not have full equality under the law. The Equal Rights Amendment will help to remedy that if it is ratified. Securing legal and civil rights has never been quick or easy, and achieving passage of the ERA is no exception.

Drafted by Alice Paul, suffragist and founder of the National Woman's Party,

On July 9, 1977, 100,000 supporters of the Equal Rights Amendment marched down Pennsylvania Avenue to the Capitol in the largest demonstration for women's rights in United States history. Dressed in white in the style of the suffrage parades, the marchers carried purple and gold banners bearing the names of more than three hundred women's organizations. © *Donna Gray*

the ERA was introduced into Congress in 1923. The original wording was altered slightly in 1944 to the form it has today (see box below). From the time it was introduced until the 1940's, the Amendment was completely buried in committee. Then began a series of attempts, which intensified in the late 1960's, to bring the Amendment to the floor of Congress for debate and vote. Its proponents were finally successful, and on March 22, 1972, the ERA was sent to the states for ratification.

Within an hour of its passage, the Amendment was ratified by the Hawaii legislature, which barely beat Nebraska in the contest to be first. Six months later, twenty states had followed suit. Initially, it seemed ratification would come easily—thirty states had passed the Amendment by the end of 1973. Only five more states were needed with six years to go. Unfortunately, as it became clear that the Amendment would soon be ratified, opposition forces organized. Amendment supporters were taken by surprise. No one was prepared for the highly organized, well-financed opposition which has arrested the progress of ratification.

Early opponents of the ERA based their arguments on the potential loss of hard-won protective legislation for women workers. Until the 1970's, many liberals, labor organizations, and women's groups opposed the Amendment for this reason. While they may have believed in the basic concept of equality for women, they did not support the Amendment. The increasing sophistication of the feminist argument, however, ultimately exposed protective legislation as a vehicle for keeping women out of higher-paying jobs and, one by one, the opponents gave up this argument—the Women's Bureau in 1969, the United Auto Workers in 1970, the National Council of Jewish Women in 1971.

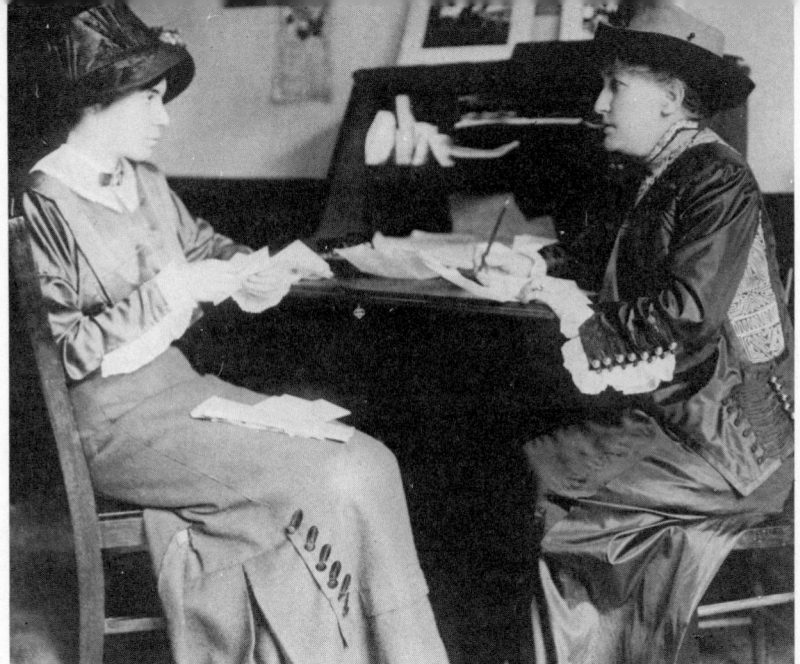

Alice Paul (1885–1977), left, and Helen Gardiner, right, working in a suffrage office in 1912. In addition to her work as a militant suffragist, Alice Paul was founder of the National Woman's Party and author of the Equal Rights Amendment. She dedicated her life to working for the Amendment but died in 1977 without seeing her goal realized. *Culver Pictures*

The new opposition, however, has never relied on such rational arguments. Rather, it appeals to and plays on the fears of those made uncomfortable by change. Representing some of the most strongly conservative forces in the country—the Mormon Church, Daughters of the American Revolution, the Ku Klux Klan, the John Birch Society—ERA opponents brought ratification to a standstill in 1977. Several states (Idaho, Nebraska, Tennessee) went so far as to rescind their approval.

Pro-ERA forces regrouped and in 1978 won a significant victory in their bid for extension. Because the Amendment specified a seven-year time limit for ratification, it would have died three states short of passage on March 22, 1979. Rather than risk failure, supporters pressed for and got legislation which extends the time limit to June 30, 1982.

The public debate over the Equal Rights Amendment has taken on the character of a pitched battle. While some segments of the women's movement would ordinarily consider it a low priority, as a change in the law rather than in actual social conditions, the attack from the right has imbued the ERA with tremendous symbolic importance. Defeat of the Amendment would be seen as the defeat of the movement. The next three years will be crucial ones for American women.

See also: Legal Status
             Right-wing Attacks

Organizations:

Common Cause
2030 M Street N.W.
Washington, DC 20036

ERA Fund
National Women's Political Caucus
1411 K Street N.W.
Washington, DC 20005

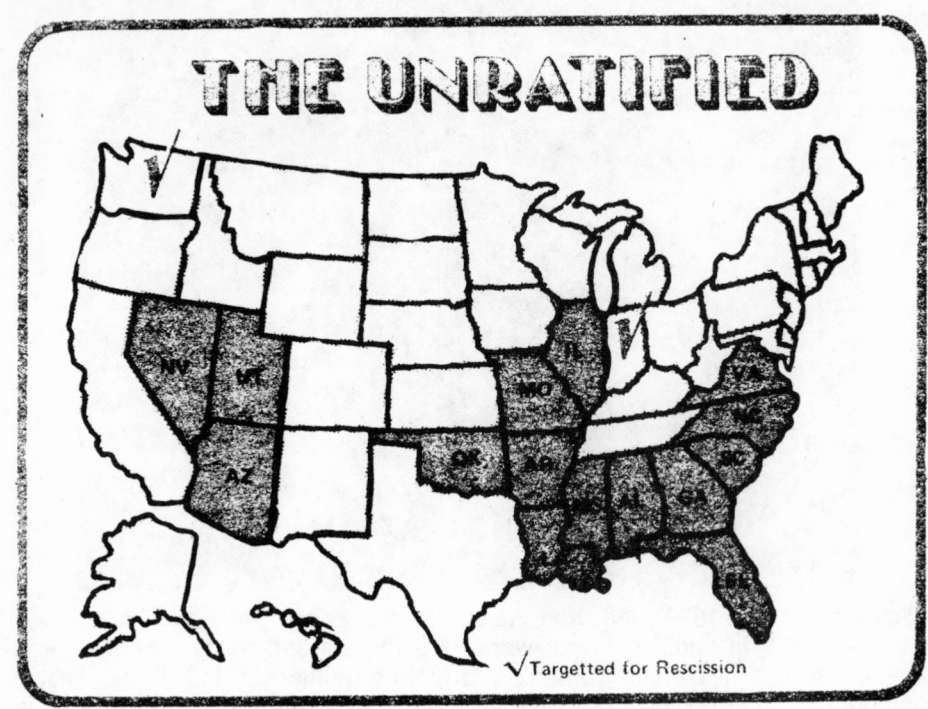

THE UNRATIFIED

√ Targetted for Rescission

The states where E.R.A. remains unratified

ERAmerica
1525 M Street N.W.
Washington, DC 20005

Housewives for the ERA
Route 3
Urbana, IL 61801

National Organization for Women Action
  Center
425 13th Street N.W.
Washington, DC 20004

National Woman's Party
144 Constitution Avenue N.E.
Washington, DC 20002

Network
1029 Vermont Avenue N.W.
Washington, DC 20005

Religious Committee for the ERA
475 Riverside Drive
New York, NY 10027

Resources:

The Equal Rights Amendment: A Bibliographical Study, compiled by Hazel
  Greenberg. Westport: Greenwood Press, 1976.
  The major bibliographic work on the Amendment, essential for serious
research.

Women's Rights and the Law: The Impact of the ERA on State Laws, by Barbara
  A. Brown, et al. New York: Praeger, 1977.
  An excellent, comprehensive treatment of the impact of the Equal Rights
Amendment. Three overview chapters discuss the general impact of the ERA,
history of the ERA, and methodology of state legislative reform. Subsequent
chapters include the following for each area of the law: background, impact of the
ERA, policy recommendations, state reform efforts.

♀ HOW WILL THE ERA AFFECT . . . ♀

FAMILY RELATIONSHIPS?

ERA will serve to strengthen the family. As it stands, most state laws require that males provide support for the home during marriage. In the event of neglect, however, women often find it difficult to receive financial assistance without first filing for divorce.

Under the Amendment, the chief wage earner would be responsible for support, yet in cases where both spouses were employed outside the home, each would be required to contribute according to their earnings. If disagreements arise in cases involving divorce or child support, court decisions would be based on each partner's financial capabilities and nonmonetary contributions to the marriage.

As nonmonetary responsibilities and services are included as major sources for support and custody allocation, the homemaker's position would be legally viewed as an important facet of our social and economic stability.

CHILD SUPPORT AND ALIMONY?

The passage of the Equal Rights Amendment would not make alimony unconstitutional, nor would it deprive women of child support or custody. Instead, the ERA would merely extend eligibility rights to men.

The welfare of the child would still be the main criterion for awarding custody; however, the ERA would challenge the assumption that sex alone determines which parent is best suited.

In the case of divorce, the Amendment prohibits a greater liability on one spouse than another for child support. Although both persons are not required to contribute the same amount of financial aid, both must take on proportional responsibilities, either in terms of money or nonmonetary services.

Community property laws, too, would be based on fair division, rather than on customary practice. In short, the ERA would make divorce laws contingent upon individual circumstances, by viewing each case in terms of two persons, rather than female/male stereotypes.

RIGHTS OF PRIVACY?

Opponents of the ERA have contended that the Amendment would require that public restrooms and similar facilities be sexually integrated. The right of privacy, first recognized by the United States Supreme Court in *Griswold* v. *Connecticut* (1965), would preclude this type of integration. Thus, undesignated bathrooms would not materialize as a result of ERA passage. States will also maintain the power to require segregation of sexes with respect to sleeping quarters in coeducational colleges, prison dormitories, and military barracks.

HOMOSEXUAL MARRIAGE?

The Amendment only requires that if state and federal governments establish laws concerning homosexual union, these laws must be made applicable to both sexes.

ABORTION?

Because laws affecting abortion can apply only to women, such statutes will not be affected by the Equal Rights Amendment.

CRIMINAL LAWS?

State laws which provide greater penalties for female law-violators than males committing the same crime (and vice versa), will be nullified by the ERA. However, the Amendment will not invalidate laws which punish crimes on the person, such as rape; these types of protective measures would merely be extended to men.

PROTECTIVE LABOR LAWS?

In the past, where physiological differences were assumed to have a significant effect on the individual capacities of women, protective labor laws were instituted. However, these laws have served to hinder a woman's chances for employment and promotion more than they have served to protect. In many cases, these laws have had a valid premise, that of serving to protect against injury, but have placed all women into stereotyped roles. ERA would not nullify any practical labor laws, it would simply extend their coverage to men.

In other words, both sexes would be subject to the same type of protection, employment would be based on individual needs and ability, rather than that evolving from a sex stereotype.

SOCIAL SECURITY?

The ERA will serve to equalize Social Security benefits. Presently, if a married woman is employed, she pays an equal percentage of Social Security tax, but receives a lower return than men in her income bracket. If a woman dies or retires, her spouse can draw on her Social Security only if he has supplied less than half of the family's income. Not until March, 1975, did the Supreme Court declare a regulation which prohibited a widower with minor children from drawing on his wife's Social Security, as unjustifiable and discriminatory.

The ERA would make the Social Security system more equitable for senior citizens and their dependents. It would also remove the dependency requirements necessary for a husband to receive his spouse's benefits.

Although some change in the system has been made, forty years have elapsed since the passage of the Social Security Act and its present, but slight, modifications. The case-by-case approach is expensive and time consuming, creating tremendous uncertainty for those whose lives are directly affected by Social Security benefits.

INSURANCE?

The ERA will require that state insurance laws prohibit companies from excluding medical coverage for sex-related disabilities, or from offering, on the basis of sex, policies of unequal terms or coverage conditions. The Equal Employment Opportunity Commission's guidelines to Title VII of the 1964 Civil

Rights Act prohibit employers from offering unequal benefits (in relation to pension and insurance), but cases are backlogged and all workers are still not covered under Title VII.

EDUCATION?

At present, most educational and vocational guidance is predicated on sex stereotypes and not on objective assessment of all students. Women are commonly discriminated against in admissions, curriculum, facilities, counseling and placement.

Although regulations concerning discrimination have been dealt with in Title IX of the Higher Education Act, the act itself is not fully conclusive, offering many exemptions and loopholes. Enforcement of the Act is also a major problem.

As teachers, women are almost universally discriminated against in hiring and salaries, particularly at the college level. Scarcely more than one high school principal in a hundred is a woman, and in elementary schools, where women compose 85 percent of the teaching force, men fill 80 percent of the principal positions.

ERA is necessary to support equal opportunity legislation such as Title IX, making these regulations stronger, while still emphasizing the need for individuality.

CREDIT PRACTICES?

There is widespread evidence of discrimination against women in granting credit by banks, savings and loan associations, credit card companies, finance companies, retail stores and the federal government. Married men can also experience hardship, as creditors do not include the working wife's salary as part of the total family income. This, of course, denies the family a higher credit rating. Unfortunately, this type of discrimination is rooted in the assumption that women of childbearing age may quit work and default on credit payments.

Although the ERA cannot have a direct effect on the private sector's credit practices, it will have a long-range effect on lessening discrimination. ERA will make available to women such public, government-insured credit programs as the FHA (Federal Housing Administration) and VA (Veterans Administration) loan programs. Moreover, the Amendment will serve to raise social consciousness by having all persons viewed as individuals under the law.

PROPERTY AND OTHER BUSINESS LAWS?

In 1971 the Supreme Court invalidated a law which arbitrarily favored men over women as administrators of estates. The ERA will go beyond that decision by invalidating all laws which restrict the right of wives to establish businesses, become guarantors, or enter into contracts. Furthermore, state property laws would be altered so that division and management of property depend on need and expertise rather than on sex.

THE MILITARY?

Significant barriers involving women's full participation exist in the armed services. At the entry level, women must meet higher standards for enlistment than men. Despite this, women's opportunity for promotion and post-service employment is far more limited. Moreover, restricted assignment policies reduce the number of training programs open to women, narrowing their range of work experiences.

The ERA would require admission of women into the military under the same conditions as men, demanding equal consideration for assignment and rank.

Under the ERA, women would be subject to the draft; however, only those persons meeting appropriate physical standards would be eligible for combat duty. (Only 14 percent of all men in the military served in combat at the height of the Vietnam war; the other 86 percent were stationed in areas around the globe, serving in support positions.) Congress can provide draft exemptions as long as they are applied to both sexes. Exemptions on the basis of parental or marital status will remain valid, but those initiated on the basis of sex will not.

Historically, women have served in forward positions as communication officers and medics. Although they have been voluntarily stationed in these areas, women have not been allowed to carry any type of weapon for defense. ERA would nullify this law, allowing women to carry arms in the interest of protection.

Reprinted from Common Cause brochure on the Equal Rights Amendment.

The Equal Rights Amendment

SECTION I

Equality of rights under the law shall not be denied or abridged by the United States or by any State on account of sex.

SECTION II

The Congress shall have the power to enforce, by appropriate legislation, the provisions of this article.

SECTION III

This amendment shall take effect two years after the date of ratification.

ESTROGEN REPLACEMENT THERAPY

IN THE EARLY 1940'S DOCTORS AND DRUG COMPANIES ANNOUNCED THAT medical science had conquered menopause—Estrogen Replacement Therapy (ERT) could prevent unpleasant climacteric symptoms. Since then, 50 percent of all postmenopausal women have undergone ERT to retard the aging process. But ERT has failed to live up to its claims and has created a new set of problems for its users.

Menopausal symptoms—hot flashes, vaginal dryness, osteoporosis and depression—can be treated by other methods (vitamins, diet, exercise—see excerpt below) which are safer than estrogens. Not only does ERT have side effects like edema, increased body weight, allergic rash, and blistering—it may be carcinogenic. Doctors are currently debating whether or not its use is linked to the increase or simply to the detection of endometrial cancer (cancer of the uterine lining). However, women who take ERT have a four to eight times greater chance of developing endometrial cancer than do nonusers. Even ERT proponents disagree about its application. Some doctors think it should begin before menopause and continue afterward, while others think it should be prescribed only after menopause begins. One medical man suggested that the treatment should span ages nine to ninety! Both pro- and anti-ERT factions agree that women with histories of cancer, cysts, or blood clots should forgo the therapy.

Before trying Estrogen Replacement Therapy, remember that the Food and Drug Administration has never approved any hormonal product as a preventive to aging in humans. Also note that although doctors are quick to prescribe ERT to relieve the discomfort of hot flashes, they do not even know what a hot flash is. Between 1903 and 1973 only five studies were made on hot flashes; medical science is still unclear about their source.

See also: Older Women

Resources:

Menopause: A Positive Approach, by Rosetta Reitz. New York: Penguin, 1979.
  A sensitive and informative book, combining original insights with the honest voices of women during their menopause. Includes excellent material on ERT alternatives.

Women's Health Care: Resources, Writings, Bibliographies, by Belita Cowan. Ann Arbor: Anshen Publishing, 1977. Order from: Belita Cowan, 3821 T Street N.W., Washington, DC 20007.
  Sections on questions and answers about menopause; estrogen therapy linked to endometrial cancer in postmenopausal women; and synthetic estrogens, DES, and cancer. Substantial materials on aging, estrogens, and cancer.

Women and the Crisis in Sex Hormones, by Barbara Seaman. New York: Rawson Associates, 1977.
  A fascinating report from the well-known women's health activist and writer. Seaman offers information on nonchemical treatments for menopausal symptoms. Highly recommended.

Women: Menopause and Middle Age, by Vidal Clay. Pittsburgh: KNOW, 1977. Order from: KNOW, P.O. Box 86031, Pittsburgh, PA 15221.
  Discusses estrogens, but also presents information on more holistic treatments for the menopausal woman.

♀ VITAMIN THERAPY FOR MENOPAUSAL SYMPTOMS ♀

Here is a suggested regimen designed for both the menopausal woman who has never taken ERT, and the one who has but is no longer taking it.

1. Vitamin E. *What to take.* Vitamin E comes as alpha-tocopherol and as mixed tocopherols. Which form is more beneficial is still debated. *How much.* 200 units (on the average), though 30 units are enough for some and up to 600 or more are required for others. *When to take.* a) After meals or bedtime snack containing fats, or b) with two lecithin capsules at any time. (Lecithin contains fatty acids which help the E to be absorbed). *Caution.* Those with heart problems, diabetes, or high blood pressure should take no more than 30 units without medical supervision. *Note.* Some women find the dry form more agreeable.

2. Vitamins B complex and C. *What to take.* Traditionally, such terms as "stress formula" or "stress supplement" are used to describe therapeutic or "high potency" vitamins that combine B complex with C. Select one that includes some folic acid and a minimum of 5 mg of B_6 (pyridoxine). The niacin should be in the form of niacinamide. A good moderate-level preparation is Plu Products' Formula 72. Some newer stress formulations may also include vitamin E, iron, or other ingredients. One such example is Lederle's Stresstabs 600 with iron. *How much.* Usually one or two daily. Read directions on the label. *When to take.* After meals. *Note.* If symptoms of water retention, weight gain, depression, hypoglycemia, or lack of dream recall suggest a deficiency, take additional B_6, from 30 to 100 mg as needed. *Note.* Other special conditions, such as joint pains, sometimes respond to additional supplements of other B's including niacinamide and pantothenic acid (see vitamin tables). *Note.* To strengthen capillaries, thereby helping to diminish hot flashes, correct gum problems and reduce excessive menstrual bleeding, or if living in a polluted city or smoking heavily, add separate C-complex (C, combined with bioflavonoids, rutin and hesperidin) or a separate bioflavonoids tablet. Another way to get the C complex factors is to eat a lot of fresh citrus fruit.

3. Vitamin D. *What to take.* D is available in separate capsules, in combined A and D capsules, and in multivitamin preparations. *How much.* 400 units daily is the recommended allowance. In winter those living in northern climates may wish to double this, unless they drink a quart of D-enriched milk every day. *When to take.* After meals or bedtime snack. Combined with calcium at bedtime may have mild sedative effects.

4. Calcium. *What to take.* Calcium is available alone as a calcium lactate, calcium carbonate, and calcium gluconate (there being little difference among them), combined with magnesium as in dolomite, or combined with vitamin D, phosphorus, and other minerals as in bone meal. We prefer calcium alone or dolomite for the menopausal woman. *How much.* 600 to 800 mg daily, which can be obtained in one large calcium tablet or in several dolomite tablets (see label). *When to take.* Plain calcium is best to take after bedtime snack along with vitamin D to take advantage of sedative effect. Dolomite may be taken in divided doses after meals.

5. Further dietary supplements. *What to take.* Depending on their own normal diet, and symptoms, women may want to consider some of the

health-food products discussed in other chapters and in the vitamin tables. Either dessicated liver or liver itself (from an organic supplier) is often reported helpful for skin and energy. It probably provides associated or undiscovered B factors that cannot be derived from vitamin products alone. Yeast and wheat germ are often beneficial and may improve the efficiency of B and E supplements.

Various minerals and trace elements (besides the all-important calcium) are often deficient at menopause and after. Moderate supplements of zinc, selenium, chromium, magnesium, manganese, iron, iodine and fluoride are all reported to benefit some women. A good multi-mineral supplement several times a week provides extra insurance.

Women who have dry scaly skin, poor night vision, or joint pains may benefit from vitamin A, 5,000-10,000 units daily (see vitamin tables).

6. Ginseng. *What to take.* Ginseng (Korean) comes in many forms. We recommend the capsules for hot flashes. If Korean ginseng has too much stimulant effect, try "Siberian ginseng" instead. Buy only from a reliable dealer and avoid combination products and teas. A capsule usually contains 8 to 10 grains, approximately 500 mg. *How much.* For women weighing 100 to 130 pounds, 2 capsules daily; 130 to 160 pounds, 3 capsules; over 160 pounds, 4 capsules. *When to take.* Before meals, in divided doses. Try to allow a few hours separation from foods or vitamins that are rich in vitamin C. *Note.* If undesired weight gain occurs, increase dose; if undesired weight loss occurs, decrease it. *Note.* Ginseng can be stopped when flashes are under control. Effects may last a month or longer. If flashes resume, ginseng can be resumed. As an herb, rather than a vitamin, greater caution needs to be exercised.

Finally, for women who want to keep their regimen as simple as possible, here is what we suggest:

1. *No Hot Flashes* (or gum problems or excess menstrual bleeding)
   — Take a good stress supplement (B complex with C) once or twice daily after meals.
   — After dinner or a bedtime snack, take a good therapeutic strength multiple vitamin, containing at least 30 units of E and 400 units of D.
   — Also add a calcium supplement.
2. *Hot Flashes*
   — Instead of a stress supplement take separate B complex and C complex twice daily after meals.
   — In addition to your daily multivitamin formula, and calcium, add 100–600 units of E or E with selenium.
   — Also take ginseng before meals.

SOURCES BY MAIL:
VITAMINS, MINERALS, GINSENG:

Willner Chemists
300 Lexington Avenue
New York, NY 10016

Tiger-Mite Health Foods
2071 Broadway
New York, NY 10023

GINSENG:

Freeda Pharmacy
36 East 41st Street
New York, NY 10017

Korean Ginseng Products
817 Lexington Avenue
New York, NY 10021

Kiehl's Pharmacy
109 Third Avenue
New York, NY 10003

SIBERIAN GINSENG AND DRY VITAMIN E:

The Solgar Company
Lynbrook, NY 11563

From *Women and the Crisis in Sex Hormones,* by Barbara and Gideon Seaman, M.D. Copyright © 1977 by Barbara and Gideon Seaman, M.D. Reprinted by permission of Rawson Associates, Publishers.

EXECUTIVE ORDER 11246/11375

EXECUTIVE ORDER 11246 WAS SIGNED BY PRESIDENT LYNDON JOHNSON ON September 24, 1965. The Order prohibits federal contractors and subcontractors receiving monies in excess of $10,000 from discriminating in employment on the basis of race, color, religion or national origin. Executive Order 11375 was issued in October 1967; it amended the original Order to include employment discrimination based on sex among the prohibitions. The Order is enforced by the Department of Labor's Office of Federal Contract Compliance and its 12 regional offices. It is implemented through rules and regulations drafted by them. These regulations are amended from time to time; such changes are printed in the *Federal Register.* As set forth in the rules and regulations, the Order has two thrusts: nondiscrimination and affirmative action. Nondiscrimination pertains to all individuals and simply states that no one shall be discriminated against on account of race, color, religion, sex or national origin. Affirmative action pertains to women and minorities, groups which have already experienced discrimination, and requires employers to take positive steps to ensure them equal employment opportunity.

See also: Affirmative Action

Organizations:

Office of Federal Contract Compliance
Employment Standards Administration
Department of Labor
Washington, DC 20210

Resources:

A Survey of Executive Order 11246, as Amended: Nondiscrimination Under Federal Contracts. Washington: Office of Contract Compliance, Department of Labor, 1975. Order from: OFCC (address above).

OFFICE OF FEDERAL CONTRACT COMPLIANCE REGIONAL OFFICES

Associate Assistant Regional Director, OFCC/ESA, Department of Labor, JFK Building, #1612-C, Government Center, Boston, MA 02203.

Associate Assistant Regional Director, OFCC/ESA, Department of Labor, 1515 Broadway, New York, NY 10036.

Associate Assistant Regional Director, OFCC/ESA, Department of Labor, Gateway Building, 3535 Market Street, Philadelphia, PA 19104.

Associate Assistant Regional Director, OFCC/ESA, Department of Labor, 1371 Peachtree Street N.E., Atlanta, GA 30309.

Associate Assistant Regional Director, OFCC/ESA, Department of Labor, 854 Everett M. Dirksen Building, 219 S. Dearborn Street, Chicago, IL 60604.

Equal Opportunity Specialist, OFCC, Department of Labor, 803 Federal Building, 1240 E. 9th Street, Cleveland, OH 44199.

Associate Assistant Regional Director, OFCC/ESA, Department of Labor, 1100 Commerce Street, FOB & U.S. Court House, Dallas, TX 75202.

Associate Assistant Regional Director, OFCC/ESA, Department of Labor, Federal Office Building, 911 Walnut Street, Kansas City, MO 64106.

Associate Assistant Regional Director, OFCC/ESA, 15412 Federal Office Building, 1961 Stout Street, Denver, CO 80202.

Associate Assistant Regional Director, OFCC/ESA, Department of Labor, Federal Building, 450 Golden Gate Avenue, San Francisco, CA 94102.

Equal Opportunity Specialist, OFCC, Department of Labor, Federal Building, 300 N. Los Angeles Street, Los Angeles, CA 90012.

Associate Assistant Regional Director, OFCC/ESA, Department of Labor, 1911 Smith Tower, 506 2nd Avenue, Seattle, WA, 98104.

FEMINIST SPIRITUALITY

FEMINISM IS DISTINGUISHED FROM OTHER IDEOLOGIES BY THE BELIEF—SHARED by many though not all feminists—that significant social change requires more than political and social action. What is required is a change in consciousness which recenters human energy into life-affirming activities instead of death-oriented technologies. Patriarchy—capitalist, communist, or socialist—uses financial and human resources to conquer nature as well as other nations. Matriarchy, feminists hope, will direct energy into harmonious relationships among people and the earth's resources.

Another name for this feminist, nonmaterialistic political philosophy is womanspirit. Womanspirit appeals especially to women whose spiritual impulses have been frustrated by traditional religions. Many women feel that Christianity and Judaism are misogynist to the core and have no liturgical, mythical, or ritual place for women. Rather than work for change from within, they prefer to develop alternatives.

Womanspirit weaves together strands of women's history and mythology. It revitalizes the Great Goddess, she who preceded patriarchal religion and whose shrines and statues are found throughout the Near and Middle East. Goddess worship, also known as the Old Religion and The Craft, was suppressed by the Hebrews, who referred to it as paganism, and by the Christians, who deemed it witchcraft. Actually, witches (the word is derived from *wicce,* meaning "wise") were not really devil worshippers: they celebrated a religion of nature, attuned to life cycles and herbal healing. Besides reclaiming the Great Goddess and the Old Religion, advocates of womanspirit study such esoterica as astrology, dreams, the I Ching, the tarot and yoga to help uncover the individual's psychic center and power source. Old rituals are also revived—celebrations at the solstice and equinox—and new rituals are created.

Like its symbol, the circle, womanspirit is embracing and unending. Unlike the cross, it is nonlinear and nonbifurcating. Indeed, spiritual feminists are anxious to overcome mind/body, subject/object dualities. Womanspirited women live on the borders of patriarchy and the women's movement; their beliefs seem frightening, irrational, and irrelevant to many members of both sexes. In the future, more people may agree that the destructive and sorry qualities of our lives are as much a result of spiritual poverty as of economic inequality and political injustice. When people realize that they are alienated from the source of life itself, cut off from love of nature and for one another, then feminist rituals for cleansing, rediscovery, and renewal will be appropriated by all.

See also: Ordination of Women
            Women and Religion

Organizations:

Foundation for the Matriarchy
P.O. Box 271
Pratt Station
Brooklyn, NY 11205

Resources:

Chrysalis (Winter 1978). Order from: Chrysalis, 635 Westlake Avenue, Los Angeles, CA 90057.

Special issue on women and spirituality. Articles are excellent and informative, and vary from Chellis Glendenning's "Star Wars and the Old Religion" to excerpts from Mary Daly's *Gyn/Ecology.* The "Women's Survival Catalog: Spirituality" covers works of fiction, nonfiction, magazines, art, theater pieces, lunar calendars and tarot.

Gyn/Ecology: The MetaEthics of Radical Feminism, by Mary Daly. Boston: Beacon Press, 1979.

Daly blasts the patriarchy with vivid descriptions of cross-cultural gynocidal atrocities and at the same time points to an alternative—a gynocentric environment. She creates words for the new realities and rituals for the new experiences.

Combining politics and spirituality, Daly offers a new world in which spiritual transformation necessitates a redefinition of political relationships.

The Matriarchist. Order from: Foundation for the Matriarchy, P.O. Box 271, Pratt Station, Brooklyn, NY 11205.

When God Was a Woman by Merlin Stone. New York: Harcourt, Brace, Jovanovich, 1976.
Provocative study of prepatriarchal religion. Helpful for reclaiming women's history and mythology.

Womanspirit. Order from: Womanspirit, Wolf Creek, OR 97497.

Womanspirit Rising: A Feminist Reader in Contemporary Religion, ed. by Carol Christ and Judith Plaskow. New York: Harper and Row, 1979.
Rituals and reflections on feminist theology and spirituality. Covers Goddess Religion, paganism as well as Judaism and Christianity.

FINANCIAL AID FOR EDUCATION

WITH COSTS OF HIGHER EDUCATION SPIRALING, THE NEED FOR FINANCIAL AID IS going to affect more and more students. Female students may find some sources of aid closed to them; many athletic scholarships, for example, are reserved for men. There has been much protest against male-only awards, though they have not been declared illegal. In 1976, the Rhodes Scholarship program, one of the most prestigious, accepted women applicants for the first time. Another sign of progress is the development of special award programs. A few of these have been initiated in recent years in response to the particular needs of women: scholarships for mature women who need additional education to return to the work force, for example. There are many sources of aid available. The following suggestions and resources should provide a guide.

See also: Continuing Education for Women
Higher Education
Sex Discrimination in Education
Title IX

Resources:

Financial Aid: A Partial List of Resources for Women. Washington: Project on the Status and Education of Women, 1978. Order from: Project on the Status and Education of Women, 1818 R Street N.W., Washington, DC 20009.
This compilation includes selected awards for undergraduate and graduate education, for returning students, minority students and for study in various fields. It also lists other guides to financial aid.

The Directory of Financial Aids for Women, ed. by Gail Schlachter. Los Angeles: Reference Service Press, 1978.
A list of scholarships, fellowships, and loans intended primarily or exclusively for women.

AIAW Directory 1978–1979. Washington: American Alliance for Health, Physical

Education and Recreation, 1977. Order from: AAHPER, 1201 16th Street N.W., Washington, DC 20036.
Lists the 180 member schools of the Association for Intercollegiate Athletics for Women, noting those which offer scholarships.

WHERE TO FIND FINANCIAL AID RESOURCES

1. Contact the financial aid director of the school you (will) attend. Inquire about any sources of assistance, including student loan programs—borrowing money may be a necessary investment in your future.
2. Contact organizations in your community, especially women's groups, unions, churches and temples, civic and fraternal groups, chambers of commerce; many have aid programs available.
3. Is there a professional association in your vocational area? Contact the local president or national office and explain your education plans and financial need. Many professional groups have scholarships or loan funds.
4. You might also consider using a computerized national scholarship research service. For example, Scholarship Search, 1775 Broadway, New York, NY 10019, will locate ten to twenty money sources for which students qualify. Write for complete information.

FLEXIBLE WORK SCHEDULES

AMERICAN WORKERS—MEN AND WOMEN—HAVE GROWN TIRED OF THE OPPRESsive forty-hour nine-to-five, Monday-to-Friday work week. Some people like to rise early and are ready to work at seven A.M. Others do their best work at night. Millions of working parents would like to be home at three P.M. when their children return from school. Some workers—women in particular—are kept out of the job market because of rigid scheduling. Experiments with flexitime and job sharing are opening doors to new working/living arrangements.

Flexible or alternative scheduling involves basically three types of systems, which can be organized in a variety of combinations:

— Part-time employment: The work is less than full-time, and two people may share one job.
— Flexitime: Varies the arrival time and departure time from the standard nine to five to an agreed-upon schedule, or the employee may set her or his own daily, weekly, or monthly schedule provided a specific total number of hours are worked or a job is completed.
— Compressed work week: A standard number of hours (35 to 40) are worked in less than the typical five-day work week.

It has been estimated that approximately 100,000 workers in this country are under some type of flexible schedule plan. Federal legislation encouraging alternative work schedules within government agencies has only recently been enacted. Private industry and organizations have been slow to adopt flexible programs on any systematic basis. Unions, while initially skeptical, have begun to consider including demands for flexible scheduling in future collective bargaining agreements.

Flexible work schedules have proved a benefit to both employers and employees in improved employee morale, decreased absenteeism and turnover, and increased productivity. Alternative work patterns can provide a real boost for women workers, since many have two jobs—paid work plus unpaid homemaking and child-care responsibilities. Not only does it allow greater control over both work and family life, but flexible scheduling allows men to participate more fully and equally in family activities and responsibilities.

See also: Legal Status

Organizations:

Catalyst
14 East 60th Street
New York, NY 10022

National Council for Alternative Work
 Patterns
1302 18th Street N.W.
Washington, DC 20036

New Ways to Work
149 9th Street
San Francisco, CA 94103

Options for Women
8419 Germantown Avenue
Philadelphia, PA 19118

Resources:

Alternative Work Patterns: General Reference Bibliography. New York: Catalyst, n.d. Order from: Catalyst (address above).

Catalyst Report on Flexitime, by Gwen Leen. New York: Catalyst, 1978. Order from: Catalyst (address above).

This report defines and explains the use of flexitime, the benefits and drawbacks, and provides guidelines to instituting it in the workplace.

Working Less But Enjoying It More, by Barney Olmsted and Marcia Markels. Palo Alto: New Ways to Work, 1978. Order from: New Ways to Work (address above).

A description of job sharing and its benefits, this booklet provides a guide to self-assessment of job sharing possibilities, redesigning your job for sharing, and approaching your employer.

HEALTH CARE

WOMEN HAVE AN ENORMOUS STAKE IN HOW AND WHERE HEALTH-CARE services are delivered; they visit doctors 25 percent more often than men do and if they are married and have children that figure rises to 100 percent. Health care in the United States is big business—$162.6 billion in 1977, according to government estimates. Understandably, the medical establishment and drug companies would like to maintain the status quo, but as women are beginning to exercise their rights as consumers, they are demanding higher quality services and safer products at affordable prices. Since health care is a necessity for all, its rallying potential within the women's movement is unique.

Women today have far more information and choice about health care than their mothers or grandmothers did. The women's self-help health movement has made real gains in democratizing and demystifying medicine. Although the Popular Health Movement of the 1830's had spawned Ladies' Physiological Societies, precursors of the modern know-your-body workshops, this tradition was lost with the consolidation of the male medical establishment after 1840. Not until the consciousness-raising groups of the late 1960's did women once again come together and discover their mutual complaint—that doctors treated them with disdain, as if they lacked the intelligence to understand their own anatomies. Angered by this arrogance, the fee-for-service mentality, and the increasing specialization of their doctors, women sought alternatives. They learned to use the speculum, an instrument through which a woman can view her own cervix, and to study medical textbooks in order to understand their bodies and how to take care of themselves.

Self-help encourages informed decision making. If a woman visits a private physician she should be aware of her rights as a patient (see box below). If she goes to a women's health clinic, she should expect and demand quality services at reasonable prices. Many women's clinics are worker- and client-controlled; their services include occupational health care, preventive health care, services for the aging, and reproductive health care. There are several hundred self-help health-care projects nationwide; many are outgrowths of successful workshops and courses. The members of the Boston Women's Health Book Collective, for example, met in 1969 at a workshop on women and their bodies. They discussed their unpleasant medical experiences and shared their feelings. Agreeing to continue their meetings, they began to research medical topics. The result of their efforts, *Our Bodies, Ourselves,* is a feminist classic which has sold more than two million copies and has been translated into thirteen languages.

Ten years have passed since the first exciting days of self-discovery. Besides opening women's health centers, advocates of the women's health movement have been working for legislative change. In the early 1970's women campaigned for access to birth-control information and for legalized abortions. The 1973 Supreme Court decision *(Roe* v. *Wade)* that struck down state abortion laws was a major victory. Today, the women's health movement continues to open new fronts on critical issues:

— Surgical abuse: Why is hysterectomy, a complex and difficult operation, the third most commonly performed surgery in United States hospitals? Why is the rate of Cesarean section births as high as 25 to 30 percent in some American hospitals?

— Drug abuse: Why are drugs prescribed up to 80 percent more frequently for women than for men?

— Sterilization abuse: Why have women been sterilized without their informed consent?

— Estrogen misuse: Why have DES, ERT and birth control pills been marketed to women when researchers have known since the 1940's that estrogens are carcinogenic?

— Discrimination against women doing research on contraceptives: In 1976 more than 80 percent of federally funded research on contraceptive develop-

© Bettye Lane

ment and evaluation was done by men. When will money be channeled to women's centers and to those whom the research will actually affect?

— Occupational health: What happens to women—and men—who work in potentially damaging environments? Can these conditions affect their reproductive and general health?

Women have also proposed alternatives to the system:

— several hundred self-help health-care projects nationwide
— books, magazine articles, newsletters, films, conferences on women's health issues
— The National Women's Health Network: a national membership organization influencing health policy and legislation affecting women
— monitoring the numbers of women working in the health-care field, pushing for more women to be admitted into medical schools (today many first-year medical school classes are 30–40 percent women)
— pressuring the Food and Drug Administration to include inserts with birth control pills and other drugs which inform the user of potential danger
— advocating homebirth and midwifery as an alternative to hospitals
— advocating national health service or national health insurance, since health-care costs are growing at the prohibitive rate of nearly 16 percent yearly

All Americans benefit from the women's health movement. Current interest in preventive medicine, nutrition, occupational health, and alternatives in childbirth springs from the consciousness raising begun by a small number of women health-care activists. These women developed an idea whose time had come: that medicine should be of the people and for the people.

See also: Abortion
            Birth Control
            Breast Cancer
            Childbirth
            DES
            Estrogen Replacement Therapy
            Psychology and Women
            Sterilization Abuse
            Substance Abuse

Organizations:

Coalition for Medical Rights of Women
3543 18th Street
San Francisco, CA 94110

Federation of Feminist Women's Health
  Centers
1112 S. Crenshaw Boulevard
Los Angeles, CA 90019

HealthRight
41 Union Square
New York, NY 10003

National Women's Health Network
2025 I Street N.W., Suite 105
Washington, DC 20006

Women's Occupational Health Resource
  Center
American Health Foundation
320 East 43rd Street
New York, NY 10017

Resources:

Away With All Pests: An English Surgeon in People's China, by Joshua S. Horn. New York: Monthly Review, 1971.
  A description of the egalitarian health-care system developed under adverse economic circumstances, but progressive social conditions, in the People's Republic of China. A movement classic which inspired many alternative health projects in the United States.

Exploratory Study of Women in the Health Professional Schools. Washington: Women's Action Program, Department of Health, Education and Welfare, 1976. Order from: Superintendent of Documents, Government Printing Office, Washington, DC 20402.
  Looks at medical, osteopathic, veterinary, dentistry, optometry, podiatry, pharmacy, and public health schools to identify and explore barriers to success which women face.

For Her Own Good, by Barbara Ehrenreich and Deirdre English. New York: Anchor Press/Doubleday, 1978.
  Newest work of this excellent investigative team. Explores the practices and philosophies of the male medical establishment in America. Discusses how women lost control of healing and helping one another.

Hysterectomy, by Susanne Morgan. Boston Women's Health Book Collective, Inc., 1978. Order from: HealthRight (address above).
  One-of-a-kind resource on the how, what, when, why of hysterectomy.

Health-PAC Packets. Order from: Health-PAC, 17 Murray Street, New York, NY 10007.

Information pack with bibliographies, editorials, bulletins on topical health-care issues.

Our Bodies, Ourselves, revised edition, by the Boston Women's Health Book Collective. New York: Simon and Schuster, 1979 To write the Collective directly: Boston Women's Health Book Collective, Inc., Box 192, West Somerville, MA 02144.

Updated in 1979, this all-purpose anthology remains an excellent resource book for all areas of reproductive health care, preventive health care, and sexuality.

Seizing Our Bodies, by Claudia Dreifus. New York: Vintage Books/Random House, 1977.

Anthology of major works on women's health-care issues. This book provides the widest view of the issues.

The Health of Women at Work: A Bibliography, by Vilma Hunt. Evanston: The Program on Women, Northwestern University, 1977. Order from: Program on Women, Northwestern University, 619 Emerson Street, Evanston, IL 60201.

Includes books, pamphlets, articles, and resources. Categories include history of working women, accidents, and many types of specific diseases.

The Hidden Malpractice, by Gena Corea. New York: Jove, 1978.

How the medical profession treats women as patients and as professionals.

The Politics of Health Care: A Bibliography, by Ken Rosenberg and Gordon Schiff. Somerville: New England Free Press, 1973. Order from: New England Free Press, 60 Union Square, Somervilla, MA 02143.

Categories include power in the health-care system, health economics, consumer-community control of health-care services, women and the health-care system, health and war, alternative health-care systems, strategies for change.

Vaginal Politics, by Ellen Frankfort. New York: Quadrangle Books, 1972.

A vintage look at women's health care and the early politics of the movement.

Women and Health. Order from: Haworth Press, 149 Fifth Avenue, New York, NY 10010.

Quarterly journal covering new research, health-care topics of interest to women, new resources, analyses of existing health-care policies, and commentary on topical health-care issues.

Women and Health Care: A Bibliography with Selected Annotations, by Sheryl K. Ruzek. Evanston: The Program on Women, Northwestern University, 1975. Order from Northwestern University, Program on Women, 619 Emerson Street, Evanston, IL 60201.

Categories include health-care issues, sexuality and mental health, women's clinics and health projects, social context of women's health care, microfilm, bibliographies, indexes, as well as books and articles.

Women's Health Care: Resources, Writings, Bibliographies, by Belita Cowan. Ann Arbor: Anshen Publishing, 1977. Order from: Belita Cowan, 3821 T Street N.W., Washington, DC, 20007.

Introduction to and excellent bibliography for all the health-care issues; includes DES, ERT, self-help, sterilization abuse, breast cancer, birth control, abortion, malpractice, women in health-care professions, substance abuse, childbirth, psychotherapy, sexuality, aging, rape.

Working For Your Life: A Woman's Guide to Job Health, by Andrea Hricko and
Melanie Hunt. Berkeley: Labor Occupational Health Project and Public Citizen
Health Resource Group, 1976. Order from: Labor Occupational Health
Project, 2521 Channing Way, Berkeley, CA 94720.

Characteristics and needs of women workers, how jobs affect health, hazards of
women's occupations, changes needed. Also available as film.

Speculums, for the woman who wants to examine her cervix, are available from:
New Moon Communications, P.O. Box 3488, Ridgeway Station, Stamford, CT
06905.

YOUR RIGHTS AS A PATIENT

YOU HAVE THE RIGHT TO KNOW:

— who is it that is treating or interviewing you and what training they've had
— what treatment your doctor wants to use, and why
— what other treatments are possible, and why this particular one was chosen
— what the side effects of the treatment are
— what the benefits of the treatment are
— whether the treatment might not work, or might leave you in a worse
condition
— how risky it will be
— how much it will cost
— whether it's covered by medical insurance
— how much it will hurt and for how long
— whether follow-up exams will be necessary
— whether you'll need to be hospitalized, and for how long

YOU HAVE THE RIGHT TO REFUSE:

— a medication or treatment
— to participate or be interviewed for research purposes
— to be examined by medical students for the purpose of medical student
training
— to have surgery until you obtain another medical opinion from an
independent physician
— to sign binding arbitration forms prior to receiving medical treatment

Reprinted from *Women and Health Care: Resources, Writings, and Bibliographies,* by Belita Cowan,
Ann Arbor, 1977.

HIGHER EDUCATION

AMERICAN WOMEN WERE FIRST ADMITTED TO INSTITUTIONS OF HIGHER EDUCATION in the mid-nineteenth century. Mt. Holyoke, the first college for women, opened in 1837. Four years earlier, women had been admitted to Oberlin College, though not on an equal basis with men, and in 1852 with the opening of Antioch College, women were given equal access to advanced learning in a coeducational institution for the first time. Since then, women have been enrolling in colleges and universities in slowly increasing numbers. In 1978, women outnumbered men for the first time, accounting for 52 percent of the undergraduate population. "Joe College is a woman" became the rallying cry.

The increase in women students has not been matched, however, by the number of women college graduates. In 1930, 40 percent of the B.A.'s awarded were earned by women; by 1971, the figure had risen to only 42 percent. A recent study showed that of the qualified male population, 65 percent entered college and 45 percent graduated; for women the findings were 50 percent and 30 percent respectively. There is a disturbing pyramid effect as the educational level increases. "The higher, the fewer" aptly characterizes women's place in educational institutions. In 1971, women were 50.4 percent of high-school graduates, 43.1 percent of those receiving B.A.'s, 39.7 of those receiving M.A.'s, and 13.4 percent of those receiving the Ph.D. Even in areas where women B.A.'s predominate, their numbers decrease sharply at the Ph.D. level:

	Library Science	Foreign Language	Fine and Applied Arts
B.A.	90%	75%	60%
Ph.D.	28%	38%	22%

There are three major barriers to women's participation in postsecondary education: discriminatory policies and practices of educational institutions, negative social constraints in the life situations of women (marriage, children), and sex-role socialization which produces negative or passive attitudes in many women.

Another contributing factor may be the lack of role models for college women— less than 25 percent of faculty members are female. Women not only account for a low percentage of total faculty, they predominate in the lower ranks. In 1974 women were 10.3 percent of full professors, 16.9 percent of associate professors, 27.1 percent of assistant professors, and 40.6 percent of instructors. Of male faculty members, 63.3 percent are tenured while only 44 percent of their female colleagues have been granted this protection. Women (and minorities) are also kept out of the administration. A 1977 study showed that of all administrative officers, 79 percent are white men, 14 percent are white women, 5 percent are minority men, and only 2 percent are minority women. Not surprisingly, women are also paid less; on the average, women faculty earn 20 percent less than men with the same job title.

In professional schools, women are beginning to increase their numbers, partially as a result of affirmative action requirements. From 1970 to 1976 the number of women admitted increased from 9 percent to 20.5 percent in medical school; from 1.4 percent to 9.7 percent in dental school; from 8.8 percent to 23.5

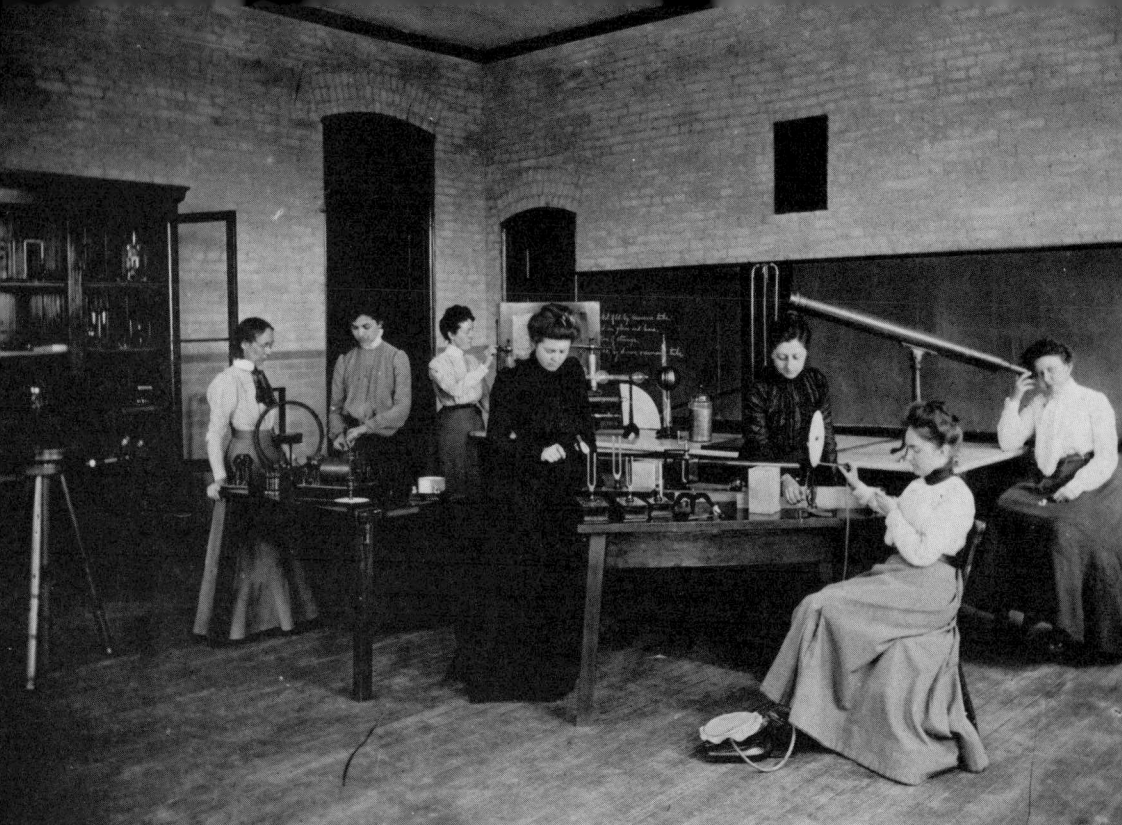

Women students in a physics class at Lake Erie College, Painesville, Ohio, at the turn of the century. *Brown Brothers*

percent in veterinary medical school; and from 7 percent to 23.3 percent in law school. Taken together, that's an average increase of slightly more than 2 percent per year; at that rate it will take many years for women to approach equity in graduate and professional education.

See also: Affirmative Action
Financial Aid for Education
Women's Studies

Organizations:

American Association of University
Women
2401 Virginia Avenue N.W.
Washington, DC 20037

American Association of Women in
Community and Junior Colleges
c/o Mildred Bulpitt
Phoenix College
1202 West Thomas
Phoenix, AZ 85013

Intercollegiate Association for Women
Students
c/o American Association of University
Women
2401 Virginia Avenue, N.W.
Washington, DC 20037

Office of Women in Higher Education
American Council on Education
1 Dupont Circle N.W.
Washington, DC 20036

Project on the Status and Education of
Women
Association of American Colleges
1818 R Street N.W.
Washington, DC 20009

Resources:

Bachelor's Degree Awards to Women, ed. by George H. Brown. Washington: National Center for Education Statistics, 1978. Order from: NCES, 400 Maryland Avenue S.W., Washington, DC 20202.

This report compares women and men B.A.'s for the years 1970–71 and 1975–76; in addition to giving overall figures, it compares field to field. It supplied many of the statistics cited above.

Barriers to Women's Participation in Postsecondary Education, by Esther Manning Westervelt. Washington: National Center for Education Statistics, 1975. Order from: NCES, 400 Maryland Avenue S.W., Washington, DC 20202.

Westervelt has reviewed and summarized the research (as of 1973–74) on institutional, social, and psychological barriers to women's higher education opportunities. The bibliography lists more than 250 items.

Higher Education Kit, ed. by Carol Parr. Washington: Women's Equity Action League, 1977. Order from: WEAL Fund, 805 15th Street N.W., Washington, DC 20005.

Presented in an easy-to-use loose sheet format, the kit includes a bibliography, a listing of key organizations, and information on federal sex discrimination laws.

Masters Degree Awards to Women, ed. by George H. Brown. Washington: National Center for Education Statistics, 1977. Order from: NCES, 400 Maryland Avenue S.W., Washington, DC 20202.

This report compares the overall number of women M.A.'s in 1970–71 and 1975–76, and also compares field to field. It supplied many of the statistics cited above.

On Campus with Women. Order from: Project on the Status and Education of Women, 1818 R Street N.W., Washington, DC 20009.

This newsletter comes with a packet of interesting offprints, reports, and brochures three times a year. Each issue is full of information, statistics and resources by and for women students and teachers in higher education.

Women in Higher Education Administration: Annotated Bibliography, ed. by Hannelore Rader. Washington: National Association for Women Deans, Administrators and Counselors, 1976. Order from: NAWDAC, 1028 Connecticut Avenue N.W., Washington, DC 20036.

Rader's bibliography covers studies of the woman administrator in higher education from 1969 to 1975.

Women's Participation in First-Professional Degree Programs in Medicine, Dentistry, Veterinary Medicine, and Law, 1969–70 through 1975–76. Washington: National Center for Education Statistics, 1977. Order from: NCES, 400 Maryland Avenue S.W., Washington, DC 20202.

The total enrollment of women, the enrollment of women in their first year, and the number of degrees awarded are compared at five-year intervals in this report. It supplied many of the statistics cited above.

HISTORY

Spurred by the issues and needs of the women's movement, women (and men) historians are writing—and rewriting—the history of American women. They are developing new approaches, perspectives, and methodologies. The standard periods of history, for example, are drawn according to significant political, economic, or military events. But significant to whom? Feminist historians are finding that the events and changes used in current periodization may be of little value in thinking about women's history. In an effort to speak meaningfully of the conditions of women's day-to-day lives, such developments as the baby bottle or adequate birth control may be more useful dividing lines than wars or changing administrations.

Within the scope of this book, it is, of course, impossible to include a section recapitulating the role of women in history. The resources below should guide the reader interested in pursuing the subject. Also, the illustrations and photographs throughout have been selected with an eye to the history of American women and the women's movement.

See also: International Women's Day
Labor Union Women
Women's Studies

Organizations:

The American Women's Museum
1805 Burning Tree Drive
Chapel Hill, NC 27514

Women's Hall of Fame
P.O. Box 335
Seneca Falls, NY 13148

Resources:

The American Woman in Colonial and Revolutionary Times, 1565–1800, by Eugenie A. Leonard, Sophie H. Drinker and Miriam Y. Holden. Westport: Greenwood Press, 1974.

Bibliography in the History of American Women, by Gerda Lerner. Bronxville: Sarah Lawrence College, 1978. Order from: Women's Studies, Sarah Lawrence College, Bronxville, NY 10708.

Bibliography in the History of European Women, by Joan Kelly. Bronxville: Sarah Lawrence College, 1976. Order from: Women's Studies, Sarah Lawrence College, Bronxville, NY 10708.

Women in Antiquity: An Annotated Bibliography, by Leanna Goodwater. Metuchen: Scarecrow Press, 1975.

Women in U.S. History: An Annotated Bibliography. Cambridge: The Common Women Collective, 1976. Order from: The Common Women Collective, 5 Upland Road, Cambridge, MA 02140.

Harriet Tubman (ca. 1820–1913), far left, with a group of slaves she helped to free. Called the "Moses of her people," Harriet Tubman is remembered primarily for her work freeing slaves. But she also served as a spy and scout in the Civil War and after the war founded a home for indigent and aged former slaves. *The Sophia Smith Collection*

Lucretia Mott (1793–1880), Quaker minister, abolitionist and women's rights advocate. Lucretia Mott and Elizabeth Cady Stanton met in London when both were refused admission to the 1840 World Anti-Slavery Convention. Unable to participate in the Convention, they made plans for the women's rights convention they called in Seneca Falls in 1848. *The Sophia Smith Collection*

Jeannette Rankin (1880–1973), standing foreground, at the National Suffrage Headquarters in 1917 just before taking her seat as the first woman in Congress. Jeannette Rankin's political career grew out of her work for woman suffrage. She served in Congress twice and has the unique distinction of having cast the sole vote against both World Wars. *The Sophia Smith Collection*

Anna Howard Shaw (1847–1919) and Carrie Chapman Catt (1859–1947) flank Susan B. Anthony in this group portrait of nineteenth-century feminists. Both women were young suffragists, called "Aunt Susan's girls," who learned to be organizers under Anthony's tutelage. Although both were trusted colleagues, the leadership of suffrage work fell to Catt upon Anthony's retirement. *The Sophia Smith Collection*

Sojourner Truth (ca. 1797–1883), a former evangelist turned abolitionist and feminist, she traveled constantly in the years before the Civil War, speaking at women's rights meetings and antislavery conventions. She was a magnetic speaker whose reputation preceded her wherever she went. *The Sophia Smith Collection*

A Susan B. Anthony (1820–1906) and Elizabeth Cady Stanton (1815–1902) were co-workers for fifty years, each complementing the abilities of the other: Stanton was the speaker and writer, Anthony the organizer. Elizabeth Cady Stanton, married and the mother of seven children, was perhaps the broader minded of the two. In addition to her work on behalf of woman suffrage, she spoke out for property rights for married women, more liberal divorce laws and clothing reform; she spoke against the Church and the Bible for limiting women's potential. Susan B. Anthony worked tirelessly for woman suffrage for more than fifty years; she crossed the country repeatedly, lecturing, organizing and raising money for the cause. Anthony also published *Revolution,* a women's rights journal, and supported labor issues. She attended her last women's rights convention at age eighty-six, the year of her death, leaving this message behind: "Failure is impossible." *Library of Congress*

B Frances Willard (1839–1898) was probably the best organizer produced by the nineteenth-century women's rights movement. Part of the national leadership of the Women's Christian Temperance Union from its inception, she constantly pushed it to adopt a broader social platform. Her motto was all-purpose: "Do everything." Under her direction, the Union supported woman suffrage and became the largest contemporary women's organization. In her later years she lived and worked in England, where her views moved even further to the left and she became a Fabian socialist. She was nearly deified by her supporters after her death, and many memorials to her remain—stained-glass windows, statues, water fountains, parks. *Culver Pictures*

C Ida Wells-Barnett (1862–1931) was born of slave parents who died, leaving her on her own, when she was only fourteen. She taught school, at the same time continuing her own education, until 1891 when she became a full-time journalist. Retaliation against her for investigative reporting on lynchings eventually forced her to move to New York. Ida Wells-Barnett helped to organize black women's associations and also worked with white women for suffrage and equal rights. *Courtesy of the University of Chicago Library, Department of Special Collections, Ida B. Wells papers*

D Margaret Fuller (1810–1850) is remembered primarily as an intellectual and Transcendentalist; she was also a journalist, feminist and revolutionary. From 1839 to 1844 she supported herself through her famous "Conversations," sometimes called the forerunner of consciousness raising. She edited the Transcendentalist journal the *Dial,* which led to a job on Horace Greeley's *New York Tribune.* Her *Woman in the Nineteenth Century* remains a feminist classic. In 1846 Fuller toured Europe, where she became involved with Italian revolutionaries, marrying the Marchese d'Ossoli. She, her husband and their child all perished in a shipwreck on their return to the United States. *The Schlesinger Library, Radcliffe College*

A

B

C

D

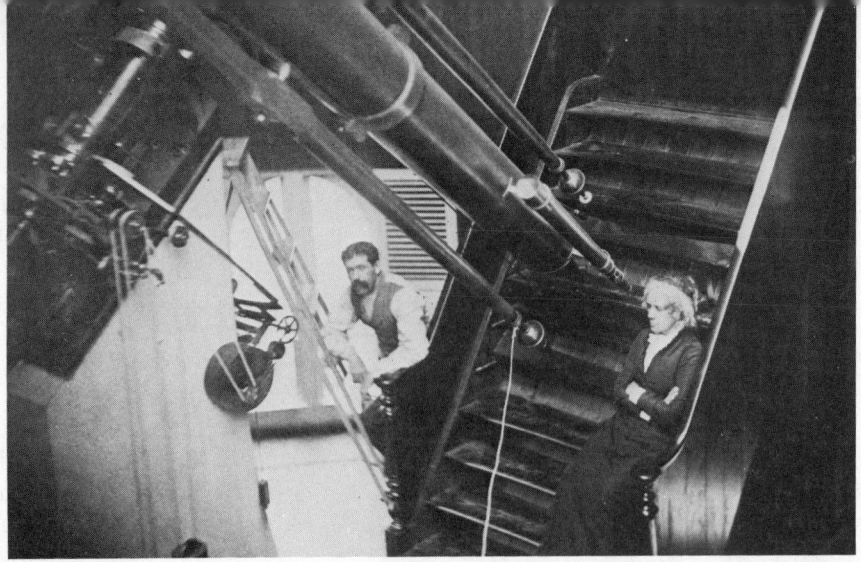

Maria Mitchell (1818–1889) was born and raised on Nantucket Island, an important whaling port; in a seafaring environment, she early learned the importance of the skies. Mitchell's interest in and knowledge of astronomy was encouraged by her father. He operated an observatory as part of the United States Coast Survey and it was there that she discovered a new comet in 1847. Matthew Vassar offered to build her an observatory with what was then the third largest telescope in the nation if she would teach at his new college for women. She agreed and trained several young women who went on to become important scientists. *Vassar College Library*

Charlotte Perkins Gilman (1860–1935), author and lecturer, is one of the foremost nineteenth-century feminist thinkers. Although not a political activist, Gilman was a socialist in sentiment. She called for day care and communal dining arrangements, calling the contemporary American home "an archaic vestige of preindustrial society." In both *Women and Economics* and *The Home,* she argued for the economic independence of women through the mechanization and/or collectivization of housework. *Brown Brothers*

HOMEMAKERS

FOR MANY AMERICAN WOMEN, HOMEMAKING IS THE PREFERRED CAREER choice. They find caring for home and family a rewarding occupation. The problem is that society does not recognize housework as work, does not value it, and does not compensate women for doing it. In a world that places a dollar value on everything, it's no wonder so many women end up feeling like "just a housewife."

The tacit assumption that homemakers "don't work" is an insidious one. In 1966, a Chase Manhattan Bank study estimated that the average homemaker works 99.6 hours per week. More recent research has shown that the woman who works outside the home also does 34 hours of housework per week. And more and more married women are seeking employment—56 percent of the female labor force is married. The fact is, *all* women are homemakers.

What about the value of housework? Estimates place the dollar amount at $250 billion annually—exclusive of child care. If the cost of raising children is added, the total doubles. This figure—the market value of women's unpaid labor in the home—is not included in the Gross National Product. Not only is the value of housework discounted, its overall role in the economy is also ignored. The unpaid labor of women in the home provides an infrastructure upon which the rest of the economy depends.

Because housework is not defined as work, women are not paid for doing it. By the same token, they are denied basic benefits. Homemakers are not entitled to vacations, nor are they eligible for workers' compensation, unemployment insurance or Social Security benefits. Some of these benefits may be provided by the husband, but they are never tied to the length or quality of the woman's service and they are never guaranteed; rather, they depend on the ability and willingness of the husband to pay for them.

Many women have become dissatisfied with these unfair conditions and have organized to demand proper benefits and in some cases wages. Other women have avoided the agitation route and have recommended more local solutions. By getting together in small groups and each one paying another to clean her house, homemakers would be able to prove they were employed and therefore qualify for government benefits. Ingenious though these measures may be, they are no substitute for a complete rethinking of the role and status of the homemaker. New social services, legislation, and government policies are necessary.

See also: Battered Women
Child Care
Displaced Homemakers
Divorce
Marriage and Family
Social Security

Organizations:

Future Homemakers of America
2010 Massachusetts Avenue N.W.
Washington, DC 20036

Martha Movement
1011 Arlington Boulevard
Arlington, VA 22209

Wages for Housework
P.O. Box 830
Brooklyn, NY 11202

Resources:

The Dollar Value of Housework, by Kathryn E. Walker and William H. Gauger.
Ithaca: New York State College of Human Ecology, 1973. Order from:
Communications Arts, 170 D-MVR, New York State College of Human
Ecology, Cornell University, Ithaca, NY 14850.
Analyzes value of housework and amount of time it takes for different-size
families, with one or two working parents.

Feminist Perspective on Housework and Child Care, ed. by Amy Swerdlow. New
York: Sarah Lawrence College, 1978. Order from: Women's Studies Program,
Sarah Lawrence College, Bronxville, NY 10708.
The proceedings of a conference, this pamphlet includes three papers giving a
personal view of housework and three papers giving an historical/theoretical view.

Houseworker's Handbook, by Betsy Warrior and Lisa Leghorn. Cambridge, 1976.
Order from: Betsy Warrior, c/o Women's Center, 46 Pleasant Street,
Cambridge, MA 02139.
This pamphlet includes an interesting mix of quotes, articles, cartoons, and
excerpts on the status of homemaker.

The Legal Status of Homemakers. Washington: Homemakers Committee, Na-
tional Commission on the Observance of International Women's Year, 1977.
Order from: Superintendent of Documents, Government Printing Office,
Washington, DC 20402.
This series of 50 pamphlets gives an overview of the homemaker's legal status
on a state-by-state basis. Specify state(s) desired when ordering.

The Sociology of Housework, by Ann Oakley. New York: Pantheon, 1974.
A fascinating study of women's attitudes about housework and their psychological identification with the role of homemaker.

Woman's Work: The Housewife, Past and Present, by Ann Oakley. New York:
Pantheon, 1974.
Oakley looks at women's role in the home historically and cross-culturally,
though most of the volume is on the contemporary British homemaker.

Working Women: Homemakers and Volunteers, ed. by Jenrose Felmley. Washington: Business and Professional Women's Foundation, 1975. Order from: BPWF,
2012 Massachusetts Avenue N.W., Washington, DC 20036.
An annotated bibliography on two groups of women who work without pay.

HELP WANTED: HOMEMAKERS

REQUIREMENTS: Intelligence, good health, energy, patience, sociability, skills: at least 12 different occupations. HOURS: 99.6 per week. SALARY: None (will be required to remain on standby 24 hours a day, seven days a week). OPPORTUNITIES FOR ADVANCEMENT: None (limited transferability of skills acquired on the job). JOB SECURITY: None (trend is toward more layoffs, particularly as employee approaches middle age. Severance pay will depend on the discretion of the employer). FRINGE BENEFITS: Food, clothing, and shelter generally provided, but any additional bonuses will depend on financial standing and good nature of the employer. No health, medical or accident insurance; no Social Security or pension plan.

Reprinted from the July 1972 issue of *Ms.* Magazine.

INCEST

INCEST BETWEEN AN ADULT AND A CHILD IS TANTAMOUNT TO SEXUAL ASSAULT. It completely violates the special trust which exists between father and daughter, adult and child. Those who practice incest with children don't need to use force: they succeed through the power of psychological coercion. Many times the victim will not understand the significance of the act; only later will the guilt, embarrassment and shame rankle in the memory.

Like other crimes of sexual violence—rape and wife abuse—incest occurs much more frequently than is reported. Some researchers estimate that more than ten million Americans may be involved. One out of ten girls is abused by age ten, and girl victims outnumber boy victims seven to one.

The psychological trauma of the victim is difficult to measure. The child is careened into an adult role of responsibility but remains dependent upon the one who has betrayed her. The depths of the betrayal are gauged by the self-destructive behavior of victims. Odyssey House, a drug-rehabilitation center in New York City, reports that 44 percent of their drug-addicted female population are incest victims. A survey of Minnesota prostitutes found that 75 percent had been victimized. Therapists note that victims who marry—locked into a pattern of self-hate and man-hating—often choose husbands who will abuse their daughters. Victims act out antisocial behavior because they feel shame and guilt. If they remain within the family situation, they fear repeated incidents and/or beatings. If the incident is reported, they face humiliation by the police and the courts—almost as devastating as the act itself.

Incest taboos exist in almost every culture, but the parties protected vary depending on family structure. All fifty of the United States have laws prohibiting sexual relations between parent and child, brother and sister. Often aunts and nephews, uncles and nieces are also off limits as sex partners.

Incest carries criminal penalties—up to fifteen years in jail—in every state, and many states have laws which stipulate that incest must be reported by any medical, social-service, school or law enforcement official who suspects it. But once a case of incest is reported, the incest victim receives treatment similar to that of the rape victim: Are you lying? Did you ask for it? She must repeat painful details in a public courtroom. In some states, the child's testimony alone is not enough to sustain a guilty verdict; in other states her testimony is not even acceptable. Even if a guilty verdict is reached, there are few treatment programs; offenders are jailed when what they need is therapy.

Incest involves the entire family; the mother is often an intimidated "silent partner" in the child's abuse. Good counseling programs provide individual therapy for each family member as well as therapy for the family group together. The Child Sexual Abuse Treatment Program in Northern California is one of the few treatment centers in the United States. It handles five hundred to six hundred cases each year and reports that the recidivism rate is quite low. By and large, incest aggressors are not disturbed or insane people. Kinsey reported that most incest abusers were more intelligent than rapists, child molesters or exhibitionists. The incest abuser is not unlike the man down the street or next door—except that the abuser does not curb his desires.

See also: Pornography
Prostitution
Rape

Organizations:

Center for Women Policy Studies
2000 P Street N.W.
Washington, DC 20036

Institute on Women's Wrongs
c/o Odyssey Institute
24 West 12th Street
New York, NY 10011

Midtown Adolescent Resource Center
Odyssey House
309-11 East 6th Street
New York, NY 10011

Resources:

Betrayal of Innocence, by Susan Forward and Craig Buck. Los Angeles: J. P. Tarcher, 1978.
This account presents case histories in the context of theories, analyses and treatment. Much solid information and good bibliography.

Conspiracy of Silence: The Trauma of Incest, by Sandra Butler. San Francisco: New Glide Publications, 1978.
Well-written and sensitive discussion about why parents, professionals, educators and other adults have been unable or unwilling to face the extent of incest abuse among children. Butler takes eloquent testimonies from child-victims, father-aggressors, and mother-witnesses and tries to break through the so-called conspiracy of silence.

♀ FACILITIES WITH INCEST TREATMENT PROGRAMS ♀

Arizona
Tucson Center for Women and Children
419 South Stone Avenue
Tucson, AZ 85701

Center Against Sexual Assault
137 West McDowell Road
Phoenix, AZ 85003

Arkansas
Ms. Sharon Pallone
S.C.A.N. (Suspected Child Abuse and
 Neglect)
Hendrix Hall
4313 West Markham
Little Rock, AR 72201

California
Henry Giarretto, Director
Child Sexual Abuse Treatment Program
Parents United
840 Guadelupe Parkway
San Jose, CA 95110

Colorado
Robert Schrant
National Center for Prevention and
 Treatment of Child Abuse
1205 Oneida Street
Denver, CO 80220

Connecticut
Ms. Norma Toteh, Director
Susanne Sgroi, M.D.
Sexual Trauma Treatment Pilot Program
94 Branford Street
Hartford, CT 06112

District of Columbia
Children's Hospital National Medical
 Center
Child Protection Center
111 Michigan Avenue N.W.
Washington, DC 20010

Florida
Dr. Dorothy Hicks, Director
The Rape Treatment Center
Jackson Memorial Hospital
1700 N.W. Tenth Avenue
Miami, FL 33136

Georgia
Rape Crisis Center
Grady Memorial Hospital
80 Butler Street S.E.
Atlanta, GA 30303

Iowa
Department of Pediatrics or Adolescent
 Clinic
University Hospital
Iowa City, IA 52242

Michigan
Bennie Stovall, Coordinator
Child Sexual Abuse Division
Children's Aid Society
71 West Warren Street
Detroit, MI 48201

Minnesota
Deborah Anderson, Coordinator
Sexual Assault Services
Hennepin County Attorney's Office
2000-C Government Center
Minneapolis, MN 55487

Child Adolescent Services
Ramsey County Mental Health Center
529 Jackson Street
St. Paul, MN 55101

Child Protection Intake Unit
Ramsey County Welfare Department
160 E. Kellogg Boulevard
St. Paul, MN 55101

Face to Face Health and Counseling
 Service
730 Mendota
St. Paul, MN 55106

Sexual Abuse Counseling Team
Wilder Child Guidance Clinic
919 Lafond Avenue
St. Paul, MN 55104

New Jersey
Mary Wells, Codirector
Family Service of Burlington County
Meadow Health Center
Woodlane Road
Mount Holly, NJ 08060

New Mexico
Family Resource Center
8016 Zuni S.E.
Albuquerque, NM 87108

New York
Brooklyn Society for the Prevention of
 Cruelty to Children
P.O. Box 423
Times Plaza Station
Brooklyn, NY 11217

James Walsh, Director
Victim's Information Bureau of Suffolk
(VIBS)
501 Route 111
Hauppague, NY 11787

Diane Meier-Erne Alliance
1654 West Onondaga Street
Syracuse, NY 13204

Ohio
Rape Prevention Program
Consultation and Education Department
Columbus Area Community Mental Health
Center
1515 East Broad Street
Columbus, OH 43205

Community Relations Department
Franklin County Children Services
1951 Gantz Road
Grove City, OH 43123

Oklahoma
C. Eugene Walker, Ph.D., Director
Pediatric Psychology Service
Oklahoma Children Memorial Hospital
Box 26901
900 N.E. 13th
Oklahoma City, OK 73104

Parents Assistance Center
2720 Classen Boulevard
Oklahoma City, OK 73106

At-Risk Parent-Child Program
Hillcrest Medical Center and the
University of Oklahoma College of
Medicine
Utica on the Park
Tulsa, OK 74104

Pennsylvania
Maddi-Jane Stern, Director of Social
Services
Center for Rape Concern
112 South 16th Street
Philadelphia, PA 19102

Tennessee
Child and Family Service
114 Dameron Avenue
Knoxville, TN 37917

Texas
Sherry Tayne, Project Director
Project S.E.Y. (Sexually Exploited Youth)
510 S. Congress, Suite 312
Austin, TX 78704

Washington
Lucy Berliner
Sexual Assault Center

Harborview Medical Center
Seattle, WA 98104

Peter Coleman, Coordinator
Child Protective Services Incest Program
Department of Social and Health Services
1301 Tacoma Avenue South
Tacoma, WA 98402

Reprinted from *Kiss Daddy Goodnight*, by Louise Armstrong. New York: Hawthorn Books, 1978.

INSURANCE

AN INSURANCE POLICY PROTECTS ITS HOLDER IN CASE OF FINANCIAL LOSS DUE
to death, accident, disability, or theft. The holder pays premiums and is promised
that a predetermined sum will be forthcoming should misfortune occur. Women,
like men, want easily obtainable, affordable, comprehensive coverage. Unlike
men, many women have found that this has been denied to them. Reports made
between 1974 and 1976 by state commissions in Pennsylvania, New York, Iowa,
New Jersey, Michigan, California, North Carolina and Arkansas shared the
conclusion that unfair sex discrimination does exist among insurance companies.
The Michigan Report (June 1975) described three types of undesirable practices:
overt discrimination—intentionally denying benefits on the basis of sex; disparate

treatment—different rules for the sexes; and smaller monthly pension payments for women because they live longer.

Pressure from the consumers' and women's movements brought these practices to light in a series of hearings on the economic problems of women before the Joint Economic Committee of Congress in 1973. It was noted that the McCarran-Ferguson Act of 1945 specifically exempted the insurance industry from federal law—thus leaving regulations up to the states. In other words, the federal laws which prohibit or control classification by sex do not pertain to the insurance industry. Sex classification may have seemed justifiable in the past when men were the primary breadwinners and their death or disability resulted in grave economic hardship. But since more women than ever are in the work force *out of economic necessity,* a woman's death or disability is equally as serious a hardship.

Insurance companies make money by risk-spreading. They use the premiums collected from many people to cover the losses of a few; obviously, those who most need protection will pay most dearly for it—the rationale behind higher rates for women's medical coverage. But, since insurance companies are profit-making ventures, they change policies when it is in their best interests to do so. Progressive forces within the industry have suggested that companies take a more equitable view of women and mount an active campaign to win their business. Some companies are recruiting women executives and writing new accounts with appeal to women. But since the industry is large and deregulated, changes are slow to come.

If women want to do more than just wait for insurance companies to change, they can push for ratification of the Equal Rights Amendment. This legislation will end the issue of sex-based classification. The ERA would permit sex as a classification in insurance tables only if it were linked to unique physical differences which make for higher risks.

See also: Equal Rights Amendment
Pregnancy Benefits
Social Security

Organizations:
Write your state Commission on the Status of Women for specific information on insurance laws in your area; see the Commissions entry for addresses.

Resources:

Sex Discrimination in Insurance, by Naomi Naierman, Ruth Brannon and Beverly Wahl. Washington: Women's Equity Action League, 1977. Order from: WEAL, 805 15th Street N.W., Washington, DC 20009.

Excellent overview of the insurance companies' discriminatory practices, and the federal legislation, judicial reviews and state insurance regulations, which have challenged the industry. Discusses avenues for future action.

U.S. Commission on Civil Rights hearings on sex discrimination in the insurance industry, 1978, produced the following reports: *An Overview Report: Discrimination in the Insurance Marketplace,* by Dr. Herbert Denenberg; *Discrimination Against Minorities and Women in Pensions and Health, Life and Disability Insurance,* by R. Minck; *Employment Patterns of Minorities and Women* in the Insurance Industry, by F. Marion Fletcher and Linda Pickthorne Fletcher; State Deregulation of the Insurance Industry, by Linda Lamel; The Treatment of Women Under Social Security, by Nancy Gordon. Order from: U.S. Commission on Civil Rights, Publications Office, 1121 Vermont Avenue N.W., Washington, DC 20425. These papers are chock-full of hard-to-find information on discrimination in the insurance industry and are understandable to the lay person.

♀ TYPES OF INSURANCE AND HOW THEY DISCRIMINATE AGAINST WOMEN ♀

Disability Insurance: Disability insurance protects an individual from loss of income due to inability to work. Disability benefits provide disabled policyholders with a monthly payment which is expressed as a fixed amount or as a percentage of monthly income prior to disability. Most insurance companies set a maximum limit to the amount of disability an individual may buy. Insurance policyholders are divided by occupational class, based on varying degrees of hazard associated with their jobs. The more hazardous the job, the lower the maximum benefits available and the higher the rates. Within each job classification, rates also vary by age and sex. In general, rates are higher among women and older people within each of the occupational classes.

Health Insurance: Health insurance is a means of protection against health care costs due to illness, injury, or other conditions requiring medical attention. Women rely on health care services more than men. In 1975, women made 48 percent more physician visits than men and were admitted to hospitals 41 percent more often. Part of this differential is due to women's unique reproductive role. Approximately 13 percent of women's physician visits and 36 percent of hospital admissions are due to gynecological or obstetrical reasons. Thus, about one-third of the sex differential in physician visits and nearly nine-tenths of the difference in hospital discharges are due to conditions related to women's reproductive function. Yet, these conditions are subject to the most serious gaps in availability and scope of health insurance and to the most prohibitively expensive premium rates.

Life Insurance: Life insurance protects against financial losses which result from death. Although most women face no difficulty in obtaining basic life insurance coverage, they have limited access to many life insurance options. When these options are offered, the premium rates are unjustifiably higher for women than for men. Basic life insurance is generally less expensive for women, but current mortality tables justify an even greater advantage.

Property and Liability Insurance: Property and liability insurance protects an insured's car, home, and other personal belongings against losses caused by accidents and other perils. In addition, it protects against suit brought by another person who may claim that the insured is responsible for damage to property or for personal injury. Premiums are based upon the frequency of claims (in this case, frequency of auto accidents, fires, thefts, etc.), the costs of settling each claim, and a variety of other factors such as sex, age, driving record, place of residence.

Reprinted from Sex Discrimination in Insurance, by Naomi Naierman, et al. Washington, 1977.

INTERNATIONAL WOMEN'S DAY

LIKE MUCH OF WOMEN'S HISTORY, THE STORY OF INTERNATIONAL WOMEN'S Day has been largely lost to us. Although feminists revived celebration of the day, March 8, in the early 1970's, the origins of the event were only partly known. The March 8 Research Project has worked to uncover and restore this piece of feminist history; it is on their work that this text is based.

The seeds for the international celebration of a day for women were planted in the United States in the early part of the twentieth century. Women in the Socialist Party were active in the women's rights movement and pressed the Party to support feminist demands. One way the Party responded was to create a special Women's Day. The resolution stated: "That we recommend, to all locals of the Socialist Party, to set aside the last Sunday in February, 1909, for the purpose of a demonstration in favor of woman's suffrage." On February 28 of that year, women participated in mass meetings in cities all across the country. The American Women's Day was a tremendous success and caught the attention of feminists and socialists around the world.

At the Conference of Socialist Women held a few days prior to the Second International Socialist Conference in Copenhagen in 1910, German socialist Clara Zetkin put forth a resolution to "internationalize" Women's Day. It passed both conferences unanimously. The slogan for the newly created International Women's Day was: "The vote for women will unite our strength in the struggle for socialism." It was first celebrated on March 19, 1911 in Germany and Austria. As more countries adopted the celebration, the list of demands grew.

Meanwhile, in the United States, it was still called just Women's Day and was observed on the last Sunday in February. In 1912, the demands included support for the Lawrence mill strikers. With the advent of World War I, many countries stopped celebrating the day. In the United States, antiwar demands were added. American women first called it International Women's Day in 1916; in both 1916 and 1917, protest against the war was a major part of the event.

International Women's Day was celebrated only sporadically during the twenties and thirties in the United States, though it was more regularly observed in European countries. Eventually, observance of March 8 died out entirely. Then, following the rebirth of the women's movement in the late 1960's, International Women's Day was revived. It is now regularly celebrated with demonstrations, rallies, teach-ins and parties in cities all across the country.

The March 8 Research Project has produced a pamphlet detailing the history of International Women's Day; it is available from: March 8 Research Project, P.O. Box 560, Old Chelsea Station, New York, NY 10011.

See also: History
            Labor Union Women
            Women's Studies

INTERNATIONAL WOMEN'S YEAR

THE UNITED NATIONS PROCLAIMED 1975 INTERNATIONAL WOMEN'S YEAR IN response to the growing consciousness of women's worldwide second-class status. That June, an international conference was held in Mexico City to launch the World Plan of Action, a series of recommendations designed to insure the equal participation of women in all facets of all societies.

American involvement began officially in January of 1975 when President Ford issued an order establishing the National Commission on the Observance of International Women's Year. The 35-member Commission immediately set to work researching and holding hearings on a full range of issues. "... *To Form a More Perfect Union,*" the Commission's final report, made 115 recommendations for the elimination of sex discrimination in all aspects of women's lives.

Not wishing to see the energy and momentum of International Women's Year go to waste, Representative Bella Abzug introduced legislation which would extend the life of the Commission and provide for a national conference of American women. The bill was signed into law in December of 1975. Public Law 94-167 appropriated five million dollars (less than five cents for each woman in the country) to be used for meetings in each of the fifty states and a national conference.

"Houston," as the conference has commonly been called, was held in that city on November 18–21, 1977. Representatives of every minority or ethnic group, religion, class, and political persuasion converged for three rewarding, frustrating, enlightening, tiring, and action-packed days. The main work of the nearly 1,800

The triumphal torch parade into Houston at the start of the National Women's Conference. Marchers in the front row are, from left to right: Billie Jean King, Susan B. Anthony (grandniece of the nineteenth-century feminist), Bella Abzug, runners Sylvia Ortiz, Pat Kokernot and Michele Cearcy, Betty Friedan. © *Diana Mara Henry, 1978*

delegates was to discuss, debate, amend, and vote on a 25-plank National Plan of Action which had been culled from the original 115 recommendations of the Commission's report.

Pro- and anti-plan forces mobilized during the course of the year as state meetings were held. Conservative organizations such as the Mormon Church, the Ku Klux Klan, and Phyllis Schlafly's Eagle Forum saw the conferences as a way to strike a blow against the progress being made by the women's movement. They were most vociferously opposed to the abortion, lesbian rights, and ERA planks. While they were able to capture some of the state conferences—seven of them defeated the plan *in toto*—they were not in the majority in Houston. The National Plan of Action as forwarded to the President and Congress calls unequivocally for full and equal rights for American women.

The Commission's "term" expired in March of 1978. But International Women's Year is still not over; two groups were formed to continue the work. The National Advisory Committee for Women, successor to the Commission, will work for implementation of the National Plan and monitor its progress; its "term" expires in the summer of 1980. The "spirit of Houston" has also been preserved in the 470-member Continuing Committee made up of delegates from around the country. The United Nations extended the original year to the International Decade for Women, 1976–1985. A second world conference will be held in 1980.

Organizations:

National Advisory Committee for Women
200 Constitution Avenue N.W., Room
  C5321
Washington, DC 20210

U.N. Branch for the Advancement of
  Women
United Nations, Room DC-1033
New York, NY 10017

U.N. Decade for Women
Centre for Social Development and
  Humanitarian Affairs
United Nations
New York, NY 10017

Resources:

The Spirit of Houston: The First National Women's Conference. Washington: National Commission on the Observance of International Women's Year, 1978. Order from: Superintendent of Documents, Government Printing Office, Washington, DC 20402.

This fat volume includes the full National Plan, a rundown of the state conferences, and a blow-by-blow report of the Houston meeting.

♀ NATIONAL PLAN OF ACTION ♀

ARTS AND HUMANITIES

The President should take steps to require that women:

• Are assured equal opportunities for appointment to managerial and upper level posts in Federally-funded cultural institutions, such as libraries, museums, universities and public radio and TV.

• Are more equitably represented on grant-awarding boards, commissions and panels.

• Benefit more fairly from government grants, whether as individual grant applicants or as members of cultural institutions receiving Federal or state funding.

Judging agencies and review boards should use blind judging for musicians, including singers, in appraising them for employment, awards, and fellowships as well as for all articles and papers being considered for publication or delivery and for all exhibits and grant applications, wherever possible.

BATTERED WOMEN

The President and Congress should declare the elimination of violence in the home to be a national goal. To help achieve this, Congress should establish a national clearinghouse for information and technical and financial assistance to locally controlled public and private nonprofit organizations providing emergency shelter and other support services for battered women and their children. The clearinghouse should also conduct a continuing mass media campaign to educate the public about the problem of violence and the available remedies and resources.

Local and State governments, law enforcement agencies and social welfare agencies should provide training programs on the problem of wife battering, crisis intervention techniques, and the need for prompt and effective enforcement of laws that protect the rights of battered women.

State legislatures should enact laws to expand legal protection and provide funds for shelters for battered women and their children; remove interspousal tort immunity in order to permit assaulted spouses to sue their assailants for civil damages; and provide full legal services for victims of abuse.

Programs for battered women should be sensitive to the bilingual and multicultural needs of ethnic and minority women.

BUSINESS

The President should issue an Executive Order establishing as national policy:

• The full integration of women entrepreneurs in government-wide business-related and procurement activities, including a directive to all government agencies to assess the impact of these activities on women business owners.
• The development of outreach and action programs to bring about the full integration of women entrepreneurs into business-related government activities and procurement.
• The development of evaluation and monitoring programs to assess progress periodically and to develop new programs.

The President should amend Executive Order 11625 of October 13, 1971 to add women to its coverage and to programs administered by the Office of Minority Business Enterprise.

The President should direct the Small Business Administration (SBA) to add women to the definition of socially or economically disadvantaged groups as published in the *Code of Federal Regulations* and take all steps necessary to include women in all the services and activities of the SBA. These steps should include community education projects to encourage women to participate in SBA programs, particularly minority women, including Blacks, Hispanic Americans, Asian Americans and Native Americans.

The President should direct all contracting agencies to increase the percentage of the annual dollar amount of procurement contracts awarded to women-owned businesses and to maintain records by sex and race or ethnicity for monitoring and evaluation.

The President should direct the General Services Administration to amend, so as to include women, the Federal Procurement Regulations requiring that all firms holding government contracts exceeding $5,000 insure that "minority business enterprises have the maximum practicable opportunity to participate in the performance of Government contracts."

The President should direct the Department of Labor, Office of Federal Contract Compliance Programs to assure that compliance officers monitor the awards of subcontracts in order to assure that women-owned businesses are equitably treated.

CHILD ABUSE

The President and Congress should provide continued funding and support for the prevention and treatment of abused children and their parents under the Child Abuse Prevention and Treatment Act of 1974.

States should set up child abuse prevention, reporting, counseling and intervention programs or strengthen such programs as they already have. Child abuse is defined, for this purpose, as pornographic exploitation of children, sexual abuse, battering, and neglect.

Programs should:

- provide protective services on a 24-hour basis;
- counsel both victim and abuser;
- create public awareness in schools and in communities by teaching how to identify and prevent the problems;
- encourage complete reporting and accurate data collection; and
- provide for prompt, sensitive attention by police, courts, and social services.

CHILD CARE

The Federal government should assume a major role in directing and providing comprehensive, voluntary, flexible hour, bias-free, non-sexist, quality child care and developmental programs, including child care facilities for Federal employees, and should request and support adequate legislation and funding for these programs.

Federally funded child care and developmental programs should have low-cost, ability-to-pay fee schedules that make these services accessible to all who need them, regardless of income, and should provide for parent participation in their operation.

Legislation should make special provision for child care facilities for rural and migrant worker families.

Labor and management should be encouraged to negotiate child care programs in their collective bargaining agreements.

Education for parenthood programs should be improved and expanded by local and State school boards, with technical assistance and experimental programs provided by the Federal government.

City, county and/or State networks should be established to provide parents with hotline consumer information on child care, referrals, and follow-up evaluations of all listed care givers.

CREDIT

The Federal Equal Credit Opportunity Act of 1974 should be vigorously, efficiently and expeditiously enforced by all the Federal agencies with enforcement responsibility.

The Federal Reserve Board should conduct a nationwide educational campaign to inform women of their rights under the law.

DISABLED WOMEN

The President, Congress, and state and local governments should rigorously enforce all current legislation that affects the lives of disabled women.

The President, Congress, and Administration should expeditiously implement the recommendations of the White House Conference on Handicapped Individuals and develop comprehensive programs for that purpose.

Disabled women should have access to education, training and employment based on their needs and interests rather than on the preconceived notions of others.

The federal government should enact legislation which will provide higher income levels so that disabled women can afford to live independently and at a decent standard of living. The disabled woman must have the right to determine for herself whether she will live in or out of an institutional setting. Funds and services should be available to make independent living a reality. Congress should appropriate sufficient funds to ensure the development of service programs controlled by disabled people.

Disabled women should have the right to have and keep their children and have equal rights to adoption and foster care.

The Congress should mandate health training and research programs focused on the health needs of the disabled.

Information developed by disabled women should be disseminated to medical professionals and women so that all women can make decisions about children based on knowledge rather than fear.

National health care legislation must provide for the unique requirements of disabled women without reference to income.

The Congress should enact legislation to remove all work disincentive for all disabled individuals who wish paid employment.

The President and the Congress should work closely with disabled individuals in the development of the welfare reform act and all other legislation concerning disabled persons.

Medicaid and Medicare should cover all the medical services and supplies that are needed by disabled women.

The President and Congress should encourage all states to utilize Title 20 funds for the provision of attendant care and other such service for disabled women.

The President and Congress should enact legislation to include disabled women under the 1964 Civil Rights Act and afford them judicial remedy.

The President and Congress and International Women's Year must recognize the additional discrimination disabled women face when they are members of racial, ethnic and sexual minority groups and appropriate steps must be taken to protect their rights.

In the passage of the National Plan of Action, the word "woman" should be defined as including all women with disabilities. The term "bilingual" should be defined as including sign language and interpreters for the deaf. The term "barriers" against women and "access" should be defined as including architectural barriers and communication barriers.

Congress and the President should support U.S. participation in and funding for the International Year of the Handicapped as proclaimed by the United Nations for 1981.

EDUCATION

The President should direct the vigorous and expeditious enforcement of all laws prohibiting discrimination at all levels of education and oppose any amendments or revisions that would weaken these laws and regulations.

Enforcement should apply to elementary, primary, secondary, post-secondary, graduate, vocational and technical schools, including sports and other programs and granting of scholarships and fellowships.

Federal surveys of elementary and secondary schools should gather data needed to indicate compliance with Federal antidiscrimination laws, and these data should be collected by sex as well as race or ethnicity. The Civil Rights Commission should conduct a study to evaluate the enforcement of laws prohibiting sex discrimination in physical education and athletics, and to consider the usefulness and feasibility of per capita expenditure in physical education and athletics as a measure of equal opportunity.

Leadership programs for working women in post-secondary schools should be upgraded and expanded, and private foundations are urged to give special attention to research on women in unions.

Bilingual vocational training, educational and cultural programs should be extended and significantly expanded, with particular attention to the needs of Hispanic Americans, Native Americans, Asian Americans and other minority women.

State school systems should move against sex and race stereotyping through appropriate action, including:

- Review of books and curriculum. The integration into the curriculum of programs of study that restore to women their history and their achievements and give them the knowledge and methods to reinterpret their life experiences.
- Pre-service and in-service training of teachers and administrators.
- Non-sexist and non-racist counseling at every level of education, with encouragement of women to increase their range of options and choices to include both

non-traditional and traditional occupations and to increase understanding of women's rights and status in various occupations.

ELECTIVE AND APPOINTIVE OFFICE

The President, Governors, political parties, women's organizations and foundations should join in an effort to increase the number of women in office, including judgeships and policy-making positions, and women should seek elective and appointive office in larger numbers than at present on the Federal, State and local level.

The President and, where applicable, Governors should significantly increase the numbers of women appointed as judges, particularly to appellate courts and supreme courts.

Governors should set as a goal for 1980 a significant increase and, by 1985, equal membership of men and women serving on all State boards and commissions. Concerted efforts should be directed toward appointing women to the majority of State boards and commissions which have no women members.

Political parties should encourage and recruit women to run for office and adopt written plans to assure equal representation of women in all party activities, from the precinct to the national level, with special emphasis on equal representation on the delegations to all party conventions.

The national parties should create affirmative action offices for women. Women's caucuses and other women's organizations within the party should participate in the selection of its personnel and in the design of its program, which should include greatly improved financial assistance for female delegates and candidates.

EMPLOYMENT

The President and Congress should support a policy of full employment so that all women who are able and willing to work may do so.

The President should direct the vigorous and expeditious enforcement of all laws, executive orders and regulations prohibiting discrimination in employment, including discrimination in apprenticeship and construction.

The Equal Employment Opportunity Commission should receive the necessary funding and staff to process complaints and to carry out its duties speedily and effectively.

All enforcement agencies should follow the guidelines of the EEOC, which should be expanded to cover discrimination in job evaluation systems. These systems should be examined with the aim of eliminating biases that attach a low wage rate to "traditional" women's jobs. Federal legislation to provide equal pay for work of equal value should be enacted.

Repeal the last sentence of Sec. 703(h) of Title VII, Civil Rights Act (1964) which limits enforcement of that law by incorporating the more restrictive standards of the Equal Pay Act.

As the largest single employer of women in the nation, the President should require all Federal agencies to establish goals and timetables which require equitable representation of women at all management levels, and appropriate sanctions should be levied against heads of agencies that fail to demonstrate a "good faith" effort in achieving these goals and timetables.

The Civil Service Commission should require all Federal agencies to establish developmental and other programs in consonance with upward mobility and merit promotion principles to facilitate the movement of women from clerical to technical and professional series, and make all Federal women employees in Grades (GS) 11 through 15 eligible for managerial positions.

Agencies and organizations responsible for apprenticeship programs should be required to establish affirmative action goals and timetables for women of all racial and ethnic origins to enter into "non-traditional" training programs.

Federal laws prohibiting discrimination in employment should be extended to include the legislative branch of the Federal government.

In addition to the Federal government, State and local governments, public and private institutions, business, industry and unions should be encouraged to develop training programs for the employment and promotion of women in policy-level positions and professional, managerial and technical jobs.

Special attention should be given to the employment needs of minority women, especially Blacks, Hispanics, Asian Americans and Native Americans, including their placement in managerial, professional, technical and white collar jobs. English-language training and employment programs should be developed to meet the needs of working women whose primary language is not English.

The Congress should amend the Veteran Preference Act of 1944 (58 Stat. 387, Chapter 287, Title V, US Code) so that veterans preference is used on a one-time-only basis for initial employment and within a three-year period after discharge from military service, except for disabled veterans. It should modify the "rule of three" so that equally or better qualified non-veterans should not be unduly discriminated against in hiring.

Title VII of the 1964 Civil Rights Act should be amended to prohibit discrimination on the basis of pregnancy, childbirth or related medical conditions.

The President should take into account in appointments to the National Labor Relations Board and in seeking amendments to the National Labor Relations Act of 1936 the obstacles confronting women who seek to organize in traditionally nonunionized employment sections.

Unions and management should review the impact on women of all their practices and correct injustices to women.

Enforcement of the Fair Labor Standards Act and the Social Security Act as they apply to household workers and enforcement of the minimum wage should be improved.

Federal and State governments should promote Flexitime jobs, and pro-rated benefits should be provided for part-time workers.

All statistics collected by the Federal government should be gathered and analyzed so that information concerning the impact of Federal programs on women and the participation of women in the administration of Federal programs can be assessed.

EQUAL RIGHTS AMENDMENT

The Equal Rights Amendment should be ratified.

HEALTH

Federal legislation should establish a national health security program. Present Federal employees' health insurance policies and any future national health security program should cover women as individuals.

Health insurance benefits should include:

- preventive health services
- comprehensive family planning services
- reproductive health care
- general medical care
- home and health support services
- comprehensive mental health services

States should license and recognize qualified midwives and nurse practitioners as independent health specialists and State and Federal laws should require health insurance providers to directly reimburse these health specialists.

States should enact a patient's bill of rights which includes enforceable provisions for informed consent and access to and patient ownership of medical records.

Federal legislation should be enacted to expand the authority of the Food and Drug Administration:

- to require testing of all drugs, devices and cosmetics by independent sources other than the manufacturers.
- to extend test periods beyond the present grossly inadequate one year or 18 months.
- to have immediate recall of hazardous, unsafe or ineffective drugs, devices and cosmetics.
- to require a patient information package insert with every drug and device marketed. This insert should include warnings about possible risks.
- to require by law the reporting of significant adverse reactions noted by physicians or by the manufacturers of drugs, devices and cosmetics.

Congress should appropriate funds for increased research on safe, alternative forms of contraception, particularly male contraception. Research to identify the risks of present forms of contraception and estrogen-based drugs should be given higher priority. Outreach programs should be established by the Department of Health, Education and Welfare to identify and provide services for victims of hazardous drug therapy.

The Department of Health, Education and Welfare should provide additional funds for alcohol and drug abuse research and treatment centers designed to meet the special needs of women.

Federal and State governments should encourage fair representation of women on all Federal, State and private health policy and planning bodies.

Congress should appropriate funds to establish and support a network of community-based health facilities to offer low-cost reproductive health services.

The President should appoint a special commission to conduct a national investigation of conditions in nursing homes and mental institutions and propose standards of care.

Congress should appropriate funds to encourage more women to enter the health professions and Congress should allocate funds only to those health professions schools whose curricula are clearly non-sexist.

The Secretary of Health, Education and Welfare should undertake a special investigation of the increase in surgical procedures such as hysterectomy, Cesarean section, mastectomy and forced sterilization.

HOMEMAKERS

The Federal Government and State legislatures should base their laws relating to marital property, inheritance, and domestic relations on the principle that marriage is a partnership in which the contribution of each spouse is of equal importance and value.

The President and Congress should support a practical plan for covering homemakers in their own right under social security and facilitate its enactment.

Alimony, child support, and property arrangements at divorce should be such that minor children's needs are first to be met and spouses share the economic dislocation of divorce. As a minimum every State should enact the economic provisions of the Uniform Marriage and Divorce Act proposed by the Commissioners on Uniform State Laws and endorsed by the American Bar Association. Loss of pension rights because of divorce should be considered in property divisions. More effective methods for collection of support should be adopted.

The Census Bureau should collect data on the economic arrangements at divorce and their enforcement, with a large enough sample to analyze the data by State.

The Federal and State Governments should help homemakers displaced by widowhood, divorce, or desertion to become self-sufficient members of society through programs providing counseling, training and placement and counseling on business opportunities; advice on financial management; and legal advice.

INSURANCE

State legislatures and State insurance commissioners should adopt the Model Regulation to Eliminate Unfair Sex Discrimination of the National Association of Insurance Commissioners. The Regulation should be amended and adopted to include prohibition of the following practices:

• denial of coverage for pregnancy and pregnancy-related expenses for all comprehensive medical/hospital care.
• denial of group disability coverage for normal pregnancy and complications of pregnancy.
• denial of health insurance coverage to newborns from birth.
• requiring dependents who convert from spouses' contracts to their own to pay increased premiums for the same coverage or be forced to insure for lower coverage.

• denial of coverage to women with children born out of wedlock and denying eligibility of benefits to such children.
• using sex-based actuarial and mortality tables in rate and benefit computation.

INTERNATIONAL AFFAIRS

Women and foreign policy. The President and the Executive Agencies of the government dealing with foreign affairs (Departments of State and Defense, USIA, AID and others) should see to it that many more women, of all racial and ethnic backgrounds, participate in the formulation and execution of all aspects of United States foreign policy. Efforts should be intensified to appoint more women as Ambassadors and to all U.S. Delegations to international conferences and missions to the United Nations. Women in citizen voluntary organizations concerned with international affairs should be consulted more in the formulation of policy and procedures.

The foreign affairs agencies should increase with all possible speed the number of women at all grade levels within the agencies, and a special assistant to the Secretary of State should be appointed to coordinate a program to increase women's participation in foreign policy and to assume responsibility for U.S. participation in and the funding of the UN Decade for Women. All concerned agencies of the Executive Branch should strive to appoint women on an equal basis with men to represent the U.S. on all executive boards and governing bodies of international organizations and on the UN functional commissions. A permanent committee composed of government officials and private members, the majority of them women, should be appointed to advise the State Department on the selection of women candidates for positions on U.S. delegations, on governing bodies of international agencies, and in the UN system.

U.N. Commission on the Status of Women. The U.S. Government should work actively for the retention and adequate funding of the U.N. Commission on the Status of Women, and it should recommend that the Commission meet annually rather than biennially.

Women in development. The U.S. Agency for International Development and similar assistance agencies should give high priority to the implementation of existing U.S. legislation and policies designed to promote the integration of women into the development plans for their respective countries. They should also continue to study the impact on women in the developing world of U.S. government aid and commercial development programs over which government has any regulatory powers. These agencies should actively promote the involvement of these women in determining their own needs and priorities in programs intended for their benefit.

Human rights treaties and international conventions on women. In pressing for respect for human rights, the President and the Congress should note the special situation of women victims of oppression, political imprisonment and torture. They should also intensify efforts for ratification and compliance with international human rights treaties and conventions to which the United States is signatory, specifically including those on women's rights.

Peace and disarmament. The President and the Congress should intensify efforts to: build, in cooperation with other nations, an international framework within which serious disarmament negotiations can occur; reduce military spending and foreign military sales, convert excessive weapons manufacturing capacity to production for meeting human needs; support peace education in schools and advanced study in the fields of conflict resolution and peace keeping.

To this end the United States should take the lead in urging all nuclear powers to start phasing out their nuclear arsenals rather than escalating weapons development and deployment, and should develop initiatives to advance the cause of world peace.

International education and communication. Government agencies, media, schools, and citizen organizations should be encouraged to promote programs of international education and communication emphasizing women's present and potential contribution, particularly in developing countries, to economic and social well-being. Improved methods should be devised for collection and dissemination of this needed information in order to make adequate data available to policy makers and the public.

International Women's Decade. The U.S. should give vigorous support to the goals of the UN Decade for Women: Equality, Development and Peace in the General Assembly and other international meetings; should give financial support to Decade activities and should participate fully in the 1980 mid-Decade World Conference to review progress toward targets set in the World Plan of Action adopted unanimously by the World Conference of International Women's Year, 1975.

MEDIA

The media should employ women in all job categories and especially in policy-making positions. They should adopt and distribute the IWY media guidelines throughout their respective industries. They should make affirmative efforts to expand the portrayal of women to include a variety of roles and to represent accurately the numbers and lifestyles of women in society. Training opportunities should be expanded so that more women can move into all jobs in the communications industries, particularly into technical jobs.

Appropriate Federal and State agencies, including the Federal Communications Commission, U.S. Commission on Civil Rights, Department of Health, Education and Welfare, Department of Justice, and State civil rights commissions should vigorously enforce laws which prohibit employment discrimination against women working in the mass media. These agencies should continue studying the impact of the mass media on sex discrimination and sex-role stereotyping in American society.

Special consideration should be given to media which are publicly funded or established through acts of Congress. Particularly, public broadcasting should assume a special responsibility to integrate women in employment and programming.

Women's groups and advocacy groups should continue to develop programs to monitor the mass media and take appropriate action to improve the image and employment of women in the communications industries. They should join the campaign to de-emphasize the exploitation of female bodies and the use of violence against women in the mass media.

MINORITY WOMEN

Minority women share with all women the experience of sexism as a barrier to their full rights of citizenship. Every recommendation in this plan of action shall be understood as applying equally and fully to minority women.

But institutionalized bias based on race, language, culture and/or ethnic origin or governance of territories or localities have led to the additional oppression and exclusion of minority women and to the conditions of poverty from which they disproportionately suffer.

Therefore every level of government action should recognize and remedy this double discrimination and ensure the right of each individual to self-determination.

Legislation, the enforcement of existing laws and all levels of government action should be directed especially toward such problem areas as involuntary sterilization; monolingual education and services; high infant and maternal mortality rates; bias toward minority women's children; confinement to low level jobs; confinement to poor, ghettoized housing; culturally biased educational, psychological and employment testing (for instance, civil service); failure to enforce affirmative action and special admission programs; combined sex and race bias in insurance; and failure to gather statistical data based on both sex and race so that the needs and conditions of minority women may be accurately understood.

Minority women also suffer from government failure to recognize and remedy problems of our racial and cultural groups. For instance:

American Indian and Alaskan Native Women. American Indian/Alaskan Native women have a relationship to Earth Mother and the Great Spirit as well as a heritage based on the sovereignty of Indian peoples. The federal government should guarantee tribal rights, tribal sovereignty, honor existing treaties and congressional acts, protect hunting, fishing, and whaling rights, protect trust status, and permanently remove the threat of termination.

Congress should extend the Indian Education Act of 1972, maintain base funding of education instead of replacing it with supplemental funding, provide adequate care through the Indian Health Service, forbid the systematic removal of children from their families and communities, and assure full participation in all federally-funded programs.

Asian-American women. Asian/Pacific American women are wrongly thought to be part of a "model minority" with few problems. This obscures our vulnerability due to language and culture barriers, sweatshop work conditions with high health hazards, the particular problems of wives of U.S. servicemen, lack of access to accreditation and licensing because of immigrant status, and to many federally-funded services.

Hispanic women. Deportation of mothers of American-born children must be stopped and legislation enacted for parents to remain with their children; citizenship provisions should be facilitated.

Legislation under the National Labor Relations Act should be enacted to provide migrant farm working women, the Federal minimum wage rate, collective bargaining rights, adequate housing, and bilingual-bicultural social services delivery.

Classification of existing Hispanic American media as "Foreign Press" must be stopped to ensure equal access to major national events.

Additionally, the Federal Communications Commission must provide equal opportunity to Hispanic people for acquisition of media facilities (radio and television), for training and hiring in order to provide Spanish language programming to this major group.

Puerto Rican women emphasize that they are citizens of the United States and wish to be recognized and treated as equals.

Black women. The President and the Congress should provide for full quality education, including special admission programs, and for the full implementation and enforcement at all levels of education.

The President and the Congress should immediately address the crisis of unemployment which impacts the Black community and results in Black teenage women having the highest rate of unemployment.

The Congress should establish a national program for the placement of "children in need of parents," preferably in a family environment, where the status of said children is affected by reason of racial or ethnic origin.

The President and the Congress should assure federally assisted housing to meet the critical need of Black women, especially of low and moderate income; should direct the vigorous enforcement of all fair housing laws; and provide the allocation of resources necessary to accomplish this housing goal.

The President, Congress and all Federal agencies should utilize fully in all deliberations and planning processes, the Black Women's Plan of Action which clearly reflects and delineates other major concerns of Black Women.

OFFENDERS

States should review and reform their sentencing laws and their practices to eliminate discrimination that affects the treatment of women in penal facilities. Particular attention should be paid to the needs of poor and minority women.

States should reform their practices where needed, to provide legal counseling and referral services; improved health services emphasizing dignity in treatment for women in institutions; and protection of women prisoners from sexual abuse by male and female inmates and by correctional personnel.

Corrections Boards must provide improved educational and vocational training in a non-stereotyped range of skills that pay enough for an ex-offender to support her family.

Law enforcement agencies, courts, and correctional programs must give special attention to the needs of children with mothers under arrest, on trial, or in prison.

States must increase efforts to divert women offenders to community-based treatment facilities such as residential and non-residential halfway houses, work release, or group homes as close to the offender's family as possible.

Disparities in the treatment of male and female juvenile offenders must be eliminated; status offenses must be removed from jurisdiction of juvenile courts; and States are urged to establish more youth bureaus, crisis centers and diversion agencies to receive female juveniles detained for promiscuous conduct, for running away, or because of family or school problems.

OLDER WOMEN

That the federal and state governments, public and private women's organizations and social welfare groups should support efforts to provide social and health services that will enable the older woman to live with dignity and security. These services should include but not be limited to:

- Innovative housing which creates as nearly as possible an environment that affords security and comfort.
- Home health and social services, including visiting nurse services, homemakers services, meals-on-wheels and other protective services that will offer older women alternatives to institutional care, keeping them in familiar surroundings as long as possible.
- Preventive as well as remedial health care services.
- Public transportation in both urban and rural areas for otherwise housebound women.
- Continuing education in order to insure that the older woman will be an informed and intelligent user of the power which will be hers by virtue of the increase of her numbers.
- Immediate inclusion of geriatric education in the curriculum and training of all medical personnel in order that the elderly will receive optimum medical attention. This applies particularly to nursing home staff.
- Bilingual and bicultural programs, including health services, recreation and other programs to support elderly women of limited English speaking ability.
- Elimination of present inequities in social security benefits.
- Recognition of the economic value of homemaking in the social security benefits.
- Passage of the Displaced Homemakers bill.
- Expansion of coverage for medical and health care costs.
- Older women should be included as active participants on all kinds of policy making positions at every level of government.
- The image of the older woman is changing and there should be wide publicity focused on this. The effective use of the media is essential to furnishing information to the older woman so as to insure her informed participation in the decision-making process which continuously affects the quality of her life and the life of her community.
- Mandatory retirement should be phased out.

RAPE

Federal, State and local governments should revise their criminal codes and case law dealing with rape and related offenses to provide for graduated degrees of the crime with graduated penalties depending on the amount of force or coercion occurring with the activity; to apply to assault by or upon both sexes, including spouses as victims; to include all types of sexual assault against adults, including oral and anal contact and use of objects; to enlarge beyond traditional common law concepts the circumstances under which the act will be considered to have occurred without the victim's consent; to specify that the past sexual conduct of the victim cannot be introduced into evidence; to require no more corroborative evidence than is required in the prosecution of any other type of violent assault; and to prohibit the Hale instruction where it has been required by law or is customary.

Local task forces to review and reform rape law and practices of police, prosecutors, and medical personnel should be established where they do not now exist. Such task forces should also mobilize public support for change. Rape crisis centers should be established (with Federal and State funding) for the support of victims and the confidentiality of their records should be assured. Bilingual and bicultural information resources should be made available where necessary.

Federal and State funds should be appropriated for educational programs in the public school system and the community, including rape prevention and self-defense programs.

The National Center for the Prevention and Control of Rape within the National Institute of Mental Health should be given permanent funding for operational costs, for staff positions, research and demonstration programs and for a clearinghouse on sexual assault information and educational material with regard to prevention, treatment of victims and rehabilitation of offenders. In addition, rape centers should be consulted by NIMH in the setting of priorities and allocation of funds. The National Center should re-evaluate priorities for disbursements to make funds available to community-based programs that provide direct services to victims. The advisory committee to the National Center should be continued in order to insure community involvement and the composition of the committee should be reviewed to assure minority representation and a majority of women.

State legislatures should expand existing victim compensation for the cost of medical, surgical, and hospital expenses; evidentiary examinations; counseling; emergency funds for housing, etc.; and compensation for pregnancy and pain and suffering.

REPRODUCTIVE FREEDOM

We support the U.S. Supreme Court decisions which guarantee reproductive freedom to women.

We urge all branches of Federal, State and local governments to give the highest priority to complying with these Supreme Court decisions and to making available all methods of family planning to women unable to take advantage of private facilities.

We oppose the exclusion of abortion or childbirth and pregnancy-related care from Federal, State or local funding of medical services or from privately financed medical services.

We urge organizations concerned with improving the status of women to monitor how government complies with these principles.

We oppose involuntary sterilization and urge strict compliance by all doctors, medical and family planning facilities with the Dept. of Health, Education & Welfare's minimum April 1974 regulations requiring that consent to sterilization be truly voluntary, informed and competent. Spousal consent should not be a requirement upon which sterilization procedures are contingent. If the patient does not speak English, appropriate staff must be found to explain the procedures and HEW regulations in the primary language of the patient.

Particular attention should be paid at all levels of government to providing confidential family planning services for teen-agers, education in responsible sexuality, and reform of laws discriminating against illegitimate children and their parents.

Programs in sex education should be provided in all schools, including elementary schools.

Federal, State and local governing bodies should take whatever steps are necessary to remove existing barriers to family planning services for all teen-agers who request them.

Each school system should assist teen-age parents with programs including child care arrangements that will encourage them to remain in school, provide educational and vocational training leading to economic independence, and teach prenatal health and parenting skills.

RURAL WOMEN

The President and Congress should establish a Federal rural education policy designed to meet the special problems of isolation, poverty and underemployment that characterizes much of rural America. Such a policy must be consciously planned to overcome the inequality of opportunities available to rural women and girls.

The Office of Management and Budget should set and enforce a policy that data collected on beneficiaries of all Federal programs shall be reported by sex, by minority status, and by urban/rural or metropolitan/non-metropolitan areas, based on a standard definition.

Data on employment of women and public programs on behalf of working women should include in their definitions farm wives and widows who perform the many tasks essential to the farm operation.

A farm wife should have the same ownership rights as her spouse under State inheritance and Federal estate laws. Tax law should recognize that the labor of a farm wife gives her an equitable interest in the property.

All programs developed on behalf of rural women should be certain to include migrants, Native Americans and Alaskans.

The President should appoint a joint committee from the Departments of Labor, Agriculture, and Justice to investigate the Louisiana sugar plantations system's violations of human rights, especially of women. This commission should also investigate conditions of other seasonal and migratory workers in all States and territories of the United States.

All programs developed on behalf of rural women should be certain to include Black, migrant, Native American, Alaskan, Asian, and Hispanic, and all isolated minorities, and that affirmative action programs be extended to include all disenfranchised groups.

SEXUAL PREFERENCE

Congress, State, and local legislatures should enact legislation to eliminate discrimination on the basis of sexual and affectional preference in areas including, but not limited to, employment, housing, public accommodations, credit, public facilities, government funding, and the military.

State legislatures should reform their penal codes or repeal State laws that restrict private sexual behavior between consenting adults.

State legislatures should enact legislation that would prohibit consideration of sexual or affectional orientation as a factor in any judicial determination of child custody or visitation rights. Rather, child custody cases should be evaluated solely on the merits of which party is the better parent, without regard to that person's sexual and affectional orientation.

STATISTICS

The Office of Management and Budget should require all departments and agencies to collect, tabulate, and analyze data relating to persons on the basis of sex in order to assess the impact of their programs on women.

The U.S. Census Bureau should aggressively pursue its efforts to reduce the undercounts of minority Americans, including Blacks, Hispanic Americans, Asian Americans, and American Indians. The Department of Health, Education, and Welfare should continue its efforts to implement the usage of special group identifiers in all vital statistics recordkeeping. These statistics should be recorded and reported by sex and subgroup.

WOMEN, WELFARE AND POVERTY

The Federal and State governments should assume a role in focusing on welfare and poverty as major women's issues. All welfare reform proposals should be examined specifically for their impact on women. Inequality of opportunity for women must be recognized as a primary factor contributing to the growth of welfare roles.

Women in poverty, whether young or old, want to be part of the mainstream of American life.

Poverty is a major barrier to equality for women. Millions of women who depend on income transfer programs or low paying jobs for their basic life support may be subject to the multiple oppression of sexism, racism, poverty and are often old or disabled.

Many other women, because of discriminating employment practices, social security laws, differential education of men and women, and lack of adequate child care are just one step away from poverty. Consequently, the elimination of poverty must be a priority of all those working for equal rights for women.

Along with major improvements of the welfare system, elimination of poverty for women must include improvements in social security and retirement systems, universal minimum wage, non-traditional job opportunities, quality child care, comprehensive health insurance, and comprehensive legal services. A concerted effort must be made to educate the public about the realities of welfare, the plight of the blind, the aged, the disabled, single-parent families and other low income women.

We support increased federal funding for income transfer programs (e.g. Social Security, SSI, AFDC). Congress should approve a federal floor under payments to provide an adequate standard of living based on each state's cost of living. And, just as other workers, homemakers receiving payments should be afforded the dignity of having that payment called a wage, not welfare.

We oppose the Carter Administration proposal for welfare reform (HR 9030) which among other things eliminates food stamps, CETA training and CETA jobs paying more than minimum wage, adequate day care and introduces "workfare" where welfare mothers would be forced to "work off" their grants which is work without wage, without fringe benefits or bargaining rights, and without dignity. HR 9030 further requires those individuals and families without income to wait weeks or even months before even the inadequate grant is available. We strongly support a welfare reform program developed from on-going consultation with persons who will be impacted. This program should be consistent with the national Academy of Science recommendation that no individual or family living standard should be lower than half the median family level (after tax); should not fall below the government defined poverty level of family income even for shorter periods; which helps support sustaining the family unit; and that women on welfare and other low income women who choose to work not be forced into jobs paying less than the prevailing wage.

Employers should, in order to improve the status of women, include the following actions:

• In order to insure that welfare and other poor are not discriminated against as an economic class, affirmative action guidelines should be drawn up to provide that all employers who are recipients of Federal and/or State contract monies be required to show that they are hiring recipients.
• The targeting of funds by local CETA advisory boards for the placement and training of women in non-traditional higher paying jobs, consistent with the original mandate.
• The Department of Labor should make a study based on a standard of comparable worth, and speedily move the implementation of that study in all government positions.
• Unions should devote additional energy to the organization of women to upgrade pay and working conditions for women in traditional employment.

Quality child care should be a mandated Title XX service, available to all families on an ability to pay basis throughout training, education, job search and employment.

Congress should encourage education of women by removing federal education grants from the expendable income classification in AFDC programs.

Comprehensive support services and social services must be provided and adequately funded.

JEWISH WOMEN

JEWISH WOMEN HAVE BUILT A SET OF COMMUNAL ORGANIZATIONS WHICH DO not handily fit under the categories of religious, volunteer, or minority. These organizations are distinguished by their commitment to the survival of Jewish culture and/or the state of Israel as well as to the improvement of life in America. And although Jewish women have formed religious groups—sisterhoods, fellowships, task forces—they have also created a network of secular organizations.

Like their Christian counterparts, middle- and upper-class Jewish women of the late nineteenth century were affected by social progressivism. Wanting to do more than just gather for cultural and recreational purposes, they organized voluntary associations in order to do social-service work. Among the first such groups was the National Council of Jewish Women (NCJW) begun in 1893; its constituency organized Jewish study groups, Sabbath schools, and immigrant aid facilities. B'nai B'rith Women, the wives of B'nai B'rith men, organized themselves in 1897. Like the NCJW, their goals were to preserve Jewish values and to enhance the quality of life for all Americans.

During the twentieth century these groups and the Women's Divisions of the American Jewish Congress and the American Jewish Committee tried to strike a balance between serving the American Jewish community, the United States, and—especially after World War II—the state of Israel. Today their programs reflect all of these concerns. Across the board, these groups support ERA and other women's issues, social justice concerns, and community involvement in the United States as well as support for health, educational and vocational institutions in Israel.

Also important on the American Jewish scene are Zionist women's organizations. Hadassah has a membership of more than 360,000 and can raise as much as $25 million each year to support medical and educational facilities in Israel. Hadassah is respected among social-service agencies for being the best-organized force in American Jewish communal life. Pioneer Women, another Zionist organization, works with a sister group in Israel. There they have initiated educational and vocational programs to improve the status and role of women.

Jewish women's organizations succeed because of volunteer power; they galvanize women who can organize their communities around issues which are important to them. These women make possible a wide range of services, from political lobbying to career counseling to aid for youth, the disabled and the elderly.

Unfortunately Jewish women are less successful at achieving positions of power within professional Jewish organizations, Jewish Federations, homes for the aged, family and child-care organizations and community councils. This situation parallels the problems of all women in social work, as documented in a recent National Association of Social Workers survey. A 1977 survey on the status of women in Jewish communal service revealed that although nearly half the staff of organizations surveyed were female, less than 1 percent of the women were executives and only 3 percent of all executive positions were held by women. Only 4 percent of women were assistant directors and 95 percent were in the two lowest categories. Economically, this means that one out of four men in Jewish community service organizations make more than $30,000 per year whereas only one out of every five hundred women do.

Since Jewish women have staffed their own organizations for more than seventy-five years they are obviously not lacking in management and administrative skills. However, when men and women compete for well-paying jobs, men invariably win out and women are relegated to lower status, lower-paying positions or to achieving rewards in a voluntary capacity.

See also: Ordination of Women
            Women and Religion

Organizations:

American Jewish Congress
National Women's Division
15 East 84th Street
New York, NY 10028

B'nai B'rith Women
1640 Rhode Island Avenue N.W.
Washington, DC 20036

Hadassah
50 West 58th Street
New York, NY 10019

National Council of Jewish Women
15 East 26th Street
New York, NY 10010

Pioneer Women
200 Madison Avenue
New York, NY 10016

Resources:

The Jewish Woman in America by Charlotte Baum, Paula Hyman, Sonya Michel. New York: Dial Press, 1976.
  Interesting social history of the Ashkenazi woman in America. Excellent bibliography of primary and secondary sources.

Lilith. Order from: Lilith, 250 West 57th Street, New York, NY 10019.
  Quarterly magazine by women committed "to the creative survival of the Jewish people, and of Israel, and to the equality and advancement of Jewish women and of all women."

The Status of Women in Jewish Communal Service. New York: National Conference of Jewish Communal Service, 1977. Order from: National Conference of Jewish Communal Service, 15 East 26th Street, New York, NY 10010.
  Findings of a survey which provided much of the information in the text above.

"Women and Social Work: Perceptions of Barriers to Administrative Advancement," by Mary Flanagan. *Womanpower,* December 1977 and May 1978. Order from: National Association of Social Workers, 1425 H Street N.W., Washington, DC 20005.
  The study of the status of women in social work cited in the text.

LABOR UNION WOMEN

WOMEN WORKERS, THOUGH CONSISTENTLY UNDER-UNIONIZED, HAVE ALWAYS been part of the American labor union scene: from the weavers of Pawtucket, Rhode Island who, in 1824, were the first women to join a strike, to the tireless

United Mine Workers organizer Mother Jones, to the founding of the Coalition of Labor Union Women in 1974.

The Daughters of St. Crispin was the first national organization of trade union women; it was founded in Lynn, Massachusetts in 1869. Without the blessing of the American Federation of Labor, working-class and middle-class women united to form the National Women's Trade Union League in 1903. Women have also worked in auxiliary organizations, often providing crucial support in an emergency situation. For example, in the United Auto Workers sit-down strike in Flint, Michigan, in 1936, wives of striking workers stood guard outside the plant, keeping out company guards and strike breakers. Unfortunately, though women have played many important roles in union history, once the unions gained power, they tended to support continued discrimination against women workers. Although the situation varies from union to union, of course, the overall pattern has been to protect the interests of the male workers by keeping women out.

Women's participation in labor unions has been influenced perhaps most heavily by the sex segregation of the labor market. Women are under-unionized because they are concentrated in clerical and service occupations—areas that unions have traditionally shown little interest in organizing. Historically, white-collar work has been seen as higher in status than the physical work performed by blue-collar workers. Indeed, it once was. In 1920, white-collar workers earned 50 to 100 percent more than factory workers; in 1952, office workers were 4 percent behind. During this period two things happened: American labor unions grew and gained tremendous strength, and the huge sexual ghetto of clerical workers developed

Members of the New York City Coalition of Labor Union Women march in a 1977 demonstration in support of the Equal Rights Amendment. © *Bettye Lane*

Union organizer Rose Schneiderman (1882–1972) speaking at a 1913 rally in New York. Schneiderman, while working in the garment industry, organized the first local of the United Cloth Hat and Cap Makers Union. A tireless organizer, she was president of the Women's Trade Union League throughout the twenties and ran for U.S. Senate on the Labor Party ticket in 1920. *Brown Brothers*

into the largest single occupational group in the country. Unfortunately, these two sectors grew independently of each other until, by 1975, two-thirds of women workers were in white-collar jobs and only 13 percent of women were unionized. Male blue-collar workers, on the other hand, accounted for 63 percent of the total male labor force and were—and are—the most highly unionized group of American workers.

A recent study of women's participation in unions from 1956 to 1976 points to some encouraging and some discouraging trends. The percentage of women workers who belonged to unions declined over the twenty-year period; in 1956, 15 percent of women workers were unionized, but only 11 percent in 1976. However, women were being unionized at a faster rate than men—union membership overall increased only 13 percent while union membership among women rose 34 percent. The seeming discrepancy is explained by the huge numbers of women going into nonunionized clerical jobs. That is, while more women were joining unions, their numbers could not keep pace with the vastly expanding nonunion female labor force.

While fewer unions had no women members in 1976 than in 1956—the figure dropped from 27 percent to 14 percent—women tended to join unions that already had substantial female memberships. In 1956, 75 percent of all union women belonged to one of seventeen unions; in 1976, 81 percent belonged to one of eighteen unions.

Women have joined associations at a much greater rate than they have joined unions. While women's participation in unions increased 10 percent from 1970 to 1976, their membership in associations increased 80 percent. However, one

Dolores Huerta, center, vice-president of the United Farm Workers, is one of the few top-ranking female labor union officials. *Wide World Photos*

organization—the National Education Association—accounts for two-thirds of all women association members. Most associations are for professional women, which still leaves millions of clerical workers unrepresented.

One of the most hopeful recent events was the formation of the Coalition of Labor Union Women (CLUW) in 1974. At its founding convention, the Coalition set forth four areas of concern: organizing nonunion workers, affirmative action, political action and legislation, and increasing the participation of women in their own unions. During the four years of its existence, CLUW has been active in supporting the demands of the women's movement and union struggles. The Coalition has the potential to be a tremendously positive force in bringing women and unions together.

See also: Earnings Gap
Nontraditional Occupations
Sex-typing of Occupations

Organizations:

Coalition of Labor Union Women
15 Union Square
New York, NY 10003

Union Women's Alliance to Gain Equality
P.O. Box 462
Berkeley, CA 94701

United Auto Workers Women's
Department
8000 East Jefferson Avenue
Detroit, MI 48214

Resources:

Organize: A Working Women's Handbook. San Francisco: Union Women's Alliance to Gain Equality, 1975. Order from: Union W.A.G.E. (address above).

This pamphlet gives guidelines and strategies for workplace organizing and includes a complete chapter on writing and negotiating a contract.

Salt of the Earth, screenplay by Michael Wilson, commentary by Deborah Silverton Rosenfelt. Old Westbury: The Feminist Press, 1978. Order from: The Feminist Press, P.O. Box 334, Old Westbury, NY 11568.

This is the screenplay of the classic 1953 film about the crucial role of women in a miner's strike in the Southwest.

"Women in Labor Organizations: Their Ranks are Increasing," by Linda H. LeGrande. *Monthly Labor Review* (August 1978).

A study of women's labor union participation from 1956 to 1976. *The Monthly Labor Review* has published at least one article on labor union women per year during the last few years. This article provided much of the information in the text above.

Workers and Allies: Female Participation in the American Trade Union Movement, 1842–1976, by Judith O'Sullivan and Rosemary Gallick. Washington: Smithsonian Institution Press, 1975.

Attractively illustrated with portraits of women from trade union history, this paperback gives a brief history of women's union activity and chronology of events. The bulk of the book is made up of biographies of living and historical figures. *Workers and Allies* provided much of the information in the text above.

♀ CHRONOLOGY: FEMALE PARTICIPATION
IN THE AMERICAN TRADE UNION MOVEMENT ♀

<u>1765</u> The first society of workingwomen, the Daughters of Liberty, is organized as an auxiliary of the Sons of Liberty, a workingman's association.

<u>1789</u> During a visit to the Boston Duck Sail Manufactory, President George Washington praises the spinners as "daughters of decayed families, and . . . girls of character."

<u>1790</u> The first textile mill is established in Pawtucket, Rhode Island, equipped with machinery designed from memory by Samuel Slater for Ezekial Carpenter. It is staffed entirely by children under twelve years of age—seven boys and two girls.

<u>1791</u> In his Report on Manufactures, communicated to the House of Representatives on December 5, Secretary of the Treasury Alexander Hamilton praises the industry of women workers, "rendered more useful . . . by manufacturing establishments than they would otherwise be."

<u>1792</u> Mary Wollstonecraft publishes *Vindication of the Rights of Women.*

<u>1793</u> Eli Whitney develops the cotton gin, reportedly from an idea of Catherine Littlefield Greene, his landlady.

<u>1810</u> The first American cigar factory, its entire work force female, opens in Suffield, Connecticut.

<u>1814</u> With the adoption of the power loom, weaving becomes a factory occupation; its first prominent female practitioner is Deborah Skinner.

<u>1824</u> Women workers strike for the first time, in Pawtucket, Rhode Island. At a meeting "conducted . . . without noise, or scarcely a single speech." One hundred and two female workers strike in support of brother weavers protesting the simultaneous reductions of wages and extension of the workday.

<u>1825</u> Women workers strike alone for the first time when the United Tailoresses' Society of New York City demands a wage increase.

<u>1828</u> Paterson, New Jersey, textile workers rally in support of the ten-hour workday.

Philadelphia and Manayunk, Pennsylvania, cotton spinners protest a wage cut of 25 percent.

Dover, New Hampshire, mill workers denounce company fines for tardiness and for talking on the job.

<u>1829</u> Taunton, Massachusetts, textile workers protest a wage reduction.

<u>1831</u> Led by Mrs. Phobe Scott, Mrs. Eliza Trulin, and Mrs. Lydabach, 1,600 members of the United Tailoresses' Society of New York City strike for a wage increase of 33⅓ percent.

<u>1833</u> Led by Susan Stansbury, Hannah Moran, and Jacob Daley, the Society of Tailoresses and Seamstresses of Baltimore, Maryland, demands a wage increase.

The Female Society of Lynn, Massachusetts, and Vicinity leads shoebinders in a strike for increased wages.

<u>1834</u> Recording industrial conditions, the British writer [and economist] Harriet Martineau visits Massachusetts factories.

The Factory Girls Association is formed by 2,500 textile workers in Lowell,

Massachusetts. Signaled by the wave of the bonnet, they walk out to protest the dismissal of a sister employee and a wage reduction of 15 percent, asserting that "none of us will . . . [return] . . . unless they receive us all as one."

In Dover, New Hampshire, 800 women strike against wage reductions and for the right to organize; they form a union embracing sister workers in Great Falls and Newmarket.

Amesbury, Massachusetts, weavers decry a company proposal to tend two looms rather than one with no pay increase.

Manayunk, Pennsylvania, mill operatives denounce a wage reduction of 25 percent.

1835   In Philadelphia 500 women, including binders, corset makers, folders, mantuamakers, milliners, seamstresses, stockmakers, and tailoresses, establish the Female Improvement Society. The organization draws up a price scale and publishes lists of employers who violate it.

Workers in twenty Paterson, New Jersey, textile mills demand that the workday be shortened from thirteen and one-half hours to eleven hours.

New York City shoebinders strike for higher wages.

The United Men's and Women's Trading Society is established.

Journeymen Segar Makers of Philadelphia declare their support for sister workers, resolving that "we recommend them in a body to strike with us and thereby make it a mutual interest with both parties to sustain each other in their rights."

1836   In Lowell, Massachusetts, the Factory Girls' Association strikes, denouncing a 12½ percent increase in the cost of room and board at the company boardinghouses.

Dover, New Hampshire, textile workers strike to protest a wage reduction.

1837   Led by Lavinia Wright and Louisa Mitchell, 1,600 members of the Tailoresses' Society of New York City strike for a wage scale.

1840   *The Lowell Offering*, the journal of female textile workers in Lowell, Massachusetts, begins publication.

1842   Chief Justice Lemuel Shaw of the Massachusetts Supreme Court endorses the worker's right to organize in *Commonwealth* v. *Hunt*, declaring that "such agreement could not be pronounced a criminal conspiracy" and that unions "far from being criminal or unlawful . . . may be highly meritorious and public spirited." His landmark decision ends the American application of the English common law of criminal conspiracy to trade unions and provides a legal foundation for unionization.

1843   Women employed in the Pittsburgh cotton mills protest an extension of the workday without pay.

1844   Pioneer labor organizer Sarah G. Bagley founds the Lowell Female Labor Reform Association; she also establishes the Lowell Industrial Reform Lyceum.

Boston seamstresses and journeymen tailors join forces to fight a wage reduction.

1845   Sarah Bagley's articles are rejected by *The Lowell Offering* editor Harriet Farley. Denouncing the journal as a company paper, Bagley on behalf of the Lowell Female Labor Reform Association acquires *The Voice of*

Industry, in which she attacks company recruiting policies, health conditions in company boardinghouses, and the company store. Appearing before the Massachusetts legislature, she testifies in favor of extension of the ten-hour workday (adopted by the federal government in 1842) to private industry, presenting a petition signed by 1,000 sister workers.

The Lowell Female Labor Reform Association elects Bagley president, Mary Eastman secretary, and Huldah J. Stone correspondent.

Female workers in five Allegheny, Pennsylvania, cotton mills strike for the ten-hour workday; they are supported by co-workers in Lowell, Massachusetts, and Manchester, New Hampshire.

The Female Industrial Association of New York City is formed; its president is Elizabeth Gray, secretary is Mary Graham, and chairman is Annie S. Stevens. Among its members are bookfolders, bookstitchers, capmakers, crimpers, dressmakers, strawmakers, and tailoresses.

1846   During the winter of 1845–1846, the Manchester, New Hampshire, Female Labor Reform Association is organized; Sarah Rumrill is elected president.

New York City seamstresses found the Shirt Sewers' Cooperative Union.

On February 21 Sarah Bagley becomes the first female telegraph operator, to the amusement of the Boston *Journal,* which speculates that "the long mooted question 'Can a woman keep a secret?' will now become more interesting than ever."

1847   Spurred by the efforts of the Female Labor Reform Association, the New Hampshire legislature enacts the ten-hour workday law.

Miss E. Kidder is elected president of the Manchester, New Hampshire, Female Labor Reform Association.

The Dover, New Hampshire, Female Labor Reform Association is established by textile workers. Miss Burnham is its first president.

1848   The Pennsylvania legislature passes the ten-hour law; when it is violated by employers, female mill workers riot, attacking factory gates with axes.

Declaring that "all men and women are created equal," Elizabeth Cady Stanton, a champion of female suffrage, and Lucretia Mott, a Quaker minister and militant abolitionist, open the first feminist convention in Seneca Falls, New York. Their Delaration of Sentiments, a paraphrase of the Declaration of Independence, castigating male tyranny, immediately unleashes a flood of ridicule.

1850   Lucretia Mott and Elizabeth Oakes Smith support a cooperative sewing shop established by a union of Philadelphia seamstresses.

1860   On January 10 the pillars supporting the central structure of the Pemberton Mills in Lawrence, Massachusetts, give way; eighty-eight working men, women, and children are killed.

On March 5 Abraham Lincoln declares his support for striking New England shoemakers and asserts his faith in unionization. "Thank God that we have a system of labor where there can be a strike. Whatever the pressure, there is a point where the workingman may stop."

Breaking a decade of silence on the part of women workers—the aftermath of the financial crisis of 1848–1849 and the subsequent replacement of Anglo-

Saxon employees by immigrants—800 female shoebinders in Lynn, Massachusetts, join 4,000 brother workers on March 7 to parade through a blinding snowstorm to demand higher wages. "American ladies will not be slaves," their banners proclaim. "Give us a fair compensation and we labour cheerfully."

1861 A massive influx of soldiers' wives and widows into the needle trades takes place.

1864 In New York City, 100 sewing-machine operators unite to collect dues and administer sick benefits; their president is M. Trimble, their secretary Ella Patterson.

1865 Philadelphia seamstresses petition President Abraham Lincoln for a living wage.

The Boston Women's Union of Pantaloon Makers is established.

Two hundred seamstresses found the Chicago Sewing Women's Protective Union.

Manufacturers, railroads, and steamship companies join forces to recruit European labor.

1866 Transcending the self-interest of male workers, the National Labor Union pledges "individual and undivided support to the sewing women, factory operatives and daughters of toil."

The Working Women's Protective Union is established, empowered to collect back wages from recalcitrant employers.

1867 The Cigarmakers International Union amends its constitution to admit blacks and women.

1868 The eight-hour federal workday is declared.

Susan B. Anthony establishes *The Revolution,* a paper printed by females and dealing with issues of interest to women workers.

The New York Working Women's Association is founded by Susan B. Anthony, Elizabeth Cady Stanton, and Augusta Lewis Troup.

Augusta Lewis Troup becomes president of Women's Typographical Union No. 1.

Despite male opposition, Stanton and Anthony are seated as delegates at the convention of the National Labor Union.

Maggie McNamara is elected head of the Brooklyn Female Burnishers' Association.

1869 The membership of the National Labor Union votes against seating Susan B. Anthony as a convention delegate. Anthony is charged with underpaying her employees at *The Revolution,* encouraging female strikebreakers, and discharging Augusta Lewis Troup from *The Revolution* because of her union activities.

The first female national union, The Daughters of St. Crispin, is organized by women shoeworkers. They elect Carrie Wilson president and Abbie Jacques secretary. On July 28 the union holds its first convention in Lynn, Massachusetts.

The International Typographical Union admits female members.

The Knights of Labor is established, its membership open to blacks and females, its policy "To secure for both sexes equal pay for equal work."

The National Colored Labor Union is founded.

Kate Mullaney of the Troy, New York, Collar Laundry Workers calls a strike.

1870 Augusta Lewis Troup is elected corresponding secretary of the International Typographical Union.

At their second convention, the Daughters of St. Crispin demand "for our labor the same rate of compensation for equal skill displayed, or the same hours of toil, as is paid other laborers in the same branches of business."

Victoria Woodhull and her sister, Tennessee Claflin, establish the first female brokerage, Woodhull, Claflin & Company, in New York City, and begin publication of *Woodhull & Claflin's Weekly,* a precursor of the "yellow journal," which features exposés of corporate fraud and political corruption, as well as articles on labor, divorce, free love, and abortion.

Victoria Woodhull declares her candidacy for president of the United States.

1871 *Woodhull & Claflin's Weekly* publishes an English translation of Karl Marx's *Communist Manifesto,* the first American press to do so.

Victoria Woodhull and Tennessee Claflin assume leadership of Section 12 of Marx's International Workingman's Party; they are later expelled.

1875 Named for the legendary Irish heroine whose reign of terror thwarted English landlords' attempts to evict indigent farmers, the Molly Maguires, a secret society of immigrant miners in eastern Pennsylvania, are penetrated by Pinkerton agent James McParlan. On the basis of McParlan's assertions, ten miners are tried, convicted, and executed.

In Fall River, Massachusetts, women textile workers vote to strike despite the acceptance of a wage cut by male employees. Later joined by their brother workers, the women win the strike.

The cigarmakers amend their constitution to prohibit local unions from discriminating against women workers.

1877 In New York City, several hundred women are recruited as strike-breakers during a work stoppage by unionized male cigarworkers. Employers hail the strike as "a blessing in disguise," because it has brought to their attention the value of female employees, "workers whose services may be depended on at low wages."

In Cincinnati, male unionists strike successfully to prohibit employers from hiring females. Commented the Cincinnati *Daily Inquirer:* "The men say the women are killing the industry. It would seem that they hope to retaliate by killing the women."

Climaxing four years of depression, a national railroad strike commences on July 16, leaving in its wake more than one hundred deaths and the massive destruction of property. In Pittsburgh, members of the Philadelphia National Guard fire upon strikers and their families.

1881 Mrs. Terence V. Powderly is admitted to the Knights of Labor.

The Federation of Organized Trades and Labor Unions of the United States and Canada, later to become the American Federation of Labor, is founded in Pittsburgh.

1883 Mary Stirling, a Philadelphia shoeworker, is the first female delegate to the convention of the Knights of Labor. Kate Dowling of Rochester, New York, is elected a delegate but does not attend.

<u>1884</u> The first female local of the Knights of Labor, the Garfield Assembly, is organized.

Louisa M. Eaton, a Lynn, Massachusetts, shoeworker, and Mary Hannafin, a Philadelphia saleswoman, are delegates to the Knights of Labor convention.

<u>1885</u> The Knights of Labor establish a committee to collect statistics on working women. Among its members are Mary Hannafin, Mary Stirling of Philadelphia, and Lizzie H. Shute of Haverhill, Massachusetts.

Charlotte Smith, president of the Women's National Labor League, attends the convention of the Federation of Organized Trades and Labor Unions of the United States and Canada.

<u>1886</u> On May 4 a bomb explodes during a protest in Chicago's Haymarket Square; seven policemen and four workers are killed. Anarchist orators are promptly seized, convicted, and executed. For years after her husband Albert R. Parsons' execution, Lucy Eldine Gonzalez Parsons proclaimed his innocence.

The American Federation of Labor, headed by Samuel Gompers, holds its first convention in Columbus, Ohio.

Women delegates to the Knights of Labor convention number sixteen, among them Elizabeth Flynn Rodgers, master workman of District Assembly No. 24, who attends with her two-week-old child. The women's department of the Knights of Labor is organized, headed by Leonora Barry, a widow with three children and master workman of District Assembly No. 65, as general investigator. Her assignment is to examine "the abuses to which our sex is subjected by unscrupulous employers" and to "agitate the principles . . . of equal pay and the abolition of child labor."

The Working Women's Society is founded by Leonora O'Reilly of the Knights of Labor, assisted by Josephine Shaw Lowell, Mrs. Robert Abbé, Arria Huntingdon, and L. S. Perkins.

<u>1887</u> Knights of Labor general investigator Leonora Barry is assisted in her documentation of the industrial exploitation of women and children by Mary O'Reilly of Providence, Rhode Island, vice-president of the Knights' women's department and a former cotton mill worker.

<u>1889</u> Jane Addams and Ellen Gates Starr open Hull House, the pioneer Chicago settlement.

<u>1890</u> Alzina Parsons Stevens, founder of the Joan of Arc Assembly of the Knights of Labor, is elected master workman of District Assembly No. 72. At the convention of the Knights of Labor, however, she declines the post of general investigator vacated by Leonora Barry.

The first fully accredited female delegate, Mary Burke of the Retail Clerks, of Findley, Ohio, attends the American Federation of Labor convention. The convention passes a resolution supporting women's suffrage and urging the appointment of female organizers.

Josephine Shaw Lowell helps to establish the Consumers League of the City of New York, dedicated to the patronage of those establishments which pay just wages and provide "reasonable hours, suitable seats, and decent sanitary conditions."

<u>1891</u> At the American Federation of Labor convention, a women's committee

headed by Eva McDonald Valesh and Ida Van Etten recommends the creation of the office of national organizer.

1892   Mary Kenney O'Sullivan of the Bindery Workers is appointed the American Federation of Labor's first female national organizer. Her activities include campaigns in Albany, Boston, New York City, and Troy, New York.

During a steelworkers' strike in Homestead, Pennsylvania, Russian immigrants Emma Goldman and Alexander Berkman misread the workers' militancy and conspire to assassinate Henry Clay Frick, an antiunion manager of the Carnegie Steel Company. The attempt, however, is abortive: Frick recovers and Berkman is sentenced to twenty-five years in prison. Despite her open avowal of participation, Goldman is never tried.

1893   An army of unemployed, led by businessman Jacob S. Coxey, marches on Washington. A company broadside is later to charge that Mother Mary Harris Jones, in 1893 a sixty-three-year-old United Mine Workers organizer, as a madam made elaborate plans for their entertainment en route.

1896   The Union for Industrial Progress is founded by Mary Kimball Kehew and Mary Kenney O'Sullivan.

1898   The National Consumers' League is founded; John Graham Brooks is elected president, Florence Kelley executive secretary. Among its goals is protective legislation for women and children.

A resolution vigorously opposed by the American Federation of Labor is placed before Congress, barring all women from federal employment and "regulat[ing] them to the home."

Charlotte Perkins Gilman publishes *Women and Economics.*

1900   Emma Goldman begins publication of *Mother Earth.*

Hannah Mahoney Nolan organizes the Steam Laundry Workers' Union of San Francisco.

1902   "Petticoat butchers" Maggie Condon and Hannah O'Day found the Maud Gonne Club in Chicago.

Local 183 of the Amalgamated Meat Cutters and Butcher Workmen of New York City is organized; Mollie Day is elected president, Maud Sutter business agent.

1903   Mother Mary Harris Jones, veteran United Mine Workers organizer, leads the March of the Mill Children, many of them victims of industrial accidents, from Philadelphia to President Theodore Roosevelt's home in Oyster Bay, New York.

On November 14, during the American Federation of Labor's Boston convention, blue-collar and bourgeois women unite to form the National Women's Trade Union League. The league is open to male and female members of all races "willing to assist those trade unions already existing, which have women members, and to aid in the formation of new unions of women wage earners." Among the officers elected are Mary Morton Kehew of Boston, president; Jane Addams of Chicago, vice president; Mary Kenney O'Sullivan of Boston, secretary; and Mary Donovan of the Boot and Shoe Workers, treasurer. Its board of directors includes Mary McDowell of Chicago; Lillian Wald of New York; Ellen Lindstrom of the United Garment Workers; Mary

Trites of the Textile Workers; and Leonora O'Reilly of the Ladies Garment Workers' Union.

1904   Local branches of the National Women's Trade Union League are established in Chicago, New York City, and Boston.

Mary McLeod Bethune opens the Daytona Educational and Industrial School for Negro Girls.

1905   The founding convention of the Industrial Workers of the World (IWW) is held in Chicago. Those in attendance include the most colorful and controversial figures in labor history: one-eyed "Big Bill" Haywood; Joe Hill; feisty Mother Mary Harris Jones; Elizabeth Gurley Flynn; Haymarket widow Lucy Eldine Gonzalez Parsons; Eugene V. Debs; and Daniel DeLeon.

The laundry workers of Troy, New York, wage an unsuccessful strike.

1906   Mother Ella Reeve Bloor assists novelist Upton Sinclair, verifying for federal investigators charges made in *The Jungle,* an exposé of immigrant exploitation by Chicago meatpackers.

In Schenectady, New York, the International Workers of the World pioneer the sit-down strike; employees of General Electric fold their arms on the job for sixty-five hours.

1907   The National Women's Trade Union League begins publication of its journal, *Life and Labor.*

During the summer the National Women's Trade Union League sponsors simultaneous conventions of female unionists in Boston, Chicago and New York City.

Margaret Dreier Robins of Chicago is elected president of the National Women's Trade Union League.

Josephine Clara Goldmark publishes *Labour Laws for Women in the United States.*

1908   The Supreme Court in *Muller* v. *Oregon,* 208 U.S. 412, upholds the constitutionality of maximum-hour laws for women workers, agreeing with Louis Brandeis that a female's "physical structure and a proper discharge of her maternal functions . . . justify legislation to protect her from the greed as well as the passion of men." Brandeis's brief is based on the research of Josephine Clara Goldmark, his sister-in-law.

1909   At a mass meeting of New York City garment workers held in Cooper Union on November 22, teenaged Clara Lemlich interrupts proceedings chaired by Samuel Gompers to declare, "What we are here for is to decide whether or not we shall strike. I offer a resolution that a general strike be declared—now!" Thus begins the "Uprising of 20,000" Jewish and Italian immigrant workers, the vast majority of whom are women. Seventy-five members of the New York Women's Trade Union League form the "mink brigade," a picket line supporting Ladies' Waistmakers' Union No. 25 against the Triangle Shirtwaist Company. Mary Dreier, president of the New York League, is arrested; because of her social standing, the arrest makes headlines.

Mary White Ovington helps to establish the National Association for the Advancement of Colored People.

1910   Margaret Dreier Robins, president of the National Women's Trade

Union League, establishes a training program for female labor organizers. Among those to participate are Louisa Mittelstadt of the Kansas City Brewery Workers; Myrtle Whitehead of the Baltimore Brewery Workers; and Fannia Cohn of the International Ladies' Garment Workers' Union.

In New York City 70,000 cloakmakers strike.

The Philadelphia needle trades' strike is strongly supported by the National Women's Trade Union League. Among the allies of Labor are Margaret Dreier Robins, national president; Mary Dreier, president of the New York League; Agnes Nestor, rank-and-file Chicago League organizer; socialite Mrs. George Biddle; settlement resident Anna Davies; and Consumers' League representative Anne Young.

During the strike by the makers of ready-made men's clothing, the Chicago United Garment Worker's District Council No. 6 appeals to the National Women's Trade Union League for speakers. In response, the league provides Margaret Bondfield and Mrs. Philip Snowden and contributes $70,000 in relief funds.

1911   On Saturday, March 25, fire breaks out at the Triangle Shirtwaist Company in New York City. The doors of the sweatshop, located on the eighth floor of a ten-story building, are locked to keep union organizers out and employees in. Attempting to escape, workers leap from the windows. The tragedy claims 143 lives. Among those witnessing the holocaust are labor journalist Mary Heaton Vorse and future secretary of Labor Frances Perkins.

1912   In Lawrence, Massachusetts, 27,000 textile workers protest the reduction in wages accompanying the American Woolen Company's compliance with a state law shortening the work week. A female picket, Anne Lo Pizzo, is shot and killed. The National Women's Trade Union League withdraws from the strike because of the dominance of the International Workers of the World, among them Elizabeth Gurley Flynn.

Elizabeth Christman is elected president of the International Glove Workers' Union.

1913   In Paterson, New Jersey, 25,000 silk workers strike to protest an increase in the number of looms to be tended. Rose Pastor Stokes is active in the protest.

Members of the International Ladies' Garment Workers Union strike in New York City.

1914   On April 20 wives and children of striking miners are slain when their tent colony in Ludlow, Colorado, is set aflame by National Guardsmen mustered to protect the properties and officers of the Colorado Fuel and Iron Company, an interest of John D. Rockefeller, Jr. Among the union organizers assisting the Ludlow strikers is Mother Mary Harris Jones.

The Women's Trade Union League establishes a school for organizers in Chicago, which continues in operation until 1926.

1915   On November 19 labor balladeer and IWW organizer Joseph Hillstrom (Joe Hill) is executed in Salt Lake City, Utah. Among his pallbearers is Elizabeth Gurley Flynn.

Charlotte Perkins Gilman and Jane Addams found the Woman's Peace Party.

1917   Pacifists Kate Richards O'Hare Cuningham and Emma Goldman are convicted of obstructing the selective service law and are incarcerated in the federal prison in Jefferson City, Missouri.

1918   In June, Secretary of Labor William B. Wilson, a former coal miner, establishes the Women in Industry division of the U.S. Department of Labor. It is administered by Mary Van Kleeck and her assistant, Mary Anderson.

1919   On August 26, United Mine Workers organizer Fannie Sellins, the widowed mother of four, is shot to death by coal company guards while leading strikers in Brackenridge, Pennsylvania.

Emma Goldman is deported to Russia on December 1.

The Women's International League for Peace and Freedom is founded.

Mother Mary Harris Jones participates in the steel strike in Pittsburgh.

1920   The women's suffrage amendment is ratified.

The Women in Industry division of the U.S. Department of Labor becomes the federal Women's Bureau.

Elizabeth Gurley Flynn helps to establish the American Civil Liberties Union.

1921   The Summer School for Women Workers in Industry is established at Bryn Mawr College by President M. Carey Thomas; Bryn Mawr Dean Hilda Smith is appointed director. Among the school's future instructors is Esther Peterson, assistant secretary of labor under President John F. Kennedy.

In North and South Carolina, 9,000 textile workers strike.

1922   Maud O'Farrell Swartz succeeds Margaret Dreier Robins as president of the National Women's Trade Union League.

1925   A resident school for workers is established at the University of Virginia.

1927   Sweetbriar College establishes its resident school for workers.

Barnard College initiates a nonresident seven-week course for New York City workers.

1929   On September 14 Ella May Wiggins, widowed mother of five and a labor balladeer, is slain by vigilantes while en route to a meeting of strikers in Gastonia, North Carolina.

1930   Ann Burlak, a secretary of the National Textile Workers' Union, is arrested in Atlanta for calling a meeting of black and white workers.

1931   Clara Holden, National Textile Workers' Union organizer, is abducted and beaten by vigilantes in Greenville, South Carolina on September 1.

Jane Addams receives the Nobel Prize for Peace.

1933   President Franklin Delano Roosevelt is inaugurated in March; as his secretary of labor, he appoints Frances Perkins.

Martha Roberts, wife of National Miners' Union organizer Robert F. Roberts, is arrested in Gallup, New Mexico, after leading wives of striking coal miners in a "Dawn Patrol."

Oberlin College establishes a School for Office Workers.

Section 7A of the National Industrial Recovery Act endorses the worker's right to unionization and collective bargaining.

The impromptu visits of First Lady Eleanor Roosevelt to coal mines inspire a cartoon by New Yorker artist Robert Day.

1935   The Social Security Act becomes law, guaranteeing help to eligible workers in times of unemployment, pensions for the elderly, and aid to dependents.

The Wagner Labor Relations Act guarantees to workers the right to unionization and collective bargaining.

1936   During an organizing campaign among Akron, Ohio, rubber workers, John L. Lewis popularizes the sit-down strike, which renders unfeasible the use of strikebreakers.

In Flint, Michigan, United Auto Workers dieworkers make effective use of the sit-down in the General Motors plant, Fisher Body Shop. Flint strikers are strongly supported by the militant Women's Emergency Brigade.

1937   Ten workers are slain and eighty wounded during a demonstration at the Republic Steel plant in Chicago. Among those injured in the Memorial Day Massacre is Lupe Marshall, a social worker and mother of three.

1938   The Fair Labor Standards Act establishes a minimum wage, minimum age, and maximum work week for employees engaged in interstate commerce.

1941   The Fair Employment Practice Committee is established by presidential mandate, its mission to investigate "discrimination in the employment of workers in defense industries or government because of race, creed, color or national origin."

1944   Women number 3,500,000 of 18,600,000 unionized workers. Their entry into the ranks of labor, like that of blacks, is spurred by the war effort.

1955   The American Federation of Labor, headed by George Meany, merges with the Congress of Industrial Organizations, led by Walter Reuther.

1959   The Landrum-Griffin bill strengthens the provisions of the Taft-Hartley Act.

1961   The minimum wage specified under the Fair Labor Standards Act is increased to $1.25 an hour; minimum wage coverage is extended to 3,600,000 workers.

1963   The Equal Pay Act of 1963, 77 Stat. 56, 29 U.S.C.S. 206, the first statutory prohibition against sex discrimination, compels employers engaged in interstate commerce to provide equal pay "for equal work on jobs the performance of which requires equal skill, efforts, responsibility, and which are performed under similar working conditions."

1964   The Civil Rights Act, Title 7, 78 Stat. 253, 42 U.S.C.S. 2000e, is enacted, establishing an Equal Employment Opportunity Commission. The sex amendment to the bill, barring discrimination according to gender, is introduced ironically by Representative Howard Smith of Virginia, but strongly supported by Representative Martha Griffiths of Michigan.

1966   The minimum wage is raised to $1.40 an hour.

1968   The minimum wage is raised to $1.60 an hour.

The Equal Employment Opportunity Commission rules that protective "laws and regulations do not take into account the capacities, preferences, and abilities of individual females and that such laws tend to discriminate rather than to protect."

1969   Mary Moultrie organizes the successful strike of 550 black women hospital workers for union representation in Charleston, South Carolina. The strike is staunchly supported by Coretta King, wife of slain civil rights advocate the Reverend Dr. Martin Luther King, Jr.

Photojournalist Jeanne M. Rasmussen records the campaign of martyred United Mine Workers' candidate Joseph "Jock" Yablonski.

1970 Dolores Huerta is elected vice president of the United Farm Workers.

Labor lawyer Bella Savitzky Abzug is elected to the 92nd Congress.

1971 Jean Maddox, labor leader of Native American ancestry, and Joyce Maupin form the Union Women's Alliance to Gain Equality (Union W.A.G.E.).

Barbara Mikulski emerges as a spokeswoman for ethnic America during her successful campaign for the Baltimore, Maryland, city council.

1973 Women Office Workers is founded.

Barbara Wertheimer becomes director of Trade Union Women's Studies for Cornell University's New York State School of Industrial and Labor Relations.

In Roanoke Rapids, North Carolina, J. P. Stevens Company employee Crystal Lee Jordan participates in the organizing campaign of the Textile Workers' Union of America and is fired.

1974 On January 19, the New York Trade Union Women's Conference is held.

The founding convention of the Coalition of Labor Union Women (CLUW) opens in Chicago on March 22. Officers elected include president Olga Madar; vice-president Addie Wyatt; secretary Linda Tarr-Whelan; and treasurer Gloria Johnson. Addressing an enthusiastic audience, Myra Wolfgang of the Hotel and Restaurant Employees' Union declares, "We didn't come here to swap recipes!"

Reprinted from *Workers and Allies*. Smithsonian Institution Press, 1975.

LANGUAGE

WHEN WOMEN BEGAN TO EXAMINE THEIR LIVES AND ENVIRONMENTS FOR MALE bias, they didn't stop with socialization, educational opportunities or employment discrimination. Sexism exists in every area of our society—right down to the English language itself. Some of the sexism is inherent in the language, some is a matter of custom and usage. Both are damaging to women and slow to change.

Sexist language takes several basic forms: 1) the male generic; 2) terms of address; 3) sexist idioms and patterns. The male generic is truly one of the most insidious examples of sexism. This usage does not actively insult women—it just ignores them. Mankind, the brotherhood of man, chairman, man-made and manpower; all these, we are to understand, actually include women. Only recently has research shown the subtle—and not so subtle—ways in which women grow up not genuinely believing that mankind includes them. And why, logically, should they? Certainly young girls have no reason to believe that they could grow up to be police*men*, sales*men* or mail*men*. Women understand, whether consciously or not, that if they are supposedly included, but are *not named*, that they are second class at best.

One of the key usages of the male generic is embedded in the language itself:

the pronoun he. There simply is no neuter personal pronoun for the third person singular, one of the most-used forms. Many remedies for this key problem have been recommended and/or tried in recent years. Students at the University of Tennessee tried using tey, ter, and tem in their newspaper in 1973. "The applicant was late for the interview because tey could not start ter car. This nearly cost tem the job." Apparently they did not find the results satisfactory, for they abandoned the experiment after three months. Another suggestion is to use "he or she," "him or her." While this solves the problem, it can become awkward if used too frequently. Some writers and editors have alternated the use of he and she randomly through the text. This can be confusing for the reader, who is not accustomed to the use of she when it hasn't been specified that the person referred to is female. Another remedy, usually used incorrectly, is the use of the plural they. "Everyone entered and took their seats" avoids the use of his, but is grammatically incorrect. One of the best ways to avoid he is to name the person (the doctor, the student, the sailor) and recast the sentence if necessary. "He needs to see his family and friends while he is in the hospital" becomes "A patient needs to see family and friends while hospitalized." Until a new word is added to the English language, there will be no single, simple alternative to the generic he. But the sensitive writer can avoid sexist usage through a combination of the above remedies.

Another major area of sexism in language involves terms of address. Men are always Mr., but women are Mrs. or Miss. There is no reason to automatically denote a woman's marital status, but not a man's; the neutral Ms. has now come into fairly common usage.

Term-of-address problems tend to crop up most commonly in business communications. If the "Dear Sir" letter must go (and it must), what should replace it? Obviously, a name would be preferable to any term, but when that's not possible, name the recipient according to the capacity in which you are writing to her or him: Dear Client, Dear Publisher, Dear Member. It may sound odd, but it won't insult your female associates.

Finally, there is the totally unnecessary sexist idiom of common usage. Lady lawyer, man and wife, the fair sex, girl Friday, and all the rest are nothing more than bad habits. They, along with the male generics, can easily be changed with just a bit of thought and time (see box below).

One of the primary weapons that has been used against feminist efforts to humanize language is ridicule. The "ladies, gentlemen and persons" jokes abound. But sexist language is not a laughing matter. Anthropologists know that language is not a neutral force in culture. It doesn't simply reflect values, it reinforces and perpetuates them. Just because something sounds odd to a conditioned ear is no reason to perpetuate harmful usage. Besides, male-biased language can be truly ridiculous. Here is an example from a group insurance brochure: "If the employee becomes pregnant while covered under this policy, he will be entitled to . . ." This stunning remark comes from a New York State Assemblyman: "Everyone should be able to decide for himself whether or not to have an abortion." A personal favorite is a letter, recently received, addressed to "Mr. Women's Action Alliance." Ridiculousness is in the eye of the beholder.

Resources:

How to Avoid Sexism: A Guide for Writers, Editors and Publishers, by Merriellyn
  Kent and Virginia Underwood. Chicago: Lawrence Ragan Communications,
  1978. Order from: Lawrence Ragan Communications, 407 South Dearborn
  Street, Chicago IL 60605.
  A useful discussion of the sexism in the English language, with many
suggestions for alternatives. Many of the examples in the text are taken from this
volume.

She Said/He Said: An Annotated Bibiliography of Sex Differences in Language,
  Speech, and Nonverbal Communication, compiled by Nancy Henley and Barrie
  Thorne. Pittsburgh: KNOW, 1975. Order from: KNOW, P.O. Box 86031,
  Pittsburgh, PA 15221.
  In addition to research findings on the ways in which men and women use
language and nonverbal clues, a section on male bias in English is included. A
very useful tool.

Without Bias: A Guidebook for Nondiscriminatory Communication. San Francisco: International Association of Business Communicators, 1977. Order from:
  International Association of Business Communicators, 870 Market Street, San
  Francisco, CA 94102.
  A brief and useful guide to avoiding race and sex bias, as well as prejudice
against the handicapped, in writing. It also includes a section on balanced visual
presentations. A summary of sex discrimination laws and a model affirmative
action plan complete the guide.

Words and Women, by Casey Miller and Kate Swift. Garden City: Anchor Press,
  1976.
  An excellent, readable analysis of the way sexist language works, and how it
affects us.

HOW TO AVOID SEXISM

Avoid	Use
authoress	author
the best man for the job	the best qualified candidate for the job, the best person for the job, or the best man or woman for the job
the better half	wife
brotherhood (and fellowship and fraternity)	friendship, unity, kinship, companionship, community, oneness, or peace
businessman	business executive, business leader, entrepreneur, manager, operator of a small business, merchant, or industrialist

camera girl	photographer
cameraman	camera operator
career girl	professional, professional woman, or name the woman's profession (i.e., lawyer)
chairman	leader or moderator (of a meeting), chair, coordinator, head (of a committee), presiding officer (of a company), or chairperson
cleaning woman or cleaning lady	house or office cleaner
co-ed	student
the common man	the average person or ordinary people
Congressman	Members of Congress or Congressional Representative
craftsman	skilled worker or name the occupation (i.e., electrician)
draftsman	drafter
the fair sex	women
fireman	firefighter
foreman	supervisor
gal, girl	woman
gal Friday	assistant
girl—as in "I'll have my *girl* do it."	secretary
housewife	homemaker, customer, shopper, or consumer
insurance man	insurance agent
ladies—when men are called *men,* not *gentlemen*	women
lady—as a modifier, as in *lady lawyer*	lawyer (or whatever the woman's occupation)
libber	feminist
the little woman	wife
longshoreman	longshore worker
mailboy	mail clerk, mail messenger
mailman	mail carrier, letter carrier, or postal worker
man—used generically	person or human being

man—used as an agent ending, as in *pipeman*	-er as an agent ending; or describe just which duties or actions are being performed (i.e., pipe adjuster, pipe agent, pipe attendant, pipe broker, pipe cleaner, pipe controller, pipe inspector, pipe installer, pipe maker, pipe patcher, pipe setter, pipe tender, pipe tester, and, most general of all, pipe worker
manned	staffed
man and wife	husband and wife, man and woman or the couple
manhood	adulthood or maturity
mankind	humanity, human beings, or people
man-made	synthetic, machine-made, or manufactured
manpower	labor force, work force, workers, human energy, or human power
a man-sized job	a big or enormous job
middleman	go-between, liaison, broker, or intermediary
milkman	milk route driver
the old lady	wife
old wives' tales	superstition or superstitious beliefs
poetess	poet
policeman	police officer
right-hand man	assistant or key person
salesman	sales clerk, sales representative, sales agent, sales person (sales people), or sales force
spokesman	speaker or spokesperson
statesman	leader, diplomat, public figure, or public servant
stewardess	cabin attendant or flight attendant
sweet young thing	young woman or girl
usherette	usher
watchman	guard
the weaker sex	women (or men, depending on your perspective)

"the wife"	wife or my wife
woman's work	This is a meaningless concept, delete altogether.
workmen's compensation	worker's compensation
workman	worker
workmanlike	competent or professional

Reprinted from *How to Avoid Sexism* (Lawrence Ragan Communications, 1978).

LEGAL STATUS

WOMEN STILL DO NOT HAVE FULL LEGAL EQUALITY. THE SPECIFIC WAYS IN which women suffer discrimination under the law are discussed in appropriate sections throughout this book. The law, of course, is constantly changing. The following is a legislative report on some of the actions of the 95th Congress that pertained to women's rights.

ERA Extension. The deadline for ratification of the Equal Rights Amendment was extended until June 30, 1982. An amendment that would have permitted states to rescind ratification was voted down by both houses.

Privacy Protection for Rape Victims. Congress passed by voice vote a bill prohibiting, in cases of rape or attempted rape, the introduction of the victim's reputation or opinionated evidence of the victim's past sexual behavior in a federal court. The bill was sponsored by Congresswoman Elizabeth Holtzman.

Domestic Violence. A bill to provide supplements to states and programs to prevent and treat domestic violence was passed by the Senate August 1. Its companion bill in the House never reached the floor for vote. The act would have provided $40 million over three years, and would have established a training program and a National Clearinghouse on Domestic Violence. Senator Alan Cranston, sponsor of S. 2759, will introduce a modified version early in 1979.

CETA. Congress voted to extend the Comprehensive Employment and Training Act, and produced a mixed blessing for women. Among the positive provisions: the definition of specially disadvantaged groups is expanded to include women, and the act calls for the elimination of artificial barriers to employment and for research on alternative working arrangements and on classifications that undervalue certain skills. More problematic are provisions targeting low-income persons and putting limits on the amount of time that can be spent in the program, both in training and on the job.

The League of Women Voters, NOW and the Center for Law and Social Policy are reviewing the impact of this legislation on women as part of an informal network of Washington based national women's organizations that meet on issues relating to women and poverty. The Women's Bureau, U.S. Department of Labor, is also preparing an analysis.

Displaced Homemakers. Legislation was passed, as part of the CETA package, that gives the U.S. Department of Labor $5 million for fiscal year 1979 to set up multipurpose centers and programs for middle-aged women displaced from their traditional homemaker roles by widowhood or divorce. Services offered to such women would include job counseling, training and placement, as well as creation of new jobs within the programs for displaced homemakers.

Full Employment. Congress passed the Humphrey-Hawkins bill, aimed at reducing joblessness. It establishes goals of a four percent unemployment rate for youth aged 16 to 20, a three percent unemployment rate for adults over 20, and a three percent inflation rate to be achieved within five years.

The legislation as it finally passed includes no provisions mandating or authorizing job programs, but rather sets up a process of planning and coordinating economic policy by which the President, Congress and the Federal Reserve Board may be accountable to the public for unemployment rates.

Women's, labor and other groups must continue pressing for programs to translate the goals of the bill into reality.

Part-Time Jobs and Flexitime. Congress passed the Federal Employees Part Time Career Employment Act, sponsored by Rep. Yvonne Burke, which calls on all government agencies to create career part-time positions at every level and sets up incentives for agencies to comply.

Congress also passed a bill authorizing a three-year experiment in flexible and compressed work schedules in the federal government. The experiment is voluntary on the part of the employees and is limited to agencies that choose to enter it. Agencies in which there are employee organizations such as unions must negotiate a written agreement to undertake the experiment.

Veterans Preference. An amendment to the Civil Service Reform Act that would have limited preferential treatment of veterans in hiring and promotion so that women, few of whom have veteran status, would have increased opportunities for federal employment, was defeated.

Pregnancy Disability. A bill to ban employment discrimination on the basis of pregnancy and to provide disability and medical benefits to pregnant workers was passed after House and Senate conferees agreed to modify anti-abortion language, ending a three-month stalemate. The compromise language allows employers to exempt elective abortions from medical coverage, except if the life of the mother is threatened or in the case of medical complications resulting from abortion. Employers, however, must provide disability and sick leave benefits to women receiving abortions and may permit health and other benefits for abortion if they wish.

Teenage Pregnancy. A Carter Administration bill to provide comprehensive care to pregnant teenagers and to prevent teenage pregnancy by authorizing funds to strengthen existing pregnancy-related community services was approved by Congress. Both houses rejected an amendment that would have required parental consultation before dispensing contraceptives to teenagers under 16, but they stopped short of approving abortion counseling. Instead, pregnant teens will be "informed of the availability" of counseling on "all options regarding their pregnancy."

Family Planning Services. Resisting efforts to weaken this program for family planning and birth control, Congress voted to extend Title X, the Family Planning and Population Research Act, which authorizes funding for three more years, beginning with $200 million in fiscal year 1979. It rejected a package of amendments that would have required parental consultation for contraceptive services to minors and would have redirected funds away from family planning services to "alternatives to abortion" projects.

Medicaid Funding for Abortions. Both houses voted to support compromise language enacted last year that allows federal funding for abortions only in limited circumstances. These include when the woman's life would be endangered if the pregnancy were carried to term, in cases of rape or incest, and where severe and long-lasting health damage would result. The key provision that many women's groups supported, to permit abortion where "medically necessary," was rejected.

The Hyde Amendment was attached to the Labor-HEW appropriations bill.

Defense Department and Abortion. Congress voted to limit coverage of abortion for military employees and their dependents by applying the Labor-HEW guidelines governing federal spending for Medicaid abortions. Military abortions, therefore, will only be reimbursed in cases of threat to the woman's life, rape or incest, or danger of severe and long-lasting damage.

The amendment was attached to the largest military defense budget ever approved.

Peace Corps and Abortion. Both the House and Senate approved an amendment to the 1979 Foreign Assistance Appropriations bill prohibiting the use of Peace Corps funds to pay for abortions for Peace Corps volunteers, with no exceptions. Such funds were used to provide abortions and related travel expenses for approximately forty volunteers in 1977.

Judgeships for Women. An Omnibus Judges bill that could lead to more women on the federal bench was passed. The legislation creates 152 new federal judgeships, the largest increase in history.

To encourage selection of judges on the basis of merit rather than politics, President Carter has established regional commissions to screen and recommend candidates for the courts of appeal. He has also issued guidelines for Senators, who select the district court judges, that encourage but do not require the Senators to base their selections on merit.

Women's groups will have to continue pressing for selection of capable women as judges and to monitor the steps taken by officials to include women and minorities on the federal bench.

Reprinted from the December 1978 issue of *Women's Agenda.*

Organizations:

American Civil Liberties Union
Women's Rights Project
22 East 40th Street
New York, NY 10016

Center for Constitutional Rights
Women's Rights Program
853 Broadway
New York, NY 10003

Congressional Clearinghouse on Women's
Rights
Contact the Clearinghouse through your
Congressional Representative.

NOW Legal Defense and Education Fund
36 West 44th Street

New York, NY 10036

Organization of Women for Legal
Awareness
94 Claremont Avenue
Maplewood, NJ 07040

Women's Equity Action League
805 15th Street N.W.
Washington, DC 20005

Women's Law Fund
620 Keith Building
1621 Euclid Avenue
Cleveland, OH 44115

Women's Law Project
112 South 16th Street
Philadelphia, PA 19102

Resources:

The Congressional Clearinghouse on Women's Rights. To order: Write your
Congressional Representative.

This excellent weekly is the best source of legislative updates on women's issues.
Operated as a service to Congress, it is available to individuals only through one's
Representative.

Women's Rights Law Reporter. Order from: WRLR, 15 Washington Street,
Newark, NJ 07102.

This quarterly is a law review for women. It carries in-depth articles on new or
proposed legislation and important cases as well as book reviews and announce-
ments.

House Computer Service

(202) 255-1772

For information on the status of any bill before Congress, call the House
Computer Service. You must know the number of the bill, or its subject or
author.

LESBIAN MOTHERS

BY CONTENDING THAT THE SEXUAL PREFERENCE OF A MOTHER WHO PROVIDES
a loving and secure environment for her children is unimportant to their welfare,
the lesbian mother represents a dramatic challenge to traditional rationales for the
nuclear family.

To date, most husbands and judges believe that the lesbian mother is unfit to
raise her children. Although numbers are hard to come by—many cases are settled

out of court and in states where there are no printed decisions news travels by
word of mouth—the majority of decisions are unfavorable to the lesbian mother.
Juries' decisions are not binding at these civil court hearings, and since each judge
has complete discretion in deciding what is in the best interests of the child,
precedent means little. Some judges have awarded children to lesbian mothers
and/or lesbian couples; others will give custody only if the mother will stop having
homosexual relationships.

Since no custody decision is ever final, one parent may return to family court if
the other parent is discovered to be gay. Although the burden of proof should be
on the court to demonstrate that having a homosexual parent is harmful to the
child, *de facto* the homosexual parent must prove that he or she will not be a
detrimental influence.

Judges consider three basic questions: will the child grow up to be a homosexual
if raised by a gay parent; will the child be unduly embarrassed or distressed by the
parent's homosexuality; will the parent or another gay adult molest the child. Gay
legal advocates have researched and answered each concern. Experts in children's
sexual orientation believe that sexual predisposition is determined between the
ages of four and a half and six, and that the influence of a gay parent will not have
an adverse effect on the child. Some children may be upset by a homosexual
parent, but this can be worked through within a loving and secure environment.
Finally, surveys—most recently reported on in Bell and Weinberg's
Homosexualities—show that a gay man is less likely than a straight man to molest a
child; women (either gay or straight) are least likely of all.

In the past lesbians have remained in unhappy marriages or led celibate lives in order to keep their children. As alternative life-styles gain acceptance, lesbians have felt freer to come out and fight, if need be, to keep their families together. Once a lesbian has custody of her children her problems do not end. Each woman must decide how and when to tell her children about her sexual identity, whether or not to introduce a lover into the household, and how to facilitate the child's adjustment to and acceptance of homosexuality. Organizations of lesbian mothers have helped women by ending their isolation and providing moral, legal, and financial support.

See also: Divorce
Lesbians

Organizations:

Lesbian Mothers National Defense Fund
2446 Lorentz Place N.
Seattle, WA 98109

National Gay Task Force
80 Fifth Avenue
New York, NY 10011

Resources:

ACLU Handbook: The Rights of Gay People, ed. by E. Carrington Boggan et al. New York: Avon Books, 1975.
Contains information on custody.

By Her Own Admission: A Lesbian Mother's Fight to Keep Her Son, by Gifford Guy Gibson in collaboration with Mary Jo Risher. New York: Doubleday, 1977.
Sensitive portrayal of a Texas lesbian's court fight and ultimate loss of her young son. Made into movie for TV, fall 1978.

Homosexualities, by Alan Bell and Martin Weinberg. New York: Simon and Schuster, 1978.
While this book contains some useful information on lesbians, it is almost entirely about gay men.

In the Best Interests of the Children, by Mary Blackman, Berkeley, 1977. Order from Iris Film Collective, P.O. Box 5353, Berkeley, CA 94705.
Annotated list of resources (individuals, groups, expert witnesses, legal counsel) and information on lesbians, lesbian mothers, and custody cases.

In the Best Interests of the Children, 16 mm. color film. Iris Film Collective, P.O. Box 5353, Berkeley, CA 94705.
Film about lesbian mothers and their custody struggles.

Lesbian Mothers Custody Cases: Who to Call for What, by Mary Hovell. Seattle, n.d. Order from: Mary Hovell, 2101 Smith Tower, Seattle, WA 98104.
Annotated bibliography and resource list of court cases.

LESBIANS

IN THEIR EXCELLENT PAMPHLET, *TWENTY QUESTIONS ABOUT HOMOSEXUALITY,* the National Gay Task Force explains:

"Homosexuality" is a term used to describe feelings or behavior and it is also used to describe individuals who have feelings of love, emotional attachment or sexual attraction toward people of their own gender. There is no neat way of compartmentalizing people as heterosexual or homosexual. Human sexual behavior and orientation, it has become evident from the studies of Dr. Alfred Kinsey and other researchers, is a continuum between exclusive heterosexuality and exclusive homosexuality in which every intermediate combination may be found. People who have romantic and sexual feelings for members of the opposite sex and for members of the same sex are often termed "bisexual" although for most people one or the other orientation predominates. Furthermore, people are not limited to a set of behavior patterns or feelings which restrict them or assign them to a particular category for life.

Lesbian, the particular name for female homosexuals, is derived from Lesbos—the Aegean isle off what is now the coast of Turkey—where the Greek poet Sappho (sixth century B.C.) lived. It is believed that Sappho headed a cult of female homosexuals, but all that remains are fragments of her love poems written to and about women.

Perhaps hoping that they would disappear, our society has long overlooked homosexuals. This is doubly true for lesbians. For example, the recent and long-awaited Kinsey Research Institute report—*Homosexualities* by Alan Bell and Martin Weinberg—almost ignores the lesbian experience. The authors apologize, stating that homosexual men are more visible and numerous than females, and that their sponsors, the National Institute for Mental Health, felt the "problems and adaptations" of men to be of "greater interest." But that does not change the situation—the most comprehensive book to date on homosexuality hardly mentions women's experiences.

Fortunately, *The Hite Report* offers new and important information on lesbianism. Eight percent of Hite's respondents were lesbians, 9 percent were bisexual. "What is different about sexual relations between women," Hite writes, "is precisely that there is no one institutionalized way of having them, so that they can be as inventive and individual as the people involved. Perhaps the two most striking specific differences from most heterosexual relationships . . . were that there were generally more feelings and tenderness, affection and sensitivity, and more orgasms." Hite also suggests that lesbianism can have political origins—a reaction against men and against women's subservient relationships to them.

Lesbians in America have had to fight for recognition and equal standing in both the gay rights movement and the feminist movement. Before these movements emerged, lesbians founded the Daughters of Bilitis, a group begun in San Francisco in 1955. Frustrated by their isolation and by the hypocritical attitudes of a prurient society, the members banded together to form a support community which would provide understanding for the lesbian way of life. Fourteen years later, in June of 1969, the gay rights movement was born. Out of the Stonewall Riots—the resistance to New York City police raids on gay bars in Greenwich Village—came a new consciousness and a sense of political solidarity. At first gay males ostracized their female counterparts. It took several years of hard work to successfully integrate women into the movement. Today the National Gay Task Force defines itself as feminist, has long-term commitments to fighting sexism and

Staff of the Lesbian Herstory Archives, a national repository for materials on lesbians (see Research and Information entry for address). © *Bettye Lane*

racism, has a board of directors which is half female, and acts as an information center for lesbian-mother custody cases.

Many straight women have felt something of a threat and an implicit condemnation when confronted with lesbianism. When lesbians identified themselves within the women's movement, Betty Friedan referred to them as "the lavender menace" and refused to lend her very influential support. A painful split developed and for several years many lesbians became separatists. They had little or nothing to do with men and straight women. During that period, much political theorizing, cultural developments, and personal growth occurred. Then some lesbian separatists began to widen their sphere of involvement. They discovered straight feminists who welcomed them and who had learned from lesbian political and cultural accomplishments. Today, there is a spirit of rapprochement between lesbian females and the women's movement. At the 1977 National Women's Conference in Houston, a platform supporting freedom of sexual preference was passed by a comfortable majority. Betty Friedan was one of the first to speak in favor of the resolution.

Today, some lesbians are deeply involved in the women's movement and/or the gay rights movement. Many believe that such coalitions will be able to fight the battles to come in American courts and legislatures. Since 1972, a number of United States cities have extended varying degrees of protection to their gay citizens (see chart below). But these laws are not uniform and are sometimes subject to repeal. And, of course, twenty-seven states still have restrictions on adult consensual acts in private.

In June 1977, Anita Bryant helped launch an antigay campaign—Save Our Children—the goal of which was to revoke Dade County, Florida's antidiscrimination laws. She succeeded. And in the wake of her victory, St. Paul, Minnesota; Wichita, Kansas; and Eugene, Oregon, repealed their antidiscrimination laws too. Not surprisingly, during the summer of 1977 a Harris Poll revealed that a majority of Americans thought gays suffer the greatest amount of discrimination of any group in the country. The National Gay Task Force launched a campaign—We Are Your Children—to counter antigay propaganda.

Fortunately the tide began to turn in 1978. Initiative 13 in Seattle would have repealed protection of gays in housing and employment *and* rescinded enforcement powers from the Office of Women's Rights. California's Proposition 6 would have required the dismissal of any teacher or school employee convicted on charges of "advocating, soliciting, imposing, encouraging, or promoting private or public homosexual acts . . . directed at or likely to come to the attention of school children and/or other employees." Both of them were voted down. At the same time the most complete gay rights bill to date was passed unanimously by the Berkeley, California, City Council.

There are still hurdles in the road ahead, however. New York City was, in 1971, the first city to introduce a Gay Rights Bill. In 1978, the bill was defeated by the City Council for the eighth time. The Supreme Court has refused to hear any gay rights cases: in November, 1972, a Washington teacher was fired for publicly admitting his homosexuality and in October, 1977, the Supreme Court refused to review the case *(Gaylord* v. *Tacoma)*. The year before, the Court had refused to review *Doe* v. *Commonwealth's Attorney,* a challenge to the Virginia state sodomy laws.

Gay women are involved in these issues as well as in court struggles for custody of their children. As more and more women come out, one realizes the truth of the lesbian motto: "We are everywhere." The lesbian population is as diverse as its straight counterpart. But gay women are united by their desire for full civil rights—as lesbians *and* as women—and by their desire for the freedom to love the person of their choice.

See also: Lesbian mothers
          Right-wing Attacks

Organizations:

Daughters of Bilitis
1151 Massachusetts Avenue
Cambridge, MA 02138

Gay Rights National Lobby
Women's Caucus
110 Maryland Avenue N.E.
Washington, DC 20002

National Gay Task Force
80 Fifth Avenue
New York, NY 10011

National Lesbian Feminist Organization
P.O. Box 14643
Houston, TX 77021

Our People's Task
114 Liberty Street
New York, NY 10006

Resources:

A Gay Bibliography. Philadelphia: Task Force on Gay Liberation, American Library Association, 1975. Order from: Task Force, American Library Association, P.O. Box 2383, Philadelphia, PA 19103.

Homosexualities, by Alan Bell and Martin Weinberg. New York: Simon and Schuster, 1978.

Long-awaited Kinsey Institute study of homosexuals in the Bay Area. Evolves a new typology for homosexuality and shows the diversity of gay life-styles. Concludes that the majority of homosexuals interviewed are as content with their life choice as are heterosexuals who were interviewed. Includes little information on lesbians.

Lesbian Health Issues: An Annotated Bibliography. Santa Cruz: Santa Cruz Women's Health Center, 1975. Order from: Santa Cruz Women's Health Center, 250 Locust Street, Santa Cruz, CA 95060.

Includes information on health-care issues specific to lesbians plus a bibliography and a list of resource people working in this area.

The Lesbian in Literature, compiled by Gene Damon and Lee Stuart. Reno: The Ladder, 1975. Order from: Naiad Press, 20 Rue Jacob Acres, Bates City, MO 64011.

Lists all known books in the English language which have lesbian characters or are concerned with lesbianism. Includes novels, short stories, poems, drama, fictionalized biography.

Lesbian/Woman, by Del Martin and Phyllis Lyon. New York: Bantam Books, 1972.

Groundbreaking classic on the lesbian life-style written by the founders of the Daughters of Bilitis—two courageous and uncompromising activists.

Our Right to Love, ed. by Ginny Vida. New Jersey: Prentice-Hall, 1978.

An excellent up-to-date anthology of issues, resources, and women within the lesbian movement. If you read only one book, this should be it.

Women Loving Women: A Select and Annotated Bibliography of Women Loving Women in Literature, ed. by Marie J. Kuda. Chicago: Womanpress, 1975. Order from: Womanpress, P.O. Box 59330, Chicago, IL 60645.

GAY RIGHTS PROTECTION IN THE U.S. AND CANADA

Date Enacted	Location	Conditions
1972	Atlanta, GA	Municipal employment (executive order)
2/72 & 1/78	New York City, NY	Municipal employment (executive order)
5/72	Washington, DC	Employment, by Board of Education
11/73	Washington, DC	Employment, housing, credit, public accommodations, education
7/72	Ann Arbor, MI	Housing, employment, public accommodations

8/72 & 7/78	San Francisco, CA	All encompassing
5/73	East Lansing, MI	Employment, public accommodations
11/73	Seattle, WA	Municipal and private employment
11/73	Toronto, ONT	Municipal employment
11/73 & 10/78	Berkeley, CA	Municipal employment, employment with private employer under city contract; all encompassing
11/73	Detroit, MI	Municipal employment
1/74	Columbus, OH	Employment, housing, public accommodations
3/74	Minneapolis, MN	All encompassing
5/74	Alfred, NY	All encompassing
8/74	Palo Alto, CA	Inclusion in jurisdiction of human rights commission
11/75	Palo Alto, CA	Employment, Board of Education
9/74	Ithaca, NY	Municipal employment
12/74	Sunnyvale, CA	Municipal employment
12/74	Portland, OR	Municipal employment
2/75	Cupertino, CA	Municipal employment
3/75	Mountain View, CA	Municipal employment
3/75	Madison, WI	Employment, housing, credit, public accommodations
7/75	Austin, TX	Municipal employment, labor union membership, employment agency referrals
8/75	Santa Barbara, CA	Municipal employment
9/75	Chapel Hill, NC	Municipal employment
11/75	Urbana, IL	Employment, credit, public accommodations
4/76	Ottawa, ONT	Municipal employment
4/76	Boston, MA	Municipal employment (executive order)
4/76	Pullman, WA	Municipal employment

5/76	Amherst, MA	All encompassing
5/76	Los Angeles, CA	Municipal employment
1/77	Tucson, AZ	Employment, housing, public accommodations
3/77	Windsor, ONT	Municipal employment
5/77	Iowa City, IA	Employment, credit, public accommodations
7/77	Champaign, IL	Employment, housing, public accommodations
12/77	Aspen, CO	All encompassing
7/75	Santa Cruz County, CA	Affirmative Action Policy
11/75	Howard County, MD	All encompassing
6/78	Ingham County, MI	All encompassing
4/76	Pennsylvania	State employment (executive order)
12/77	Quebec, Canada	Employment, public accommodations, housing

STATES WITH NO RESTRICTIONS ON ADULT CONSENSUAL SEX ACTS

Alaska	Iowa	Ohio
California	Maine	Oregon
Colorado	Massachusetts	South Dakota
Connecticut	Nebraska	Vermont
Delaware	New Hampshire	Washington
Hawaii	New Jersey	West Virginia
Illinois	New Mexico	Wyoming
Indiana	North Dakota	

MARRIAGE AND FAMILY

THERE HAS BEEN MUCH CONCERN IN RECENT YEARS ABOUT THE CONDITION OF the American family. It has been attacked by some as a source of oppression, and praised by others as our most important institution. It is said to be in crisis, on the decline—some say that it is threatening to disappear altogether. Whether you're for it or against it, you can't ignore it.

Much of this cacophony and disagreement stems from different conceptions of what "family" means. If family means two parents, two (or more) children, father as breadwinner, mother at home, then the family *is* on the decline. Only 15.9% of American households conform to the nuclear family ideal: father as sole provider, mother at home with one or more children. Although most Americans do marry and have children, today's mother is a working mother. In 1976, 54 percent of mothers of school-age children worked outside the home. So, in fact, the nuclear family model with "proper" division of labor by sex is fading from the American scene. But does that mean the end of the family? What about the 18.5 percent of American families in which both parents work? What about those children living with their single mothers—6.2 percent of American households—are they not growing up in a "family" setting? What about the millions of unmarried men and women and gay couples who live together—with or without children—could they not be considered a family unit?

Those who fear and deplore the decline of the nuclear family often speak as if an age-old, basic human unit were passing from existence. In fact, the modern nuclear family is simply that—modern. Far from the "natural," prehistoric form it is often made out to be, the two-parents-with-two-children family is a product of nineteenth-century industrialization. Previous to that, families were much larger units, including several generations and serving a different function. In preindustrial America, families were producing units. Each member of the family was important, contributing to the production of necessary goods and therefore to the support of the family. With improved technology, production of goods was taken out of the home and the family became a consuming unit. There was no longer a need for extra hands to help with the work; rather, they became extra mouths to feed on a now limited income, and the American family contracted in size.

The shift in makeup and function of the family had a profound effect on the status of women. Where they had once been respected producers of necessary family goods—and often surplus goods to sell—they became consumers and maintainers. Having a wife at home who did not work—in some cases not even the housework—became a badge of status for men, a demonstration of their wealth. In a society which ascribes status by cash value, the role and position of women in society and within the family was seriously devalued.

The legal status of married women has also changed over the course of American history. Our legal system is based on English common law as set forth in 1765 by William Blackstone. It stipulated that upon marriage, the man and woman became one—and the one was the husband. Blackstone stated: "The very legal being or legal existence of the woman is suspended during the marriage." This meant that married women had no right to sue, own property or make contracts in their own name.

The legal situation of married women was improved in the mid-nineteenth century through the passage of reform legislation. Married Women's Property Acts were passed in all of the fifty states, but many legal limitations persist today. Some states continue to limit a wife's freedom to enter into contracts; in other states she must get court approval before she can open her own business. In still other jurisdictions a wife cannot sell her own property or use it as collateral without the consent of her husband.

A married woman has no guaranteed right to choose her own residence. Some states allow separate domiciles under certain circumstances, but nearly half automatically assume the domicile of the husband to be that of the wife. Legal residence is important in voting, running for public office, and receiving lower tuition rates at state schools, among other things.

A wife is legally required to be sexually available to her husband and except in Oregon may not press charges for rape. Nor have women received legal protection against the physical abuse of their husbands, though this is beginning to change.

While a husband is legally bound to support his wife, the courts have been unwilling to define what constitutes an acceptable level of support. A few dramatic cases of wives living at the level of bare subsistence despite their husband's wealth have come to light over the years. The courts have declined to interfere on the grounds that it is not their place to tell a husband how to treat his wife.

Certainly it is safe to say that most women are unaware of the legal compromises imposed upon them when they marry. Some women's groups have suggested that couples be given full information on the legal consequences of marriage at the time they apply for a license. This would be a useful interim measure until married women are treated equally under the law.

See also: Battered Women
Divorce
Homemakers
Lesbian Mothers

Organizations:

National Alliance for Optional Parenthood
3 North Liberty Street
Baltimore, MD 21201

Resources:

The Changing Family: Making Way for Tomorrow, ed. by Jerald Savells and Lawrence Cross. New York: Holt, Rinehart, and Winston, 1978.

This anthology includes nearly fifty articles on past, current, and future changes in the American family, breaking down sex roles, remaining single, sex in marriage, childlessness, communal living.

Feminist Perspectives on Housework and Child Care, ed. by Amy Swerdlow. New York: Sarah Lawrence College, 1978. Order from: Women's Studies, Sarah Lawrence College, Bronxville, NY 10708.

The proceedings of a conference, this pamphlet includes three papers giving a personal view of housework and three papers giving an historical/theoretical view. The historical papers provided the basis of some of the text above.

For Better, For Worse: A Feminist Handbook on Marriage and Other Options, by Jennifer Baker Fleming and Carolyn Kott Washburne. New York: Charles Scribner's Sons, 1977.

After several years of counseling women going through separation and divorce, the authors wanted to provide some advice on avoiding marital problems in the first place. They discuss women's legal status in marriage, lesbian relationships, money problems, and wife abuse, among other things.

The Legal Status of the Homemaker. Washington: Homemakers Committee, National Commission on the Observance of International Women's Year, 1977.

Order from: Superintendent of Documents, Government Printing Office, Washington, DC 20402.

These excellent pamphlets give a comprehensive overview of the legal status of married women in each of the fifty states. They can provide specifics for the general conclusions cited above.

Marriage: Focus on Change, by Elizabeth Wright. Washington: Women's Equity Action League Fund, n.d. Order from: WEAL Fund, 805 15th Street N.W., Washington, DC 20005.

This short report summarizes the issues concerning women and marriage and makes international comparisons. It includes a bibliography.

Origin of the Family, Private Property, and the State, by Frederick Engels. New York: International Publishers, 1972.

The Marxist classic on the history of the family, based on the anthropological research of Lewis Morgan, which provided the theoretical basis for most contemporary feminist thinking on the family and women's status.

"Who is the *Real* Family?" *Ms.* 7(2): p. 43, August 1978.

Woman's Work: The Housewife, Past and Present, by Ann Oakley. New York: Pantheon, 1974.

Oakley looks at women's role in the home historically and cross-culturally, though most of the volume is on the contemporary British homemaker.

THE AMERICAN FAMILY

Father as sole wage earner, mother as full-time homemaker, at least one child	15.9%
Both father and mother as wage earners, at least one child	18.5%
Married couples with no children or no children living at home	30.5%
Single mothers with one or more children at home	6.2%
Single fathers with one or more children at home	0.6%
Unrelated persons living together	2.5%
Single-person households	20.6%
Female- or male-headed households that include relatives other than spouses or children	5.3%

Statistics are from the *U.S. Statistical Abstract, 1977* as printed in the August 1978 issue of *Ms.*

MINORITY WOMEN

ASIAN-AMERICAN, BLACK, HISPANIC, AND NATIVE AMERICAN WOMEN TO-gether make up at least 19 percent of the female population of the United States, representing diverse heritages, histories, traditions, cultures, and languages. They share a common problem—triple jeopardy—race, sex, and the resulting economic discrimination.

The first stumbling block to addressing the problems and concerns of minority women is the lack of adequate statistical information. All minorities are undercounted in the census, and employment figures available from the Department of Labor do not adequately delineate by race and sex. Asian-Americans, blacks, and Native Americans are grouped together under the category of minority while Hispanics are counted as white. Information is more current for some groups than others. As a result it is difficult to draw an accurate and detailed picture of the status of minority women or to make comparisons by race and national origin. But even with the little information available we can see that, as a group, minority women are economically worse off than white women, whose incomes are less than those of both minority and white males.

Asian-American women represent a diverse population of differing cultures and languages. The statistics available are incomplete and primarily deal with Chinese, Japanese and Filipinos. The Asian-American population in this country also includes Koreans, Indians, Pakistanis, Vietnamese, and Pacific Islanders. The female and male ratios for the various Asian groups are imbalanced as a result of immigration patterns. Early laws restricted immigration of the wives of Chinese and Filipino men coming to this country. In more recent years large numbers of Korean, Vietnamese and Japanese women came to this country as the brides of American servicemen. As a result, about half of the Asian women in this country are foreign born, suffering from extreme isolation—from their own cultures as well as American culture—handicapped by language barriers as well as by race and sex discrimination.

Asian-American women have one of the highest rates of employment in the country—fifty percent—and as a group they have a high level of educational achievement. The well educated tend to be underemployed in clerical positions while their less educated sisters are working in factories and service-related industries.

Black women are a part of the largest and, as a result of the civil rights movement, the most recognized and vocal minority group. Black women have been maligned by social scientists as the matriarchs and emasculators of black men. They have been unfairly identified as the primary beneficiary of affirmative action: "Black women get the jobs—after all, one black woman can be counted twice, as minority and female, for affirmative action purposes." In actuality black women are worse off than either white women or black males—remaining at the bottom of the employment and economic ladder. Overall, black women tend to be employed in greatest numbers in service occupations such as hospital work, food service, custodial work and household work. These occupations account for 36.8 percent of black women workers. Another 25 percent were employed in clerical jobs in

Median annual earnings of women and men who worked year round, full time by race and Spanish origin, 1975

Sex and earnings	White	Black	Spanish origin			
			Total	Mexican-American	Puerto Rican	Other
WOMEN						
Worked year round, full time in 1975[1] (thousands)	15,371	2,043	636	326	82	229
Percent	100.0	100.0	100.0	100.0	100.0	100.0
Under $2,000[2]	4.5	4.2	4.6	5.8	2.5	3.5
$2,000 to $4,999	15.4	21.4	23.0	27.6	18.5	18.4
$5,000 to $9,999	54.6	53.2	58.0	55.2	64.2	60.5
$10,000 to $14,999	20.3	18.4	12.9	10.1	14.8	14.9
$15,000 to $24,999	4.7	2.8	1.6	0.9	—	2.6
$25,000 or more	0.5	0.1	0.2	0.3	—	—
Median annual earnings, 1975	$ 7,441	$7,223	$6,388	$5,945	$7,144	$ 6,758
MEN						
Worked year round, full time in 1975[1] (thousands)	33,975	2,775	1,511	907	201	404
Percent	100.0	100.0	100.0	100.0	100.0	100.0
Under $2,000[2]	2.1	1.8	1.5	1.4	1.5	1.5
$2,000 to $4,999	4.1	10.8	7.7	9.6	5.0	5.0
$5,000 to $9,999	23.3	40.0	46.3	45.8	57.2	41.6
$10,000 to $14,999	33.0	32.9	28.7	27.6	27.9	32.2
$15,000 to $24,999	28.8	13.5	13.4	13.6	7.5	16.1
$25,000 or more	8.6	0.9	2.3	1.9	1.0	4.0
Median annual earnings, 1975	$12,877	$9,098	$9,413	$9,247	$8,512	$10,197

[1] The survey was conducted in March 1976 and counted persons 16 years and over as of the survey date who worked 50 to 52 weeks in 1975, usually full time (35 hours or more per week).

[2] Includes workers with no earnings or a loss.

1977. Black women thirty-five and under tend to be more concentrated in clerical jobs, bringing them closer to par with white women. While this does indicate some job mobility, it is within sex-typed jobs only.

Hispanic women are of Spanish origin, including Mexican-American, Puerto Rican, Cuban, Central and South American. They totaled more than 5.7 million in the United States in 1977. Like their Asian-American sisters, each subgroup represents distinct cultures, interests, problems and needs, making it difficult to discuss Hispanic women as a homogeneous group. They do share economic deprivation and other problems related to language and cultural differences; they are often torn between demands of their own and Anglo culture.

Mexican-Americans are currently the second largest minority group in the United States. Mexican-American women, or Chicanas, are slightly less represented in the labor force than all other women, with 42 percent employed in 1975. Of the families headed by Chicanas, almost half were below the poverty level in 1974.

The day-to-day reality of cultural bias and racial discrimination is very evident in the harassment of Chicanas—threats of deportation. The stigma of the illegal alien lingers and threatens Mexican-Americans regardless of their actual legal status.

Puerto Rican women, on the other hand, are United States citizens at birth, though they are viewed as "aliens" by many because of language and cultural

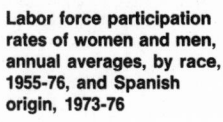

Labor force participation rates of women and men, annual averages, by race, 1955-76, and Spanish origin, 1973-76

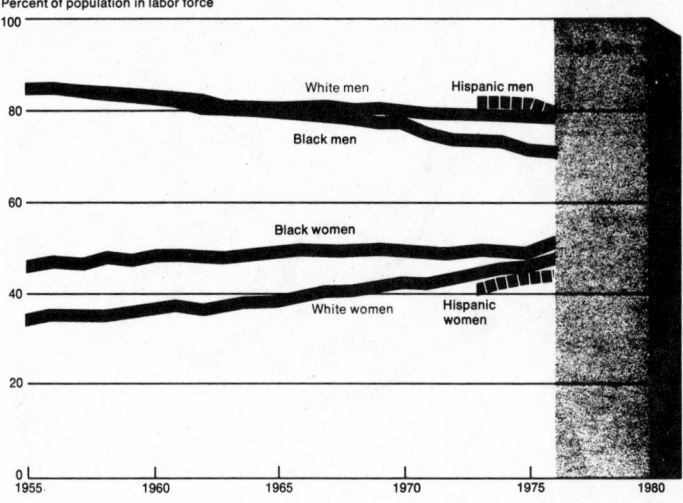

differences. Only 34 percent of Puerto Rican women were in the labor force in 1975; this is a smaller proportion than that for Hispanic women as a whole or for all women. They tended to be employed as operatives (29 percent) more than as clerical workers (26 percent) or service workers (26 percent).

Native Americans are the smallest and poorest of all minorities in this country. Based on the most recent available information (1970) Native American women account for more than half of the approximately 798,119 American Indians. The most recent data from the Women's Bureau (1970) indicates that 36 percent of all Native American women had no incomes at all. For those who were working, the median income was $1,697. Twenty-six percent were operatives, 19 percent were service workers, 14 percent were household workers, and only 9 percent were clerical workers. Contrasted with occupations for all women—35 percent clerical and 17 percent service workers—we see that Native American women are concentrated in the lowest paying of all sex-typed jobs.

Two extreme stereotypes about Native American women persist—the beautiful maiden Pocahantas and the fat drudge squaw—and both are an insult to Indian women and their cultures. Of the more than seven hundred tribes, many have retained much of their cultural heritage despite rigid governmental control and intervention in daily life and tribal customs. While some tribes are patriarchal and patrilineal, others have retained egalitarian and matrifocal and/or matrilineal structures.

Sexism and racism are often compared, and too often thought of as applying to two distinct groups. Little has been done to examine their combined impact. As a group minority women have the lowest income and the highest rate of unemployment in the country. Not only have they been forgotten by our institutions, often minority women have been the victims of abuse by these institutions.

Health care is an area of neglect and sometimes outright abuse. Minority

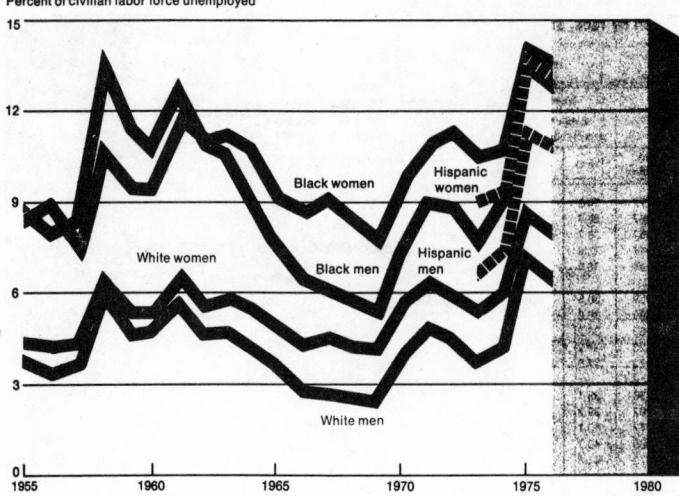

Percent of civilian labor force unemployed

Unemployment rates of women and men, annual averages, by race, 1955-76, and Spanish origin, 1973-76

Black women

Hispanic women

White women

Black men

Hispanic men

White men

women are more likely to be sterilized than white women. Native American women are sterilized more frequently than any other group. Because they are disproportionately poor, minority women have been hurt the most by the cutoff of federal funds for abortion. Poor women are faced with forced pregnancy or life-threatening self-induced or illegal abortions. Minority women have a shorter life expectancy: 72.3 years as opposed to 77.2 years for white women. This, coupled with the higher rates of maternal and infant mortality among the minorities, point toward the damages wrought by racism and sexism in combination.

The concerns of minority women were strongly in evidence at the 1977 National Women's Conference in Houston, Texas. A coalition of minority women's caucuses formed to create a new minority plank to replace the deficient one in the proposed Plan of Action (see box below). The joining together of Asian-American, black, Hispanic, and Native American women was a momentous occasion for those present at the Conference and a symbol of hope for real collective efforts of women of all races, creeds and national origins.

See also: Abortion
   International Women's Year
      (National Plan of Action)
   Older Women
   Rural Women
   Sterilization Abuse
   Welfare and Poverty
   Women's Movement
   Working-class Women

Organizations:

Asian-American Women
Council of Asian-American Women
3 Pell Street
New York, NY 10013

Organization of Chinese-American Women
1443 Rhode Island Avenue N.W.
Washington, DC 20005

The Organization of Pan Asian-American
  Women
719 Fern Place N.W.
Washington, DC 20012

Black Women
Black Women Organized for Action
P.O. Box 15072
San Francisco, CA 94115

Black Women's Community Development
  Foundation
1028 Connecticut Avenue N.W.
Washington, DC 20036

Links
1522 K Street N.W.
Washington, DC 20005

National Alliance of Black Feminists
202 South State Street
Chicago, IL 60604

National Association of Negro Business
  Professional Women's Clubs
1806 New Hampshire Avenue N.W.
Washington, DC 20009

National Black Feminist Organization
4812 46th Street N.W.
Washington, DC 20016

National Council of Negro Women
815 Second Avenue
New York, NY 10017

National Hook-Up of Black Women
2021 K Street N.W.
Washington, DC 20006

National Organization on Concerns of
  Black Women
3958 Louise Street
Lynwood, CA 90262

National Association of Colored Women's
  Clubs
5808 16th Street N.W.
Washington, DC 20011

National Association of Negro Business
  and Professional Women
3905 Georgia Avenue N.W.
Washington, DC 20011

Hispanic Women
Comisión Femenil Mexican Nacional
379 South Loma Drive
Los Angeles, CA 90017

Mexican-American Legal Defense and
  Education Fund
Chicana Rights Project
201 N. St. Mary's Street
San Antonio, TX 78205

Mexican-American Women's National
  Association
P.O. Box 23656
L'Enfant Plaza Station S.W.
Washington, DC 20024

National Chicana Foundation
1005 South Alamo
San Antonio, TX 78210

National Conference of Puerto Rican
  Women
P.O. Box 4804
Washington, DC 20008

Native American Women
Cante Ohitika Win (Brave Hearted
  Women)
P.O. Box 474
Pine Ridge, SD 57770

Women of All Red Nations
c/o Lorelei Means
General Delivery
Porcupine, SD 57779

Resources:

American Indian Women. Washington: Women's Bureau, Department of Labor,
  1977. Order from: Women's Bureau, Office of the Secretary, Department of
  Labor, Washington, DC 20210.
  A statistical profile of Native American women.

Black Macho and the Myth of the Superwoman, by Michelle Wallace. New York:
  Dial, 1978.
  This book looks at the myths surrounding black women and what it means to
live with those myths.

The Black Woman and the Black Family: A Bibliography, compiled by Phyllis Rauch Klotman and Wilmer H. Baatz. New York: Arno Press, 1978.

Black Women in White America: Documentary History, by Gerda Lerner. New York: Random House, 1973.

A compilation of documents of black women from 1811 to 1971, providing a firsthand account of the lives of black women.

Black Women Makers of History: A Portrait, by George F. Jackson. Sacramento, California: Fong and Fong, 1977. Order from: G. F. Jackson Book Co., 8438 Center Parkway, Sacramento, CA 95832.

Bibliographical portraits of black women and their contributions to American society from the 1700's to the present.

Cante Ohitika Win, prepared by Geraldine Janis and Vernona Kills Right. Pine Ridge, South Dakota: Cante Ohitika Win, 1977. Order from: Cante Ohitika Win, P.O. Box 474, Pine Ridge, SD 57770.

A pamphlet about the women of the Pine Ridge Reservation, and their group Cante Ohitika Win (Brave Hearted Women).

Daughters of the Earth, the Lives and Legends of American Indian Women, by Carolyn Neithammer. New York: Macmillan, 1977.

A well-researched account of the lives of Native American women, including a comprehensive bibliography.

Enlarging the American Dream, by Donna Hart. Washington: Project on the Status and Education of Women, 1977. Order from: Project on Status and Education of Women, American Association of Colleges, 1818 R Street N.W., Washington, DC 20009.

Reprinted from *American Education,* this article takes a look at those problems of minority women that are specifically related to educational needs and offers recommendations.

A Guide to Conducting a Conference with American Indian Women in Reservation Areas. Washington: Women's Bureau, Dpartment of Labor, 1978. Order from: Women's Bureau, Office of the Secretary, Department of Labor, Washington, DC 20210.

I Am the Fire of Time, ed. by Jane B. Katz. New York: Dutton, 1977.

An anthology of writings of Native American women, including oral histories in prose, poetry, song and prayer.

Minorities and Women: A Guide to Reference Literature in Social Sciences, by Gail Ann Schlachter with Donna Belli. Los Angeles: Reference Service Press, 1977.

An annotated bibliography covering fact books, biographical, documentary, directory and statistical sources.

Minority Women's Organizations, a Partial Annotated List. Washington: Project on the Status and Education of Women, n.d. Order from: Project on the Status and Education of Women, 1818 R Street N.W., Washington, DC 20009.

Minority Women Workers: A Statistical Overview. Washington: Women's Bureau, Department of labor, 1977. Order from: Women's Bureau, Office of the Secretary, Department of Labor, Washington, DC 20210.

© Diana Davies

Problems and Issues Facing Chinese-American Women. Washington: Organization of Chinese-American Women, 1977. Order from: Organization of Chinese-American Women (address above).

A paper describing the major issues facing Chinese-American women.

Profile of the Chicana: A Statistical Fact Sheet, March 1975, prepared by Elizabeth Waldman. San Francisco: Mexican-American Legal Defense and Education Fund, 1978. Order from: Mexican-American Legal Defense and Education Fund, 28 Geary Street, San Francisco, CA 94108.

Puerto Rican Women in the United States: Organizing for Change. Washington: National Conference of Puerto Rican Women, 1977. Order from: National Conference of Puerto Rican Women (address above).

A conference report containing selected papers examining the status of Puerto Rican women today.

Puerto Rican Women: Some Biographical Profiles, by Carmen Delgado Votaw. Washington: National Conference of Puerto Rican Women, 1978. Order from: National Conference of Puerto Rican Women (address above).

The Spirit of Houston. Washington: National Commission on the Observance of International Women's Year, 1978. Order from: Superintendent of Documents Government Printing Office, Washington, DC 20402.

Includes a discussion of the development of the minority women's caucus at the national conference, and the "Black Women's Plan of Action."

Women of Puerto Rican Origin in the Continental United States. Washington: Women's Bureau, Department of Labor, 1977. Order from: Women's Bureau, Office of the Secretary, Department of Labor, Washington, DC 20210.
A statistical portrait of Puerto Rican women.

NAME CHANGES

IN 1855 LUCY STONE BECAME THE FIRST AMERICAN WOMAN TO KEEP HER NAME after marriage; it has taken more than one hundred years for considerable numbers of women to follow suit. Adopting the husband's family name is a custom rather than a law. Today there is no state which absolutely requires a woman to do so. In isolated pockets throughout the nation, however, local officials may require a woman to use her husband's name. For instance, a state court in Kentucky upheld the automobile licensing bureau's demand that a woman use her married name; but such instances are rare.

Names are determined by usage. As long as there is no attempt to defraud, a woman can use whatever name she chooses and whichever title: Ms., Miss, or Mrs. Choosing a name for children from divorced homes may be a thorny issue if the mother has kept or taken back her family name. If the child has already used the father's name, judges tend to retain it as long as the father displays an active interest in the child's welfare.

Organizations:

Center for a Woman's Own Name
261 Kimberley
Barrington, IL 60010

Lucy Stone (1818–1893), nineteenth-century abolitionist and women's rights activist, retained her name when she married Henry B. Blackwell in 1855. Women who followed her lead were called "Lucy Stoners." *The Sophia Smith Collection*

NONSEXIST EDUCATION

ONE OF THE MOST DISTURBING ASPECTS OF SEX BIAS IN EDUCATION IS HOW early the sex-role stereotyping begins and how quickly children learn what behavior is—and is not—considered sex-appropriate. Recent studies have shown that by as early as age three, children have a complex and rigid set of beliefs about male and female roles. Chances are, these biased beliefs will receive the stamp of approval when the child enters the preschool classroom—dolls and kitchen equipment in one corner, blocks and trucks in the other. And unless the teacher is aware of and concerned about nonsexist education, he or she will probably only reinforce the sex-role stereotyping already begun. Perhaps no other educator is as important to role-free learning as the early childhood teacher. If a child's nonsexist education begins at the nursery school or kindergarten level, there is that much less to "unlearn" later on.

Because textbooks are not used on the preschool level, the emphasis falls on the toys and games used, and especially on the teacher's behavior. The preschool teacher should never give children the impression that he or she disapproves of certain activities because of gender; indeed, efforts should be made to encourage boys and girls to explore new areas. Teachers can, for example, legitimize doll play in the eyes of little boys and open up the block corner to girls. The instructional materials which are used in the preschool classroom—pictures, puzzles, lotto games, flannelboard people—should be carefully selected; nonsexist materials are available.

On the elementary and secondary level, textbooks remain the major teaching tool. Their purpose is to impart certain knowledge or skills—the facts of American history, how to spell or add. But those are not the only lessons taught; textbooks also carry what sociologists call "latent content"—social values and rules for appropriate behavior. Blacks and other racial minorities were first to examine this "hidden curriculum"; they found they were not included in it.

Since about 1969, numerous studies have been done on everything from elementary readers to senior high history texts, documenting the biased lessons taught about women. One of the most comprehensive studies examined the most widely used elementary textbooks in five subjects: social science, spelling, science, reading, and math. The books were considered for their presentation of age, sex, and race, and the results were discouraging all around. Males were pictured in 69 percent of the illustrations and females in 31 percent. As the grade level increased, the percentage of females pictured dropped; by grade six, only 20 percent of the pictures were of women and 80 percent were of men. If race is added to the equation, the percentage drops again—nonwhite males were pictured 18 percent of the time and nonwhite females only 7 percent of the time.

This *absence* of women from textbooks is the first problem, and it has been documented for all grade levels and subjects. A second problem is how the few women or girls who are included are portrayed. A 1972 study of 134 elementary readers looked at what men and women in the stories did; they found men working in 147 different jobs and women in only 26—and these 26 were clearly sex-typed occupations such as nurse, telephone operator, and secretary. Examination of story themes in this same study revealed a disturbing trend illustrated by these examples: "Boy saves dog from raft, Boy receives sled for passing a test, Boy uses intelligence to get rid of bothersome crab; Girl is sick and gets a doll, Girl's doll is sick, Girl's pet angers father and she makes peace between them." Overall, boys are portrayed as intelligent, brave, helpful, and active; girls as passive, domestic and incompetent.

What can be done—is being done—to end the lessons of the hidden curriculum? In many cities around the country—from Berkeley to Kalamazoo to New York— groups of parents, teachers, and concerned citizens have joined together to put pressure on school districts and textbook publishers. They are urging schools to examine books for damaging attitudes before they make purchasing decisions, and urging publishers to eliminate sex-role stereotypes in future editions.

Unfortunately, textbooks are not revised very often and those new editions which have appeared since this agitation began have not shown a great deal of improvement. Furthermore, this is one area where there is no recourse to the law. Curriculum is the one major area exempt from the law prohibiting sex discrimination in education. Sex bias in instructional materials was deliberately ignored in the Title IX regulations—despite the extensive documentation of its existence— because it was felt that federal guidelines governing textbook publishers would constitute a breach of First Amendment rights. The preamble to the Amendment does recognize biased curriculum as an important issue and recommends regulation on the state level. About half of the states have passed some form of law or regulation calling for review of textbooks, and many publishers have adopted guidelines for their writers and editors. Despite these beginning efforts, there is not a significant body of commercially produced nonsexist material; most of the available curricular material has come from educational organizations, small publishers, women's groups, and individual teachers.

See also: Sex roles
Women's Studies

Organizations:

Council on Interracial Books for Children
Racism and Sexism Resource Center for Educators
1841 Broadway
New York, NY 10023

The Feminist Press
P.O. Box 334
Old Westbury, NY 11568

Nonsexist Child Development Project
Women's Action Alliance
370 Lexington Avenue
New York, NY 10017

Resource Center on Sex Roles in Education
National Foundation for the Improvement of Education
1201 16th Street N.W.
Washington, DC 20036

Women on Words and Images
P.O. Box 2163
Princeton, NJ 08540

Resources:

Biased Textbooks: Images of Males and Females in Elementary School Textbooks, by Lenore J. Weitzman and Diane Rizzo. Washington: Resource Center on Sex Roles in Education, 1974. Order from: Resource Center (address above).

The study cited in the text above. Results and suggestions for change available in pamphlet form.

Dick and Jane as Victims: Sex Stereotyping in Children's Readers. Princeton: Women on Words and Images, 1975. Order from: Women on Words and Images (address above).

A classic among textbook studies, *Dick and Jane* provided much of the information in the text above.

Feminist Resources for Schools and Colleges: A Guide to Curricular Materials, ed. by Merle Froschl and Jane Williamson. Old Westbury: The Feminist Press, 1977. Order from The Feminist Press (address above).

This annotated bibliography provides an updated listing of nonsexist curriculum for all levels, as well as readings on the various aspects of sexism in education.

Guidelines for Creating Positive Sexual and Racial Images in Educational Materials. New York: School Division, Macmillan, 1975. Order from: Macmillan Publishing Co., 866 Third Avenue, New York, NY 10022.

Many publishers of textbooks have developed guidelines for writers and editors in an effort to remove race and sex bias. Macmillan's *Guidelines* are recommended because they cover race as well as sex, discussing each of the minority groups in some detail.

High School Feminist Studies, ed. by Carol Ahlum, et al. Old Westbury: The Feminist Press, 1976. Order from: The Feminist Press (address above).

This volume provides the high school teacher with 25 outlines for courses on women in history and literature. A review of sexism in high school texts is also included.

Non-sexist Education for Young Children: A Practical Guide, by Barbara Sprung. New York: Citation Press, 1975. Order from: Women's Action Alliance, 370 Lexington Avenue, New York, NY 10017.

An excellent source for the preschool teacher or parent, this volume suggests nonsexist teaching methods, describes several units of study, and includes resource listings on nonsexist materials and picture books. The only source of its kind.

TABS. Order from: TABS, 744 Carroll Street, Brooklyn, NY 11215.

TABS is a new quarterly of nonsexist curriculum, reviews of new materials, and reports on successful programs, with a pull-out poster in each issue.

Local Education Activists

Change for Children
2588 Madison Street, #226
San Francisco, CA 94110

Cornelia Wheadon Task Force
% Women's Liberation Center
2214 Ridge Ave
Evanston, IL 60201

Emma Willard Task Force
P.O. Box 14229
University Station
Minneapolis, MN 55414

Feminist Resources for Equal
  Education
P.O. Box 3185
Saxonville Station,
Framingham, MA 01701

Feminists Northwest
5038 Nicklas Place N.E.
Seattle, WA 98105

♀ MATERIALS QUESTIONNAIRE ♀

Yes No

1. Are women and men from diverse cultural and ethnic back- ___ ___
   grounds portrayed in a wide range of roles, including nontraditional ones? (Are women present as authors in literature
   anthologies, as scientists in science books; as leaders, reformers,
   pioneers, etc. in history books; as managers in business education books, and as machinists, farmers, heroes, and mayors? Are
   men present as homemakers, secretaries, elementary school
   teachers, telephone operators, clerks, and fathers?)

2. How well integrated into texts are the comments on women? ____ ____ Are the comments bunched into a separate "women's page," chapter, or paragraph? Are women of different race, religious, and ethnic groups included?

3. Does the author make generalizations about "man"? Does ____ ____ "man" mean "human" or "male"? If it means "human," are the activities, characteristics, etc. described or pictured common to both sexes? If it means "males" is equal coverage given to "woman"? (The "generic" usage of "man" and "mankind" should be replaced by "human," "humankind," and "people," since "man" and "mankind" are ambiguous, and worse, it makes many girls and women feel excluded and dehumanized.)

4. Count the pictures of people in materials. Are females half of the ____ ____ total? Do women, men, girls, and boys represent diverse racial, religious, ethnic, and class backgrounds? In pictures which illustrate both females and males, are females independently significant, or are they appendages to male characters?

5. Does content focus as often on females as on males? Does the ____ ____ material portray females and males of diverse racial, religious and ethnic groups, with their similarities and differences, in such a way as to build positive images?

6. How much emphasis is given to traditional "female" values, such ____ ____ as compassion, consideration and tenderness, as opposed to traditional "male" values such as assertiveness, risk-taking and strength? Are these values offered as ideals for both sexes?

7. Are males shown reading, admired for their school achieve- ____ ____ ment? Or do the pictures or story suggest that boys are too active and mischievous to be successful in school?

8. Does the story line show subtle bias? For example, do males ____ ____ (especially white males) have the power and make decisions? Do females of minority groups function in subservient positions?

9. Are the achievements of girls and women based on their own ____ ____ initiative and intelligence, or is their success due to their good looks or to their relationships with males? Would the story be essentially the same if the gender, or ethnic group, of the ____ ____ characters were reversed? If not, is there stereotyping that suggests a negative image of females? males? people of particular ethnic groups?

10. When boys and girls have different viewpoints, are the girls' ____ ____ behaviors looked upon as "problems" to be "solved"? Are girls expected to "act like boys" in order to be accepted as their comrades or as equals? Are sensitive boys labeled "sissies"?

11. Does the material assist students to clearly recognize and to ____ ____ accept basic similarities among all members of the human race, and the uniqueness and worth of every individual, regardless of sex, race, religion, age, or class background?

12. Does the material present a significant number of instances of ___ ___ fully integrated human groupings (sex, age, race, class) and settings to indicate equal status and nonsegregated social relationships?

13. Are quotations, references, and extra reading recommendations ___ ___ authored by women as well as by men? How many of the authors are ethnic minorities?

14. Are examples of women and men used equally to illustrate ___ ___ theories and ideas? In examples or illustrations, are females shown in passive behavior and males in more active situations as heroes, authors, researchers, doers, and accomplishers? Do women have names, or are they known as "Mother," or as "___'s wife"?

15. Does the material show *awareness* of a variety of people? Is ___ ___ more than one minority group shown? Are women of several physical types portrayed? Or are the women all young, pretty, slim?

16. Does the material acknowledge the validity of a variety of life- ___ ___ styles? Are adults who have chosen not to marry or have children portrayed favorably? When families are portrayed, do family relationships show individuals subordinated to one another because of sex? Are first-born children girls as often as boys? Are children and adults portrayed in single-parent families and in extended families (grandparents and other relatives, divorced and remarried parents, more than one family living together)? Does the portrayal emphasize the positive aspects of such family arrangements rather than suggesting that such arrangements are necessarily damaging to children?

17. Do sex education and family living materials limit their discus- ___ ___ sion to heterosexual, married relationships?

18. Are terms such as "the weaker sex" and "the little woman," ___ ___ etc., used? Are women referred to as "wives" as often as men are referred to as "husbands?"

19. Does personification of inanimate objects and animals involve ___ ___ the female with sex stereotypes?

20. Are there stories, reading selections, activities, and study units ___ ___ which discuss and criticize sex and race stereotyping?

Questionnaire prepared by Feminists Northwest as part of Project Awareness.

NONTRADITIONAL OCCUPATIONS

MORE AND MORE OF THE WOMEN ENTERING THE WORK FORCE ARE BEGINNING to consider traditionally male occupations of all types. They have begun to take themselves seriously as workers and are finally entering the higher-paying fields. Government affirmative action requirements have also contributed to this trend.

Just what is a nontraditional job? For the purposes of one government project, any occupation with a smaller percentage of women than the percentage in the labor force nationally was defined as nontraditional. At that time, 38 percent of the work force was female (today, it's 42 percent). Thus, any field with a lower proportion of women workers was considered nontraditional. Overall, there are three occupational areas in which women are severely underrepresented: certain professions (law, medicine, engineering); the higher, management levels of business; and the skilled trades (plumbing, construction, electrical work).

While women have entered the professional ranks, they have done so only in certain fields. In 1970, 30 percent of male professionals were in such areas as medicine, law, and engineering, while only 2 percent of women professionals were. More specifically, women were only 11.3 percent of doctors, 7.1 percent of lawyers, and 1.1 percent of engineers in 1975.

These percentages are changing slowly. At this point, the most notable changes are in school enrollment figures. In 1966, only 5.9 percent of women freshmen planned careers in male-dominated fields; by 1975 the proportion was up to 16.9 percent. One year later the percentage rose again to 19.4 percent. In 1977, women were 25 percent of the entering classes in medical schools nationwide. The nation's law schools had entering enrollments which were 23.4 percent female in 1974. Although it has a lower female population, overall, engineering has also seen gains. The number of women studying engineering quadrupled from 1972 to 1977.

Information on women in the management strata of business is much more difficult to collect and assess. Neither "business" nor "management" are very precise terms; there are many different industries, types of work, levels of decision making, and salary scales involved. One study estimated that in 1970 only 2 percent of management positions were held by women. Another found less than 1 percent in top management slots and 6 percent in middle levels. The chart below indicates a figure higher than either of these. The discrepancies are probably attributable to different definitions of management.

We do know that women are making a few small inroads, however. Again, one can look to school enrollments. In 1971, 3.9 percent of the M.B.A.'s awarded went to women; in 1976 it was 11.6 percent. Several important sex discrimination suits have been settled in women's favor in recent years, and this too contributes to greater recruitment and promotion efforts. American Telephone and Telegraph, for example, sponsors a course for its female employees—the Womanagement Process—which helps them to develop managerial skills. Many other such courses are available through business schools or consulting firms. Catalyst, a women's organization concerned with career development, maintains a résumé file for corporations that would like to appoint a woman to their board of directors.

Interestingly enough, it is in the lower-status jobs that women face some of the greatest barriers. The construction site projects an aura of a tough, male environment. The work is hard, dirty, and sometimes dangerous. Women have to learn to use tools and machines that are unfamiliar to them. Nothing in their socialization or education prepares them for this kind of work. Yet, many women are moving into the trades because they're tired of dead-end clerical jobs and they want to earn a decent wage.

Some of the women who pioneered in the skilled trades have quit their jobs to

Culver Pictures

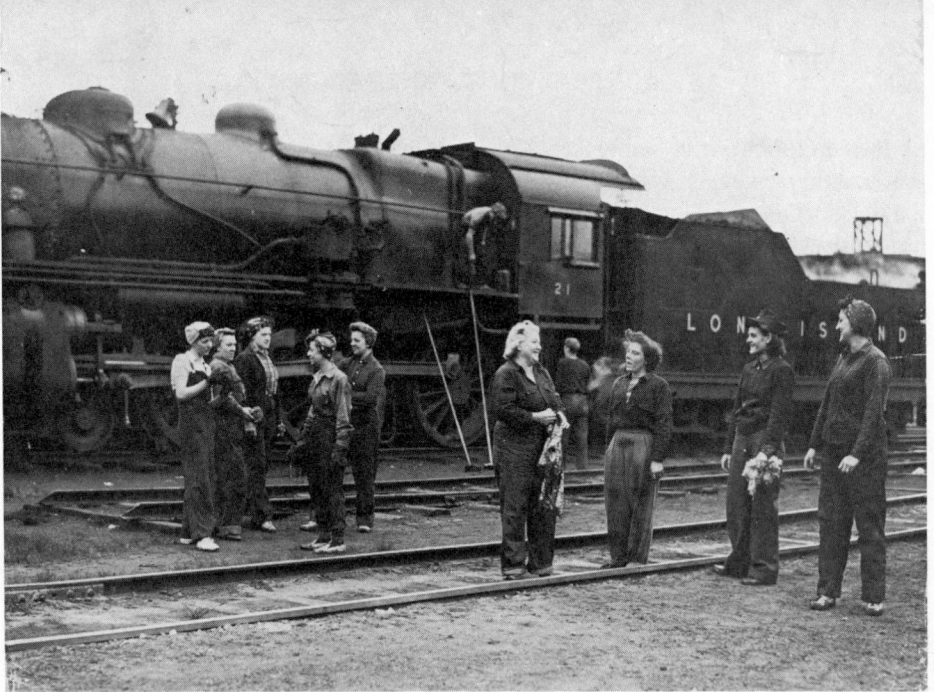

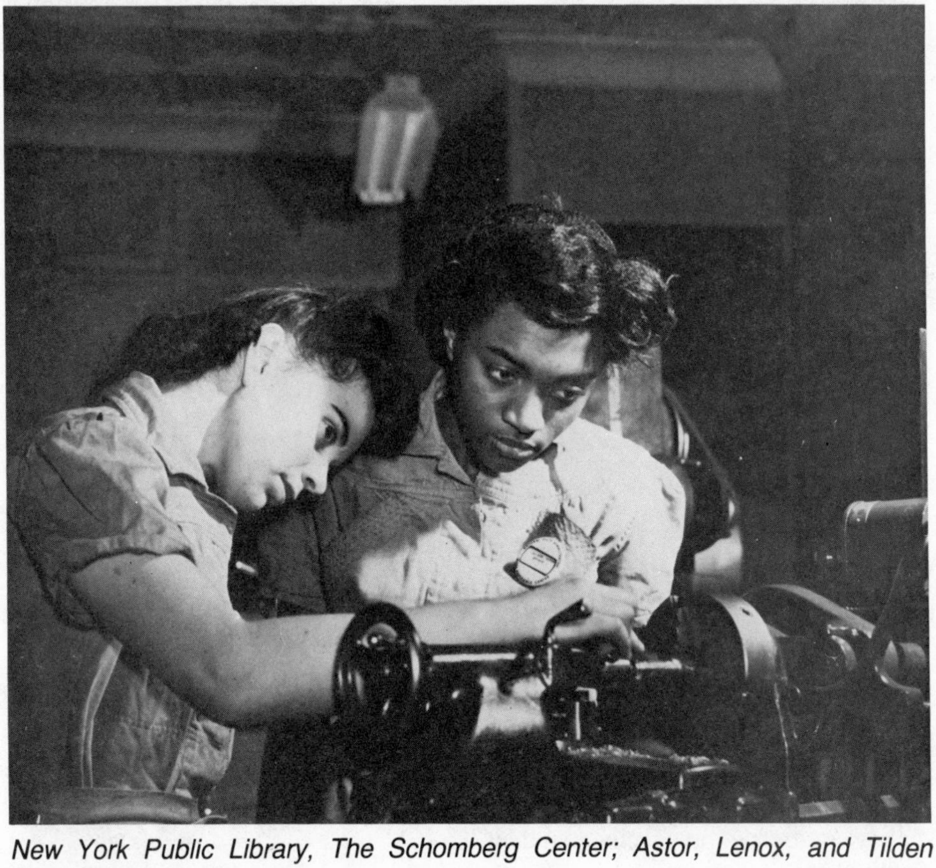

New York Public Library, The Schomberg Center; Astor, Lenox, and Tilden Foundations.

open recruitment and training centers to bring in more women (see box). They realized that tokenism was not enough. The centers recruit women who are ready for a job change, help them select an appropriate trade, and enroll them in an apprenticeship program. Apprentices earn a minimum of five dollars an hour during the two to five years they spend learning their trade. With the apprenticeship completed, the craftworker is eligible for an even higher hourly wage and the security of membership in a union.

Government affirmative action guidelines were recently revised for women in the trades. On federally funded construction projects (contracts in excess of $10,000) regulations require that women make up 3.1 percent of the workers by March, 1979, 5.1 percent by 1980, and 6.9 percent by 1981. Increased numbers of women must also be enrolled in apprenticeship programs—the apprenticeship population must be 20 percent female by 1979. These goals should not be difficult to meet. In 1974, the fourteen major trades (representing two-thirds of all apprentices) received fourteen female applicants for every woman apprentice. The ratio for men was two applicants for every one apprentice.

While it is encouraging to see the gains women are making, they must always be kept in perspective. First, they were attained only through constant struggle and agitation. It is probably safe to say that AT&T would not have instituted management training for women staff if the company had not been sued. Assuming that the battle is won is a sure road to defeat. Second, the actual degree of change must never be overestimated. An occasional bank president or corporate board member does not offset the millions of women in low-paying, dead-end jobs.

See also: Affirmative Action
           Career Development
           Higher Education
           Sex-typing of Occupations
           Vocational Education

Organizations:

Catalyst
14 East 60th Street
New York, NY 10022

Federation of Organizations for
  Professional Women
2000 P Street N.W.
Washington, DC 20036

Minority Women Employment Program
40 Marietta Street N.W.
Atlanta, GA 30303

Recruitment and Training Program
162 Fifth Avenue
New York, NY 10010

Resources:

The Managerial Woman, by Margaret Hennig and Anne Jardim. New York: Anchor/Doubleday, 1977.

One of the best books available on the subject, *The Managerial Woman* reports on a study of 25 successful women and how they "made it."

Medicine: A Woman's Career. New York: American Medical Women's Association, 1977. Order from: AMWA, 1740 Broadway, New York, NY 10019.

Advice to the prospective student on training, course requirements, and financial aid sources.

Recruiting Women for Traditionally "Male" Careers: Programs and Resources for Getting Women into the Men's World. Washington: Project on the Status and Education of Women, 1977. Order from: Project on the Status and Education of Women, 1818 R Street, N.W., Washington, DC 20009.

This nine-page pamphlet discusses career programs and materials generally as well as giving advice and information on the specific areas of law, medicine, engineering and science, and math. A final section describes materials designed for minority women. An excellent guide.

A Woman's Guide to Apprenticeship. Washington: Women's Bureau, 1978. Order from: Women's Bureau, Office of the Secretary, Department of Labor, Washington, DC 20210.

This excellent pamphlet provides basic background information on: choosing and getting into a trade; relevant government agencies; and federal laws concerning apprenticeship. Any woman considering the skilled trades would do well to start here.

Women in Non-Traditional Occupations—A Bibliography. Washington: Bureau of Occupational and Adult Education, 1976. Order from: Superintendent of Documents, Government Printing Office, Washington, DC 20402.

This bibliography includes sources on women's employment in any field in which they are less than 38 percent of the total. It includes three sections: Overview, Women in the Skilled Trades, and Women in Professional Occupations.

Women in Science and Technology: A Report on an MIT Workshop, prepared by Edith Ruina. Cambridge: Massachusetts Institute of Technology, n.d. Order from: Edith Ruina, Women in Science and Technology, Room 10-140, MIT, 77 Massachusetts Avenue, Cambridge, MA 02139.

Focusing on high schools and employers, this report makes recommendations on how to bring more women into the scientific and engineering fields.

Working for You: A Guide to Employing Women in Non-Traditional Jobs. Washington: Wider Opportunities for Women, n.d. Order from: Wider Opportunities for Women, 1649 K Street N.W., Washington, DC 20006.

A technical assistance guide for employers, this pamphlet gives good advice on how to integrate the skilled trades.

SKILLED TRADES TRAINING CENTERS

All-Craft Center
19 St. Marks Place
New York, NY 10003

Bay Area Construction Outreach
367 Second Street
Oakland, CA 94607

Better Jobs for Women
1038 Bannock Street
Denver, CO 80204

Coal Employment Project
P.O. Box 3403
Oak Ridge, TN 37830

The Committee for Women in
   Nontraditional Trades
c/o Lefcourt, Kraft and Arber
150 Nassau Street
New York, NY 10038

Although it is commonly believed that women are too frail to handle certain jobs, the urgent need for their labor in wartime overshadows such sentiments. During both World Wars, American women took over defense and industrial jobs of all types, entering the labor force by the thousands. "Rosie the Riveter," the nickname for women workers in World War II, did her part only to be sent back to the home when the war was over.

Mechanica
42-24 University Way
Seattle, WA 98105

Monmouth Apprenticeship Center
1 Main Street
Eatontown, NJ 07724

National Urban League
Leap Apprenticeship Outreach Program
500 East 62nd Street
New York, NY 10021

Skilled Jobs for Women
111 South Hamilton Street
Madison, WI 53703

Third World Jobs Clearinghouse
15 Worcester Street
Boston, MA 02118

Wider Opportunities for Women
1649 K Street N.W.
Washington, DC 20006

Women in Community Service
1730 Rhode Island Avenue N.W.
Washington, DC 20036

Women in Construction Program
11 Beacon Street
Boston, MA 02108

Women in the Trades
11-29 Catherine Street
Brooklyn, NY 11211

Women in Apprenticeship Program
25 Taylor Street
San Francisco, CA 94102

Women in Apprenticeship Project
80 Fifth Avenue
New York, NY 10003

Women Working in Construction
1649 K Street N.W.
Washington, DC 20006

Women's Apprenticeship Outreach Service
Department of Industry
Labor and Human Relations
819 North 6th Street
Milwaukee, WI 53203

Women's Enterprises of Boston
755 Boylston Street
Boston, MA 01226

YWCA
600 Lexington Avenue
New York, NY 10022

Young Women's Company
328 East 12th Street
Tucson, AZ 85719

A home demonstration agent in the mountains of Kentucky, this woman had ridden more than one hundred miles when this picture was taken in 1920. She carried all the equipment she needed in her work assisting rural people with farming, sanitation and other problems. *Culver Pictures*

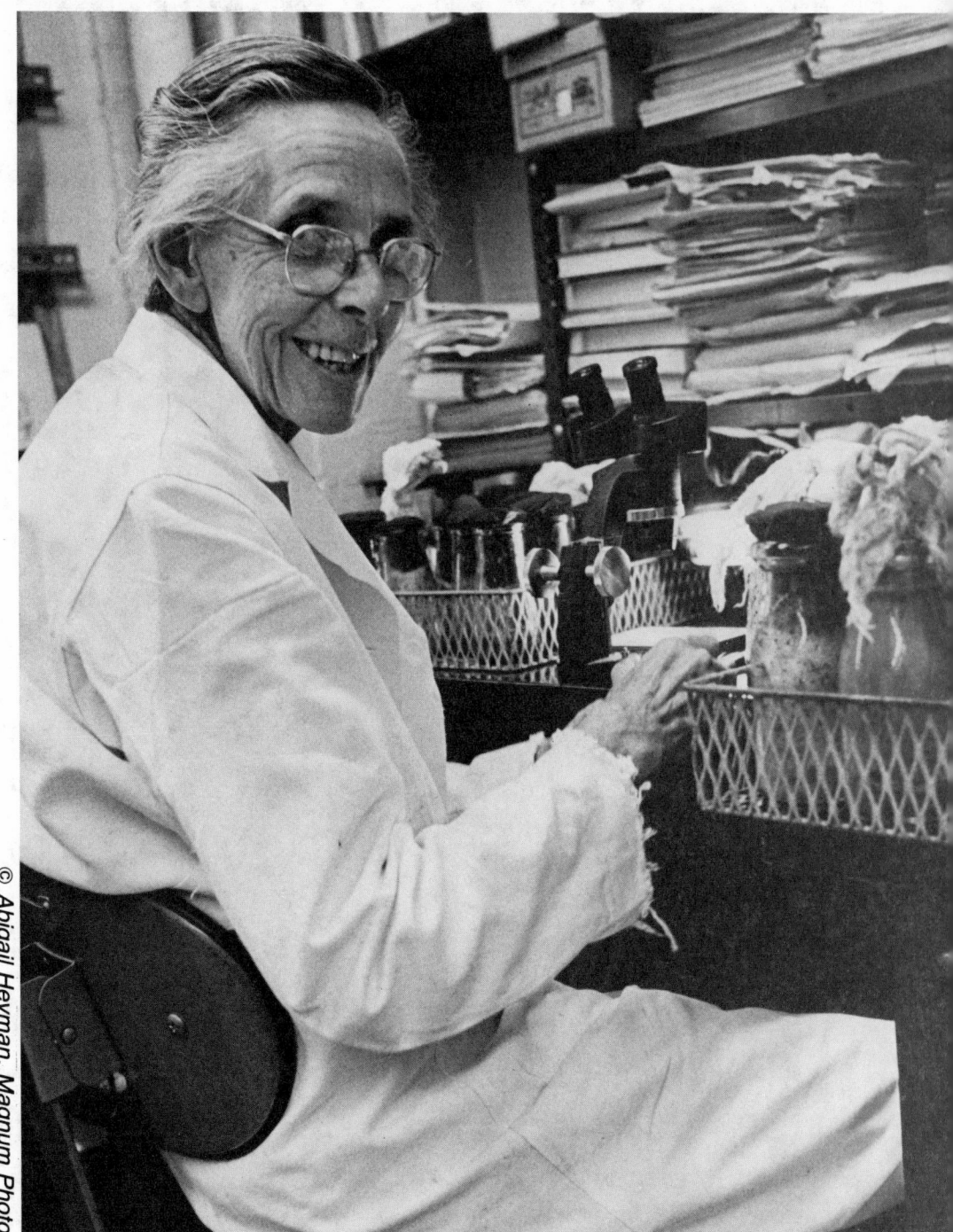

© Gail Bryan, 1976

© Bettye Lane

© Martha Tabor

OLDER WOMEN

JUST AS PEOPLE FIRST LAUGHED AT THE IDEA OF SEXISM, SO DID THEY AT THE idea of ageism. "You're not serious. Not another 'ism'! Don't be ridiculous," were common replies to the latest discovery of discrimination. But older women are serious—deadly serious—for when the two "isms" of sex and age intersect, they produce double discrimination. In a society that overvalues youth, aging can be problematic for everyone, but it is especially hard on older women.

First of all, because women live longer than men, they make up a greater proportion of the elderly population. Fifty-nine percent of those over sixty-five are women. As the years advance, the ratio increases. By age eighty-five women outnumber men by two to one. Women also tend to be considered "old" at an earlier age than men are. A man in his mid-forties to fifties is considered to be in his prime; he is probably at the height of his professional and economic success. His wife, on the other hand, will be losing her primary function of child rearer and may begin to look old to her husband. Many men in their middle years are attracted by younger women and often divorce and remarry "downward." It is wrenching to see how quickly women in our society go from sex object to obsolescence. Once they have fulfilled their traditional functions as child bearers and rearers, women are relegated to the scrap heap.

Women find that a lifetime of discrimination catches up with them very quickly as they grow older. Things they may have been unaware of suddenly become serious problems. This is especially true of the woman who has fulfilled all of society's expectations. No longer young, and therefore unattractive by social standards, she loses her role as sex object. Her lifelong economic dependence can be disastrous, especially when she is divorced or widowed. She probably has few job skills and little or no work experience. Finally, she may find herself isolated and alone with no one to turn to for help.

Despite the passage of the Age Discrimination in Employment Act, older women still find employment hard to come by. Employers are often reluctant to "invest" in older workers—male or female—who theoretically have fewer years to give than younger employees. This prejudice is intensified in the case of older women. Most people in a position to hire are male and most men, whether consciously or not, will prefer a younger woman. For the decade before retirement, ages 55 to 65, the unemployment rate for women is more than double that for men.

The results of a lifetime of sex discrimination are seen most clearly in an older woman's economic status. Women over sixty-five had the lowest median annual income of any group in the United States in 1975. At approximately $1900 per year, it was half of the income level for men of that age. In that same year, 16 percent of white women sixty-five years old and over lived below the poverty level, while 39 percent of black women in that age group did. Supplemental Social Security payments are available to elders who have little or no income; 70 percent of those receiving SSI are women.

Because women usually outlive their husbands, their later years are often ones of isolation and loneliness. In 1975, 53 percent of older women were widowed, while 79 percent of older men were married. Most women can expect to live the last decade of their lives as widows. More women than men are placed in

At seventy-two years of age, free-lance photographer Lottie Jacoby covered the 1976 Democratic National Convention. © *Bettye Lane*

institutions; they made up 75 percent of the nursing home population in 1973. This is despite the fact that many of them could and would prefer to live at home, given adequate support services.

One of the most distressing facts about the situation that older women face is that few women are aware of what's in store for them until it hits. Eliminating discrimination against women in education, employment, and family law during their younger years will help eliminate many of the problems older women face today. If they no longer spent their lives as economic dependents, but instead learned to support themselves and plan for their older years, their lot would be significantly improved. In the meantime, adequate income, at-home housekeeping services, comprehensive health care, community-based information and social support are desperately needed if older women are to live their last years with dignity.

See also: Displaced Homemakers
          Estrogen Replacement Therapy
          Social Security

Organizations:

Gray Panthers
3700 Chestnut Street
Philadelphia, PA 19104

National Action Forum for Older Women
Health Sciences Center
State University of New York
Stony Brook, NY 11794

National Senior Citizens Law Center
1200 15th Street N.W.
Washington, DC 20005

Older Women's League Educational Fund
3800 Harrison Street
Oakland, CA 94611

Pension Rights Center
1346 Connecticut Avenue N.W.
Washington, DC 20036

Transit, the National Institute for
  Transition
22 Monument Square
Portland, ME 04111

Resources:

Age Is Becoming: An Annotated Bibliography on Women and Aging, compiled by Interface Bibliographers. Oakland: NOW Task Force on Older Women, 1976. Order from: Glide Publications, 330 Ellis Street, Sa Francisco, CA 94102.

For the Woman over 50: A Practical Guide for a Full and Vital Life, by Adele Nudel. New York: Taplinger, 1978.
Written by an older woman who had been active in the civil rights and peace movements, encouraging older women to throw off the old stereotypes and live full lives. Full of specific information and advice.

Mature Women Workers: A Profile. Washington: Women's Bureau, Department of Labor, 1976. Order from: Women's Bureau, Office of the Secretary, Department of Labor, Washington, DC 20210.
A pamphlet providing statistics on older women's income, occupation, marital status, education, living arrangements, and labor force participation rate.

National Policy Concerns for Older Women: Commitment to a Better Life. Washington: Federal Council on the Aging, 1977. Order from: Superintendent of Documents, Government Printing Office, Washington, DC 20402.
A report on hearings held during 1975 (International Women's Year) on the

concerns of older women. Background information, selections from the testimony and lists of recommendations make up each section; the sections include income, health care and living arrangements, advocacy and legal aid, role in community life.

Older Women. Madison: Women's Education Resources, University of Wisconsin Extension, 1978. Order from: University of Wisconsin Extension, Communication Arts, 217 Lowell Hall, 610 Langdon Street, Madison, WI 53706.

This excellent packet of materials includes a fact sheet, a bibliography, and reprints of several fine articles on older women. Highly recommended.

Senior Citizens: A Guide to Entitled Benefits, ed. by Mary F. Tripp. San Carlos: White Oak Publishing, 1977. Order from: White Oak Publishing, P.O. Box 566, San Carlos, CA 94070.

An excellent guide for elders on the array of social services available to them. The complications of Social Security, Medicare, Medicaid, SSI, and other government programs are explained in clear English and large type. A state-by-state directory of information centers for older citizens is also included. Very useful.

INCIDENCE OF POVERTY AMONG MATURE WOMEN IN 1974 BY WORK EXPERIENCE AND RACE
(PERSONS 45 YEARS OF AGE AND OVER AS OF MARCH 1975)

Work experience and race	Percent below poverty level				
	45 years and over	45 to 54 years	55 to 59 years	60 to 64 years	65 years and over
All women	12.7	8.4	10.7	11.6	18.3
Worked in 1974	6.3	5.2	6.6	7.2	9.5
Year round full time	2.8	2.4	3.1	3.1	4.9
Did not work in 1974	17.0	13.3	15.6	14.9	19.6
White women	10.7	6.2	8.9	9.6	16.3
Worked in 1974	4.7	3.6	4.9	5.7	7.6
Year round full time	2.2	1.8	2.4	2.8	4.7
Did not work in 1974	14.6	9.9	13.4	12.6	17.5
Minority women	31.1	26.4	27.7	29.7	39.4
Worked in 1974	19.3	17.3	20.5	21.2	24.3
Year round full time	7.6	6.9	10.3	6.7	8.7
Did not work in 1974	40.4	40.5	38.4	36.0	42.1

Source: U.S. Department of Commerce, Bureau of the Census: Current Population Reports, P-60, No. 102. Reprinted from *Mature Women Workers: A Profile.* Washington, Women's Bureau, 1976.

ORDINATION OF WOMEN

NINETEENTH-CENTURY AMERICAN REVIVALISTS, BELIEVING THAT THE SPIRIT could strike anyone, anyplace, anytime, permitted women to preach. Recently founded denominations like the Christian Scientists and the Shakers had female founders; the Quakers made no sex distinctions whatever. In 1853, Antoinette Brown Blackwell became the first woman ordained by a mainline Protestant church. But there are no historical parallels to the unprecedented numbers of women seeking ordination today.

A 1925 survey on the status of women in the church discovered that of 114 denominations, 44 gave equal status to women ministers. A similar study done in 1949 noted that although there was a shortage of ministers, women were underutilized and were hired only by churches that felt that they could not afford to be choosey. As late as 1970 women fared better in the legal and medical professions than in the ministry, and even when their numbers began to rise, women had smaller congregations, lower budgets, and lower salaries than men. Data gathered in 1973 revealed that on the average a woman had a congregation of 123 people, a budget of $17,000, and a salary of $6,510. Her male counterpart led 313 people, managed a budget of $35,800, and made $10,345. The most recent (1977) statistics profile 211 denominations; of these, 76 had female ministers, 87 did not. The other 48 either have no ministers or did not provide information.

Women ministers accounted for only 4 percent of the clergy in those denominations which ordained them. Their greatest number, 31.8 percent, were in Pentecostal denominations. Another 29.9 percent were in social welfare groups such as Volunteers of America or the Salvation Army, 17.4 percent were in mainline denominations, and 20 percent were scattered. Seminary enrollment of women was found to be up 118.9 percent since 1972 but women seminarians are flexible about career options. Many prefer nontraditional ministries in hospitals, prisons, and social justice programs.

Catholicism has been constant in its refusal to ordain women. But since Vatican II, Roman Catholic women in America have pressed for equality and for admission to the priesthood. Leading feminist theologians Mary Daly and Rosemary Radford Reuther are Catholics who have grown restless waiting for change. In 1975, 2,100 people gathered in Detroit for a conference on the ordination of women; in 1976, a 19-member commission was formed to continue the work of the Women's Ordination Conference. Within a year the Vatican declared itself against the ordination of women. A Gallup Poll taken in 1975 found that 29 percent of Roman Catholics in the United States believed that women should be ordained; by 1977 the figure had risen to 41 percent.

Reform Jews have been open to the possibility of women rabbis for many years—though one was not ordained until 1972. Since then the Hebrew Union College has ordained a handful of women and others have received rabbinic degrees from the Leo Baeck Institute in London and the Reconstructionist Rabbinical College in Philadelphia. Enrollments are up at rabbinical schools, and women now account for 25 percent of the student population. These women will face a competitive job market, for unlike Protestants, rabbis rarely enter nontraditional ministries. They prefer the pulpit and leave the social work to the highly organized Jewish community-service groups.

Three of the first women to be ordained as Episcopal priests conduct services. Left to right, they are: Alison Cheek, Carter Heyward and Jeannette Piccard. © *Cary Herz*

In January 1979, following a fourteen-month study, a special committee of the Rabbinical Assembly (representative of Judaism's Conservative wing) recommended that women be ordained as rabbis. Hopefully the movement's rabbinical college, Jewish Theological Seminary, will concur with this decision and admit women. Even if they do not agree, women who are trained at Reform rabbinical colleges may receive private ordination from a committee of Conservative rabbis. Since Conservative Judaism is the largest denomination among American Jewry— 52.8 percent of religiously affiliated Jews are Conservative, 34.3 percent are Reform, 12.9 percent are Orthodox—ordaining women could significantly improve the status of women within the community. Acceptance of women's equality has accelerated rapidly over the past two decades within the Conservative camp. Before 1955 women were not allowed to read from the Torah at services; many hope that before 1985 women will be conducting the worship service.

See also: Feminist Spirituality
Jewish Women
Women and Religion

Organizations:

Priests for Equality
3311 Chauncey Place
Mt. Rainier, MD 20822

Women's Ordination Conference
34 Monica Street
Rochester, NY 14619

Women's Rabbinic Alliance
c/o Hebrew Union College
40 West 68th Street
New York, NY 10023

Task Force on Women and the Ministry in any Protestant denomination; ask your local minister where your denomination's headquarters are.

DENOMINATIONS ORDAINING WOMEN TO THE FULL MINISTRY
(INCLUDES ONLY THOSE WITH MEMBERSHIPS GREATER THAN ONE MILLION)

Denomination	Year Reported	Total Membership	Total Clergy	Authorized Women's Ordination	Total Women Clergy	Chief Women Pastors
African Methodist Episcopal Church	1951	1,166,301	7,089	1948	84(e)	45(e)
American Baptist Church	1976	1,593,574	8,566	100+ years	157	
African Methodist Episcopal Zion Church	1973	1,024,974	6,873	nineteenth century	65(e)	
American Lutheran Church	1976	2,402,261	6,625	1970	18	13
Assemblies of God	1977	1,302,318	13,684	1914	1,572	176
Christian Church (Disciples of Christ)	1976	1,278,734	6,793	1888	388	20
Episcopal Church	1976	2,882,064	12,240	1977	94	1
Lutheran Church in America	1976	2,974,749	7,695	1970	55	32
Southern Baptist Convention	1976	12,917,992	55,100	1964	20	
United Church of Christ	1976	1,801,241	9,607	1853	400	39
United Methodist Church	1975	9,861,028	35,488	1956	319	200
United Presbyterian Church in the USA	1976	2,607,321	13,772	1956	295	63

(e) *estimate by church official*

Reprinted from *Women Ministers in 1977* by Constant Jacquet, Jr. New York, 1977.

Resources:

Face to Face: An Interreligious Bulletin, special issue: *Women and the Religious Communities* (Spring 1978). Order from: Anti-Defamation League, 315 Lexington Avenue, New York, NY 10016.
Excellent digest of articles about issues facing women religious. Covers sexist language, community participation, women in the ministry. Selections from Jewish, Catholic, Protestant and Greek Orthodox writers.

Women and the Priesthood: An Experimental Vision, ed. by Ann Marie Gardiner. New York: Paulist Press, 1976.
Proceedings of the Detroit Ordination Conference.
The Women's Ordination Conference is preparing the proceedings from their November 1978 conference for publication; write for details, address above.

Women Ministers in 1977, by Constant H. Jacquet, Jr. New York: National Council of Churches, 1978. Order from: Office of Resources, Evaluation and Planning, National Council of Churches, 475 Riverside Drive, New York, NY 10027.
This summary provided much of the information in the text above.

Women of Spirit: Female Leadership in the Jewish and Christian Traditions, ed. by Rosemary Reuther and Eleanor McLaughlin. New York: Simon and Schuster, 1979.
Excellent essays on female leaders of the church and synagogue. Includes women in the early Christian community, the late patristic age, medieval Christianity, the counter Reformation, antebellum United States, and the present day Jewish, Protestant and Catholic communities.

PACIFISM AND FEMINISM

ARE WOMEN BIOLOGICALLY REVERENTIAL TOWARD LIFE AND THEREFORE "natural" pacifists? Or does their ignorance of government and world affairs allow them a naive faith in peace? Since the nineteenth century, American feminists have included world peace in the list of social changes which would follow on the heels of their success. This claim appeared shaky in the early twentieth century when some feminists—eager to deny innate differences between the sexes—realized that they couldn't have it both ways. But such inconsistencies did not blunt the edge of their convictions; in 1915 Crystal Eastman, Lillian Wald, and Jane Addams organized the Women's Peace Party.

The pacifism which these women espoused, like their feminism, was an attempt to restructure social and political priorities in order to better serve human needs on a global scale. Their hope was to use the Women's Peace Party as a base to rid the world of war. But political friction was built into the movement. Crystal Eastman, for one, felt strongly that socialism was sympathetic to an agenda of equal rights for women and world peace. Ms. Eastman and other like-minded women supported the Bolshevik Revolution while denouncing World War I. Others, Lillian Wald for example, felt compelled to back President Wilson and to support the war. In time the war split the women's movement: some women joined the national effort and others remained staunch pacifists.

Eastman's support for socialism alienated many founding members of the Women's Peace Party. These women withdrew and from the organization's ashes arose a new group—the Women's International League for Peace and Freedom (WILPF). Ironically, when Eastman tried to put feminism on the WILPF agenda, the group decided to concentrate solely on peace issues. By the 1920's, no group linked feminism and pacifism.

From the 1920's to the 1960's little was heard from feminist-pacifists. Feminism—as an active social movement—was lost amidst the Twenties, the Depression, the Second World War. Pacifism, because of leftist sympathy for the Loyalist cause in the Spanish Civil War and the threat of fascism in World War II, became unpopular.

In the early Sixties, the protest surrounding the arms race and nuclear weapons testing motivated a group of women to add their dissent. Women Strike for Peace, mothers fearful of the side effects of fallout on their children, lobbied for a ban on atmospheric testing, for disarmament, and for an end to the arms race. Currently they are trying to educate Americans about the dangers of the neutron bomb.

Women Strike for Peace and Women's International League for Peace and Freedom were joined by many other groups—such as Another Mother for Peace and the National Council of Jewish Women—in the late 1960's to protest the war in Vietnam. The antiwar movement had two effect on women: it provided longtime pacifists and leftists with a new platform and an attentive constituency,

Women march in a peace parade in 1915, the year the Women's Peace Party was formed. Within two years, the entry of the United States into World War I pressured many women pacifists to eschew their ideals for the sake of the national war effort. Those who remained on the side of peace were accused of being unpatriotic. *Culver Pictures*

and it educated a new breed of young women. These young leftists learned how to organize and, after experiencing the frustrations of working under male leadership, decided to organize for their own cause: feminism.

Today pacifism *per se* is not a strong current within feminist circles, but concerns similar to those of early feminist-pacifists are echoed in the National Plan of Action. Plank 13 calls for building international cooperation, disarmament negotiations, reductions in military spending, and peace education. A Peace Caucus gathered at Houston to remind women that "Peace is a Woman's Issue."

See also: Women's Movement

Organizations:

International Roster of Women Scholars
and Professionals
148 N Street
South Boston, MA 02127

Women Strike for Peace
145 South 13th Street
Philadelphia, PA 19107

Women's International League for Peace
and Freedom
1213 Race Street
Philadelphia, PA 19107

Resources:

Movers and Shakers by June Sochen. New York: Quadrangle Books, 1973.

Traces the rise of feminism and feminists from the turn of the century to the early 1970's. Puts feminism in perspective with other social change movements, showing interaction between different political groups and trends.

The New Woman in Greenwich Village, 1910–1920 by June Sochen. New York: Quadrangle Books, 1972.

Chapter 5, "The Challenge of War," provides an explanation of the intricacies of and interfaces between feminism, pacifism, socialism and liberalism before and during World War I. It shows where each of the feminists stood and why, and it provided much of the information in the text above.

POLITICS

MANY NINETEENTH-CENTURY FEMINISTS BELIEVED THAT WINNING THE RIGHT to vote would provide women with the political power necessary to protect their interests. But the ballot box was not enough. Women individually cannot combat the politics of sexism—the sexism that keeps women in a second-class position and limits women to their biological role; the sexism that relegates women's concerns to the level of "personal problems," denying that they are public issues; the sexism that keeps women out of public life.

Women won the right to vote in 1920 after more than seventy years of organizing for suffrage. The Equal Rights Amendment was first introduced into Congress in 1923 and has yet to be adopted. As of the 1978 elections, there is only one woman in the United States Senate and only 16 women in the House of Representatives. Women account for only 8 percent of all public officials.

Women have always worked in traditional party politics, but usually as volunteers, rather than as paid campaign staff. The national parties have begun to respond to the demands of their women members for better representation. In

1976, women were 34 percent of the delegates at the Republican Convention. Because of constant agitation, the Democrats will require that half the delegates to the 1980 Democratic National Convention be women.

Although women are still in the minority in public life, more women are running for office and getting elected (see box). Women have been more successful on the local level, sometimes running as third-party candidates, getting support from liberal and left parties. In presidential elections, women have been nominated only on third-party or independent tickets. Women's groups also are working to get more women appointed and elected, and to make all public officials accountable on women's issues.

Despite finding themselves excluded from the traditional avenues of political participation, women have persevered, organizing to bring issues such as suffrage, equal rights, equal pay, day care and reproductive freedom to the public. They have influenced legislation and public policy.

Women's organizations have historically been the guiding force and vehicle for the political participation of many women. Not only the formally structured and national organizations, but local *ad hoc* groups as well serve as political advocates and pressure groups; organize lobbying efforts; hold rallies, marches and demonstrations; testify before Congressional committees; and run campaigns for public support of issues as well as for candidates for public office. Women's groups have worked in coalition with each other and with civil rights, liberal, and left groups, rallying support for issues of mutual concern. While their visibility may be low, women are concerned, politically active citizens.

See also: Legal Status
            Pacifism and Feminism
            Volunteerism
            Women's Movement

Women marching in one of many demonstrations to demand votes for women.
Brown Brothers

Organizations:

Center for American Woman and Politics
Eagleton Institute
Rutgers University
New Brunswick, NJ 08901

Democratic National Committee
Women's Division
1625 Massachusetts Avenue N.W.
Washington, DC 20036

League of Women Voters
1730 M Street N.W.
Washington, DC 20036

Midwest Academy
600 West Fullerton
Chicago, IL 60614

National Federation of Republican Women
310 First Street S.E.
Washington, DC 20003

National Woman's Party
144 Constitution Avenue N.E.
Washington, DC 20002

National Women's Agenda Coalition
Women's Action Alliance
370 Lexington Avenue
New York, NY 10017

National Women's Education Fund
1410 Q Street N.W.
Washington, DC 20009

National Women's Political Caucus
1411 K Street N.W.
Washington, DC 20005

Women's Campaign Fund
1521 New Hampshire Avenue N.W.
Washington, DC 20036

Women's Equity Action League
805 15th Street N.W.
Washington, DC 20005

Resources:

Campaign Workbook. Washington: National Women's Education Fund, 1978.
  Order from: National Women's Education Fund (address above).
  A looseleaf how-to guide to running a campaign, whether local or statewide, with special attention to the problems and experiences of women candidates.

Everywoman's Guide to Political Awareness, by Phyllis Butler and Dorothy Gray.
  Millbrae: Les Femmes, 1976. Order from: Les Femmes, 231 Adrian Road, Millbrae, CA 94030.
  A how-to guide to political activism for the citizen and the candidate; includes resource lists of political groups, political parties, women's political organizations and resources, and college courses.

Getting Her Elected, by Susanne Paizis. Sacramento: Creative Editions, 1977.
  Order from: Creative Editions, P.O. Box 22246, Sacramento, CA 95822.
  Written by a woman who unsuccessfully campaigned for the California State Senate, this guide offers other young women firsthand information on campaigning for office.

A Portrait of Marginality, ed. by Marianne Githens and Jewel L. Prestage. New
  York: David McKay, 1977.
  Although aimed at academics, this comprehensive anthology looking at the political participation of women provides interesting insights into the influences on women.

The Political Participation of Women in the United States: A Selected Bibliography,
  by Christine Li. Metuchen: Scarecrow Press, 1977.

Women in Elective and Appointive Office. Madison: Women's Educational
  Resources, University of Wisconsin Extension, n.d. Order from: Communica-

tions Program, University of Wisconsin Extension, 217 Lowell Hall, 610 Langdon Street, Madison, WI 53706.

An information packet containing publications and film lists, articles, a fact sheet, a teaching guide on getting legislation introduced, supported and passed, and other resources.

Women in Public Office, prepared by the Center for the American Woman and Politics. Metuchen: Scarecrow Press, 1978.

An extensive directory of women in public office, including federal and state levels, and an analysis of women in office.

PROFILE OF WOMEN IN PUBLIC OFFICE

American women are making small but steady gains in winning national office. Those elected do bring a special women's viewpoint to their jobs. They are also self-confident and ambitious, but convinced that their climb toward leadership is being hampered by male party leaders.

The numbers of women in public office have increased on every level except Congress. Today, more than 9 percent of state legislators are women, as are nearly 11 percent of state cabinet and executive officials, 3 percent of county commissioners and approximately 8 percent of mayors and members of township councils. In summary, women hold 6 to 10 percent of all offices surveyed, compared to 4 to 7 percent in 1975. The most dramatic increase is at

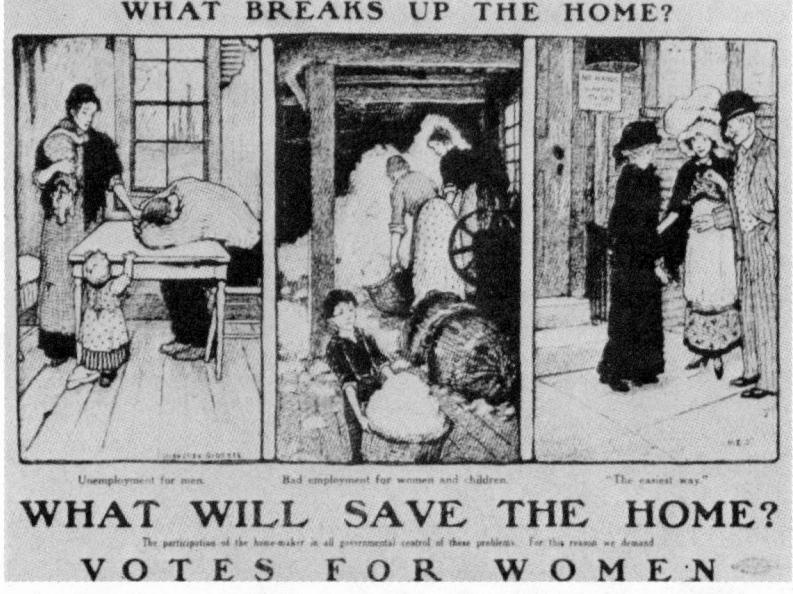

As this poster indicates, suffragists began to rely on women's special role as homemakers as a primary argument for woman suffrage in the later years of the campaign. Turning the "moral purity" argument on its head, they insisted that women's higher moral nature was a reason to give women the vote, not to deny it. *Brown Brothers*

the local level, where women have [increased] their strength by at least one-third since 1975.

The viewpoint of women in public office is most likely to be feminist and more liberal than that of their male colleagues, regardless of political party. Large majorities of women at every level of office support ratification of the federal ERA, oppose a constitutional ban on abortion and favor extension of social security to homemakers. Women officeholders are far more likely than their male colleagues to agree that government and industry should do more to promote women's rights.

Although polls of the general public show women to be no different or slightly more conservative than men on most issues, 30 percent of women officeholders designate themselves as liberal, as contrasted with only 22 percent of men officeholders.

Women officeholders are more likely than men to support legislation banning mandatory retirement, to agree that busing is desirable to achieve racial balance in the schools, and to oppose severe penalties as a way of dealing with crime. And larger proportions of women than men say they would like to hold other offices in the future.

Although a majority of women officeholders, except for Congresswomen and state legislators, are in their first terms, they are not political neophytes. They have as much experience in political parties and more experience in public offices than women who were elected before 1975.

Reprinted from the November 1978 issue of *Women's Agenda* and based on *Women in Public Office*, Scarecrow Press, 1978.

♀ HOW TO MOVE WOMEN INTO APPOINTIVE OFFICE ♀

If women are to participate in public affairs in proportion to their 53 percent representation in the population and if the female perspective is to be a significant component of public policy and practice we must increase the numbers of women in public life. During recent years more women have won elective offices, but not yet in proportion to their numbers. However, there is another avenue to adequate representation: the appointment of more women to the numerous boards and commissions which advise and set policy at all levels of government. The fact that women have yet to be found in representative numbers in important appointive positions is a challenge to all who believe in equal representation.

WHAT DO OFFICIALS CONSIDER WHEN MAKING APPOINTMENTS?

Competency. Officials prefer to appoint a *competent* person who will be a credit and not an embarrassment to the appointer and whose appointment will receive public acclaim.

Demonstrated by past performance, competency is the ability to:

— Understand the political climate, especially that of the appointing official;
— Be committed to public good;

— Understand basic facts and issues;
— Be responsible in attendance and participation;
— Express ideas without creating undue hostility;
— Carry out appointive tasks; and
— Garner public support for decisions and recommendations.

Representation of a Constituency. Government heads are also concerned with appointing individuals who are leaders of a particular group or organization and who, thus, represent a *constituency*.

Often the appointing official views this constituency as potentially supportive of his/her programs and possibly of election to future office. Balance may also be a concern—to appoint a board or commission whose membership would include representation from a wide spectrum of interest groups, citizenry, political parties, and geographic backgrounds.

An individual has a constituency when he/she is recognized as an outstanding advocate of a group's special concerns. For example, an individual with a constituency is one who:

— Is an effective member of a women's organization: a state, county or city commission on women, a professional group, a labor union, a business organization, a parent-teacher organization, a veteran's auxiliary, a minority organization, a farm organization, or a church group;
— Has waged or managed an effective campaign for public office;
— Has organized an effective citizen's group for needed change;
— Is recognized as an advocate for an ethnic or minority group;
— Is an outstanding member of his/her profession; or
— Is an active political party worker.

HOW CAN AN ORGANIZATION INCREASE THE NUMBER OF WOMEN IN APPOINTIVE POSITIONS?

Develop a Roster or Talent Bank. Establish a card file of women candidates for appointment that contains candidate's major interests, a list of various positions for which she might qualify, and names of widely respected references with addresses and phone numbers.

However, remember that this file is only one resource for providing names of women candidates. More important than information in a card file are recommendations from individuals who know the candidate personally and whose judgment in such matters is reliable.

Don't be disappointed if your candidate is not selected. Try and try again. Don't forget to commend the appointing officials, if your candidate is selected, by letter or public announcement if appropriate.

Promote a Calendar of Appointments. A calendar should include a list of appointive positions, terms of offices, current appointees, appointing officials, legislative or other official confirmation if required, qualifications, job descriptions if possible, and pay and expenses if provided.

An organization can make a significant public contribution by setting up and maintaining a calendar, but it is a time-consuming procedure for a citizen group. Alternatives include:

— Persuading another more appropriate public or private agency to perform this service;
— Initiating and supporting legislation which would require governmental units to maintain a calendar and make it available to the public; or
— Acquiring a list from another organization.

Monitor Upcoming Appointments.

— Keep careful watch of upcoming vacancies at least several months ahead to provide adequate time to promote a candidate.
— Check news and other sources for vacancies created by resignation or death.

Mount a Campaign on Behalf of a Candidate. An organization must decide whether it is more effective to develop a public or private approach or a combination of the two.

If a private approach is selected, then the organization might decide to:

— Ask an intermediary with special influence to propose and endorse the candidate to the appointing official;
— Write a letter to the official with careful documentation of a candidate's qualifications; and
— Ask other groups to work for the candidate. (However, an organization does not wage a public effort.)

If the organization decides to use a public approach, then it could:

— Meet with other organizations to select a mutually agreed-upon candidate;
— Form a committee to back appointment;
— Circulate petitions on behalf of the candidate;
— Solicit members of participating organizations to write to the appointing official (these must never be form letters); and
— Utilize the media to promote the candidate through letters to the editor, participating in talk shows and news releases.

Promote Affirmative Action in Appointments. Local political parties can encourage and assist formation of a women's caucus or committee as an appointive or a voluntary group and can:

— Develop a local roster of women candidates;
— Develop and use a calendar of appointments;
— Propose and support local women for appointment; and
— Monitor and report results to officers and membership.

Remember that women who are active in local party politics can have significant influence on an appointing official, especially when they are members of the same political party.

WHAT CAN AN INDIVIDUAL DO TO SEEK APPOINTIVE OFFICE?

— Be politically active and work hard to elect a candidate seeking election to an office which has appointive responsibilities. If your candidate wins and you have the competency, you stand an excellent chance for an appointment.

— Know the formal, and, if possible, the informal requirements for the position.

— Send a detailed résumé of your qualifications to the appointing official documenting your competence and your constituency(ies), especially as related to the appointing official's goals, past election and political future.

— Send a detailed résumé of your qualifications to the organizations whose support you seek, emphasizing your appointment as a means of reinforcing mutual interests.

— Persuade others whose opinion is respected by the appointing official, particularly party activists, to speak on your behalf. Don't overlook other intermediaries who have political influence.

Prepared by Women's Education Resources, University of Wisconsin Extension, for the National Commission on the Observance of International Women's Year.

PORNOGRAPHY

UNTIL RECENTLY, FEW FEMINISTS GAVE MUCH THOUGHT TO THE PROBLEM OF pornography. Indeed, during the height of the so-called sexual revolution, to complain about pornography was to place yourself in the camp of moralizers, prudes and reactionaries. The growing confidence of the feminist movement and the increasingly sadistic nature of pornography have combined to move many women off the fence.

Modern pornographic images have changed greatly in the last twenty years. In the early 1950's, *Playboy* spreads featuring frontal nudity were considered titillating. As competitors vied for a share of the market, one magazine showed female genitalia, another offered lesbianism, a third photographed actual copulation.

Two recent trends in the "kink wars"—child pornography and sadomasochism—are particularly offensive. The case against child pornography is clear-cut. Child models, usually peddled by their parents, are often also prostituted by their elders and/or are victims of incest. Congress recently passed a law which made proven involvement with the production and sale of explicit sex pictures of children a felony.

Sadomasochistic pornography is more difficult to curb; for one thing, the models are above the age of consent. The reason why models do consent to being whipped, tortured, or defecated on is difficult to understand. But the effect of sadomasochistic pornography on viewers is apparent.

The first national conference, "Feminist Perspectives on Pornography," met in San Francisco in November 1978. In defining pornography, the "What Is Pornography?" workshop stressed the violence so common today: "Sexual material depicting or supporting violent or coercive or nonconsensual acts when an imbalance of power is implied or explicit in such a way as to endorse or recommend the behavior." Feminists are not against mutually enjoyed sexuality. They are opposed to the violent degradation of women.

Men—and women—are bombarded by images of coercive and violent behavior toward women, offered not only in porno films and stag magazines, but increasingly in store windows, on billboards and record jackets. A boutique in Cambridge, Massachusetts, decorated its windows with a murder in progress: a female mannequin stuffed into a garbage can had a pair of beautiful shoes tied around her neck. In 1976, Women Against Violence Against Women, a Los Angeles group, campaigned to have a billboard removed from Sunset Strip which depicted a bound and bruised women. The caption read: "I'm black and blue from the Rolling Stones and I love it." In 1977, a San Francisco-based group, Women Against Violence in Pornography and Media, protested the Max Factor "Self Defense" ad campaign for a skin moisturizer whose slogan is: "A pretty face isn't safe in this city. Fight back with self defense."

Why brutality chic? This name for the genre, more pleasant-sounding than sadomasochism, was coined during the hype for Helmut Newton's *White Women,* a 1975 high-fashion photographic essay on torturing and mutilating women. Many feminists think that brutality chic is a backlash against the women's movement. To assert themselves, men resort to the bottom line of their "superiority"—physical strength.

Women have a right to be frightened. Linking sexuality to violence encourages rape, wife abuse, incest, and murder. A study done with prison inmates by *TV Guide* in January 1977 demonstrated that there is a correlation between television and violence. Asked if they were influenced by television in committing crimes, 17 percent of men who committed assaults said yes, 6 percent of murderers said yes, and 5 percent of rapists admitted the link.

Women have mounted effective campaigns against rape and wife abuse. Curbing pornography is more difficult because it raises the specter of censorship and trespasses on the First Amendment. Participants in "Obscenity: Degradation of Women Versus Right of Free Speech," a colloquium sponsored by New York University Law School, plumbed this dilemma. Lisa Lerman, conference coordinator, posed the question: "How (can we) mitigate the adverse effects of pornography on society without offending the First Amendment?" So far, there is no single feminist perspective on how to accomplish this, and probably there never will be. Antipornography organizers have sponsored demonstrations, economic boycotts, picket lines, exposés and civil disobedience. Some have argued that enforcement of current obscenity laws is the answer. Although the Supreme Court defined as obscene, materials "utterly without redeeming social values," few cases are brought—or won—against pornographers.

The Supreme Court's 1974 decision to leave the definition of obscenity to local standards raises difficult questions. Who sets the standards? Whose "social values" are adhered to? Recently, conservative forces in several communities banned *Our Bodies, Ourselves* from schools and public libraries as part of a nationally coordinated effort. Do these communities consider the book to be "utterly without redeeming social value?" Why have pornographic magazines prominently displayed on newsstands in the same communities rarely been attacked? Feminists are questioning whose standards—and whose interests—are being upheld in obscenity cases. They also understand that censorship is dangerous to all. If "pornography" is banned, their literature may be the first to go.

One explanation for the protection of pornography is its economic clout. According to the California Department of Justice, the pornography industry grosses more than $4 billion yearly—more than the record and movie industries combined! *Forbes* (September 18, 1978) estimated that the ten leading men's magazines generate close to $475 million in revenues, adult films take in $365 million and "Pleasure Chest" shops, specializing in sex toys, account for another $100 million. Adult bookstores in large cities which feature short-loop porno films (25¢ for two minutes) can bring in more than $10,000 each day.

In the war against pornography, feminists are up against enormous obstacles: a huge and powerful industry, a male-dominated legal system, and a sexist society with a voracious market for pornography. Added to this is the danger of jeopardizing the First Amendment. But the days of looking the other way are over; women adamantly refuse to be depicted as—to be treated as—victims. Accepted is Robin Morgan's thesis: "Given the current marketing of cruelty, one can only conclude that pornography is indeed the theory and battery, rape and molestation and other increasing crimes of sexual violence are not so coincidentally the practice."

See also: Battered Women
Incest
Prostitution
Rape
Right-wing Attacks
Sexuality

Organizations:

Women Against Violence Against Women
1727 North Spring Street
Los Angeles, CA 90012

Women Against Violence in Pornography and Media
P.O. Box 14614
San Francisco, CA 94114

Resources:

Bibliography: Violence Against Women, Mass Media Violence. Los Angeles: Women Against Violence Against Women, n.d. Order from: WAVAW, 1727 North Spring Street, Los Angeles, CA 90012.

First Feminist Papers on Pornography, ed. by Women Against Violence in Pornography and Media. New York: William Morrow and Co., forthcoming.

Ms., special issue: Erotica and Pornography—Do You Know the Difference? (November 1978).

WOMEN AGAINST VIOLENCE AGAINST WOMEN CHAPTERS

Boston WAVAW
c/o The Cambridge Women's Center
46 Pleasant Street
Cambridge, MA 02139

Columbia WAVAW
UMC Women's Center
Columbia, MO 65201

Ithaca WAVAW
c/o 412 Hillview Place
Ithaca, NY 14850

Knoxville WAVAW
c/o 4901 Shady Dell
Knoxville, TN 37914

New Orleans WAVAW
P.O. Box 15018
New Orleans, LA 20175

New York City WAVAW
c/o Metrolines
164 West 21st Street
New York, NY 10011

Philadelphia WAVAW
c/o The Working Group on Battered
  Women
P.O. Box 12233
Philadelphia, PA 19144

Rhode Island WAVAW
c/o Stockwood, MacKenzie
Simmons Lake Drive
Johnston, RI 20919

PREGNANCY BENEFITS

ON OCTOBER 31, 1978, PRESIDENT CARTER SIGNED INTO LAW A BILL WHICH requires employers to pay sick leave and disability benefits for all absences due to pregnancy and abortion. The bill—an amendment to Title VII of the Civil Rights Act of 1964—adds practices that discriminate on the basis of pregnancy to the definition of sex discrimination. It reverses the 1976 Supreme Court decision, *General Electric* v. *Gilbert,* which held that withholding sickness and accident benefits from a pregnant worker did not violate Title VII.

According to Congressional testimony, 95 percent of women can work until labor pains begin. As long as a woman can work, she ought to be hired, retained or promoted at her job—pregnancy notwithstanding. The new regulation, based on this line of thinking, also guarantees that if a working women is disabled because of childbirth or pregnancy, her employer must give her the same rights— seniority, sick pay, disability and health benefits, a job upon return—which would be extended to any similarly disabled non-pregnant employee. Furthermore, the employer must pay pregnancy-related health benefits on the same basis as benefits for men. If a woman is permanently disabled by childbirth or pregnancy, she is entitled to the same right to retire on long term disability benefits as a man disabled by a nonwork-related cause would have.

The new amendment also covers abortion, with one exception. The employer does not have to pay for an abortion unless the mother's life is endangered. Naturally, this clause has been criticized by women who feel that abortion, a legitimate health-care expense, should be the woman's prerogative and should be available on demand. The new amendment does stipulate that the employer must pay for sick leave and disability benefits as well as hospital and medical expenses, should there be complications after an abortion. It also prohibits employers from terminating or denying a job to a woman who has exercised her right to abortion. Nor may co-workers harass her for her choice. Despite the discrimination implicit in the abortion section, its actual effect may be limited. Many employers will prefer to cover the lower costs of abortion—about $175—as opposed to $1,200 for childbirth.

Twenty-five states and the District of Columbia have their own laws prohibiting discrimination in pregnancy without any abortion exception. (The twenty-five states are: Alaska, California, Colorado, Connecticut, Hawaii, Illinois, Indiana, Iowa, Kansas, Kentucky, Maine, Maryland, Massachusetts, Michigan, Minnesota, Missouri, Montana, New Jersey, New York, Oklahoma, Oregon, Pennsylvania, South Dakota, Washington and Wisconsin.)

See also: Abortion
             Health Care
             Insurance
             Legal Status

Organizations:

Campaign to End Discrimination Against Pregnant Workers
1126 16th Street N.W.
Washington, DC 20036

Resources:

Pregnancy Benefits and Discrimination Rules with Explanation and State Survey. Chicago: Commerce Clearinghouse, 1978. Order from: Commerce Clearinghouse, 4025 West Patterson Avenue, Chicago, IL 60641.

Full report on the requirements of the new law, employee benefits, conforming benefits plans, compliance actions, leave privileges of federal employees, survey of state laws, 1978 amendment to 1964 Civil Rights Act, House and Senate Committee reports, legislative history.

PROSTITUTION

CURRENT STATE LAWS PROHIBITING PROSTITUTION VIOLATE THE FEMINIST tenet that every woman has a basic and fundamental right to control her own body. Furthermore, the laws are applied unfairly since only the prostitute—virtually never the client—is subject to them.

But biased behavior toward prostitutes is not surprising given the confluence of religion and sexism in American society. The traditional religious position strictly prohibits sexual relations outside of marriage. When the state assumed responsibility for civil legislation, this moralistic judgment passed into secular law. Some states forbid the performance of sex acts for money, others have laws against solicitation, still others make loitering with the intent to engage in prostitution a crime. In 1949, the United Nations passed a resolution calling for the decriminalization of prostitution; most members states complied. But American prostitutes, working at the intersection of desire and disapprobation, still risk prosecution and jail as criminals in forty-nine states. Only in Nevada is prostitution legal—and there it is controlled by businessmen and the state government for their own profit. In 1975 gross revenues from prostitution nationally were estimated at $9 billion. This may be a motive for legalization in more states—hefty sums could be made by licensing the trade.

However, prostitution is "on the books" in forty-nine states, and its practitioners are regularly harassed and arrested. According to one study, Seattle spends more than $1 million yearly arresting prostitutes. In New York City each arrest, booking, and jailing costs more than $2000. And the rate of recidivism among these women is almost 100 percent.

Not only is prostitution illegal, but the law is enforced in a discriminatory manner. In the United States, nearly 500,000 women work as prostitutes. The bulk of their clients are white, middle-class men aged thirty to sixty years. But when police make arrests, they rarely book the customer; instead they go after the woman. The streetwalker, often uneducated and from a minority background, suffers most. Black prostitutes are arrested nine times more frequently than white women.

The American Civil Liberties Union and other progressive lawyers and social activists are working nationally to strike down prostitution laws on the grounds that they are unconstitutional. They argue that with the exception of child prostitution, sex for a fee is a private arrangement between two consenting adults—a victimless crime. The laws against prostitution violate equal protection, privacy, and due process regulations, and inflict cruel and unusual punishment.

Prostitutes have organized too. COYOTE (Call Off Your Old Tired Ethics) is an advocacy group dedicated to eliminating all laws dealing with prostitution and some of the criminal justice system's abuse in the treatment of arrested streetwalkers. COYOTE founder Margo St. James allies herself foursquare with the feminist movement. In November 1977 she raised the issue of decriminalization at the National Women's Conference in Houston and received widespread support.

Mari Maggu of SCAPEGOAT—a New York City-based organization for women who want to leave "the life"—stated that she would prefer a world without prostitution, but until then decriminalization would be a step in the right direction. SCAPEGOAT has provided day care, housing, doctors, lawyers, education, and consciousness-raising groups for more than 3,000 women who wanted to reenter "straight" society.

SCAPEGOAT and COYOTE perform complementary tasks. In a just society no woman would have to sell her body. But many do, in this society, because it can be lucrative. A high-priced call girl may earn upwards of $75,000 a year; even a streetwalker may turn hundreds of dollars over to her pimp in a week. Compared to the $8,814 median income of women in 1977, it is possible to understand why many women stay in "the life."

But prostitution is hard and dangerous work. A streetwalker must be constantly on guard, deciding quickly who is a client, and who a cop or a dangerous criminal. Besides threats from the vice squad, prostitutes must be wary of would-be rapists, robbers, muggers and murderers. Streetwalkers are easy prey because their outlaw status makes it difficult for them to seek or expect police protection.

While they seem to be safeguarded by their pimps, prostitutes are in fact the victims of a classic protection racket. Prostitutes (with the exception of a few high-priced call girls) are forced to align themselves with pimps—if they work alone they face harassment and beatings from the pimps who control the trade.

Few prostitutes have a kind word to say about pimps. An inexperienced streetwalker may mistake a pimp's solicitations for love and affection, but her romantic illusions are soon dispelled. The pimp-prostitute relationship may well be the archetype for sexual exploitation. These men live off women's bodies; they do little more than make certain their women are on the street earning their daily quota, which for the most part winds up in the hands of the pimps, the landlords who rent apartments to the women, and the cops who are paid to look the other way.

In a society in which all things may become commodities to be sold for profit, sex is no exception. Today, women's sexuality is itself used to sell many products—from cars to records to shampoo. In the process of selling merchandise, women's bodies become so objectified that it's a short psychological leap from selling the image of the body to selling the body itself. It is ironic that advertisers freely use women's bodies to sell products and make money, but when women attempt to use their own bodies to make money for themselves, they are arrested.

Although a case can be made for allowing adult women to engage in prostitution, there is no justification for the sexual use of children. Many runaways attracted by the excitement of city life, and incest victims escaping from abusive home situations, are picked up by pimps who exploit the child's need for love and security. During 1976, nine girls under the age of sixteen and 1,165 girls aged sixteen to twenty were arrested for loitering for illegal purposes in midtown Manhattan. Young women under the age of 21 comprised 20 percent of all prostitute-related arrests in New York City and many more, working in massage parlors, go unnoticed.

The first center in the United States to help child prostitutes and children involved in pornography opened in New York City in January 1979. The program, Midtown Adolescent Resource Center, is a federally funded pilot program; its aims are to rescue children from sex exploitation, to campaign for legislative hearings on child abuse, and to identify anyone who exploits young people sexually.

The sexual double standard would have us believe that men should enjoy and participate in sexual activities, but women should not. The mother-madonna image is idealized and the whore is treated with contempt. The stigma attached to the label "whore" still circumscribes women's behavior, restricts their mobility and fosters a tension between straight women and prostitutes. Relaxed sexual mores have lessened these effects, but divisions between women along these lines still exist. Some feminists argue that wife and whore are two sides of the same coin. Both trade in sexual services; one receives a wedding ring and respectability, the other cash. This may be crudely put, but it points up the need for all women to recognize a common problem—the straitjacketing effect of sexual stereotyping.

See also: Criminal Justice
              Incest
              Pornography
              Sexuality

Organizations:

COYOTE
P.O. Box 26354
San Francisco, CA 94126

Midtown Adolescent Resource Center
Odyssey House
309–11 East 6th Street
New York, NY 10003

SCAPEGOAT
1540 Broadway
New York, NY 10036

Resources:

Hardwork, 16 mm. color film. Order from: COYOTE, address above.
  Film on the work of COYOTE, Margo St. James and decriminalization of prostitution.

Hustling for Rights, by Marilyn Haft. New York: American Civil Liberties Union, 1974. Order from: ACLU, 22 East 40th Street, New York, NY 10016.

The Lively Commerce: Prostitution in the U.S., by Charles Winnick and Paul Kinsie. New York: Signet, 1972.

The Politics of Prostitution, by Marilyn Haft et al. Seattle: Social Research Associates, 1975. Order from: Social Research Associates, 335 N.E. 53rd Street, Seattle, WA 98105.
  Comments on current legal status, how to effect change, feminism and prostitution.

Prostitution: An Illustrated Social History, by Vern Bullough and Bonnie Bullough. New York: Crown Publishers, 1978.
  Comprehensive study of prostitution from its ancient origins to the present day. By using anthropological and sociological methodologies, the writers describe the role of women and cultural attitudes toward sexuality in each society which they discuss.

PROSTITUTE RIGHTS ORGANIZATIONS

Alley Cat
Prostitution Education Project
Ann Arbor, MI
(313) 428-7233

Beaver
c/o Toronto Wages for Housework
P.O. Box 38, Station E
Toronto, Ontario, Canada

Cat
8730 Wilshire, 5E
Beverly Hills, CA 90022
(213) 657-1738

Florida COYOTE
P.O. Box 22762
Ft. Lauderdale, FL 33335
(305) 462-5522

Mike Whitty
University of Detroit
40001 W. McNichols
Detroit, MI 48221

OCELOT
3932 Warwick, #6
Kansas City, MO 64111
(816) 735-7638

PROWL
P.O. Box 157
Spokane, WA 99210

PUMA
102 Church Street, Rm 780
Boston, MA 02114
(617) 220-2965

Seattle COYOTE
P.O. Box 4255
Seattle, WA 98105

Spread Eagles
135 11th Street N.W.
Washington, DC 20001
(202) 833-2634

Reprinted from the Spring 1978 issue of *COYOTE Howls*.

PSYCHOLOGY AND WOMEN

FREUD LAID THE FOUNDATION FOR THE DEVELOPMENT OF MUCH OF THE prevalent theory on female psychology. In discussing female psychological development as the result of biological and emotional inferiority to males, he wrote, "She feels herself at a great disadvantage, . . . and falls a victim to penis-envy, which leaves ineradicable traces on her development and character-formation, and, even in the most favorable instances, [this] is not overcome without a great expenditure of mental energy." This thinking has been criticized as biological determinism—which concludes that women are little more than victims of their biology. Further it implies that only exceptional women can overcome the emotional handicap of their biological deformities to achieve full humanity.

Psychological theory since Freud has continued to support sex stereotypes—women as expressive, men as instrumental—rather than analyzing the origins and implications of sex-typed behavior. Not only psychoanalytic theory, but all branches of psychology—clinical, experimental, developmental—have been guilty of sexism either by ignoring sex as a variable or by failing to control for sex bias in research. However, much of this thinking has come into question recently. Feminists have challenged, for example, Freud's definition of the clitoral orgasm as infantile (active, masturbatory) and the vaginal orgasm as mature (passive, receptive) along with its corollary that to become emotionally mature a woman must develop a receptive and compliant personality. Feminists have protested that this concept subverts the female personality. Masters and Johnson's research into sexuality dealt it another blow with their findings that there is no basis in biology for Freud's theory. Their research uncovered no distinction between vaginal and clitoral orgasm; physiologically, the nature of orgasm is the same regardless of the stimulation used to produce it.

Similarly, Maccoby and Jacklin have found that most sex-role differences (with the possible exception of aggression and visual-spatial ability) have little basis in biology. They locate the source of existing differences in an acculturation process whereby the child develops concepts of masculine and feminine behavior and then identifies with the appropriate sex. In addition, other research has shown that there is a greater range of difference within each sex than between the sexes.

Acceptance of proscribed behavior based on sex limits women as well as men. Phyllis Chesler points out in her book *Women and Madness* that research indicates that therapists have a psychological double standard for men and women. One study asked clinicians to indicate the traits of healthy mature adults, healthy mature males, and healthy mature females. They reported different standards for men and women. The healthy adult and healthy male corresponded, while the healthy female was defined as submissive, emotional, dependent.

Many feminists have pointed out that such biased standards of mental health limit the therapeutic profession's ability to respond to the needs of women patients. The statistics seem to substantiate this. Not only are women hospitalized more frequently and for longer periods than men, but they also have lower rates of recovery even compared to males with the same diagnosis. Taking this argument further, some feminists have suggested that psychology, as practiced on women, has served as a means of social control. Women who cannot or will not conform to societal standards of appropriate female behavior are threatened with and subjected to institutionalization, drug and shock therapy, and psychological intimidation.

Feminists are working to change this. They are studying and criticizing the theoretical and scientific basis for what has passed for theory on the psychology of women. And efforts are being made to develop new theories. While some are looking at sex-role socialization and its impact on personality, others have turned around the negative implications of sex differences to suggest that there is a distinct and positive female psychology of nurturance and cooperation. They locate the problem in the negative values attached to these so-called feminine traits and seek to identify the origin of those values as well as redefine them.

Alongside these efforts, feminist therapists are working to develop new models of therapy. Many have incorporated techniques from consciousness-raising groups—using nonauthoritarian interaction between therapist and client. Their model of female behavior is expanded to include anger, aggression, assertiveness and competence as legitimate forms of expression. And they often recommend that the potential client shop around for a therapist in whom she can place her confidence. If you are in therapy or considering therapy and want to locate a feminist therapist, contact your local women's center. Many cities also have feminist therapy referral services—consult your phone book or the resources listed below.

See also: Health Care
            Sex Roles
            Sexuality

Organizations:

National Association of Feminist
   Therapists
Boston Regional Association of Feminist
   Therapists
234 Putnam Avenue
Cambridge, MA 02139

Resources:

Counseling Women: A Bibliography. Boston: Womanspace: Feminist Therapy Collective, 1975. Order from: Womanspace: Feminist Therapy Collective, 636 Beacon Street, Boston, MA 02215.

Female Psychology: The Emerging Self, by Sue Cox. Chicago: Science Research Associates, 1976.
   This comprehensive anthology covers much of the current criticism of psychol-

ogy's analysis of women and offers feminist perspectives toward a new psychology.

Feminism as Therapy, by Anica Vesel Mander and Anne Kent Rush. New York: Random House, 1974.
A look at therapy from a feminist perspective; this book defines the use of feminism in therapy and describes it as a life process.

Feminist Therapy Roster. Seattle: Association for Women in Psychology, 1979. Order from: Laura Brown, Department of Psychology, NI-15, University of Washington, Seattle, WA 98195.
A roster of state and regional coordinators who can provide referrals to feminist therapists in their area; it also includes a guide to choosing a therapist.

Issues in the Psychology and Counseling of Women: Additional Resources. Boston: Womanspace: Feminist Therapy Collective, 1976. Order from: Womanspace: Feminist Therapy Collective, 636 Beacon Street, Boston, MA 02215.
A nineteen-page bibliography.

Notes of a Feminist Therapist, by Elizabeth Friar Williams. New York: Praeger, 1976.
Williams defines feminist therapy and explores concerns of women in therapy—love, sex, work, motherhood, loneliness, depression and more.

Psychoanalysis and Feminism, by Juliet Mitchell. New York: Pantheon, 1974.
Mitchell offers a complex analysis of Freudian theory which retains his concept of psychoanalysis and asserts the validity of his theoretical construction as a description of patriarchy.

Psychoanalysis and Women, ed. by Jean Baker Miller. Baltimore: Penguin Books, 1973.
This anthology provides a thorough look at the issues in psychoanalytic theory as they affect women.

The Psychology of Sex Differences, by Eleanor Emmons Maccoby and Carol Nagy Jacklin. Stanford: Stanford University Press, 1974.
For the serious student of psychology, this book provides a close examination of the research on sex differences and includes an exhaustive (more than 200 pages) annotated bibliography of research published since 1965.

Psychology of Women, by Juanita H. Williams. New York: Norton, 1977.
Williams, a clinical psychologist, examines the psychology of women from a biosocial context.

Too Much Anger, Too Many Tears, by Janet and Paul Gotkin. New York: Quadrangle, 1977.
A personal account of Janet Gotkin's ten years as a mental patient.

Toward a New Psychology of Women, by Jean Baker Miller. Boston: Beacon Press, 1976.
Miller examines the psychological constraints of existing sex roles and offers a new framework.

Women and Analysis, ed. by Jean Strouse. New York: Grossman, 1974.
This anthology provides a comprehensive selection of essays from theorists such

as Freud, Deutsch, Jung, Horney plus critiques of their work by Mitchell, Janeway, Mead, Stoller and more.

Women and Madness by Phyllis Chesler. Garden City: Doubleday, 1972.
With a mix of mythology, literature and science, Chesler explores the concept of madness as it is applied to women.

Women: Ethnicity and Counseling. Boston: Womanspace: Feminist Therapy Collective, 1977. Order from: Womanspace: Feminist Therapy Collective, 636 Beacon Street, Boston, MA 02215.
A twenty-four page bibliography.

Women: Sexuality, Psychology and Psychotherapy. Boston: Womanspace: Feminist Therapy Collective, 1976. Order from: Womanspace: Feminist Therapy Collective, 636 Beacon Street, Boston, MA 02215.
A twenty-nine page bibliography.

RAPE

FORCIBLE RAPE IS ONE OF THE MOST COMMON AND THE FASTEST GROWING OF violent crimes in the United States today. From 1970 to 1975 the number of rapes reported increased by 48 percent. Unfortunately, no statistics are really accurate, because most rapes go unreported. Estimates place the number of rape victims at as high as 200,000 annually.

Rape—symbolic of much that is wrong in our sexist society—was an early issue of the women's movement. It has been the subject of some of the most vigorous and insightful feminist thinking, the cause of extensive organizing across the country, and the focus of controversy among feminists, liberals, and leftists. The definition, function, and public consciousness of rape have been completely transformed by the women's movement.

Before the women's movement, rape was rationalized away through a variety of sometimes contradictory arguments and myths. The basic conception of rape fell into one of two categories: rape as the result of overwhelming sexual passion and rape as the result of a sick or deranged mind. The first conception served nicely if the victim was sexually experienced and the latter if she was a virgin.

In the first instance, the rapist was excused because he was at the mercy of the savage male sex drive, which was considered to be uncontrollable. This conception saw rape as somehow "natural" and also conveniently put at least half the blame on the victim. She was either provocatively dressed or acting in a seductive manner—in some way "asking for it." Since she had provoked the male, it was only fair that she should reap the consequences. Other myths buttressed this concept of rape—the belief that no woman could be raped against her will and, most useful and universal of all, that secretly, all women want to be raped in the first place.

The second definition of rape held that it was committed only by sexual perverts—maniacs who bore no resemblance to the average man. While this view of rape does not blame the victims, it also relieves men of a great deal of responsibility. The rapist becomes subhuman—not really a man at all.

There is, in fact, a third sort of "noncategory" of rape explanation: that rape

doesn't really exist at all; that women are natural liars and that they will use the accusation of rape to get back at men. This argument posits that the real victims of rape are not women, but falsely accused men.

Rape had previously been raised as a political issue only in the context of false accusations against men. Leftist and civil rights groups had been concerned for many years with rape in the South, where black men *were* often falsely accused, convicted, and sentenced to death. But this use of women by racist judicial systems is a way in which one powerless group has been pitted against another. Women had little to gain from these kangaroo courts (and ultimately much to lose), for it was not their own welfare that was at issue. Rather, the rape of white women was seen as defacing the property of men—it was white men who were "avenged" by the wrongful killing of blacks.

Until the consciousness-raising sessions of the early 1970's, women were as apt to believe traditional myths about rape as men were. Because they had never shared their fears and experiences, women had no basis on which to build a new perspective. In 1971, one of the earliest—and still one of the finest—feminist statements on rape appeared in *Ramparts* magazine. Susan Griffin's "Rape: The All-American Crime" denied the myths and began to build a feminist definition of rape.

First of all, rape is a crime of violence, *not* the result of sexual passion. The rapist's purpose is to defile and humiliate. Statistics indicate that 71 percent of all rapes are premeditated; often the victim is enticed to a prearranged place. This hardly supports the theory of the impulsive, passionate rape. Also, physical force is used in about 85 percent of all rapes, often with a weapon. The violence manifest in rape is immediately apparent to the victims, many of whom report fearing for their lives.

Secondly, the average rapist is not a sex maniac or deviant. Early research showed that 60 percent of the rapists studied were married and had normal sex lives. Subsequent studies have confirmed that the psychological profile of the rapist does not differ markedly from the norm.

Finally, does rape really exist only in the minds of vengeful women? A survey of rape statistics for New York City in 1975 showed that 3.4 percent of rape charges were "unfounded," a rate comparable to other felonies. But an "unfounded" case does not constitute a false report. Enforcement officials, after hearing the victim's story and examining the evidence, may not agree that the act committed qualifies as rape; in their estimation, the victim may have complied in some way or they may not consider the case prosecutable, and so they declare the case unfounded. Only .4 percent were false reports in the sense of the myth. Studies also show that the rapist is a stranger in about 80 percent of the reported cases, thereby eliminating personal revenge as a motive in the majority of cases from the outset.

Feminists view rape as the logical conclusion of sexism, as society's attitude toward women carried into action. It is one of the most insidious forms of social coercion, a constant reminder to women of their vulnerable condition. Rape is the one weapon all men hold over all women regardless of other circumstances. Despite the illegality of rape, the lack of medical, police, legal, and judicial support for the victim has amounted to the *de facto* legal and social sanction of rape.

Many rape victims do not report the crime because of the trauma of the court appearance and the low conviction rate (see chart below). Regional studies show conviction rates of as low as 10 percent. The FBI estimates that only 51 percent of reported rapists are arrested, that 76 percent of those are prosecuted, and that a full 47 percent of those are acquitted. And, compared to the chart below, these estimates are high. The woman's sexual history will be used as evidence against her while the rapist's previous arrest record will likely be ruled inadmissible. Until recently, the following advice of a seventeenth-century jurist was routinely read to the jury: "a charge such as that made against the defendant in this case is one which is easily made and once made, difficult to defend against, even if the person is innocent. Therefore, the law requires that you examine the testimony of the female person named in the information with caution." It is no wonder so many victims end up feeling that they have been raped twice—once privately by the rapist and once publicly by the court.

The women's movement has been successful in making some changes in the victim's post-rape experience. Many police departments have instituted all-female sex crimes units. Most major American cities have rape crisis centers which offer care and counseling to traumatized victims, where a woman will be given the psychological support she needs as well as information on how to report the crime. A staff member will often be available to accompany her to the hospital and police station. Continuing support groups are often available to help the woman work through her feelings over time.

In addition to providing direct services, women's groups have also taken other actions. A Wisconsin judge was recently recalled for suggesting that a fifteen-year-old rapist was only reacting normally to our sexually permissive society. (The youth was put on probation for his crime.) Many women's groups have worked to have rape laws rewritten; in many states (New York, Connecticut, and Iowa are examples) the corroboration-by-a-witness clause, unnecessary in the case of other violent crimes, has been removed from the law. A Texas group, calling itself the Kitty Genovese Project after a rape-murder victim, publishes and distributes the names of local rapists. Self-defense training for the individual woman is another essential part of anti-rape efforts. With rape the fastest growing of violent crimes, it is unlikely that women's efforts against rape will soon end.

See also: Battered Women
              Incest
              Legal Status
              Pornography
              Self-Defense

Organizations:

Feminist Alliance Against Rape
P.O. Box 21033
Washington, DC 20009

National Center for the Prevention and
   Control of Rape
National Institute of Mental Health
5600 Fishers Lane
Rockville, MD 20852

National Communications Network for the
   Elimination of Violence Against Women
4520 44th Avenue South
Minneapolis, MN 55406

Resources:

Aegis. Order from: Feminist Alliance Against Rape (address above).
   Subtitled the "Magazine on Organizing to Stop Violence Against Women," *Aegis* is the publication of the National Communications Network described above.

Against Our Will: Men, Women and Rape by Susan Brownmiller. New York: Simon and Schuster, 1975.
   The major feminist statement on rape to date. Required reading.

Forcible Rape: An Analysis of Legal Issues prepared by Battelle Memorial Institute Law and Justice Study Center, 1978. Order from: Superintendent of Documents, Government Printing Office, Washington, DC 20402.
   One of an eleven-part series, this pamphlet discusses the reasons for changing rape laws, summarizes the kinds of changes that have been made or are desirable, and gives a state-by-state overview of current rape law.

Freeing Our Lives: A Feminist Analysis of Rape Prevention. Columbus: Community Action Strategies Against Rape, 1978. Order from: Women Against Rape, P.O. Box 02084, Columbus, OH 43202.
   One of the better pamphlets on prevention, this booklet discusses community strategies women can implement to help one another. It also includes a thorough discussion of the role rape plays in our society.

The Rape Bibliography: A Collection of Abstracts. St. Louis: St. Louis Feminist Research Project, 1976. Order from: St. Louis Feminist Research Project, 4431

McPherson, St. Louis, MO 63108.

One of the most comprehensive compilations, *The Rape Bibliography* includes abstracts of research on legal, medical, psychological, and sociological aspects of rape. There is a final section on popular works.

Rape: The Price of Coercive Sexuality, by Lorenne Clark and Debra Lewis. Toronto: The Women's Press, 1977. Order from: Canadian Women's Educational Press, 280 Bloor Street West, Toronto, Ontario, Canada.

Written by two feminist criminologists, this is the report of their research on rape in Toronto. A very important new work.

FLOW OF RAPE CASES
THROUGH THE CRIMINAL JUSTICE SYSTEM

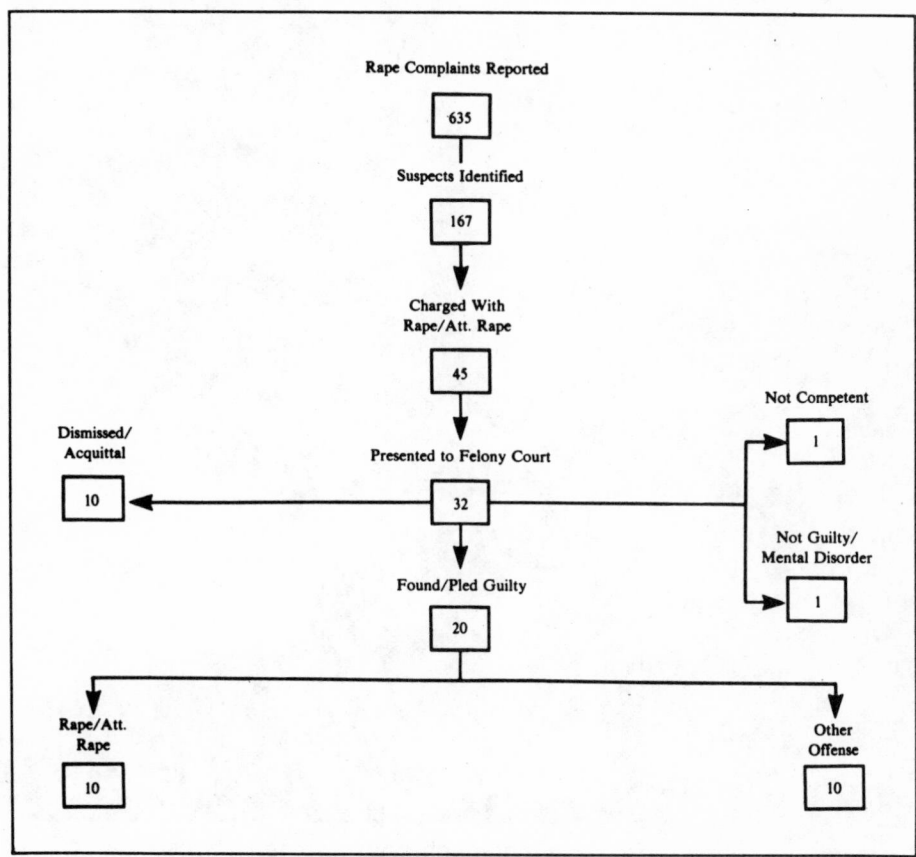

Reprinted from *Forcible Rape: An Analysis of Legal Issues,* prepared by Battelle Memorial Institute Law and Justice Study Center for the U.S. Department of Justice. Chart is based on data from King County (Seattle, Washington), 1974 and Jackson County (Kansas City, Missouri), 1975.

Catalyst is a national organization which helps women choose, launch and advance their careers. Its library is the major national clearinghouse on careers, career education and employment for women. Hundreds of women use the information center each year.

RESEARCH AND INFORMATION

ONE OF THE HALLMARKS OF THE WOMEN'S MOVEMENT HAS BEEN THE DIVERSITY of perspectives, approaches, and projects it has taken up. While some women's groups have been primarily political, others have concentrated on providing services. There has also been a strong information and research arm. Although women scholars have sometimes been criticized by activists for being "armchair feminists," they have made a valuable contribution to the women's movement. In fact, the researchers and information providers have been an integral part of the women's movement from the beginning.

Women's research and information projects vary enormously in size and sophistication. The basic information provider to and about the women's movement is the local women's center. Found in small and large cities all across the country, women's centers are able to provide referrals to services and women's organizations in local areas. They may also provide a small resource collection, counseling, or other programs. National information centers have also been formed, usually in specific subject areas (see box below). A number of research centers have also been established over the years, some independent, some located at colleges and universities. These too differ in size and subject specialty.

In 1975, the women's research and information centers formed a national network, the Women's Information Services Network, to facilitate information exchange, identify common needs, and work together on projects which meet these needs. We are in an age in which "knowledge is power" and access to and control over information is crucial to effective functioning. The women's movement has responded to this challenge with its own vital and invaluable information community.

See also: Women's Centers
          Women's Studies

Organizations:

Institute for Studies in Equality
926 J Street
Sacramento, CA 95814

Women's Action Alliance
370 Lexington Avenue
New York, NY 10017

Women's Information Services Network
P.O. Box 31635
San Francisco, CA 94131

Resources:

New Feminist Scholarship: A Guide to Bibliographies, compiled by Jane Williamson. Old Westbury: The Feminist Press, 1979. Order from: The Feminist Press, P.O. Box 334, Old Westbury, NY 11568.

A comprehensive, annotated bibliography of bibliographies in women's studies.

With Reference to Women: An Annotated Bibliography of Reference Materials on Women compiled by Linda Seckelson-Simpson. Evanston: Northwestern University, 1975. Order from: Library, Northwestern University, Evanston, IL 60201.

This excellent guide lists general and specialized reference sources in five subject areas. Each entry is carefully annotated.

Women's Information Services Network Directory. San Francisco: WISN, forthcoming. Order from: Women's Information Services Network (address above).

A directory of women's information and research centers across the country. Each entry describes in some detail the services and resources available.

Women's Studies: A Guide to Reference Sources, compiled by Kathleen Burke McKee. Storrs: University of Connecticut Library, 1977. Order from: University of Connecticut Library, Acquisitions Department, Box U-T, Storrs, CT 06268.

An excellent guide to reference works, this paperback describes library catalogs, handbooks, directories, statistical sources, indexes, abstracts, and bibliographies.

INFORMATION AND RESEARCH CENTERS

Catalyst
14 East 60th Street
New York, NY 10022

Schlesinger Library
Radcliffe College
3 James Street
Cambridge, MA 02138

The Feminist Press
P.O. Box 334
Old Westbury, NY 11568

Center for Women Policy Studies
2000 P Street N.W.
Washington, DC 20036

SPRINT
Women's Equity Action League
805 15th Street N.W.
Washington, DC 20009

Clearinghouse International
Eleanor Association
16 North Wabash
Chicago, IL 60602

Institute for Education and Research
on Women and Work
Cornell University
7 East 43rd Street
New York, NY 10017

Lesbian Herstory Archives
215 West 92nd Street
New York, NY 10025

Business and Professional Women's
Foundation
2012 Massachusetts Avenue N.W.
Washington, DC 20036

Center for Research on Women in
Higher Education and the
Professions
Cheever House
Wellesley College
Wellesley, MA 02181

Center for the American Woman and
Politics
Rutgers University
New Brunswick, NJ 08901

Sophia Smith Collection
Smith College Library
Northampton, MA 01060

Women's Collection
Northwestern University Library
Evanston, IL 60201

Center for Research on Women
103 Polya Hall
Stanford University
Stanford, CA 94305

Center for the Sociological Study of
Women
605 Prince Lucien Campbell Hall
Eugene, OR 97403

New Alexandria Library for Lesbian
Women
3523 North Halsted
Chicago, IL 60657

RIGHT-WING ATTACKS

WHEN THE SECOND WAVE OF AMERICAN FEMINISM BEGAN IN THE 1960's, ITS opponents believed that the bra-burners could be ridiculed out of existence. But feminists, schooled by the civil rights and antiwar movements, were not intimidated by crude jokes or abusive remarks. They built institutions, organizations, communications networks, and political lobbies; within ten years the national consciousness toward women had changed drastically. Hard work bore fruit: the 1973 Supreme Court decision striking down state abortion laws, the passage of important educational and employment legislation, support for the ERA. These successes and more have made feminism a target of the right wing.

More than a dozen right-wing groups operate nationwide. Some sell an entire platform which includes states' rights, the centrality of the family, and an end to federal involvement in the business sector. Others harp on single issues: abortion, bussing, unions, taxes.

Various right-wing political action committees (PACs) have annual budgets of several million dollars. Among these are the Committee for the Survival of a Free Congress (CSFC) which rates congressional voting records from a conservative standpoint, and the National Conservative Political Action Committee (NCPAC) which provides campaign services to right-wing candidates. Another group with a general conservative program, Young Americans for Freedom, attracts conservative high-school and college youth. Single-issue groups include the National Right to Work Committee (anti-union), the Council for National Defense (arms spending over social services), TRIM (Tax Reform Immediately), and the Right to Keep and Bear Arms Political Victory Fund.

Often called the "new" right because of its use of modern technology and well-

The Gurus of the New Right Maintain a Tight Web of Relationships

They serve on one another's governing bodies, trade contributions of money and skill, and support each other's special interests in a variety of ways.

AAUCG
Richard A. Viguerie, Rep. Steve Symms, Roger Stone, Sen. Jesse Helms

NRTWC
Richard A. Viguerie, M. Stanton Evans, Reed Larson, Hugh Newton, Rep. Steve Symms, Rep. Ben Blackburn

MANION
M. Stanton Evans, Reed Larson, Sen. Jesse Helms, Howard Phillips, Phyllis Schlafly, Rep. Phillip Crane, Clarence Manion

CFTR
M. Stanton Evans, Roger Stone, Joseph Coors, Charles Black

ACU
Richard A. Viguerie, M. Stanton Evans, Rep. Steve Symms, Howard Phillips, Phyllis Schlafly, Rep. Phillip Crane, Joseph Coors, Charles Black, Rep. Lawrence P. McDonald

YAF
Richard A. Viguerie, M. Stanton Evans, Reed Larson, Rep. Steve Symms, Howard Phillips, Phyllis Schlafly, Rep. Phillip Crane, Charles Black, Rep. Lawrence P. McDonald

CSFC
Richard A. Viguerie, Rep. Steve Symms, Sen. Jesse Helms, Joseph Coors, Rep. Lawrence P. McDonald, Paul Weyrich

HERITAGE
Richard A. Viguerie, Hugh Newton, Rep. Steve Symms, Rep. Ben Blackburn, Rep. Phillip Crane, Joseph Coors, Paul Weyrich

NCPAC
Richard A. Viguerie, Roger Stone, Sen. Jesse Helms, Joseph Coors, Charles Black

CC
Richard A. Viguerie, Rep. Steve Symms, Rep. Ben Blackburn, Howard Phillips, Joseph Coors, Charles Black, Rep. Lawrence P. McDonald, Paul Weyrich

BIRCH
Phyllis Schlafly, Clarence Manion, Joseph Coors, Rep. Lawrence P. McDonald

organized campaigns, the new right's ideology is not significantly different from that of the "old" right. Both exploit middle-class economic fears of being caught between the demands of the poor and rising inflation, and social fears about the loss of traditional values. First, the economic: the value of the dollar is plummeting, minorities and women are competing for increasingly hard-to-find jobs, the welfare rolls seem to be growing as the specter of recession draws nearer. Second, the social: the availability of birth control; abortion-rights demands; increasing numbers of divorces and of women who work; the growth of feminism; and demands by homosexuals for civil rights are seen as threats to the nuclear family. Among the right wing's solutions to these economic and social concerns is its program for women. They want women out of the labor market, confined to the home, raising children and keeping house. They uphold the ideal of the nuclear family, the privileges of the husband and the subordination of the wife. This formula sounds uncomfortably similar to the Nazi slogan, *"kinder, küche, kirche"*—children, kitchen, church.

Special campaigns are directed at pulling women into the conservative camp. STOP ERA, "Right to Life" groups, and the Eagle Forum have been successful at identifying women who are frightened by social change and political responsibility. STOP ERA, a conservative coalition, includes, among others, the Daughters of the American Revolution, Young Americans for Freedom, National Council of Catholic Women, the Women's Christian Temperance Union, the Mormon Church, the Union of Orthodox Jewish Congregations, and the Parent-Teacher Associations in Illinois and Texas. Some of the false claims used to pull women into opposition organizations are that the ERA will permit homosexuals to marry, will eliminate single-sex bathrooms and dormitories, will end a husband's financial responsibilities to his wife, and will make it difficult for a woman to receive alimony and child-care payments in case of divorce. Still others claim that the ERA will take jurisdiction over marriage, property rights, divorce and child custody away from the states and give it to the federal government. To stop ERA, money is poured into campaigns to influence the citizenry and legislatures of unratified states. In the July 1977 issue of *Ms.* magazine, Lisa Cronin Wohl described the pressure that powerful Mormon leaders brought to bear on members of the Nevada state legislature in order to defeat ratification.

The so-called Right to Life groups seek to deny women the right to abortion. In St. Paul, Minnesota, "Right to Lifers" intimidatingly photographed women entering a Planned Parenthood abortion clinic and also made telephoned threats to clinic volunteers. A group of anti-abortion women in Rochester, New York, chained themselves to fixtures in a hospital examination room during an anti-abortion demonstration. In 1977 and 1978, six firebombings and more than a dozen cases of violence against abortion clinics were documented by the National Abortion Rights Action League. Another technique of harassment is to threaten Catholic doctors and medical personnel with excommunication if they perform or help with abortions. "Right to Lifers," bankrolled by the Catholic Church, the Mormon Church, and insurance companies, attended pre-Houston state women's conferences *en masse.* The Mormon Church made certain that sparsely populated Utah (less than one million residents) had the largest convention (14,000 people) which voted down all the recommendations of the National Plan of Action.

At a political workshop at the National Right to Life convention in June 1978, Dr. Robert Sassone counseled ". . . espionage is not illegal or immoral . . . have some of your members join the local NOW. You don't think we'd have gotten this far without people at the top of the opposition." A few who attended this conference tried to influence the rightists to adopt anti-nuclear energy and anti-capital punishment platforms as consonant with a genuine concern for life. But the official line nixed the linkage: "Unborn life is perfect, whereas born life is imperfect."

Anti-abortion forces pushed legislative and judicial campaigns in 1978. Their strong turnout in New York State gave them third place on the ballot—displacing the Liberal Party. Their opposition also helped to defeat two progressive senators, Don Fraser of Minnesota and Dick Clark of Iowa, in the November elections. During the 95th Congress they had ninety-five anti-abortion bills introduced and succeeded in attaching amendments to the Labor-HEW appropriations bill and the military defense budget which severely limit federal funding for abortions. Only if the mother's life is endangered, when rape or incest has occurred, or when severe and long-lasting physical damage would result can federal moneys now support abortion. An amendment to the Foreign Assistance Appropriations bill forbade the use of federal funds to pay for abortions for Peace Corps volunteers *with no exceptions*. To get their bill passed, proponents of the pregnancy disability amendment had to accept compromise language which allows employers to exempt abortions from medical coverage except when the mother's life is endangered.

The Eagle Forum is headed by Phyllis Schlafly. Besides opposing ERA, this group tries to remove what they consider to be obscene literature from community libraries and the classroom. During 1977–78, Forum members and sympathizers in Illinois, Maryland, Massachusetts, and Texas claimed that the feminist health classic *Our Bodies, Ourselves* encouraged "perversions" like masturbation, homosexuality, and premarital sex. Although this attention caused the book's sales to rise, it was barred from the shelves of several libraries—despite letters of support from medical professionals, church leaders, and educators.

Lately the right has targeted gay people as well as feminists, since they too challenge the concept of the nuclear family. Anita Bryant's Save Our Children campaign led to the repeal of antidiscrimination laws which protected the civil rights of gays in Dade County, Florida; Wichita, Kansas; St. Paul, Minnesota; and Eugene, Oregon. Initiative 13, a referendum proposed by Save Our Moral Ethics in Seattle, Washington, attempted to repeal gay rights statutes and to eliminate the enforcement power of the Office of Women's Programs in one stroke. Fortunately, the attempt was defeated.

The right employs many tactics. Campaigns by Save Our Children, STOP ERA, and Right to Life deepen the fears of unsophisticated women by insisting that if feminism succeeds they will no longer be supported by their husbands or allowed to be housewives and mothers. Feminists are made to appear out of touch with women when hitherto silent housewives speak out against women's equality. These women picket, write letters, and attend and disrupt women's conferences, meetings and conventions. Toll-free hotlines give instructions and addresses. At state International Women's Year conferences, right-wing women were assisted in their attempts to take over the conferences by their leaders' familiarity with parliamentary procedure, their use of walkie-talkies to stay in communication, and their willingness to disrupt workshops. Feminists were outraged at their opponents' reliance on male floor leaders.

Women on the right find reenforcement for their views in the church and their cultural milieu. The Mormon and Catholic Churches are particularly influential in trying to defeat ERA and pro-choice movements and they send the message from the pulpit and in informal gatherings. Marabel Morgan, author of *The Total Woman,* has given voice to sexual politics that are compatible with the social perspective of the "new" right. Women, she counsels, should take care of the home, the children, and do everything possible to please their husbands. Morgan stresses that this runs the gamut from black lace negligees and sex-on-demand to professional housekeeping.

Recently the right has been trying to organize a constitutional convention to amend the United States Constitution. Its strategy is two-pronged: fourteen states have agreed to a convention to consider a "Human Life" (i.e., anti-abortion) amendment and twenty-eight states have asked for a convention to balance the federal budget, a euphemism for cutting nearly all spending for social services. If six more states agree, Congress must pass legislation which prepares the way for a convention. Although the right insists that a constitutional convention would only insert a "pro-life" or balanced-budget amendment into the Constitution, insiders whisper that major changes could be effected and that the hidden agenda is to "reexamine" and revise the Bill of Rights. Sounds impossible? The times, afflicted by rising inflation, the threat of deep economic crisis, and social dysfunction, are ripe for the right. Of late, they have defeated or rescinded progressive efforts before liberals knew what had hit them.

See also: Abortion
Affirmative Action
ERA
International Women's Year
Lesbians
Politics
Sexuality
Women's Movement

Organizations:

National Organization for Women Action
   Center
425 13th Street N.W.
Washington, DC 20004

National Women's Political Caucus
1411 K Street N.W.
Washington, DC 20005

Women's Lobby
201 Massachusetts Avenue N.E.
Washington, DC 20002

Resources:

A Citizen's Guide to the Right Wing. Washington: Americans for Democratic Action, 1978. Order from: ADA, 1411 K Street, N.W., Washington, DC 20005.
   Tries to alert the citizenry about what the right is up to, how it gets its money, what particular groups and individuals on the right are doing.

"America's New Right," by Andrew Kopkind. *New Times* (September 30, 1977).

Crusader Kopkind sets out to understand what is in the hearts—and on the minds—of the right in middle America.

RURAL WOMEN

THERE IS NO STANDARD DEFINITION OF "RURAL," EITHER IN THE UNITED States or elsewhere, and consequently there is no precise calculation of the size of the American rural population. The U.S. Bureau of the Census, in its current Population Reports, uses a three-way division of the national population, allowing for residence in the central cities, in suburban areas, and in non-metropolitan areas.[1] (Non-metropolitan areas are counties which contain no city of 50,000 residents or more.) Under this classification, which is at best approximate, 61.5 million people live in central cities, 80 million in the suburbs, and nearly 66 million people in non-metropolitan areas.

About one-third of America's population, then, can be considered rural. To give this figure of 66 million more meaning: it is larger than the total population of the one hundred largest cities in the country, larger than the population of any country in Europe, and the equivalent of the population of the ninth most populous country in the world.[2]

Women and girls comprise slightly more than half of this population, or 34 to 35 million. This total number of rural women is a sizable one, and one clearly worthy of attention. And, contrary to the trends of the past, it is a total that recently has been increasing: "Since 1970, changes in rural and urban population flows have occurred so rapidly that non-metropolitan areas are not only retaining people but are receiving an actual net immigration as well."[3]

This rural population is a dispersed and diverse one. Its largest clusters—which are not necessarily discrete—are: Farm, Rural Black, Rural Spanish-origin, Migrant, Native American and Native Alaskan, and Appalachian. These can be sketched briefly as follows.

In 1920, nearly 32 million Americans lived on farms. Today, the farm population is estimated at less than 9 million, or about 5 percent of the total population. According to the most recent information from the Census Bureau and the Department of Agriculture, it is young people and blacks who are leading the current decline in farm population. States with the most farms, although not necessarily the most farm acreage, include Illinois, Indiana, Iowa, Kentucky, Minnesota, North Carolina, Ohio, Tennessee, Texas and Wisconsin, all of which

[1]Much of the data for this paper was taken from the Census Bureau's September 1975 Special Studies, "Social and Economic Characteristics of the Metropolitan and Non-Metropolitan Population: 1974 and 1970." Other publications and abstracts from the Bureau of the Census were also used. No attempt has been made to challenge any of the figures, although unemployment data for both rural individuals and females are often questioned on the grounds that the method and bases used to determine unemployment rates exclude many who should be counted. The federally established "poverty line" is also regarded by many as unrealistically low.

[2]Swanson, Gordon I., *Rural Education News*, Vol. 22, #1, March 1970. Cited by Lewis R. Tamblyn in "Inequality: A Portrait of Rural America," Rural Education Association, Washington, DC, 1973.

[3]Beale, Calvin L. and Glenn V. Fuguitt, "The New Pattern of Nonmetropolitan Population Change," Center for Demography and Ecology, Working Paper 75-22, University of Wisconsin, Madison, 1975. Data confirmed by 1974 Appalachian Regional Commission Report.

On small family farms where every hand is needed, women work just as hard as men, and at many of the same jobs. © *Sylvia Johnson, Woodfin Camp and Associates*

Not all rural women live and work on small family farms; thousands of women, most of them Mexican-Americans, travel across the country following the ripening crops. These farm workers are among the most poorly paid of all Americans. © *George Ballis, National Land for People*

have more than 100,000 farm units. Average income of farm families fluctuates; the 1973 figure was $11,639, and the 1974 figure $9,211. With respect to educational attainment, statistics show that in 1970, 31 percent of the farm residents had completed high school, 7 percent had one to three years of college, and 4 percent had four or more years of college.

There are 23.5 million black Americans. Five million or 22 percent of them are classified as rural. Predominant concentrations of rural blacks are in regions identified as the coastal plain tobacco and peanut belt, the old coastal plain cotton belt, and the Mississippi delta. A significant number also live in the Ozark-Ouchita uplands, the southern Appalachian coalfields, and the Blue Ridge, Great Smokies and Great Valley.[4] Black ownership of land has diminished to less than half of what it was in 1950.[5] The annual income of a rural black family headed by a male is $6,641; for female heads the figure slips to $3,780. About 25 percent of rural blacks have completed high school.

Two million, out of a total of 10.7 million people of Spanish origin, live in rural areas of the United States. These include Chicanos, Cubans, Latin Americans, Mexicans, Mexican-Americans, Puerto Ricans, and "others." They are concentrated most heavily in the Southwest, from California to Texas. An estimated 8 percent of all Spanish-origin people in the country are agricultural workers. Educational attainment figures show that 24 percent of all the men and 31 percent of the women are high school graduates and roughly one-fourth have had less than five years of school.

About 800,000 agricultural workers follow the crops. They are based primarily in southern and central California, the Rio Grande Valley of Texas and southern Florida. Many are Spanish-speaking. Migratory workers engage in a common occupation, but have little cohesion as a group. "Each harvest collects and regroups them. They live under common conditions, but create no techniques for meeting common problems. The public acknowledges the existence of migrants yet declines to accept them as full members of the community."[6] Income data for migrant farm workers is given in "daily" wages. In 1973, that wage averaged $9.10 a day for workers 14 to 19 years of age, and $12.05 a day for workers over 20. The total of paid working days in a year is extremely low—generally less than 25 per person, so it is usually necessary for every family member to take work where available.

Today there are about 800,000 United States citizens who consider themselves Native Americans or Native Alaskans. They are concentrated primarily in Arizona, Oklahoma, New Mexico, California and Alaska, although significant populations also live in Minnesota, North Carolina, South Carolina, South Dakota, Washington and Wisconsin. About 500,000 live on, or adjacent to, reservations. Overall 70 percent of this population is rural and 30 percent is urban. Native Americans have the distinction, among all American minorities, of having

[4]Tamblyn, Lewis R., "Inequality: A Portrait of Rural America," op cit., p. 8.
[5]Toward a Platform for Rural America, "Report on the First National Conference on Rural America, April 14–17, 1975," Rural America, Inc. and Rural Housing Alliance, Washington, DC, 1975.
[6]National Advisory Commission on Rural Poverty, "The People Left Behind," 1967, cited by Tamblyn, op. cit.

the least education, the lowest income, the highest infant mortality and the shortest life expectancy.[7]

Appalachia refers to an economically deprived region delineated in the Appalachian Regional Development Act of 1965, containing 397 counties in 13 Eastern states. Those states which include portions of Appalachia are: Alabama, Georgia, Kentucky, Maryland, Mississippi, New York, North Carolina, Ohio, Pennsylvania, South Carolina, Tennessee, Virginia and West Virginia. The total population approachs 20 million people. The average income in 1973 was $3,098. For the region as a whole, one quarter of the people live in poverty. In some states—Kentucky and Mississippi, for example—the percentage of families living in poverty is as high as 39 percent and 34 percent, respectively. Literacy rates in Appalachia are below the national average.

In general, these and other rural Americans have a higher incidence of social problems and receive a lower per capita share of federal dollars designed to meet those problems than the rest of the population.[8] Poverty, illiteracy, malnutrition, underemployment, infant mortality, economic exploitation, migration and lack of opportunity are all appreciably more prevalent in rural than urban areas. And the more sparsely settled and removed from the population centers an area is, the higher the incidence of poverty and its concomitant circumstances.

To these broad characteristics of rural life can also be added the special hardships of life in the clusters of subgroups described above, which make up so large a percentage of our rural population: the racism to which rural blacks, Native Americans and Alaskans, and Spanish-speaking people are subjected; the language barriers of the Spanish, Asian and other groups for whom English is a second language, the debilitating and demoralizing effect of transience on the migrant population; the chronic unemployment and welfare dependency in Appalachia.

Organizations:

Council on Appalachian Women
P.O. Box 490
Mars Hill, NC 28754

National Rural Center
1828 L Street N.W.
Washington, DC 20036

Rural American Women
1522 K Street N.W.
Washington, DC 20005

Women Involved in Farm Economics
P.O. Box 172
Crook, CO 80726

Resources:

Annotated Bibliography of Women in Rural America; with a Review of the

---

[7] *Ibid.*

[8] McClellan, John L. (Chr., Committee on Government Operations), Foreword to Tamblyn, "Inequality: A Portrait of Rural America." Documentation appears in some twenty pages of tables in that publication. While the concerns of this report extend beyond the rural poor, it may be useful to note the most concentrated areas of rural poverty: Southeast and Southcentral regions; Appalachia; Black Belt of the South; Ozark region; Southwest Mexican and American Indian populations; Northern Great Lakes region of Michigan, Wisconsin and Minnesota; northern New England and New York; and Indian population of the Upper Great Plains.

Reprinted from *Educational Needs of Rural Women and Girls*. Washington: National Advisory Council on Women's Educational Programs, 1977.

Literature About Women in Rural America, by Lynda Joyce. University Park: Department of Agricultural Economics and Rural Sociology, 1976. Order from: Department of Economics and Rural Sociology, Agricultural Experimental Station, Pennsylvania State University, University Park, PA 16802.

Country Women. Order from: Country Women, P.O. Box 208, Albion, CA 95410.

A monthly magazine focusing on country life as an alternative lifestyle for women and featuring articles on a variety of topics; includes creative writing.

Educational Needs of Rural Women and Girls, by Kathryn F. Clarenbach. Washington: National Advisory Council on Women's Educational Programs, 1977. Order from: National Advisory Council on Women's Educational Programs, 1832 M Street, N.W., Washington, DC 20036.

This report on the Council's investigation of the educational needs of rural women and girls provides good background information, recommendations and a program-focused bibliography.

Hillbilly Women, by Kathy Kahn. New York: Avon, 1974.

This book records the personal stories of the women of southern Appalachia. Insightful and moving.

Research on Appalachian Women and Girls. Washington: Association for the Development of Education, n.d. Order from: ADE, 1522 K Street N.W., Washington, DC 20005.

A research report covering issues such as health care, education, employment; includes recommendations and a bibliography.

Rural Women Workers in the Twentieth Century: An Annotated Bibliography, by Collette Moser and Deborah Johnson. East Lansing: Michigan State University, Department of Agricultural Economics, 1973. Order from: Department of Agricultural Economics, College of Agriculture and National Resources, Michigan State University, East Lansing, MI 48823.

A comprehensive bibliography including both farm and nonfarm work, household and manual labor.

SELF-DEFENSE

MANY BOOKS ON SELF-DEFENSE COUNSEL THE PROSPECTIVE VICTIM TO RUN. IF escape is impossible, she must rely on her knowledge of self-defense. Self-defense as it is taught today is usually a mixture of Eastern martial arts—judo, karate, tae kwon do, jujitsu, aikido—and street fighting, none of which employ weapons.

During the early days of the women's movement, feminists organized self-defense classes to learn how to defend themselves from rapists and muggers. These classes are successful in changing many women's attitudes from helplessness to self-confidence; often, the difference between a victim and a nonvictim is the attitude that she projects. When a woman is committed to self-defense her mental alertness and discipline are as important as her physical conditioning. Her reflexes must be exact; the mind must know that it can depend on the body. The woman

A self-defense display at a rally for International Women's Day, Cambridge, Massachusetts, March 1978. © *Peggy McMahon*

must also accept that in defending herself, she may cause pain to her attacker. This is often difficult for a woman to do, since it means overcoming all of her social conditioning.

Recently, the plea of self-defense has been used in court by women like Roxanne Gay and Pat Evans, who were accused of killing their husbands after sustaining repeated physical abuse, as well as Joan Little, Inez Garcia, and Yvonne Wanrow, who allegedly killed the men who raped or attempted to rape them. Some of these women have been acquitted, and their cases have helped to establish women's legal right to self-defense.

See also: Battered Women
Pornography
Rape

Organizations:

Center for Constitutional Rights
Women's Self-Defense Law Project
853 Broadway
New York, NY 10003

Resources:

In Defense of Ourselves, by Linda Sanford and Ann Fetter. New York: Doubleday, 1979.
Workbook on self-defense focuses on defending oneself against rape.

Practical Self-defense for Women, by Judith Lushsinger. Minneapolis: Dillon Press, 1977. Order from: Dillon Press, 500 South 3rd Street, Minneapolis, MN 55415.

An illustrated manual showing how to achieve holds and how to hurt an attacker.

Representation of Women Who Defend Themselves In Response to Physical or Sexual Assault, by Elizabeth M. Schneider, Susan B. Jordan and Cristina C. Arguedas. New York: Center for Constitutional Rights, 1978. Order from: Center for Constitutional Rights, 853 Broadway, New York, NY 10003.

This informative pamphlet covers the historical, social and legal background as well as the legal defense theories and strategies for cases of self-defense in response to physical and sexual assault.

SEX DISCRIMINATION IN EDUCATION

WOMEN AND GIRLS EXPERIENCE SEX DISCRIMINATION IN EDUCATION AS STU-dents and as teachers, at all levels from preschool to postgraduate, in educational programs and in extracurricular activities. Sometimes discriminatory behavior takes a subtle form—when an elementary school teacher asks for "two strong boys" to help carry heavy equipment and at the same time tells girl students that it's not "ladylike" to play active games. Sometimes the discrimination is more blatant—as when a woman faculty member is denied tenure because of anti-nepotism rules. Blatant or subtle, the following patterns can be found in virtually every school and college across the country: sex-role stereotypes enforced by teacher behavior, biased textbooks and curricular materials, sex-segregated courses, sex-segregated schools, virtually no extracurricular athletic opportunities for girls, expulsion of pregnant students, sex-biased vocational and academic counseling, higher college admissions standards for women, discrimination in student financial aid, lower salaries for women teachers, women faculty concentrated in lower ranks and underrepresented in administration.

A few specific examples will illustrate the patterns listed. In one southwestern school district, out of a total $10 million worth of athletic facilities and equipment, girls were allowed the use of only the tennis courts and balls. An American Council on Education study done in 1972 revealed that of 188,900 freshmen surveyed, 44 percent of the women had a B+ grade point average, while only 29 percent of the men did. Half of 136 different vocational courses nationwide have enrollments of 90 percent one sex or the other, and girls are concentrated in those courses which lead to low-paying jobs. Research from the National Education Association shows the following figures for elementary and secondary schools in 1970–71: women were 67.2 percent of teachers, 15.3 percent of principals, 15 percent of assistant principals, and 0.6 percent of superintendents. None of these statistics correlate with women's educational background: women earned 74 percent of B.A.'s in education, 56 percent of M.A.'s in education, 20 percent of M.S.'s in education administration, 21 percent of the Ph.D.'s in education and 8.5 percent of the Ph.D.'s in education administration.

Most of this discrimination is now against the law, but the practices and patterns run deep and the laws only have begun to be enforced. The laws that exist were *passed* only through the agitations of concerned parents and citizens, women's

OVERLAP OF EMPLOYMENT COVERAGE IN FEDERAL LAWS AND REGULATIONS CONCERNING SEX DISCRIMINATION IN EDUCATIONAL INSTITUTIONS

	Equal Pay Act Amended	Executive Order 11246 Amended	Public Health Service Act Title[1] VII & VIII	Title VII Civil Rights Act, 1964 Amended	Title IX Education Amendments 1972
Recruitment		X	X	X	X
Hiring		X	X	X	X
Salary	X	X	X	X	X
Back Pay	X	X[2]		X	X
Assignment/Job Classification		X	X	X	X
Promotion		X	X	X	X
Tenure		X	X	X	X
Grants/Awards[3]	X[4]	X	X	X	X
Termination		X	X	X	X
Anti-Nepotism Policy		X	X[5]	X	X
Marital Status		X		X	X
Family Status[6]		X		X	X
Pregnancy/Maternity		X	X	X	X
Medical Benefits	X	X	X[7]	X	X
Retirement Benefits[8]	X	X	X[7]	X	X
Insurance Benefits[9]	X	X	X[7]	X	X
Grievance Procedures			X	X	X
Affirmative Action Programs[10]		X		X[11]	X[11]

[1] Applies only to professional and other staff who work directly with applicants or students in health-related training programs.

[2] E.O. 11246 will pursue back pay only if not covered at the time by Title VII, EPA, or National Labor Relations Act.

[3] Financial support for training, attending professional meetings, conferences and related activities, selection for tuition assistance, sabbaticals and leaves to pursue training.

[4] Depending upon type of award and degree of employer control.

[5] Not specifically stated, but may be implied.

[6] Parental status, head of household or principal wage earner.

[7] Public Health Service Act — Regulations state the "(f)ringe benefits available by virtue of employment may not be discriminatory", but it does not identify specific fringe benefits as does Title IX and E.O. (Federal Register, Vol. 40 No. 130, July 7, 1975).

[8] EEOC requirements stronger than others.

[9] Insurance includes life, accident and hospital.

[10] Not required by Title VII, but may be ordered if discrimination is found.

[11] May be ordered if discrimination is found.

This chart was prepared for WEAL by Dr. Norma K. Raffel for a study done under contract with the National Commission on the Observance of International Women's Year and is printed and distributed by the WEAL Educational and Legal Defense Fund, 733 15th Street, N.W., Suite 200, Washington, D.C. 20005. It may be reproduced in whole or part without permission, provided credit is given to WEAL Fund.

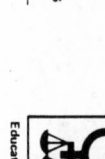

WOMEN'S EQUITY ACTION LEAGUE

Educational and Legal Defense Fund

organizations, and the students and teachers themselves; they will be *enforced* only through constant monitoring by these same groups and individuals.

See also: Affirmative Action
Financial Aid for Education
Title IX
Women's Educational Equality Act

Organizations:

American Federation of Teachers
Women's Committee
1816 Chestnut Street
Philadelphia, PA 19103

National Coalition for Women and Girls in Education
c/o Leslie Gladstone
Women's Equity Action League
805 15th Street N.W.
Washington, DC 20005

Women Educators
P.O. Box 218
Red Bank, NJ 07701

Women's Educational Equity
Communications Network
Far West Laboratory
1855 Folsom Street
San Francisco, CA 94103

Resources:

And Jill Came Tumbling After: Sexism in American Education, by Judith Stacey, et al. New York: Dell, 1974.

This anthology includes materials on sexist education from preschool to the graduate level. An annotated bibliography completes the volume.

Federal Laws and Regulations Concerning Sex Discrimination in Educational Institutions. Washington: The Project on the Status and Education of Women, 1977. Order from: the Project, address above.

This poster-sized chart includes Executive Order 11246, Title VII of the Civil Rights Act, the Equal Pay Act, Title IX of the Education Amendments of 1972, Titles VII and VIII of the Public Health Service Act.

A Handbook of State Laws and Policies Affecting Equal Rights for Women in Education. Denver: Equal Rights for Women in Education Project, Education Commission of the States, 1975. Order from: Education Commission of the States, 300 Lincoln Tower, 1860 Lincoln Street, Denver, CO 80203.

Although the Project is no longer in existence, this excellent *Handbook* is still being distributed. In a state-by-state listing, "laws, executive orders, regulations, guidelines, administrative structures and procedures" which relate to employment, admissions, and access to programs are summarized. Each state's chapter includes the following sections: State labor laws, Fair employment practices legislation, State anti-discriminatory agency, Administrative promulgations pursuant to state fair employment practices legislation, other pending or passed legislation, Equal Rights Amendment, Elementary and secondary level education policies, State commission on the status of women.

Resources for Ending Sex Bias in Schools. Washington: Project on Equal Education Rights, 1978. Order from: PEER, 1029 Vermont Avenue N.W., Washington, DC 20005.

This free listing includes books and other resources for the teacher, parent or

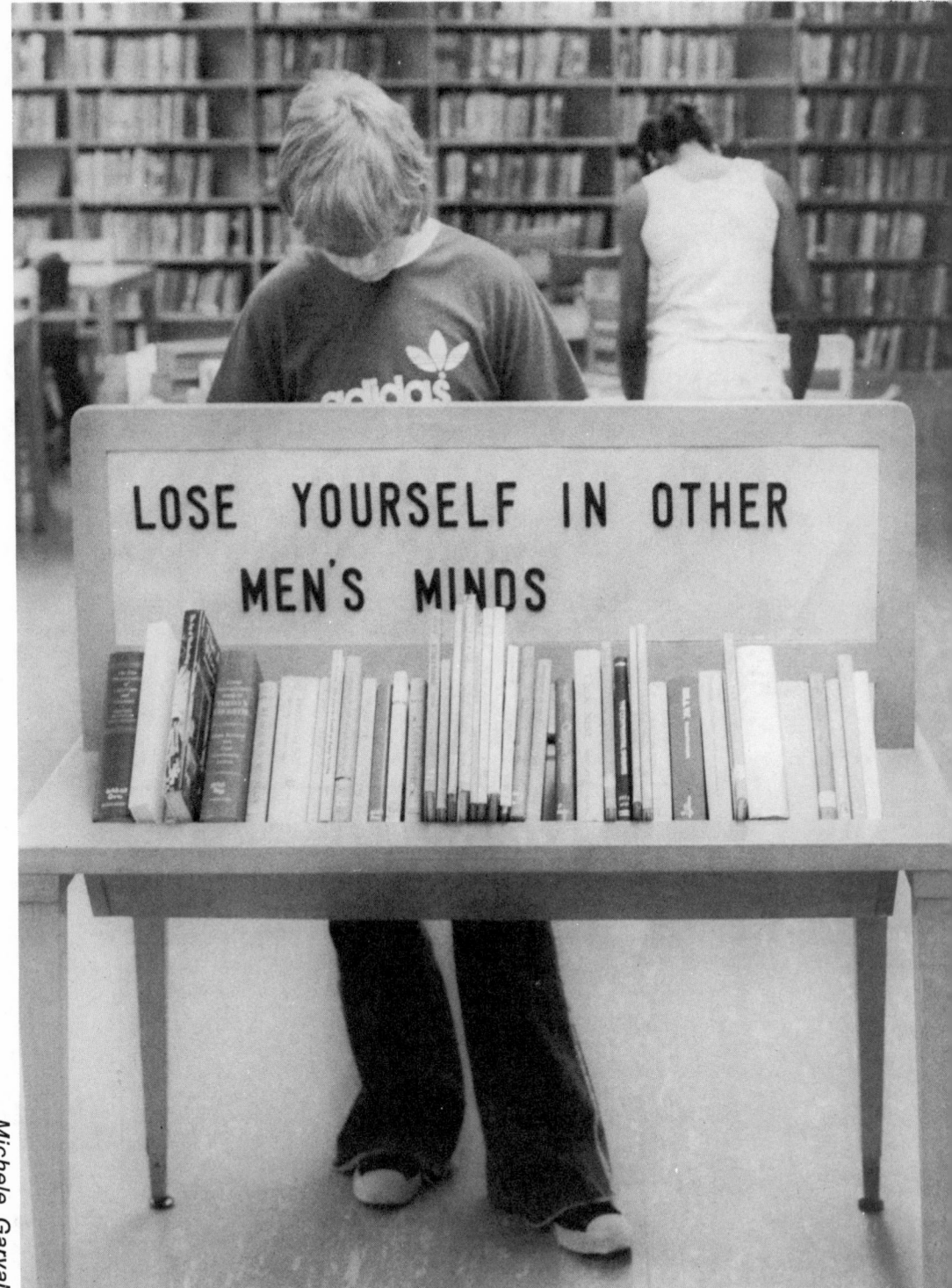

LOSE YOURSELF IN OTHER MEN'S MINDS

Michele Garval

Sexism Project of Southeastern Public Education Program of the American Friends Service Committee

concerned citizen, to help them understand the sex bias in our educational system and find appropriate ways to combat it. It is updated periodically.

Sexism in School and Society, by Nancy Frazier and Myra Sadker. New York: Harper and Row, 1973.

Written by an educator and a journalist, this volume gives a good general introduction to the forms sexism takes in educational institutions at all levels, and relates it to the sexism in the larger society.

SEX ROLES

BEGINNING WITH THE PINK AND BLUE BLANKETS IN WHICH NEWBORN BABIES are wrapped, everything in their environment conspires to transmit all-important sex-role messages. Unless they are consciously attempting to break down sex-role stereotypes, most parents begin treating their child according to its sex from birth. A full-blown but unconscious set of expectations settles in. Little boys will be expected to show bravery and curb their tears, they will be encouraged in rough, active play and will be dressed accordingly. Their misbehaviors will be less severely chastised—boys will be boys, after all—and they will be helped into independence and self-confidence. Little girls, on the other hand, will be allowed and encouraged to show fear and depend on others. They will be taught to think of themselves as too fragile to take part in most "boys' games" and will often be dressed for nothing other than quiet, indoor play. A more rigid set of rules for

behavior will be imposed on them; little ladies simply don't do certain things.

Most children learn very quickly to conform to these rules. As they grow, everything in their environment will confirm past lessons—the toys they are given, the books they read, the TV shows they watch, the friends they play with. Psychologists estimate that a full set of sex-appropriate behaviors has been internalized by age three. When they enter school they will find an atmosphere of institutionalized sex-role conditioning.

Sex-role stereotyping is so deeply woven into the fabric of our society that most parents aren't even aware of it. Sex roles are seen as innate and biological rather than learned. This is the Catch-22 of sex roles. Adults prefer to believe, for example, that little girls naturally want to play with dolls. They remain oblivious to everything in the little girl's life which carefully instructs her to play with dolls, including their own expectations. And then when little girls do show a marked preference for doll play they claim with satisfaction that it is only natural. Probably the most basic and valuable dissent made by the women's movement— the one from which all other arguments proceed—is that against biological determinism. Little girls do *not* naturally play only with dolls, anatomy does *not* have to be destiny.

Finally, what about the quality—and equality—of sex roles? What do boys experience as they grow into men, girls as they grow into women? What are the implications of two thoroughly different roles?

First of all, separate is not equal. In addition to learning the masculine role, boys also learn that they belong to the superior sex. For them, the conditioning experience is one of affirmation and approval. Girls do not receive such positive messages. In fact, their apprenticeship to womanhood is fraught with frustration. For strong-willed girls, sex-role socialization can amount to little more than breaking their spirits.

One of the classic pieces of sex-role research provides a grim insight into society's opinion of the sex roles it prescribes. Seventy-nine psychologists, psychiatrists, and social workers were given a list of personality traits. They were asked to assign the traits to any of three categories: "mature, healthy, socially competent male," "mature, healthy, socially competent female," or "mature, healthy, socially competent adult." Their responses were overwhelmingly consistent. The "mature, healthy, socially competent adult" and the healthy adult male were nearly indistinguishable. Compared to the healthy adult standard, however, the adult female was not healthy, mature *or* socially competent.

Conditioning women to believe that they are inferior and to feel dependent lays the foundation for a whole range of sex discrimination. Here are a few examples of how early conditioning operates in later life.

— Women are trained from infancy to perform household chores; through toys and play at a young age to helping out at home as teenagers to marrying and becoming homemakers. This lengthy apprenticeship is not required by the complexity of the work; rather the long training period is required to condition women into feeling that these chores are theirs by nature.

— Women are conditioned to think of themselves as future mothers and homemakers (men, as people and workers). When they must enter the paid labor force, as so many now do, they have few job skills, but more importantly, they lack a self-image of themselves as workers and so will not have the same aspirations as men.

— Women are also conditioned to be passive and to accept authority, which in our society is male. This feeds into every type of sexism and sex discrimination.

— Sex-role conditioning keeps women physically weak and underdeveloped, barring them from certain kinds of work, but more importantly, leaving them unable to protect themselves.

With something as deep-seated as sex-role socialization is in our society, just recognizing its existence is half the battle. Many parents, educators, and others responsible for the training of young children are beginning to understand the crippling limitations that sex roles impose. Treating children as the unique individuals they are will help them to grow into their fullest, freest selves.

See also: Nonsexist Education
Psychology and Women

Organizations:

Nonsexist Child Development Project
Women's Action Alliance
370 Lexington Avenue
New York, NY 10017

Women on Words and Images
P.O. Box 2163
Princeton, NJ 08540

Resources:

Channeling Children: Sex Stereotyping on Prime Time TV. Princeton: Women on Words and Images, 1975. Order from: Women on Words and Images, address above.

Recognizing that television plays an important part in the lives of most children, this study details and analyzes the sex-role messages that are broadcast daily.

Right from the Start: A Guide to Nonsexist Child Rearing, by Selma Greenberg. Boston: Houghton Mifflin, 1978.

Written by a feminist early childhood educator, this guide gives parents all the advice and encouragement they will need in raising nonsexist children. Delightful to read; a must.

Sex Roles: A Journal of Research. Order from: Plenum Publishing, 277 West 17th Street, New York, NY 10011.

The major scholarly quarterly reporting new research; a fine way to keep abreast of the latest findings.

Sex Roles: A Research Bibliography, ed. by Helen Astin. Washington: National Institute of Mental Health, 1975. Order from: Superintendent of Documents, Government Printing Office, Washington, DC 20402.

With 450 entries, this is probably the most comprehensive bibliography of research into sex roles available, though it is becoming dated.

Sex-Role Stereotypes and Clinical Judgments of Mental Health, by Inge K. Broverman, et al. Pittsburgh: KNOW, 1970. Order from: KNOW, P.O. Box 86031, Pittsburgh, PA 15221.

The study cited in the text.

SEX-TYPING OF OCCUPATIONS

SEX-TYPING OF OCCUPATIONS HAS BEEN REDISCOVERED RECENTLY AS AN added wrinkle in the various layers of sex discrimination in employment. Urging women to move out of the home and into the paid labor market is not sufficient if the goal is economic equality and independence for women. In fact, there is no such thing as *the* labor market. Sex-typing is so thorough that one can say there are—and always have been—two labor markets, a male one and a female one.

As early as 1846, American women protested the sex-typing of occupations which kept them economically dependent on their husbands—or, if they were less fortunate, in dire poverty.

> Men have monopolized almost every field of labor. They have taken the learned professions. They have entered every department which commerce opens, and indeed, almost every place where skill and talent is required, they have excluded women . . . and have only left to them the unmolested possession of the nursery. Women are thus limited to a few employments, hence these are overstocked with laborers . . . It will avail little merely to denounce the oppression . . . The great work to be accomplished is to increase the number of employments which shall be accessible to women and then to encourage the daughters of the land to undertake them. Does anyone ask "Would you have them plead at the bar, or follow the plough?" I frankly answer "Yes."[1]

A recent study found that from 1900 to 1960, more than half of all women consistently were employed in occupations that were at least two-thirds female. Furthermore, between 30 and 50 percent of them were in occupational areas that were 80 percent or more female. Neither of these statistics has changed. The occupations open to men and women in their respective labor markets have changed somewhat over the years—women were the first factory workers and men were the first clerical workers, for example. But the consistent and pervasive sex-typing has not disappeared. The dual labor markets have remained intact.

If one studies in detail the male/female ratios within each occupational area, even greater sex segregation appears. According to the chart, for example, women are 43 percent of professional workers—a rate slightly higher than their participation in the labor force overall. A breakdown by profession reveals a more accurate picture (see table on page 263).

An even more detailed analysis could be made. Take the field of teaching, for example, a traditional occupation for women. In 1975, women were 98.6 percent of preschool teachers, 85.4 percent of elementary school teachers, 49.2 percent of secondary teachers, and only 31.1 percent of college and university teachers. The higher the level, the lower the number of women. Analysis of particular schools or universities, from the lowest teacher to the highest administrator, reveals a similar pattern. This is true from profession to profession, from institution to institution, from department to department.

The sex-segregated nature of women's employment has been sadly overlooked in recent years. Two other, more dynamic trends have captured public attention

---

[1]From an 1846 issue of the *Advocate;* quoted in Barbara J. Berg, *The Remembered Gate: Origins of American Feminism,* New York: Oxford University Press, 1978.

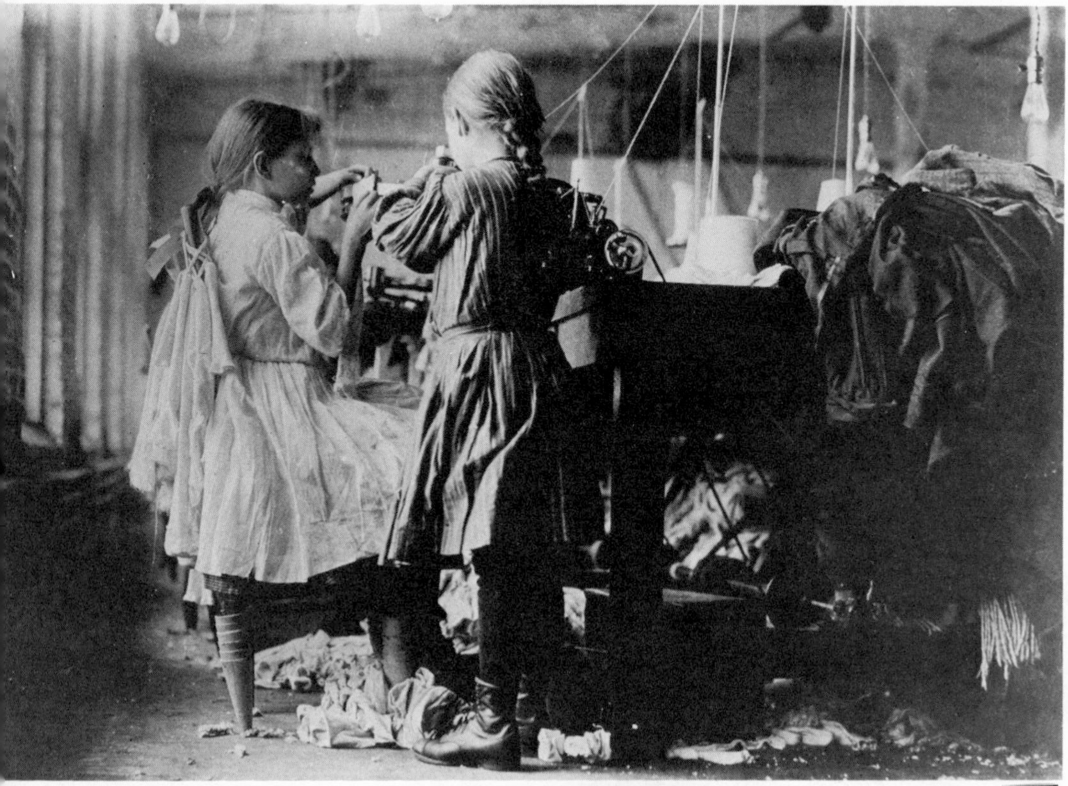

Brown Brothers

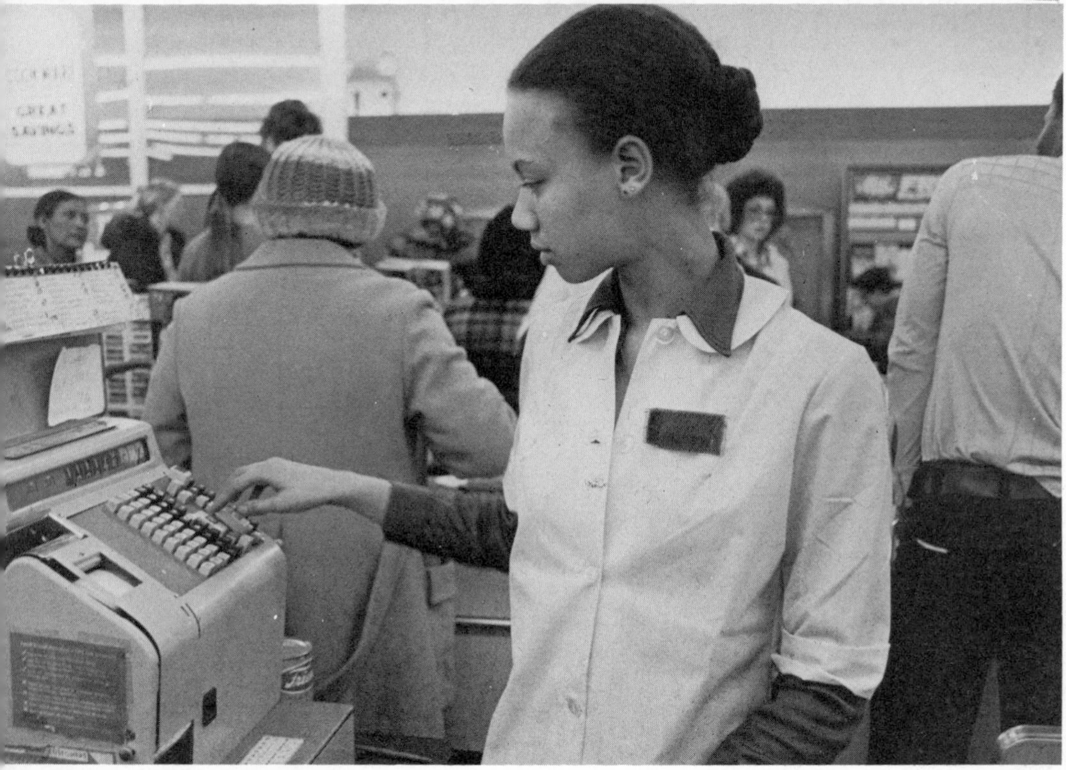

© Peggy McMahon

Field % Women	
Nursing	97.0%
Librarianship	81.1%
Teaching	70.6%
Social work	60.8%
Medicine	11.3%
Law	7.1%
Architecture	4.3%
Engineering	1.1%

instead: the tremendous rate at which women are entering the labor force and the inroads they have made into male-dominated fields. Although no one has made the connection directly, the concomitant occurrence of these two circumstances hints that one leads to the other. That is, it is suggested that all of those women who are going to work—an increase of twelve million women during the past decade—are finding jobs as doctors and plumbers and managers in business. In fact, the majority of women entering the labor force are taking the same jobs women have always held—office work, teaching, waitressing, nursing.

Equal pay for equal work doesn't mean much to women who are only competing with other women for the same low-paying clerical jobs. Their problem is not that men are being' paid more for doing the same work—their problem is that "women's work" does not pay as well as "men's work." The combination of a sex-segregated work force with the influx of large numbers of unorganized women into the labor force keeps women's wages low. Workers in female-dominated professions have begun to understand this and to do something about it.

Librarians, for example, have recently shifted away from comparing the salaries of women librarians with those of men in the profession, to comparing the average salary of a librarian with the average salary in a similar-level male-dominated profession. While there *is* sex discrimination within the field, librarianship is also a depressed occupation because it is 81.1 percent female. In California, librarians in city and county systems compared their pay scales with those of male-dominated professions requiring similar education and experience. They found a wage differential of 21 percent. In other comparisons, they found discrepancies as high as 64 percent. In 1976, a group of nurses brought a suit charging that salary scales were kept unfairly low for women's occupations. They lost their case; the judge complained that equalizing pay scales could destroy the entire economic system. *Fortune* magazine estimated that closing the earnings gap would add $150 billion to payrolls nationally. This points up the substantial material obstacles standing in the way of equality for women in the United States.

With a few isolated exceptions, trade unions have been uninterested in organizing service and clerical workers—the two areas in which women workers are concentrated. So women have created their own unions and associations—with

Lewis W. Hine, courtesy Tennessee Valley Authority

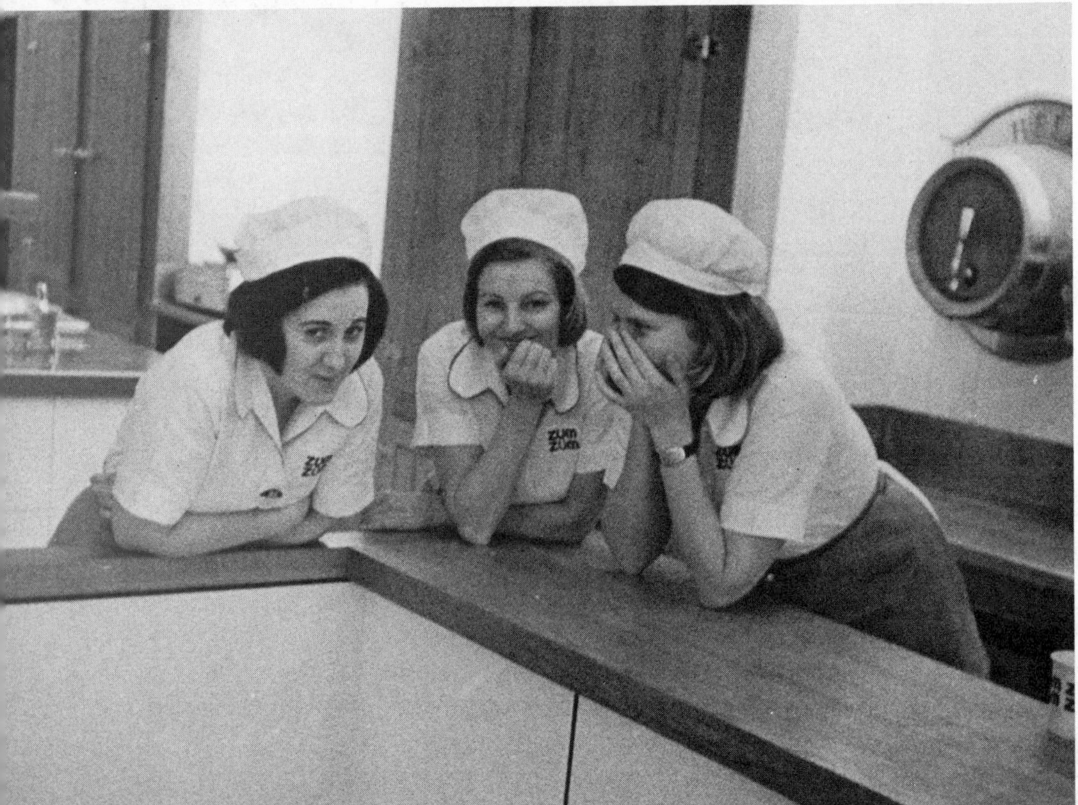

© Ronnie Ginnever

names like Nine to Five, Women Library Workers, and National Committee on Household Employment. Recently, a number of local organizations for clerical workers united nationally. We can expect to hear more from and about these spirited new unions.

See also: Earnings Gap
Labor Union Women
Nontraditional Occupations
Vocational Education

Organizations:

National Committee on Household Employment
7705 Georgia Avenue N.W.
Washington, DC 20012

Women Library Workers
P.O. Box 9052
Berkeley, CA 94709

Working Women—National Association of Office Workers
1258 Euclid Avenue
Cleveland, OH 44115

Resources:

Pink Collar Workers, by Louise Kapp Howe. New York: G. P. Putnam's Sons, 1977.

An instant classic on the world of women's work. Howe discusses beauticians, sales workers, waitresses, office workers, and homemakers. It provided much of the information for the text above.

NCHE News. National Committee on Household Employment, address above.
National news on the organizing of household workers.

Women Private Household Workers: A Statistical and Legislative Profile.
Washington: Women's Bureau, 1978. Order from: Women's Bureau, Department of Labor, Washington, DC 20210.

This pamphlet is in two parts: statistics on wages, working conditions, age of workers, etc., and the latest legislation on social security, minimum wage requirements and unemployment insurance coverage.

Working Women Newsletter. Order from: Working Women, address above.
The newsletter of the recently formed coalition of clerical workers' organizations, Working Women.

OFFICE WORKERS' ORGANIZATIONS

Women Office Workers
680 Lexington Avenue
New York, NY 10022
212-688-4160

Cleveland Women Working
1258 Euclid Avenue
Cleveland, OH 44115
216-566-8511

Interfaith Project On Working Women
Tabernacle Church
3700 Chestnut Street
Philadelphia, PA 19104
215-561-1873

Dayton Working Women
YWCA Building, #318
141 West Third Street
Dayton, OH 45412
513-228-8587

Nine to Five
c/o Boston YWCA
140 Clarendon Street
Boston, MA 02116
617-536-6003

Office Workers of New Haven
P.O. Box 754
New Haven, CT 06103
203-789-8295

Hartford Office Workers
% CWEALF
57 Pratt Street
Hartford, CT 06103
203-247-6090

Sixty Words Per Minute
1346 Connecticut Avenue N.W.,
   #1025
Washington, DC 20036

Women Employed
37 South Wabash
Chicago, IL 60603
312-372-7822

Women Organized for Employment
127 Montgomery Street
San Francisco, CA 90104
415-982-8963

Cincinnati Women Working
% YWCA
9th and Walnut Street
Cincinnati, OH 45202
513-381-6003

Working Women
Women's Center
21 Elliot Street
Brattleboro, VT 05312
802-257-7858

New Hampshire Association of
   Working Women
8 N. Main Street
Concord, NH 03301
603-224-4104

Worcester Women Working
YWCA Box 127
2 Washington Street
Worcester, MA 01608

12 to 1
111-A Draper Hall
University of Massachusetts
Amherst, MA 01003

Rhode Island Working Women
62 Jackson Walkway
Providence, RI 02903
401-861-2910

SEXUAL HARASSMENT ON THE JOB

SEXUAL HARASSMENT ON THE JOB IS ONE OF THE FACTS OF WOMEN'S LIVES
recently transformed from the status of "personal problem" to "issue." *Redbook*
magazine surveyed its readers on the hazards of sex in the office in 1976. More
than 9,000 women responded and 90 percent said they had experienced some form
of sexual harassment. Fifty percent said they—or someone they knew—had quit a
job because of sexual harassment. Other less extensive surveys have produced
similar results.

Just what is sexual harassment? A good definition is "unsolicited nonreciprocal
male behavior that asserts a woman's sex role over her function as worker."
Sexual harassment can take many forms—leering looks, too-familiar remarks
about appearance, repeated requests for dates, a pat on the behind, the threat of

Women workers have had to deal with unwanted sexual attentions whenever and wherever they have worked, as this 1909 postcard demonstrates. This young woman has the right approach.

rape. There will always be some form of sexual behavior between men and women on the job; it becomes sexual harassment when the woman does not want it and can't stop it.

For many women, sexual harassment stands between them and their paychecks. They fear that protest or refusal will lose them a raise, a promotion or the job itself. In some cases they are told as much—point blank. Male bosses or supervisors have a great deal of power over the working lives of their female employees, and a discouraging number of them abuse it regularly.

What can a woman do? Ultimately, her only choice may be to put up or to quit, but she should try first to hang on to both her integrity and her job. The first recommendation is a firm no. Confront the harasser head-on and tell him his attentions are not appreciated. Many activists recommend writing a note for documentation purposes. Talk to other women; chances are that you are not alone. It is more difficult to dismiss the complaint of several women than of only one. If there is a sympathetic supervisor or personnel officer, she or he may be able to help. Grievance procedures and legal action may be used. For this documentation is essential, so keep a diary.

Although there is disagreement in the courts as to whether sexual harassment constitutes sex discrimination, there has been one victory. Diane Williams, an information specialist in Washington, DC, lost her job when she refused the attentions of a supervisor. (Ironically, she had been employed by the U.S. Department of Justice!) She sued under Title VII of the Civil Rights Act and was awarded $16,000 in back pay. The legal route is an unpleasant one. As in rape cases, a woman's entire sexual history may be revealed in the courtroom. But it is one of the few avenues of redress open to women who have already lost their jobs.

Organizations:

Alliance Against Sexual Coercion
P.O. Box 1
Cambridge, MA 02139

Working Women United Institute
593 Park Avenue
New York, NY 10021

Resources:

Sexual Harassment: A Hidden Issue. Washington: Project on the Status and Education of Women, 1978. Order from: Project, Association of American Colleges, 1818 R Street N.W., Washington, DC 20009.

This pamphlet focuses on the campus situation, where female students may be harassed by male professors and have their grades threatened. Includes a rundown of the legal situation and a list of organizations.

Sexual Harassment at the Workplace. Cambridge, Mass.: Alliance Against Sexual Coercion, 1977. Order from: AASC (address above).

A good guide to the issue, this pamphlet dispels some of the myths, gives current and historical background, and discusses the legal options.

Sexual Shakedown: The Sexual Harassment of Women on the Job, by Lin Farley. New York: McGraw-Hill, 1978.

The first full-length treatment of the subject by an early pioneer in organizing against sexual harassment. A must.

SEXUALITY

FOR CENTURIES WHAT CONSTITUTES "SEX" HAS BEEN DEFINED BY MEN AND largely controlled by them. Feminism has encouraged the exploration of female sexuality: expanding the boundaries of human sexual experience and sensitizing men and women to the similarities as well as the differences between the sexes.

Male dominance has generally followed women right into the bedroom; what could and should be a joyful and pleasure-filled experience has more often been painful. Women were socialized to be passive—especially so in sexual matters—while men learned to be aggressive. People were taught that the male sex drive was strong while women's was weak, if not nonexistent. Neither women nor men were well informed about female anatomy and sexuality or, if women did know, they were usually afraid to speak up. Thus "sex" was considered to have taken place when intercourse was successfully completed by male orgasm. The woman involved might have experienced nothing—or climaxed half a dozen times. Either way, it didn't matter: sex was defined by male pleasure. What women need to achieve sexual satisfaction in heterosexual relationships was never seriously investigated; that women could find sexual pleasure with other women or by themselves was not taken seriously. Male-oriented definitions of sexuality did not allow for sex without men. Even the pioneering Kinsey Research Institute is guilty: their new book, *Homosexualities*, treats homosexuality almost exclusively as a male experience.

Freud codified the male-oriented view of sexuality, calling the vaginal orgasm mature and the clitoral orgasm adolescent. Actually, he only hallowed a phallic fantasy: since a man reaches orgasm by penile thrusting, something was wrong with the woman if she did not. For years women struggled against an imposed frigidity. Psychoanalysis flourished but, alas, relatively few sexual relationships between men and women did.

Then, in 1970, Ann Koedt challenged Freud in her article, "The Myth of the Vaginal Orgasm." She said: "There is only one area for sexual climax . . . the clitoris. All orgasms are extensions of sensations from this area. Since the clitoris is usually not directly stimulated in conventional sexual positions we are left 'frigid.'" A complete redefinition of sex and sexuality—on women's terms—was required.

This redefinition—and rediscovery—of female sexuality was accomplished through consciousness-raising, sex workshops, and research. The pioneering work of Masters and Johnson was built on by women like Betty Dodson, whose Bodysex Workshops help women learn sexual pleasure from masturbation. Women have also stopped defining sexuality as just heterosexuality; bisexuality and lesbianism are also options. Any form of sexuality which encourages women to feel good about their bodies and themselves is becoming acceptable.

One of the key steps to redefining female sexuality was discarding the word frigid. It suggests a total lack of sexual feeling or response, and gave women little hope of ever reaching fulfillment. "Preorgasmic," its replacement, is more accurate and hopeful. Many women have learned what brings sexual pleasure and orgasm, and they no longer will settle for male-defined sexual relationships.

Women's changing sexuality was reported on by Shere Hite in 1976. Using information collected from more than three thousand women nationally, *The Hite Report* confirmed the new thinking about female sexuality. Women, she discovered, are not frigid; they generally achieve orgasm easily through masturbation. Of the 82 percent of women who masturbate regularly, 95 percent could bring themselves to climax successfully. Only 30 percent reported regular orgasm from heterosexual intercourse. Hite also noted that lesbian and bisexual women found considerable sexual satisfaction through inventive sex play and awareness of their partners. Neither Dodson nor Hite suggests doing away with men; they do encourage expanding the limits of sexuality for all people. Underlying their work is the notion that a satisfied woman will enhance the pleasure of her partner—male or female—as much as her own.

See also: Birth Control
Incest
Lesbians
Pornography
Prostitution
Psychology and Women
Rape
Right-wing Attacks

Organizations:

Sex Information and Education Council of the United States
84 Fifth Avenue
New York, NY 10011

Resources:

Eve's Garden, a pleasure boutique for women. Write for their catalog. Eve's Garden, 246 East 51st Street, New York, NY 10022.

For Yourself: Fulfillment of Female Sexuality—A Guide to Orgasmic Response, by Lonnie G. Barboch. New York: Doubleday, 1975.
An excellent self-help book on how women can achieve orgasm.

The Hite Report, by Shere Hite. New York: Macmillan, 1976.
Rambling, exciting, affirming report on women's sexuality. Hite draws conclusions, but much of the book is from the women themselves.

Liberating Masturbation: A Meditation on Self-Love, by Betty Dodson. New York: Bodysex Designs, 1974. Order from: Bodysex Designs, 121 Madison Avenue, New York, NY 10016.

Our Bodies, Ourselves, by the Boston Women's Health Book Collective. New York: Simon and Schuster, 1976.
Well-written section on exploring female sexuality. Also includes an article written by lesbians about their sexuality.

The Myth of the Vaginal Orgasm, by Anne Koedt. Somerville: New England Free Press, 1970. Order from: NEFP, 60 Union Square, Somerville, MA 02143.

The Nature and Evolution of Female Sexuality, by Mary Jane Sherfey. New York: Vintage Books, 1973.
Good companion to Hite; clear presentation of anatomy.

Women: Sexuality, Psychology, and Psychotherapy. Boston: WomanSpace: Feminist Therapy Collective, 1976. Order from: WomanSpace: Feminist Therapy Collective, 636 Beacon Street, Boston, MA 02215.
A twenty-nine page bibliography.

SOCIALIST FEMINISM

SOCIALIST FEMINISM—AS BOTH THEORY AND PRACTICE—IS STILL IN THE developmental stage. Since the nineteenth century, feminists have attempted to work within socialist movements, with varying degrees of success. But from the feminist point of view, early Marxists did not provide theory adequate to the needs of women's liberation. This is what socialist feminists are attempting to do; to create a genuine synthesis of Marxism and feminism. While many socialists and many feminists urge them to declare primary allegiance to one "ism" or the other, socialist feminists believe the two are inextricably linked. Radical Women, one socialist feminist group, puts it this way: "Authentic socialism and principled feminism are consistent, interdependent, and harmonious at every point."

Although socialist feminists may disagree among themselves on many fine points of theory and strategy, they do share certain basic assumptions. They all trace women's second-class status to capitalism, which depends for its survival on the exploitation of working people and on the special exploitation of women. In order to maintain profits, women must be kept either outside the paid labor force or in the lowest-paying jobs. In either case, women are saddled with the unpaid jobs of child care, housekeeping, and food preparation. Thus, the profit system cannot give women full economic equality and survive. The only solution, socialist feminists believe, is the overthrow of the capitalist states, the nationalization of industry, and the institution of a socialist government.

But socialist feminists want to take theory—and practice—beyond the socialist argument. Nationalizing the economy does not automatically lead to the liberation of women; in Juliet Mitchell's words: "The overthrow of the capitalist economy and the political challenge that effects this do not in themselves mean a transformation of patriarchal ideology." While recognizing the gains made by women within existing socialist countries, socialist feminists maintain a critical stance. Socialist governments have not always treated women in ways that inspire the confidence of American feminists.

And socialist and left groups as they existed in the United States in the 1960's were not only male-dominated but male chauvinist as well. Early feminists were criticized for dividing the movement; women's issues were considered petty, secondary, or, worst of all, bourgeois. Socialist feminists believe that a strong, independent, mass feminist movement must be a constant force in the struggle for socialism. Only then will the kind of socialism that socialist feminists desire result. One socialist feminist, Barbara Ehrenreich, described it this way:

We aim to transform not only the ownership of the means of production, but the totality of social existence . . . we have room within our Marxist framework for feminist issues which have nothing ostensibly to do with production or "politics," issues that have to do with the family, health care, "private" life. Furthermore, in our brand of Marxism, there is no "woman question" because we never compartmentalized women off to the "superstructure" or somewhere in the first place.

In July of 1975, socialist feminists met at a national conference sponsored by a coalition of independent socialist feminist women's unions. Many of these independent organizations no longer exist, and now many socialist feminists belong to and operate within organizations such as the New American Movement. There are still antagonisms between socialists and the women's movement, but socialist feminists are helping to patch up old disagreements and forge a new perspective: a more feminist socialism and a more socialist feminism.

See also: International Women's Day
              Women's Movement

Organizations:

Coalition of Grass Roots Women
1133 Broadway
New York, NY 10010

New American Movement
Socialist Feminist Commission
7125 McPherson Boulevard
Pittsburgh, PA 15208

Radical Women
3815 5th Avenue N.E.
Seattle, WA 98105

Women for Racial and Economic Equality
266 West 23rd Street
New York, NY 10011

Resources:

Capitalist Patriarchy and the Case for Socialist Feminism, by Zillah R. Eisenstein. New York: Monthly Review Press, 1979.

A collection of writings on socialist feminist theory providing an analysis of history and women's roles, revolutionary models and their implications for America.

The Curious Courtship of Women's Liberation and Socialism, by Batya Weinbaum. Boston: South End Press, 1978. Order from: South End Press, P.O. Box 68, Astor Station, Boston, MA 02123.

Female Liberation as the Basis for Social Revolution, by Roxanne Dunbar. Somerville: New England Free Press, n.d. Order from: New England Free Press, 60 Union Square, Somerville, MA 02143.

An early article, criticizing the antifeminist left.

Feminism and Socialism, ed. by Linda Jenness. New York: Pathfinder Press, n.d. Order from: Pathfinder Press, 410 West Street, New York, NY 10014.

Marxism and Feminism, by Charnie Guettel. Toronto: Women's Press, 1974. Order from: Women's Press, 250 Bloor Street West, Toronto, Ontario, Canada.

Guettel gives a critical summary of the major Marxist-feminist statements to date.

Origin of the Family, Private Property and the State, by Frederick Engels. New York: International Publishers, 1972.

The first Marxist treatment of women, a classic with which current theorizing begins.

Radical Women Manifesto: Theory, Program and Structure. Seattle: Radical Women, 1973. Order from: Radical Women, 3815 Fifth Avenue N.E., Seattle, WA 98105.

The theoretical statement and program of one independent socialist feminist group.

Socialism, Anarchism and Feminism, by Carol Ehrlich. Baltimore: Research Group One, 1977. Order from: Vacant Lots Press, 2743 Maryland Avenue, Baltimore, MD 21218.

An anarchist-feminist's perspective on socialism and feminism.

Women: The Longest Revolution, by Juliet Mitchell. Somerville: New England Free Press, 1966. Order from: New England Free Press, 60 Union Square, Somerville, MA 02143.

One of the first theoretical statements attempting to reconcile feminism and socialism. Mitchell has refined her position since then, but the pamphlet still makes interesting reading.

Women's Consciousness, Man's World, by Sheila Rowbotham. Baltimore: Penguin Books, 1973.

Rowbotham examines women's condition in class society and integrates feminist analysis into a socialist construction for social change.

Women's Estate, by Juliet Mitchell. New York: Pantheon, 1971.

Mitchell puts forth a synthesis of structuralist theory and feminist consciousness to provide a framework for a socialist feminist theory of women's oppression.

Working Papers on Socialism and Feminism. Chicago: New American Movement, n.d. Order from: NAM, 1643 N. Milwaukee Avenue, Chicago, IL 60647.

An anthology of articles on theory, strategy and NAM resolutions. Includes Barbara Ehrenreich's "What is Socialist Feminism?" quoted above.

SOCIAL SECURITY

IN 1935 THE SOCIAL SECURITY ACT MADE PROVISIONS FOR WAGE-RELATED retirement benefits for workers; amendments adopted in 1939 granted benefits for an insured worker's wife, and survival benefits for his widow, children under eighteen, and dependent parents. Today Social Security covers 90 percent of all jobs and provides benefits to 95 percent of the aged. Social Security is the only income security—however inadequate—many elderly Americans have; it also assures disability and survivors' insurance for workers, and protection against hospital and medical-care costs for people over 65 and the long-term disabled.

Designed in the 1930's, the Social Security program reflects the mores of the times: in particular, the traditional concept of the family as including a working husband and a nonworking wife. Today the changing roles of women have invalidated such assumptions. Women have joined the labor force in unprece- dented numbers—in 1977 56 percent of all women aged twenty to sixty-four worked—and have tended to remain employed despite pregnancy, childbirth, and childbearing. Nevertheless, a woman's wage, on the average, is 60 percent of a man's. Economic parity is not complete. Another difference is that homemakers are being reevaluated as economic contributors to the family; studies estimate the value of their labor at as high as $18,000 per year. Also the divorce rate is up—as many as 30 percent to 40 percent of current marriages will end in divorce. Divorced women are likely to work in order to support themselves and their dependents.

The dramatic entry of women into the workplace, the reevaluation of the homemaking role, and the changing structure of the American family raise three basic issues for redesigning Social Security:

— what are fair retirement benefits, given the different earning capacities of single workers and two-earner couples relative to the one-earner couple?
— what inconsistencies exist in protecting full-time or part-time homemakers?
— are there instances of sex discrimination in the Social Security system?

Some changes have been effected and some instances of sex discrimination have been eradicated. In 1977 the laws changed so that benefits would not decrease if a widow(er) remarried after the age of sixty. Also, as of January 1979, the length of marriage required for divorced women to receive ex-spouses' benefits dropped from twenty to ten years.

On August 26, 1977, President Carter requested all executive-branch depart- ment and agency heads to review and to identify any regulations, guidelines, programs, or policies which resulted in unequal treatment based on sex. In April,

1978, the Department of Health, Education, and Welfare Task Force on the Treatment of Women Under Social Security identified ten problematic issues related to women, families, and single workers.

1. low return on contributions of second working spouse
2. fairness between one- and two-earner couples
3. fairness between surviving spouse of one and two-earner couples
4. fairness to single workers
5. lack of coverage in the home
6. lack of protection for disabled homemakers and survivors of deceased homemakers
7. durability of marriage requirements for eligibility as a divorced wife or as a survivor of a divorced wife
8. inadequacy of benefits for divorced wife
9. dependent status of divorced and separated wives
10. disability protection for widows or divorced homemakers

Although the issue has been identified and proposals for change have been made, no systematic overhauls have been forthcoming. The Task Force report called for a study of proposals to eliminate dependency and sex discrimination under Social Security. At present several suggestions have been made. One would allow all Social Security credits and benefits to be shared between spouses regardless of how much either had earned. A second would create a two-tier system whereby every retired person—including those not currently eligible for such benefits—would receive a minimum benefit at age sixty-five, plus whatever extra benefits had accrued to him or her during his or her work life. A third option is to assign homemaking a cash value and to place homemakers under Social Security, thereby entitling them to retirement benefits. Hopefully the new proposals will be presented to the public as well as to politicians and policy makers, so that recipients can help to design a viable program. As it is, benefits barely allow most elderly people to live at the poverty line.

See also: Displaced Homemakers
Employment
Marriage and Family

Organizations:

Pension Rights Center
1346 Connecticut Avenue N.W.
Washington, DC 20036

Resources:

Report of the HEW Task Force on the Treatment of Women Under Social Security.
Washington: Social Security Administration, 1978. Order from: Social Security Administration, 6401 Security Boulevard, Baltimore, MD 21235.

BENEFICIARIES AND AVERAGE BENEFIT AMOUNTS BY SEX OF INSURED WORKER

Beneficiaries	Male Workers		Female Workers	
	number (in thousands)	Average benefit	number (in thousands)	Average benefit
Retired workers	9,512	$265	7,868	$210
Dependents:				
Spouses:	2,888	122	12	108
Children	617	92	38	—
Disabled Workers	1,877	286	887	213
Dependents:				
Spouses	481	68	(41)[1]	78
Children	1,293	74	1,203	74
Child Survivors	2,458	170	401	121
Widowed mothers and fathers	564	170	9	100
Disabled surviving spouses	122	157	(235)[1]	141
Aged surviving spouses	3,916	223	4	196
Aged dependent parents[2]	19	197	—	—
Men	1	178	—	—
Women	18	198	—	—

[1] Numbers in parentheses are actual numbers, not in thousands

[2] Data not available by sex of deceased worker

SPORTS

"IT'S OKAY FOR GIRLS TO BE TOMBOYS UNTIL ABOUT AGE TWELVE; AFTER THAT they must adopt more appropriate feminine behavior and learn to act like ladies." Well, the ladies are rebelling. The Association for Intercollegiate Athletics for Women (AIAW) has 100,000 members, while the all-male National Collegiate Athletic Association (NCAA) has 170,000 members. After barnstorming for many years, women now have broken into professional team sports—the Women's Professional Basketball League played its first game in December 1978. Individual women, perhaps caught up in the current fitness craze, are participating in large numbers in marathon running competition. There are increasingly visible numbers of positive role models for women athletes: Billie Jean King, Nancy Lopez, Olga Korbut, Mikki Gorman, Carol Mann and more.

A group of young runners working out at the 1977 Colgate Women's Games, a major amateur track and field event. © *Cary Herz*

While professional sports continues to be largely an all-male club, physical education and athletic programs in educational institutions have been shaken up, if not changed, by Title IX of the Education Amendments of 1972, which stipulates that there shall be no sex discrimination in any educational program or activity receiving federal financial assistance. The public schools and most of the country's 2,500 colleges and universities are affected, including their athletic programs. As could be expected, these changes have not been easily accepted by the powerful all-male NCAA, which has worked to protect the interests of men's college athletic programs, the training grounds of big-money professional sports. The Department of Health, Education and Welfare (HEW) is charged with enforcing Title IX. So far it has been slow to act in providing clear regulations or effective enforcement. One provision of Title IX gave colleges and universities until July 1978 to evaluate and develop programs in compliance with HEW guidelines. However, HEW has seldom scrutinized these programs for compliance. To date no schools have suffered a funding cut, although it is clear that most are not in compliance.

According to AIAW, women's intercollegiate sports received about 10 percent of the amount budgeted for men's programs—up from approximately 1 percent in 1972. The Project on the Status and Education of Women reports that one state university women's program received nine-tenths of 1 percent of the two-million dollar athletic budget, though the undergraduate population was 40 percent female. And at another major university 1,300 times more was spent for men's athletics than for women's.

The federal regulations do provide for separate teams in contact sports, but do not require equal expenditures—HEW "may consider the failure to provide necessary funds for teams of one sex in assessing equality of opportunity for members of each sex." Not only have few programs been examined for "equality of opportunity"; women's groups argue that the guidelines are so vague as to stack the deck in favor of the institution. It is too easy to avoid making substantial changes, and women still can't get the kind and quality of athletic programs they want and need.

Those concerned with the future direction of women's sports have raised many difficult questions: Should women emulate a male model of organized sports? Should the so-called feminine attributes of cooperation and agility be down-played in favor of more "masculine" traits of competition and strength? How much of what happens in organized sports is tied to profits? Can women's athletic programs avoid these pitfalls and create a corruption-free model for sports events? The answers have yet to surface.

But one thing is clear: women—no longer content to be cheerleaders—are creating a revolution in sports just by their sheer numbers.

If you are concerned about sex discrimination in sports or want to know more about what women in sports are doing, contact the groups below.

See also: Title IX

Organizations:

Association for Intercollegiate Athletics for
  Women
1201 16th Street N.W.
Washington, DC 20036

Center for Women and Sport
White Building
Pennsylvania State University
University Park, PA 16802

National Association for Girls and Women
  in Sports
1201 16th Street N.W.
Washington, DC 20036

Project on the Status and Education of
  Women
1818 R Street N.W.
Washington, DC 20009

SPRINT
Women's Equity Action League Fund
805 15th Street, N.W.
Washington, DC 20005
(call their toll-free number, 800-424-5162,
  for up-to-the-minute information on
  Title IX)

Women's Sports Foundation
195 Moulton Street
San Francisco, CA 94125

Resources:

Equality in School Athletics: A Guide, by Joyce R. Countiss. New Brunswick: Training Institute for Sex Desegregation of the Public Schools, 1977. Order from: Training Institute for Sex Desegregation, University Extension Division, Federation Hall, Douglass College, Rutgers University, New Brunswick, NJ 08903.

This guide, designed to aid schools in creating equitable athletic programs for both sexes, covers educational and legal considerations, interscholastic and intramural programs, and program administration.

Equity in Sport for Women, by Patricia L. Geadelmann, et al. Washington: American Alliance for Health, Physical Education and Recreation, 1977. Order from: AAHPER, 1201 16th Street N.W., Washington, DC 20036.

This book is a tool for understanding and eliminating sex discrimination in athletic programs of educational institutions.

GirlSports, by Karen Folger Jacobs. New York: Bantam Books, 1978.

Jacobs interviews fifteen young athletes involved in such sports as gymnastics, baseball, ice skating and water polo; must reading for young women.

Sports Kit. Washington: Women's Equity Action League, 1978. Order from: WEAL, 805 15th Street N.W., Washington, DC 20005.

A packet of information on women, sports, and Title IX; includes bibliographies, associations and organizations, and action suggestions for individuals and groups.

Update on Title IX and Sports, Number Two. Washington: Project on the Status and Education of Women, 1979. Order from: Project on the Status and Education of Women (address above).

The Project prepares periodic updates covering the implementing regulations for Title IX as they relate to athletic programs.

What Constitutes Equality for Women in Sports? Washington: Project on the Status and Education of Women, 1974. Order from: Project on the Status and Education of Women (address above).

A comprehensive guide to Title IX as it relates to athletic programs; discusses noncompetitive and competitive sports, funding, administrative structures, and employment.

Women's Sports Magazine. Order from: Women's Sports Foundation (address above).

Women and Sport: From Myth to Reality, ed. by Carole A. Oglesby. Philadelphia: Lea and Febiger, 1978.

An eye-opener, the collection of articles informs the average person, the student and the researcher on what's happening in sports and how it affects women, the myths about women in sports and what the future holds for sports feminism.

♀ PHYSIOLOGICAL DIFFERENCES BETWEEN THE SEXES ♀

It has sometimes been argued that vigorous physical activity renders women sterile or otherwise damages them. This belief, as well as a number of more subtle myths, has certainly been disproven. These myths include the following:

Myth • Participation in athletics might damage a woman's reproductive organs. In fact, many gynecologists believe that vigorous activity improves the muscular support in the pelvic area. The uterus is one of the most shock-resistant internal organs and is considerably more protected than male genitalia.

Myth • Athletic activity causes menstrual problems and impedes menstrual regularity. In fact, the reverse appears to be true.

Myth • Women can't reach peak performance during menstruation. In fact, although there is a great deal of variability among women, women Olympic athletes have won competitions and broken records during all stages of their menstrual cycles.

Joan Joyce is one of the top three softball pitchers and the greatest woman pitcher in the world. Her team, the Raybestos Brakettes, have been the national champions of the Amateur Softball Association every year from 1971 to 1976.
© *Cary Herz*

Myth • Female bones are more fragile than male bones. In fact, they are on the average smaller, not more fragile.

Myth • Women are more likely to be injured in sports. In fact, the injury rate per participant is lower for girls than boys in both contact and noncontact sports.

Myth • Females should not play contact sports because they might damage their breasts. In fact, medical and athletic authorities argue that breast protectors could be designed for women, just as various protective equipment has been designed for men's organs.

Myth • Women who engage in strenuous athletics develop bulging muscles. In fact, given the same amount of exercise, the development of bulging muscles depends primarily on the amount of male hormones a person has.[1]

Before puberty, males and females are nearly identical in their physical abilities. Tests of strength, muscular endurance, cardiovascular endurance and motor performance show few differences between the sexes up to this age. Beyond that age, however, the male becomes considerably stronger, possesses greater muscular and cardiovascular endurance and is more proficient in almost all motor skills. These differences increase in magnitude with time, and the female tends to plateau between the ages of ten and fourteen. According to Dr. Jack Wilmore, however:

> Recent evidence . . . indicates that these differences may be more of an artifact of social or cultural restrictions imposed on the female either at or just prior to the outset of menarche, than a result of true biological differences in performance potential between the sexes.[2]

A major physiological difference between adult women and men is that men on the average are larger and heavier than women. The average woman, on the other hand, is more flexible and has better balance. Women in sport point out that most sports emphasize and reward traits in which men tend to excel.

Averages can be misleading. Although a superbly fit adult female may be at a real disadvantage competing with a superbly fit adult male in athletic contests which depend primarily on speed and strength, she might well out-perform an *average* male. In the words of Dr. Thomas E. Shaffer:

> . . . while there are very significant sex-related differences between males and females, it should be borne in mind that there are undoubtedly greater differences between the third and the ninety-seventh percentile in each sex than there are differences between the average female and the average male in terms of physical performance.[3]

---

[1]Kathleen M. Engle, "The Greening of Girl's Sports," *Nation's Schools,* September 1973, p. 29; and interview with Dr. H. Royer Collins, *Nation's Schools,* September 1973, p. 30.
[2]Jack W. Wilmore, "Strength, Endurance and Body Composition of the Female Athlete," paper presented at the American Medical Association's 15th National Conference on the Medical Aspects of Sports, Anaheim, California, December 1, 1973.
[3]Thomas E. Shaffer, "Physiological Considerations of the Female Participant," in Women and Sport: A National Research Conference, ed. Dorothy Harris (State College, Pennsylvania, 1972), p. 330.

In other words, *all* men are not superior to *all* women in *all* athletic skills. There is a good deal of overlap in ability between the sexes, so that a sizable number of women outperform a number of men.

Excerpted from *What Constitutes Equality for Women in Sport?*, prepared by the Project on the Status and Education of Women.

STERILIZATION ABUSE

WHILE SOME WOMEN FIND IT DIFFICULT TO CONVINCE THEIR DOCTORS TO sterilize them, others are coerced into accepting sterilization. In recent years, women's groups have documented and publicized the extent to which sterilization abuse occurs.

In 1977, the Center for Constitutional Rights and the American Civil Liberties Union surveyed 64 teaching hospitals and discovered that 33 percent of consents for sterilization came from women in labor, and 58 percent from women who had just had abortions. Many doctors are reluctant to prescribe sterilizations for private patients, but are eager to perform them on their public charges. A 1972 study for *Family Planning Digest* found that doctors suggested the pill 73 percent of the time, the IUD 15 percent of the time, and sterilization 6 percent of the time to private patients. But to welfare mothers, they prescribed sterilization 77 percent of the time. By 1968, 35.3 percent of women of reproductive age in Puerto Rico had been sterilized; today almost 20 percent of Native American women have been sterilized. It is not surprising that many women's and civil rights groups believe that sterilization abuse is an insidious form of imposed population control.

Sterilization abuse is considered to have occurred if:

— a woman agrees to sterilization without informed consent; there is lack of understanding that the results are permanent, that major surgery may be involved, that there are other alternatives
— such information is not presented in the individual's native language
— the individual is threatened with termination of welfare payments or medical benefits
— the individual chooses sterilization but is discouraged or prevented from receiving it
— the individual is sterilized because abortion is unavailable and birth control is too costly

HEW's 1978 guidelines for informed consent apply to federally financed sterilizations, 10 percent of the annual total. (Write HEW Office of Population Affairs, Rm. 722H, 200 Independence Ave. S.W., Washington, DC 20201.)

See also: Birth Control
Health Care

Organizations:

Association for Voluntary Sterilization
Women's Caucus
708 Third Avenue
New York, NY 10017

Committee to End Sterilization Abuse
P.O. Box A244
Cooper Station
New York, NY 10003

Resources:

Workbook on Sterilization Abuse. Bronxville: Ad Hoc Women's Studies Committee Against Sterilization Abuse, 1978. Order from: Women's Studies, Sarah Lawrence College, Bronxville, NY 10708.

♀ STERILIZATION ABUSE: THE LAW ♀

As a first step to fight sterilization abuse, a public law, Public Law 37 (PL 37) was passed by the New York City Council in 1977. The law provided the following rights and conditions for sterilization.

— A person must be 21 and legally competent to consent to be sterilized
— Freedom from threats of withdrawal of medical or social benefits if the person decides not to be sterilized
— To be consulted by a qualified person other than the doctor doing the operation, in the person's preferred language or using a translator
— To have a witness of the person's own choosing, a friend, relative or spouse, during the counseling session and signing of the consent
— To have the sterilization no matter how many children the person has, even none, and to make the decision free from the veto of husband or wife
— To have the standardized consent form that permits the doctor or hospital to do only the requested sterilization
— To have a copy of the consent form available for the person's study at his/her own convenience
— To be free from pressure or coercion, especially if the person is in the hospital for abortion or childbirth
— To have at least 30 days in which to think the decision over and discuss it with others
— To be given information about the risks, benefits and alternatives to sterilization, including the different sterilization methods for men and women as well as temporary methods of birth control
— To have temporary methods of birth control during the waiting period
— To have the right to change one's mind any time before the operation
— To have all questions answered to the person's satisfaction

WHAT CAN YOU DO?   Always get the names of the doctors, nurses, or counselors, keep track of the dates when you visited them and hold on to any documents they give you.

Learn your rights under PL 37. If you are not given all the consideration and information just described . . . If someone threatens you or pressures you, especially during labor or abortion . . . If you are told that you must have a sterilization for your health (sterilization does not cure any illness, it will only keep you from having children) or because you have had babies by Cesarean section . . . If someone is in a great hurry to get you sterilized . . . If you have been sterilized without your knowledge or against your will . . .

Report it immediately to stop it from happening. Get a second medical opinion if you are in doubt. There is no hurry, because sterilization is never an emergency. You may be able to bring legal action.

Reprinted from *Sterilization: What You Need to Know Before Making a Decision,* Committee to End Sterilization Abuse, address above.

SUBSTANCE ABUSE

THE INCIDENCE OF SUBSTANCE ABUSE—THE DESTRUCTIVE USE OF ALCOHOL and drugs—is on the increase among women. Thirty to forty million Americans, most of them women, suffer from iatrogenic, that is, doctor-induced, drug abuse. Nearly half the nation's ten million alcoholics are women. What's worse, pills and liquor are a lethal combination, and unfortunately women are cross-addicted more frequently than men.

Pharmaceutical companies take advantage of the medical convention that women are especially prone to psychosomatic illnesses. They sell their products to doctors with the promise that a prescription will relieve boredom, anxiety, or depression. Doctors seem to agree; prescriptions to women account for 60 percent of psychotropic (mood-altering) drugs, 71 percent of antidepressants, and 80 percent of amphetamines. Many women develop drug habituations and then need to raise their dosage in order to maintain a sense of well-being. According to emergency room statistics, 90 percent of drug overdoses involve women who have taken legal substances.

A doctor may prescribe a mood-altering drug for depression and, left on her own, an unhappy woman may also turn to drink—unaware that the combination is likely to kill her. Because society stigmatizes alcoholic women more than alcoholic men, the scope of this problem remains hidden. As recently as 1970, only twenty-nine English-language studies had been done on female drinkers.

Recent studies suggest that women drink because they are unhappy. According to Edith Hornik in *The Drinking Woman,* a specific situation such as moving, divorce, miscarriage, or menopause may act as a catalyst for feelings of inferiority, frustration, or loneliness among women at home. The working woman who drinks has similar feelings, but they are triggered by different situations: she may drink to be one of the boys or to loosen up and feel more feminine. Unlike male alcoholics, who tend to drink in bouts and prefer beer, female alcoholics are generally steady drinkers and incline toward hard liquor and wine.

Studies done by Alcoholics Anonymous demonstrate that alcoholism among women cuts across racial, religious, social and economic lines. Of women seeking treatment, 40 percent are housewives, 20 percent are sales and clerical workers, 20 percent are executives and professionals, 10 percent are semi-skilled, and 10 percent are in other jobs. Women aged twenty to twenty-nine make up the highest proportion of heavy drinkers by age; unfortunately, this corresponds to prime childbearing years. Offspring of alcoholic women are prone to fetal alcoholic syndrome in which alcohol penetrates the placental barrier and inhibits intra-uterine growth. Besides suffering from congenital defects, children from alcoholic families are often neglected or abused; one-third of child-abuse cases are alcohol-related.

Women substance abusers need special treatment programs which link drug habituation and alcoholism, which offer modalities of treatment unlike the aggressive, confrontative models (which work for some men), and which provide for child care, employment counseling, nutrition counseling, and medical attention. In addition to developing treatment programs for the individual abuser, feminists and health-care activists have begun to analyze the social matrix which breeds substance abuse among women in the first place.

See also: Health Care

Organizations:

Alcohol, Drug Abuse and Mental Health Agency
Women's Council Building 36
9000 Rockville Pike
Bethesda, MD 20014

National Clearinghouse for Alcohol Information
Women's Program
9119 Gaither Road
Gaithersburg, MD 20760

National Council on Alcoholism
Office on Women
733 Third Avenue
New York, NY 10017

National Institute on Drug Abuse
Program for Women's Concerns
5600 Fishers Lane
Rockville, MD 20852

National Women's Drug Research
Coordinating Project
1015 E. Huron Street
Ann Arbor, MI 48104

The Other Victims of Alcoholism
P.O. Box 921
Radio City Station
New York, NY 10019

Women for Sobriety
P.O. Box 618
Quakertown, PA 18951

Resources:

The Drinking Woman, by Edith Lynn Hornik. New York: Association Press, 1977.

An easy-to-read text about the hazards of cross-addiction and substance abuse, the hidden addict, and the need for the addicted women to face her situation and seek help.

Drugs, Alcohol, and Women: A National Forum, prepared by National Institute on Drug Abuse, Project for Women's Concerns. Washington: National Research and Communications Associates, 1975. Order from: National Research and Communications Associates, 4201 Connecticut Avenue N.E., Washington, DC 20008.

Considers innovative planning, national legislation, youthful abusers, service delivery, future strategies.

Drugs, Resources, and Women's Health: An Alliance of Regional Coalitions. Washington: National Research and Communications Associates, 1978. Order from: National Research and Communications Associates, 4201 Connecticut Avenue N.E., Washington, DC 20008.

Information on organizing strategy, gaps in current knowledge, necessary changes.

Turnabout: Help for a New Life, by Jean Kirkpatrick. Garden City: Doubleday, 1978.

By the founder of Women for Sobriety, the book discusses the problems and cures for the woman alcoholic.

Women and Alcohol: A Bibliography. Hartford: Connecticut State Alcohol Council, 1976. Order from: Connecticut State Alcohol Council, 90 Washington Street, Hartford, CT 06115.

Women and Drug Concerns Bibliography, compiled by Ruth Hargraves and Muriel Nellis. Washington: Department of Drug and Alcohol Concerns, United Methodist Church, 1974. Order from: Board of Church and Society, Department of Drug and Alcohol Concerns, United Methodist Church, 100 Maryland Avenue N.E., Washington, DC 20002.

TITLE IX

EVER SINCE *BROWN* v. *BOARD OF EDUCATION,* THE 1954 SUPREME COURT decision mandating desegregation of public schools, a great deal of legislation has been passed attempting to ensure equal educational opportunity. With the heightened consciousness brought about by the women's movement in the late 1960's, many women (and men)—teachers, students, parents—began to examine schools and colleges for sex bias and discrimination. They found a disturbingly *institutionalized* pattern of sex-role stereotyping and discrimination. After a series of hearings in which this discrimination was brought to the attention of Congress, Title IX of the 1972 Education Amendments was passed. It states: "No person in the United States shall, on the basis of sex, be excluded from participation in, be denied the benefits of, or be subject to discrimination under any education program or activity receiving Federal financial assistance." Regulations which provide for the implementation of Title IX were drafted by the Office for Civil Rights and signed into law on July 21, 1975. One of the most—if not the most—sweeping of sex discrimination laws went into effect.

Title IX provides for equal opportunity in five basic areas: "admissions to most education institutions [some were exempted]; access to and treatment in curricular and extracurricular programs and activities; treatment under regulations and policies governing student benefits, services, conduct, and dress; access to employment in education agencies and institutions; terms, conditions, and benefits of such employment."

While Title IX may be one of the most sweeping of sex discrimination laws, it is also one of the most poorly enforced. Several monitoring projects have sprung up in different areas around the country, and the results are not encouraging. The most comprehensive national report was made by the Project on Equal Education Rights (PEER) in 1977. Its title, *Stalled at the Start,* says it all. Blaming the Office for Civil Rights, PEER made the following conclusions based on their study:

— HEW brought relief to few of the citizens who asked for help in gaining equal treatment;
— most people who filed complaints met with long delays;
— most investigations were cursory;
— HEW has done almost nothing to enforce Title IX besides work on complaints;
— yet HEW *has* had enough staff to enforce Title IX;
— indecision has been a major obstacle to action.

Without the force of authority from above, the local school districts have been discouragingly lax in responding to requirements of Title IX. They learned quickly that there was, in fact, no need to comply. Not until "the last minute of the last day," the comment of one school superintendent, sums up the intention of many.

An attorney for a school board in Mississippi advised them to do nothing "until people in the community get wind of it." People in the community have gotten wind of it. If you believe that Title IX is not being enforced in your local schools, contact one of the organizations listed below, form a monitoring project, or use the guide to file your complaint.

See also: Affirmative Action
Financial Aid for Education
Nonsexist Education
Sex Discrimination in Education
Sports
Vocational Education
Women's Educational Equity Act

Organizations:

American Association of University
  Women
2401 Virginia Avenue N.W.
Washington, DC 20037

Office for Civil Rights
Department of Health, Education and
  Welfare
Washington, DC 20201

Project on Equal Education Rights
NOW Legal Defense and Education Fund
1029 Vermont Avenue N.W.
Washington, DC 20005

Resources:

Almost as Fairly: The First Year of Title IX Implementation in Six Southern States. Atlanta: Southeastern Public Education Program, American Friends Service Committee, 1977. Order from: Southeastern Public Education Program, 52 Fairlie Street N.W., Atlanta, GA 30303.

Complying with Title IX: A Resource Kit, prepared by the Resource Center on Sex Roles in Education. Washington: Office of Education, Department of Health, Education and Welfare, 1976. Order from: Superintendent of Documents, Government Printing Office, Washington, DC 20402.
This series of twelve pamphlets is the most comprehensive guide to the law available. Items may be ordered individually or as a set; write for compete information.

Final Title IX Regulation Implementing Education Amendments of 1972. Washington: Office for Civil Rights, Department of Health, Education and Welfare, 1975. Order from: Public Affairs, Office for Civil Rights (address above).
A complete listing of the regulations with a fact sheet and question-and-answer-style explanation of compliance.

PEER Perspective. Order from: Project on Equal Education Rights (address above).

This quarterly newsletter provides the best ongoing coverage of Title IX implementation, compliance problems and successes. It also includes a valuable resource listing.

Stalled at the Start. Washington: Project on Equal Education Rights, 1977. Order from: Project on Equal Education Rights (address above).

The most comprehensive and telling document to date on the status of Title IX. It provided much of the information in the text above.

Title IX Kit. Washington: Project on the Status and Education of Women, n.d. Order from: Project on the Status and Education of Women, 1818 R Street N.W., Washington, DC 20009.

The Kit includes, among other things, three bibliographies of reading on Title IX.

Title IX Enforcement Record

Only one in 5 of the 858 complaints filed in 4 years had been resolved by the fall of 1976.

The cases HEW did resolve waited an average of 14 months for final action.

Complaints that were still open in June, 1976, had been pending an average of 16 months.

Only 61 cases—7.1 percent of all the complaints—were investigated and resolved within 6 months.

22 percent of all complaints filed were dropped without an investigation. About 60 percent of those cases could and should have been investigated.

The total case load of complaints filed against public schools was just over 5 complaints per investigator each year.

Excerpted from *Stalled at the Start*, Project on Equal Education Rights. Washington, 1977.

♀ ANYONE'S GUIDE TO FILING A TITLE IX COMPLAINT ♀

Different treatment based on a person's sex by schools, colleges and other institutions receiving federal education aid is illegal in the United States under Title IX of the Education Amendments of 1972.

The U.S. Department of Health, Education and Welfare (HEW) is charged with making sure that schools and colleges stop discriminating because of a person's sex. But HEW's civil rights office depends on citizens around the country to let it know when these institutions may be breaking the law.

If you believe your school is treating students or employees unfairly on account of their sex, you might want to go directly to school authorities, and ask them to change. If that approach doesn't work, or you would rather go to the government first (which is your right), here's how to ask HEW for help.

Who Can File a Title IX Complaint?   Anybody—an individual citizen or a group—can ask HEW to check into possible violations of Title IX. Both students and employees are directly protected by the law, and can file charges, known as "complaints."

However, you don't have to be a victim of discrimination yourself to file a complaint. Parents, community organizations and ordinary interested citizens may ask HEW to investigate possible violations.

One more point. If you are concerned that you might be harassed if you alone file a complaint (employers sometimes give workers trouble to persuade them to withdraw their complaints), try to get an organization in your area to file for you. Local chapters of such groups as the National Organization for Women (NOW), the American Civil Liberties Union (ACLU), the American Association of University Women (AAUW), and the Women's Equity Action League (WEAL) might be willing to press your case. In any event, harassment itself is a violation of Title IX. If you are harassed, be sure to tell HEW to add that charge to your complaint.

Is There a Deadline?   Generally, you must file a Title IX complaint within 180 days after the discrimination occurs. But, if the discrimination is ongoing—certain classes are closed to boys or girls, or the girls' athletics program is inferior to the boys'—you can file a complaint at any time.

Is There a Required Form?   No. A letter to HEW's Office for Civil Rights explaining why you believe your school or college is violating the law is all it takes. You have to include certain basic information which HEW needs to proceed with its investigation. Sometimes HEW will send back a form for you to complete to provide that information, but usually a letter is enough.

A recent court order set standards for HEW's investigation of complaints, including what information HEW must have to consider a complaint "complete." Although HEW must give you a reasonable chance to fill in any missing details from an "incomplete" complaint, you will save yourself time and effort if you include all the necessary information in your first letter.

Here's what must be in your letter:

— The name and address of the school district, college or other institution you believe is discriminating by sex;
— A general description of the person or persons suffering from that discrimination (you don't have to give HEW names or addresses, although, if there are only one or two victims of specific acts of discrimination, it would be helpful if you did);
— The approximate date the discrimination happened, or if it's still going on;
— Your name, address, and, if possible, a telephone number where you can be reached during the day;
— Enough information about the discrimination for HEW to understand what happened.

In addition to those basic requirements, it's a good idea to give HEW the names, addresses, and telephone numbers of others who may have additional information about the charges. Explain why HEW should talk with them. Also, if you know about written sources of information—student or employee manuals, or school board budget documents that might help HEW in its investigation—you should call them to HEW's attention.

If your complaint involves an emergency—you or someone else is about to be fired or suspended from school, for instance—label it so, and ask HEW to act fast. HEW doesn't have to move faster in emergencies, but knowledge that prompt action could keep someone from serious academic or financial injury might prod the government into a quicker response.

HEW is required to keep you informed about the progress and results of its investigation. If the government turns up information that goes against your charges, you must be given a chance to counter it with evidence of your own. You also must be given a copy of the formal "letter of findings" from the investigation. *If you request* them, HEW must give you copies of its correspondence with the school or college you complained about concerning what must be done to correct any violations HEW found.

Where Do I Send the Complaint?   Address your letter to the director of the HEW regional Office for Civil Rights with jurisdiction over your state (see below).

You might also want to send copies to your representatives and senators in Congress, the members of the school board of trustees, local newspapers and local organizations which might be interested—unless you want your identity as the person who filed the complaint to be kept confidential.

Send PEER a copy of your complaint. Unfortunately, we can't offer much assistance to individuals; there just aren't enough of us to go around. But we can push HEW for stronger enforcement in general if we know better what's happening around the country.

What About Privacy?   HEW is supposed to keep confidential the identity of the person or group who files a complaint, unless this information must be disclosed during the course of an investigation.

But if you want your name withheld, it's a good idea to stress that in your letter to HEW. And ask HEW to tell you in advance if there are plans to reveal your name.

On the other hand, publicity can often work to your advantage. Individuals and groups can sometimes pressure institutions into quickly changing unfair practices simply by generating interest in the charges. Sometimes those changes occur before HEW has a chance to investigate.

What If There's More Than One Instance of Discrimination?   If you believe there's a pattern of discrimination against girls and women throughout the school, school district or college, say so in the complaint. Describe each kind of discrimination, and ask HEW to look into them all.

Even if you just want to end one particular discrimination problem—someone has been barred from a course because of her sex, for instance—try to show it's not an isolated incident. Your case will be stronger if you can show a general pattern of unfair treatment of women and girls (or men and boys).

What Will HEW Do with the Complaints?   After receiving your complaint letter, HEW must promptly write you back acknowledging it. If HEW needs more information to begin an investigation, the letter to you must spell out what is required.

Once your complaint is "complete," HEW will tell you if it will be investigated immediately, or some time in the future. *Don't give up!* HEW will get around to your case, and when it does you will be asked if you are still interested. HEW probably won't go ahead unless you say so, but remember: The government does the investigating; you need only get involved as much as you wish. Also, there are others coming along behind you who are also being discriminated against. You can help them merely by telling HEW to proceed; it takes no more than a fifteen-cent stamp.

If you happen to move, when you tell your friends the news, send a letter to HEW, too. Explain that you're still interested in seeing your complaint resolved, and include your new address.

When HEW begins an investigation, it has 90 days to determine if the school or college complained about is in fact violating the law. If you wish, you have the right to be interviewed, and to have HEW talk with anyone else who might know about the discrimination. You also must be given a chance (if you desire) to challenge any conclusions reached by HEW that conflict with your charges.

HEW must give you a copy of its formal "letter of findings" to the institution. After that HEW has 90 days in which to negotiate an agreement with the institution to correct any violations. You must be kept advised about the status of the negotiations and the corrective action being sought. *If you request it,* HEW must give you copies of correspondence with the institution concerning the negotiations.

If HEW agrees to accept less than you would like to correct a violation, HEW must let you make your case for stronger corrective action.

At the end of the negotiation period, if HEW has not been able to settle the case, it has 30 days in which to begin formal enforcement proceedings that could lead to that institution losing its federal money.

HEW may stretch these time frames if a necessary witness is unavailable due to summer vacation. But under no circumstances may HEW delay more than 30 days after the end of summer recess.

Is It Worth It to File a Complaint?   You alone can decide, but there are some very good reasons for doing so.

— If you have been pressuring a school district or college to end sex-biased practices and have met strong opposition to change, then sometimes the act of filing a complaint with the government will break the resistance.
— HEW does carry a lot of weight when it does an investigation. It can cut off federal dollars to a school district or college that refuses to change.
— HEW's estimation of the public demand for an end to sex discrimination in education is based in large part on the number of Title IX complaints filed. The more complaints HEW receives, the more likely it is that HEW will devote greater energy and resources to enforcing Title IX.

Remember: Filing a complaint need not require that you spend a lot of time. HEW must let you get involved if you choose, but if you would prefer to keep a low profile and let HEW do it all, that's okay, too.

WHERE TO SEND YOUR COMPLAINT:

REGION I: Connecticut, Maine, Massachusetts, New Hampshire, Rhode Island, Vermont
John G. Bynoe, Director
Office for Civil Rights, DHEW
140 Federal Street, 14th Floor
Boston, MA 02110
(617) 223-6397

REGION II: New Jersey, New York, Puerto Rico, Virgin Islands
William R. Valentine, Acting Director
Office for Civil Rights, DHEW
26 Federal Plaza, Room 33-130
New York, NY 10007
(212) 264-4633

REGION III: Delaware, Maryland, Pennsylvania, Virginia, Washington, DC, West Virginia
Dewey Dodds, Director
Office for Civil Rights, DHEW
3535 Market Street
Philadelphia, PA 19101
(215) 596-6771

REGION IV: Alabama, Florida, Georgia, Kentucky, Mississippi, North Carolina, South Carolina, Tennessee
William Thomas, Director
Office for Civil Rights, DHEW
101 Marietta Street N.W.
Atlanta, GA 30323
(404) 221-2954

REGION V: Illinois, Minnesota, Wisconsin
Kenneth A. Mines, Director
Office for Civil Rights, DHEW
300 South Wacker Drive, 8th Floor
Chicago, IL 60606
(312) 353-2520

Michigan, Ohio, Indiana
Ortha Barr, Chief, Elementary and Secondary Education

Office for Civil Rights, DHEW
55 Erieview Plaza, Room 222
Cleveland, OH 44114
(216)-522-4970

REGION VI: Arkansas, Louisiana, New Mexico, Oklahoma, Texas
Dorothy Stuck, Director
Office for Civil Rights, DEW
1200 Main Tower Building, 19th Floor
Dallas, TX 75202
(214) 767-3951

REGION VII: Iowa, Kansas, Missouri, Nebraska
Taylor D. August, Director
Office for Civil Rights, DHEW
1150 Grand Avenue, 7th Floor
Kansas City, MO 64106
(816) 374-2474

REGION VIII: Colorado, Montana, North Dakota, South Dakota, Utah, Wyoming
Gilbert D. Roman, Director
Office for Civil Rights, DHEW
1961 Stout Street
Denver, CO 80294
(303) 837-2025

REGION IX: Arizona, California, Hawaii, Nevada
Floyd L. Pierce, Director
Office for Civil Rights, DHEW
100 Van Ness Avenue, 14th Floor
San Francisco, CA 94102
(415) 556-8586

REGION X: Alaska, Idaho, Oregon, Washington
Marlaina Kiner, Director
Office for Civil Rights, DHEW
1321 Second Avenue
M/S 508
Seattle, WA 98101
(206) 442-0473

Guide prepared by Project on Equal Education Rights (address above).

TITLE VII

TITLE VII OF THE CIVIL RIGHTS ACT OF 1976 PROHIBITS DISCRIMINATION IN employment on account of sex, race, color, religion or national origin. Title VII applies to private employers, employment agencies, labor organizations, and labor-management apprenticeships or training programs. Specifically excluded are religious institutions, *bona fide* private clubs, and Indian tribes. Covered under the Act are employees, job applicants, union members, applicants for union membership, apprentices, and apprenticeship applicants. The Act created the Equal Employment Opportunity Commission (EEOC) and gave it the authority to receive, investigate, and conciliate complaints. EEOC also has the right to sue on behalf of complainants.

Under the leadership of Eleanor Holmes Norton, the EEOC has undergone a complete reorganization since September 1977. New procedures for processing complaints were developed and tested in field offices and are now in effect in an expanded field structure of fifty-nine bureaus. The backlog of cases has been cleared and should not be a problem in the future due to the greater efficiency of the new procedures. The Commission also hopes to initiate class action against discriminatory patterns and practices, in an effort to further affirmative action on a large scale. Finally, the EEOC has assumed jurisdiction over laws previously enforced by other agencies. Enforcement of the Equal Pay Act was transferred from the Department of Labor, responsibility for federal employees was transferred from the Civil Service Commission, and overall coordination of federal programs was taken over from the Equal Employment Opportunity Coordinating Council. This reorganization and consolidation of equal employment opportunity enforcement should have a profound effect on affirmative action in the years to come.

See also: Affirmative Action

Organizations:

Equal Employment Opportunity Commission
2401 E Street N.W.
Washington, DC 20506

Resources:

EEOC: The Transformation of an Agency. Washington: Equal Employment Opportunity Commission, 1978. Order from: EEOC (address above).
   A brief guide to the new Commission, this pamphlet describes the new procedures and jurisdictions.

Know Your Rights: What You Should Know About Equal Employment Opportunity. Washington: Equal Employment Opportunity Commission, 1977. Order from: EEOC (address above).
   This little pamphlet explains what constitutes discrimination, and how and where to file a charge; it includes a list of EEOC district offices.

VETERANS' PREFERENCE

ONE GOVERNMENT OFFICIAL STATED RECENTLY THAT IF SCRUTINIZED AS A private corporation, the federal government would be found guilty of affirmative action violations. The largest employer in the nation, with 2.8 million civilian employees, its record on the employment of women is poor.

One of the major obstacles to equitable employment of women within the federal government is veterans' preference (see below). Veterans, 98 percent of whom are men, hold 48 percent of all federal jobs, but comprise only 25 percent of the total national work force. Women, on the other hand, comprise only 30 percent of government employees while they are 42 percent of the work force. Veterans hold 65 percent of all jobs at the top three levels of the federal government, while women hold less than 3 percent of these jobs. Of those who pass the Civil Service Professional and Administrative Career Examination (PACE), 41 percent are women. However, only 27 percent of those are hired. Veterans are 20 percent of those who pass; 34 percent of veterans who pass are hired.

Originally intended to compensate men who interrupted their careers for wartime service, veterans' preference has become a barrier to equal employment opportunities for women. The preference system adds five points to test scores (out of a possible score of 100) for most veterans and 10 points for disabled veterans. Veterans also have retention rights where there is a reduction in force. In other words, veterans are the first hired and the last fired!

Reform efforts have been made. President Carter proposed as part of the Civil Service Reform Act of 1978, a modified system that would regulate the use of the preference for able-bodied veterans, increase employment opportunities for disabled and Vietnam veterans, and reduce the discriminatory effects against women. Specifically, it would have established a time limit on hiring, promotion, and retention preference as well as limit this to a one-time-only use for nondisabled veterans. Mae Walterhouse of Federally Employed Women, testifying in favor of the legislation, stated, "Let me make it clear that FEW does not oppose veterans' preference where necessary to compensate for a sacrifice by a veteran for the public good. We can understand the hardship faced by Vietnam veterans or veterans of earlier conflicts, who had difficulty finding jobs upon their separation from service. For this reason, we would accept a compromise under which a one-time use of the veterans' preference for initial hiring would be permitted. . . . However, a person who chooses a military career is not making a sacrifice and should not be entitled to veterans' preferences." While changes were made in favor of disabled veterans, reforms affecting women were lost.

Veterans' preference is also used by state governments in their employment practices. Regulations vary from state to state: Oregon has veterans' preference limited to one-time use, while Massachusetts ranks any veteran with a passing score of 66 above a nonveteran with a score as high as 99. In June of 1979 the Supreme Court upheld the Massachusetts law allowing veterans to be hired in preference to nonveterans regardless of test scores. While the Court ruled that the law was gender neutral and not discriminatory in intent and therefore not unconstitutional, the Justices conceded that it does overwhelmingly benefit men and gives veterans "more than a square deal." This ruling is likely to have a negative impact on future efforts to change veterans' preference laws.

Federally Employed Women is continuing efforts to reform the veterans' preference system. They have formed a coalition of forty women's and civil rights groups working to get new legislation introduced.

See also: Affirmative Action
          Legal Status

Organizations:

Federally Employed Women
485 National Press Building
Washington, DC 20045

Resources:

Introducing the Civil Service Reform Act. Washington: U.S. Civil Service
    Commission, 1978. Order from: Superintendent of Documents, U.S. Govern-
    ment Printing Office, Washington, DC 20402.

This pamphlet explains the reorganization of the Civil Service Commission under the Civil Service Reform Act and includes guidelines for Veterans' Preference and Benefits.

*Testimony of Federally Employed Women, Inc. (FEW) Before the Subcommittee
    on Civil Service, Committee on Post Office and Civil Service, House of
    Representatives, April 12, 1978, on H.R. 11280, A Bill to Reform the Civil
    Service Laws.*

Unpublished testimony of Mae. M. Walterhouse, representing Federally Employed Women's position on veterans' preference. Provided much of the information for the text above.

Veterans Preference. Washington: Federally Employed Women, n.d. Order from
    Federally Employed Women, address above.

This informative brochure details the veterans' preference regulations, the impact on women's employment in the federal government, and FEW's position and recommendations for change.

♀ VETERANS' PREFERENCE LAW ♀

The Veterans' Preference Act of 1944 was enacted by Congress following World War II to facilitate the reentry of veterans into the work force. Current civil service policy is still based on this 1944 law, which entitles a veteran to employment and retention preference in competitive service. This is how veterans' preference works:

— 10 points automatically are added to the passing score of a civil service
   employment applicant who was *disabled* on account of military service.
— 5 points automatically are added to the passing score of a *nondisabled*
   applicant.
— Disabled veterans with 10 point preference automatically are placed at the
   top of most civil service registers for which they are qualified.
— Veterans with preference may not be passed over to select a nonpreference

eligible applicant unless the Office of Personnel Management or an agency under delegate authority approves the reason for "pass-over."
— During government job layoffs (RIFs) veterans are the last workers to lose their jobs.

EFFECT ON VIETNAM-ERA VETERANS

Existing data indicate that veterans' preference has not substantially helped the Vietnam-era veterans.

— While 50% of federal employees are veterans, only 10% are Vietnam-era veterans.
— The 8 million Vietnam-era veterans must compete for jobs with the 20 million older veterans who served in other wars or in peacetime.
— Although Vietnam-era veterans are 30% of the total veterans, they hold less than 18% of the federal jobs held by veterans in the civilian work force.

This is not because Vietnam-era veterans don't want federal jobs, but because even with preference, they cannot compete with the more experienced, older veteran who also enjoys lifetime preference. In 1977, Vietnam-era veterans were only 42% of the new hires, compared to 58% pre-Vietnam or career military veterans.

Vietnam-era veterans will benefit from modification of veterans' preference since the proposed changes will substantially reduce the pool of preference eligibles from 30 million to 10 million, by eliminating the 20 million nondisabled veterans who served in earlier wars or peacetime and have readjusted to civilian life years ago.

PROPOSED CHANGES IN VETERANS' PREFERENCE LAW

1. 5 point preference would be available to nondisabled veterans for *one time* successful use during a full 15 years following discharge (or until 1985, whichever comes later). Disabled veterans will continue to have 10 points added to their passing scores and would rise to the top of employment registers for which they qualify.
2. Disabled veterans would have lifetime preference protection against layoffs. Nondisabled veterans would have absolute job protection for 8 years following appointment. Thereafter, they would have the same retention rights as their nonveteran co-workers, on the basis of quality of performance and length of service (military and federal).

These changes do not interfere with the current 10 point derivative benefits for spouses, widows, widowers and mothers of deceased or disabled veterans who apply for civil service positions.

Reprinted from *Veterans' Preference Fact Sheet*, prepared by Federally Employed Women.

VOCATIONAL EDUCATION

WOMEN ARE ENTERING THE LABOR FORCE IN EVER-INCREASING NUMBERS; 90 percent of all women now work at some time during their lives. Enforcement of affirmative action regulations will open up more and more jobs in the skilled trades to women. Adequate vocational preparation is imperative if women are to take advantage of these opportunities. Unfortunately, vocational education has been one of the areas with the most entrenched sex discrimination. This discrimination has taken the following forms: single-sex vocational schools, sex-segregated courses, biased career education materials, negative attitudes of counselors and teachers.

Single-sex vocational schools were outlawed under Title IX and were given until 1979 to integrate. Vocational courses are not only sex-segregated, they are *sex-typed*, as the accompanying chart indicates. Nearly half of all female students enrolled in vocational courses are in home economics—a field which does not even lead to work outside the home. These girls are learning nothing that will prepare them for paid employment. Those female students who are learning a job skill are preparing themselves for the lowest paying work. Clerical workers earn from about $96 to $115 a week; skilled trades workers such as electricians, masons, and plumbers, on the other hand, average $269 to $285 a week.

Career education materials overwhelmingly support this division of labor by sex. A recent study showed that of 1,121 occupations considered (more than 80 curricular pieces were reviewed), only 69 were portrayed as open to both men and women. And again, low-paying jobs were designated as appropriate for women: "If you're a girl you'd probably rather handle curlers than tools."

Sex discrimination in vocational education is not legal. In 1976, new legislation (the Education Amendments of 1976) revised and extended existing laws covering vocational education to include specific mandates to end sex discrimination. The Vocational Education Amendments provide for, among other things, federal investigation of the extent of sex bias, the collection of vocational education statistics by race and sex, the submission by states of one- and five-year plans detailing equal access procedures and the appointment of a Sex Equity Coordinator in each state. This is another area of education where legislation has been passed, but not enforced. Citizen monitoring will be necessary if the laws are to be implemented and the discrimination halted.

See also: Nontraditional Occupations
Sex Discrimination in Education
Title IX

Organizations:

Center for Vocational Education
Ohio State University
1960 Kenny Road
Columbus, OH 43210

Federal Education Project
Lawyers Committee for Civil Rights Under Law
733 15th Street N.W.
Washington, DC 20005

Resources:

Help Wanted: Sexism in Career Education Materials. Princeton: Women on Words and Images, 1975. Order from: WOWI, P.O. Box 2163, Princeton, NJ 08540.

This excellent study documents the different kinds of sexism found in vocational education materials. It is also available as a slide show.

How To Erase Sex Discrimination in Vocational Education, by Patricia Beyea and Geraldine O'Kane. New York: Women's Rights Project, American Civil Liberties Union, 1977. Order from: ACLU, 22 East 40th Street, New York, NY 10016.

The ACLU guide provides analysis and documentation of sex discrimination in vocational education, a complete explanation of the Vocational Education Amendments, and step-by-step advice on how to organize on the local level. Recommended.

Resources on Eliminating Sex Role Stereotyping in Vocational Education, ed. by Faith Justice and Wesley Budke. Columbus: Center for Vocational Education, 1977. Order from: Dissemination and Utilization, National Center for Vocational Education (address above).

Recently updated, this resource list includes organizational listings of state, local and national projects, bibliographies and nonprint media as well as nonsexist career education materials.

Sex Equality in Vocational Education: A Chance for Educators to Expand Opportunities for Students, by Barbara G. Schonborn and Mary L. O'Neil. San Francisco: Women's Educational Equity Communications Network, 1978. Order from: WEECN, Far West Laboratory, 1855 Folsom Street, San Francisco, CA 94103.

An excellent overview describing problems with discrimination, explaining the laws that have been passed, and providing advice and resources to educators attempting to comply.

PERCENTAGE DISTRIBUTION OF ENROLLMENT IN VOCATIONAL EDUCATION AREAS BY SEX—1975

Program	Percent male	Percent female
Agriculture	90.8	9.2
Distribution	57.2	42.8
Health	28.3	71.7
Home Economics	18.1	81.9
Office	30.7	69.3
Technical	89.3	10.7
Trade and Industrial	87.4	12.6

Source: Unpublished report by Harold Duis, *Comparative Analysis of Vocational Education Enrollments by Sex in Fiscal Years 1972 and 1975.* Washington: Bureau of Occupational and Adult Education, Office of Education.

VOLUNTEERISM

VOLUNTEERISM—DIRECT ACTION TO IMPROVE COMMUNITY AND INDIVIDUAL welfare—was a hallmark of American life even before the Revolutionary War. The pioneer spirit, religious conviction and social and economic necessity predisposed people to help one another. Visitors to the U.S. were impressed by the vitality of volunteer associations, but not until the Civil War did Americans themselves realize volunteerism's financial and morale-building potential. The U.S. Sanitation Commission, a volunteer corps dedicated to improving health conditions in army camps and hospitals, raised $25 million dollars, a fantastic sum in those days, to accomplish its goals.

Local branches of the Sanitation Commission were staffed by women volunteers who extended their roles as nurturer and comforter from the immediate family to the soldiers in their care. After the war, women continued to volunteer in activities for social amelioration: Clara Barton began the American Red Cross, Dorothea Dix championed the rights of the insane, Lillian Wald worked with the urban poor. Also during the nineteenth century, white, educated, financially secure women, denied access to political parties and professions, formed volunteer associations of their own in order to participate in political reform and social change. Examples of these crusades were the Women's Christian Temperance Union, the National American Women's Suffrage Association and inner-city settlement houses like Jane Addams' Hull House. As the years passed much of this work was accomplished or taken over by government and social service agencies, and the focus of volunteer work shifted to community and religious-group involvement. While the patterns of women's volunteer work changed, their commitment to it did not.

Angry attacks from feminists in the early 1970's in conjunction with rising inflation changed the face of volunteerism in the United States. In 1971 and 1974, the National Organization of Women denounced volunteerism as exploitation of women, an extension of the housewife role of working without pay or recognition. In fact, NOW claimed, wealthy volunteers added injury to injustice by taking jobs away from the poor. NOW has since modified its stance, but the die was cast. Volunteerism lost prestige, and women who had been happy to give time to the church, the hospital, or the local political campaign rethought their options. At the same time, the economy had become so inflated that many families were ripe for an extra income.

Since then, volunteerism has been rethought and recast. The new emphasis is on professionalization—considering the volunteer experience a career ladder to a paying job. The volunteer expects regular, agreed-upon hours, job supervision, a job description, references, and perhaps academic credit. Moreover, the professional volunteer will not do just anything—she or he wants an interesting, challenging experience that includes learning as well as doing.

Recruiting volunteers and keeping them happy is crucial to more than seven million volunteer-staffed groups as well as to social and cultural institutions who use volunteers as the backbone of their operation. Estimates of the number of volunteers range between thirteen million and seventy million Americans who work six billion people-hours yearly. Their efforts are worth more than twenty-six billion dollars each year.

Greenwich Settlement House, New York City. Middle- and upper-class women became pioneers in social work through their volunteer work in settlement houses. In addition to educational and recreational programs for children, they provided English courses and job training to adults and spoke out against the poor living and working conditions of the immigrant and laboring classes. *Brown Brothers*

The most recent, comprehensive study of volunteerism in America was made by ACTION, the federal government's volunteer agency, in 1974. The study discovered that most volunteers are white, middle- to upper-class women between the ages of twenty-five and forty-four. The preferred volunteer activity was religious work and the most cited rationale for service was the desire to help others. These conclusions may still hold true, but trends have significantly changed since 1974. New sources of volunteers have sprung up among men, minorities, youth, and the elderly. Many prefer community work and counseling; religious organizations complain that their services are withering for lack of staff. And as mentioned, women and youth in particular pick volunteer activities with one eye to their career and another to helping the community.

Changes in volunteerism have had an impact on corporations and on local, state and federal governments. Three hundred United States corporations encourage their employees to take time off in order to work in the community. The Department of Labor and the Civil Service Commission accept volunteer work as *bona fide* job experience. In future, the thrust will be to persuade small businesses and more local governments to do the same. Volunteers are urged to document their activities and to insist to their employers that their service is serious. Such innovations are welcome; women, in particular, stand to benefit.

See also: Career Development
Continuing Education for Women
Employment
Jewish Women
Politics

Organizations:

Alliance for Volunteerism
1214 16th Street N.W.
Washington, DC 20036

Association of Junior Leagues
825 Third Avenue
New York, NY 10022

National Center for Voluntary Action
1214 16th Street N.W.
Washington, DC 20036

Women in Community Service
1730 Rhode Island Avenue N.W.
Washington, DC 20036

Resources:

Americans as Volunteers. Washington: ACTION, 1975. Order from: Superintendent of Documents, Government Printing Office, Washington, DC 20402.
The study cited in the text, which provided much of the information for this article.

How to Get College Credit for What You Have Learned As a Homemaker and Volunteer, by Ruth Ekstrom, Abigail Harris, and Marlaine Lockheed. Princeton: Educational Testing Service, 1977. Order from: Educational Testing Service, Princeton, NJ 08541.
Practical guide to determine what experiences can be considered for college credit and how to ascertain competency.

Voluntary Participation Among Women in the United States: A Selected Bibliography, 1950–1976. New Brunswick: Center for the American Woman and Politics, Rutgers University, 1976. Order from: CAWP, Rutgers University, New Brunswick, NJ 08901.
Includes the nature, extent, and political impact of American women's voluntary activities; ideology, motivations, and rewards. Lists bibliographies, directories, periodicals, books, monographs, articles.

WELFARE AND POVERTY

IT IS NO NEWS TO THE NEARLY TEN MILLION WOMEN WHO LIVE BELOW THE federal poverty line—$6,200 in 1978—that women are victimized by the lack of job-training programs, day care, and funding for abortion. Of the 25.9 million Americans categorized as poor in March 1976, 9.4 million were women, 11.1 million were children, and 5.4 million were men. Women's incomes are 60 percent of men's, women comprise two-thirds of all minimum-wage earners, and account for 80 percent of workers in eight of the ten lowest-paying occupations. But, as dismal as these statistics are, even low-paying employment is impossible for women who are single heads of households with young children to care for.

Mothers who can't work because their children are too young to go to school or to be left alone, receive Aid to Families with Dependent Children (AFDC). Like food stamps, Medicare, and aid to the disabled, AFDC is a form of welfare. Each state has its own AFDC program; therefore the fifty states have widely varying eligibility qualifications and benefits. The federal government gives the state a grant based on the state's expenditures and administrative costs. In 1978, President Carter introduced a welfare reform bill which would have set a floor for assistance at $4,200. The bill died because of its twenty-billion-dollar price tag.

In 1977, 3.6 million families (3.3 million adults and 7.8 million children) received AFDC. Ninety-seven percent of the adult recipients were women heads of households. These women must cope daily with the problems of poverty: inadequate health-care services, poor education, substandard housing, and lack of job skills. Such women are candidates only for low-level jobs, which pay little and offer no job security; seven out of ten women heads of households who do find jobs work as clerical staff or as household workers. Given the low wages of these jobs, many women opt for public assistance. That way they can take care of their children and their homes full-time.

A 1970 survey of welfare mothers revealed that 80 percent would prefer to work rather than to receive public assistance. But these women need job training, counseling, and child care so that they can compete for good-paying, interesting jobs. The federal government has proposed "workfare" instead of welfare. In exchange for assistance, recipients would have to accept low-paying, low-level jobs. This is hardly the route out of poverty.

In ten years, the number of female-headed families has risen ten times faster than the number of families with two parents. Unfortunately, one out of three families headed by women live below the poverty line as opposed to one out of nine male-headed families and one out of eighteen two-parent families. As one welfare activist quipped: "Every woman is just a man away from welfare." Too glib? Not really. Any woman can become pregnant, divorced, or widowed, and—unable to find a job or an alternative means of support—be forced to accept welfare. Programs guaranteeing adequate jobs and income are important not only for women currently on welfare, but for all women.

See also: Child Care
Child Support
Continuing Education for Women
Displaced Homemakers
Divorce
Employment
Minority Women
Working-Class Women

Organizations:

National Community Action Task Force on Women in Poverty
c/o Bolliger
824 North Cooper
Peoria, IL 61606

National Women's Program Development
P.O. Box 9385
San Antonio, TX 78204

Network
1029 Vermont Avenue N.W.
Washington, DC 20005

Women in Community Service
1730 Rhode Island Avenue N.W.
Washington, DC 20036

Resources:

Annual Report of the Social Security Administration for Fiscal Year 1977. Washington: Committee on Ways and Means, House of Representatives, 1978. Order from: Superintendent of Documents, Government Printing Office, Washington, DC 20402.
Statistics, legislation, program policy, and planning.

"To Promote the General Welfare" . . . *Unfinished Agenda.* Washington: League

of Women Voters, 1977. Order from: League of Women Voters, 1730 M Street N.W., Washington, DC 20036.

Chock-full of information, this small pamphlet describes who the poor are, what the assistance reforms do and what reforms are needed.

A Welfare Mother, by Susan Sheehan. Boston: Houghton Mifflin, 1976.

This in-depth portrait of a welfare mother in New York is a welcome change of pace from studies and statistics. Sheehan's book fleshes out the studies with a taste of humanity.

WOMEN AND DEVELOPMENT

DEVELOPMENT—THE ECONOMIC IMPROVEMENT AND INDUSTRIALIZATION OF poor countries—has been part of the foreign affairs program of Western nations during most of the twentieth century. These programs have taken various forms—cash grants, the loan of agricultural and planning experts, the donation of machinery. Called missionary at best and imperialist at worst, government-sponsored development programs have been criticized by leftist and socialist groups over the years. Now, a new voice has joined the chorus. Feminist scholars have begun to look at the effects development programs have had on women and they have not been pleased with what they see.

According to recent research, the sins of development planners are of both types: omission and commission. On the omission side is an almost universal ignorance of the special role women play in their countries. Women are assumed to be unimportant in the economic life of the nation and they are given no consideration in development planning.

First of all, developers tend to see only an unsophisticated and impoverished economy. They are insensitive to the unique cultural, social, and religious life which varies from country to country—and to women's role within it. In a subsistence economy, every able-bodied person makes a valuable contribution—women included. When this fact is ignored, women are not only excluded from plans for improvement, they may actually lose the economic status they have. As the country industrializes, women are no longer needed for at-home production of small goods. Because they are not seen as workers by Western developers, there is no place for them in developing industry either. They are usually excluded from vocational training programs and from agriculture as it mechanizes.

The sexism inherent in the efforts of Western developers obviously proceeds from their own experience and beliefs—as do their sins of commission. Along with economic aid, developing countries also find themselves the recipients of a full set of Western social and cultural ideas. They must come to resemble the developed countries socially as well as economically. This kind of cultural imperialism can have a disastrous effect on women in many societies. Development programs create economies and cultures riddled with the same sex discrimination women in the West are now battling so intensely.

Feminist researchers have presented some fundamental challenges to development planners. They have called for a realignment of priorities which would place "improved human well-being" above strict economic goals. They urge a holistic approach which would gauge the social and psychological results of economic "improvements." Ultimately, they refuse to believe that "development" has taken place when a country's Gross National Product improves at the expense of its female population.

Organizations:

International Women's Tribune Center
305 East 46th Street
New York, NY 10017

Overseas Education Fund
League of Women Voters
2101 L Street N.W.
Washington, DC 20037

Secretariat for Women in Development
New TransCentury Foundation
1789 Columbia Road N.W.
Washington, DC 20009

U.N. Branch for the Advancement of
  Women
United Nations, Room DC-1033
New York, NY 10017

Resources:

Development As If Women Mattered: An Annotated Bibliography with A Third World Focus, compiled by May Rihani. Washington: Overseas Development Council, 1978. Order from: Overseas Development Council, 1717 Massachusetts Avenue N.W., Washington, DC 20036.

An excellent source for new research into women and development. Ms. Rihani's introduction summarizes the issues succinctly and forms an important part of the basis for the text above.

Integration of Women in Development: Why, When, How, by Ester Boserup. New York: United Nations Development Programme, 1975.

This little pamphlet gives a good basic introduction to the issue of women and development, and includes a section of proposals for action.

International Directory of Women's Development Organizations. Washington: Agency for International Development, 1977. Order from: Women in Development, Agency for International Development, Department of State, Washington, DC 20523.

The directory includes local and national women's organizations for nearly 300 countries, as well as international women's organizations and international resources.

Women and World Development, ed. by Irene Tinker, Michele Bo Bramsen, Mayra Buvinic. New York: Praeger, 1976.

Based on a seminar on women and development sponsored by the American Association for the Advancement of Science, this volume includes a dozen research papers, the proceedings of the conference, and an extensive annotated bibliography. The text above is based in part on the introduction to this volume.

WOMEN AND RELIGION

IN THE INTRODUCTION TO *WOMANSPIRIT RISING,* CAROL CHRIST AND JUDITH Plaskow point out:

Feminists have charged that Judaism and Christianity are sexist religions with a male God and traditions of male leadership that legitimate the superiority of men in family and society. This new challenge to traditional faiths just confirms the view of some feminists that society has outgrown its need for religion. They agree with Freud and Marx that religions keep people dependent on authority and thwart their desire to improve their material situations. Other feminists, however, are convinced that religion is profoundly important. For them, the discovery that religions teach the inferiority of women is experienced as a betrayal of deeply felt spiritual and ritual experience. They believe that the history of sexism in religions shows how deeply sexism has permeated the human psyche but does not invalidate human need for ritual, symbol, and myth.

Feminists of both persuasions often recount that their disenchantment with religion began with their sense of exclusion from leadership positions, male-oriented liturgical and God language, and the theological community's systematic blindness toward women's experiences.

The history of Western religion begins with the migration of the Hebrew people into the land of Canaan during the second millennium before the common era. Merlin Stone, in her book, *When God Was a Woman,* describes how Yahwist (Hebrew) religion accelerated the downfall of woman-oriented pagan religions. Yahweh, the archetypal male deity—man of war, storm-god—led his people into a new land and helped them to subdue and conquer it. Once the Hebrews settled in, they gave up their nomadic existence to establish cities and social networks. In time they needed a lawgiver God more than a man of war. Out of this need evolved a new vision of God—that of the priests and the halakhah.

Under halakhah, Scriptural law, woman is treated differently than man. Specific religious laws define her rights in marriage and the respect she is due as wife and mother. But she may not testify in court and she is exempt from most liturgical and ritual responsibilities other than lighting Sabbath candles (and keeping Sabbath and other holy days), making the home kosher (and supervising the family's adherence to Jewish law and custom), and observing the laws of personal hygiene. Because of her exemption from most of the commandments the Jewish woman is, virtually, denied positions of public leadership. But providing a Jewish home and educating her children are vital to the community's survival; Orthodox Jews insist that "an electrician is not a carpenter" and that women are separate but equal.

Christianity, in its first revolutionary flush, tried to undo some of Judaism's strict attitudes toward sex-role differentiation. Like many heretical and apocalyptic sects set over and against society, Christianity inverted social norms by empowering the powerless. For a time, women could participate equally with men and could even lead rituals. But this period was short-lived—only seventy-five years out of Christianity's two-thousand-year history. As Christianity lost its renegade status and gained power in its own right, women lost their equality.

Another blow to women's equality, says theologian Rosemary Ruether, was the political upheavals, migrations, and breakdowns in tribal culture during the first millennium of the common era, factors which gave rise to dualistic thinking. Early Christianity internalized the supposed dichotomy between heaven/earth, mind/body, spirit/flesh, man/woman. Thus ended a holistic approach to life and began a history of hierarchical relationships. One of the most destructive polarities was set up between spirituality and sexuality. Eve was blamed for the downfall of humanity and female sexuality was condemned as shameful.

In consequence, the medieval religious tradition was not charitable in its outlook toward women. Mary may have been worshiped and idealized but she was hardly a role model whom women could emulate. Women did find independence within convents; women's education and culture survived in these autonomous religious enclaves.

Possibly the happiest note to sound in fifteen hundred years came when Martin Luther nailed his theses to the door at Wittenberg. By sanctifying marriage and motherhood, Luther helped to elevate the status of women.

The egalitarian spirit of colonial North America also boosted the status of women in religion. New religions founded by women took root and grew in American soil. Mary Baker Eddy started the Christian Scientists, still in force today, and Ann Lee founded the Shakers, largest and most successful of American communitarian sects. In 1853, Antoinette Brown Blackwell was the first woman ordained in a traditional Protestant denomination. Kathryn Kuhlman and Ruth Carter Stapleton developed ministries as faith healers. Two American women have been canonized by the Roman Catholic Church: Mother Cabrini and Elizabeth Seton.

Many of today's religious women are concerned with a broad social justice agenda: they form action-oriented task forces to promote peace, justice, and equality worldwide. Church Women United works at the community level, setting up centers that combat drug abuse, establishing re-entry programs for women ex-offenders, and providing expanded health-care services. The Unitarian Universalist Women's Federation has been active in dealing with the concerns of the elderly; women in the United Church of Christ have devoted time and energy to an enlightened exploration of human sexuality. The Institute of Women Today, a Chicago-based ecumenical group, does outreach work with women in prisons.

Religious women's groups also work in coalitions. The public education campaign on infant-formula sales abuse in developing nations and the boycott of Nestlé products was spearheaded by several orders of Roman Catholic sisters and Church Women United. Similar campaigns have been launched to eradicate world hunger, to divert military spending to human services, and to improve the status of women worldwide, including ratification of the ERA in the United States.

Women actively involved in religion are waging the same battles that feminists fight in society-at-large. Religious feminists want to eliminate sexist language from the Bible and in liturgies, to recast patriarchal myths, and to gain positions of leadership and authority within their institutions.

They are also struggling to integrate a viable spirituality with their social and political point of view. A tension exists between women who see their experience as a journey from oppression to liberation and who, like Mary Daly, opt for a new feminist theology, and those who think that women's traditional roles—wife and mother—can be creatively reappropriated. Another debate centers on whether religion should promote male/female equality or female ascendency. Plaskow and Christ note:

Those feminists who work within the biblical traditions tend to call for equality in religious rituals and symbolisms, while those whose theological or spiritual reflection is primarily rooted in the women's movement, especially in consciousness-raising groups, more often call for at least temporary ascendency of women and the female principle . . .

The fundamental commitment that feminists in religion share to end male ascendency in society and religion is more important than their differences. Time will tell which strategies prove most effective in achieving the shared goal. What is clear is that, if feminists succeed, religion will never be the same again.

See also: Feminist Spirituality
Ordination of Women

Organizations:

Center of Concern
Women's Project
3700 13th Street N.E.
Washington, DC 20017

Church Women United
475 Riverside Drive
New York, NY 10027

Episcopal Women's Caucus
935 East Avenue
Rochester, NY 14607

Institute for Women Today
1340 East 72nd Street
Chicago, IL 60619

Leadership Conference of Women
Religious
1302 18th Street N.W.
Washington, DC 20036

Lutheran Church Women
2900 Queen Lane
Philadelphia, PA 19129

National Assembly of Women Religious
1307 S. Wabash
Chicago, IL 60605

National Coalition of American Nuns
1307 S. Wabash
Chicago, IL 60605

National Sisters Communication Service
1962 South Shenandoah
Los Angeles, CA 90034

St. Joan's International Alliance
435 West 119th Street
New York, NY 10027

Union of American Hebrew Congregations
Task Force on Equality of Women
838 Fifth Avenue
New York, NY 10021

United Church of Christ
Advisory Committee on Women and
Society
297 Park Avenue South
New York, NY 10010

Unitarian Universalist Women's Federation
25 Beacon Street
Boston, MA 02108

United Methodist Church
National Commission on the Status and
Role of Women
1200 Davis Street
Evanston, IL 60201

United Methodist Church
Women's Division of Board of Global
Ministries
475 Riverside Drive
New York, NY 10027

United Presbyterian Church
Council on Women and the Church
475 Riverside Drive
New York, NY 10027

Women's Ecumenical Consulting Group
475 Riverside Drive
New York, NY 10027

Resources:

Face to Face: An Interreligious Bulletin. Special issue: *Women and the Religious Communities* (Spring 1978). Order from: Anti-Defamation League, 315 Lexington Avenue, New York, NY 10016.

Articles on women in Roman Catholicism, Protestantism, Judaism and Greek Orthodoxy. Discusses women's social and religious status within these traditions.

Sexist Religion and Women in the Church, ed. by Alice Hageman in collaboration with the Women's Caucus of the Harvard Divinity School. New York: Association Press, 1974.

Excellent resource book. Essays provide an introduction to religious women's issues: ministry, black women in the church, religious socialization of women, religion and sexuality, women in Judaism, sexism in the Church.

Sixth Edition of the Annotated Bibliography on the Jewish Woman, by Aviva Cantor. Fresh Meadows: Biblio Press, 1978. Order from: Biblio Press, P.O. Box 22, Fresh Meadows, NY 11365.

Listings of books, papers, pamphlets, articles on Jewish women in the categories of history, religion and law, U.S. and Canada, Holocaust and Resistance, Israel, children's literature, fiction and nonfiction.

When God Was a Woman, by Merlin Stone. New York: Harcourt Brace Jovanovich, 1976.

Provocative study of prepatriarchal religion. Helpful for reclaiming women's history and mythology.

The Woman's Bible, by Elizabeth Cady Stanton. Reprint of the 1895 edition. New York: Arno, 1972.

Woman: A Theological Perspective, compiled by Claire B. Fischer and Rochelle Gatlin. Berkeley: Center for Women and Religion, Graduate Theological Union, 1977. Order from: Graduate Theological Union, Center for Women and Religion, 2465 LeConte Avenue, Berkeley, CA 94709.

Womanspirit Rising, edited by Carol P. Christ and Judith Plaskow. San Francisco: Harper and Row, 1979.

Excellent reader of feminist theology. Covers several basic concerns: does theology speak to women's experience, can we reappropriate the past, how do we reconstruct traditions, how do we create new ones.

Women and Religion: Selected Bibliography, 1965–1972, by Elizabeth Farians. Cincinnati, 1973. Order from: Elizabeth Farians, 6125 Webbland Place, Cincinnati, OH 45213.

Women of Spirit, ed. by Eleanor McLaughlin and Rosemary Ruether. New York: Simon and Schuster, 1979.

New anthology covering women in Christianity and Judaism from the early Church to the present day. Excellent material on women and ordination in the Catholic and Episcopal churches, and on women rabbis.

GLOSSARY OF SUBSTITUTE TERMINOLOGY

Masculine Terms	*Substitutes*
Lord	God, Almighty, Blessed One, Eternal, Divine, Guardian, Creator, Redeemer, Ruler, Protector, Heavenly One, Maker, Holy One, Most High, Exalted

Masculine Terms	Substitutes
Father	One, God, Parent, Maker, Creator
Heavenly Father	Heavenly One
man, fellow man	humanity, people, us
children of men	men and women, thy children, people
sons of men	human beings, generations
God and Father	Our God (in Heaven)
fathers	ancestors, forebears, patriarchs and matriarchs
Abraham, Isaac and Jacob	add: Sarah, Rebecca, Leah and Rachel
King	ruler, sovereign
kingdom	rule, reign, realm
brotherhood or fellowship	kinship, community, unity
He	second person pronoun —Thou (You) God
His	Thy, God's, Your
brethren	brothers and sisters, one
Master	Ruler
House of Jacob	House of Israel
God of Jacob	God of our ancestors, God of Israel
Shield of Abraham	Shield of our ancestors

Reprinted with the permission of the compilers, The Task Force on the Equality of Women in Judaism, New York Federation of Reform Synagogues.

WOMEN BUSINESS OWNERS

WOMEN HAVE OWNED AND OPERATED BUSINESSES IN THIS COUNTRY throughout its history. Since the colonial period, wives and daughters have worked in family businesses and widows have taken them over entirely.

Recently, there has been a renewed interest in entrepreneurship among women. From 1972 to 1977, the growth rate for self-employed women was three times that for men. Yet, the estimate of one million women-owned firms indicates that women still account for only a small portion of the total business picture. In 1972, women-owned firms accounted for 4.6 percent of all United States companies, and 3 percent of all receipts. The National Association of Women Business Owners estimates that for every thirty cents earned by a woman business owner, her male counterpart earned, on the average, a hundred dollars. This discrepancy is partly explained by the kinds of businesses women own—primarily retail trade and services rather than the more lucrative heavy industry or manufacturing. Seventy-one percent of women-owned businesses have fewer than five employees. Finally, the majority of women-owned businesses, 98 percent, are sole proprietorships. All these factors add up to one thing: the businesses women own are small, in size and in profit.

Organizations:

American Woman's Economic
Development Corporation
1270 Avenue of the Americas
New York, NY 10020

National Association of Negro Business
and Professional Women's Clubs
1806 New Hampshire Avenue N.W.
Washington, DC 20009

National Association of Women Business
Owners
2000 P Street N.W.
Washington, DC 20036

National Federation of Business and
Professional Women's Clubs
2012 Massachusetts Avenue N.W.
Washington, DC 20036

Office of Minority Business Enterprise
U.S. Department of Commerce
Washington, DC 20230

Office of Women in Business
Small Business Administration
Washington, DC 20416

Resources:

The Bottom Line: (Un)Equal Enterprise in America. Washington: Task Force on Women Business Owners, 1978. Order from: Superintendent of Documents, Government Printing Office, Washington, DC 20402.

Report of the Task Force's study of women business owners; reveals patterns of discrimination, educational limitations, lack of information on women entrepreneurs, and more.

A National Index of Women-Owned Businesses. Washington: National Association of Women Business Owners, forthcoming.

NAWBO has recently launched the *Index* project and plans to publish three metropolitan-wide directories in 1979, for Washington/Baltimore, Boston, and Chicago. Write to them (address above) for more information.

Small Business: Look Before You Leap; A Catalog of Information To Help You Start and Manage Your Own Small Business, ed. by Louis Mucciolo. Order from: Marlu, P.O. Box 11, Dobbs Ferry, NY 10522.

This catalog is a useful guide to books, pamphlets, services, agencies, and organizations that can help the entrepreneur start and manage a small business. A brief chapter on women business owners describes books and organizations especially geared to women, but points out that the whole book is useful to everybody. Written in nonsexist language, *Look Before You Leap* is a good starting place for the prospective businesswoman.

Statement. The monthly newsletter of the National Association of Women Business Owners, address above.

Women-Owned Businesses 1972. Washington: Office of Minority Business Enterprise, 1976. Order from: Government Printing Office, Superintendent of Documents, Washington, DC 20402.

This report, while a bit dated, is the most comprehensive source of statistical information on women business owners, and supplied the information in the text above.

WOMEN'S ARTS AND MEDIA

THE WOMEN'S MOVEMENT HAS DEVELOPED SINCE THE 1960'S AS A REMARKABLY self-contained whole. That is, as feminists became progressively more dissatisfied with male-biased services, products, and entertainment—culture—they created their own. Feminist publishers, music companies, art galleries, film producers, and theater groups began to spring up and flourish all across the country.

These women-owned cultural enterprises have played an array of roles. In addition to the most obvious function of providing feminist books, art, and music for an ever-growing (and appreciative) audience, these institutions have provided an outlet for women whose work would otherwise go unnoticed and unrewarded. They have provided a place for women to learn technical skills they would have little or no opportunity to learn elsewhere. In fact, many of the feminist art and media groups have made a conscious decision to pass on valuable technical expertise in order to keep the culture coming. Because of their feminist principles, most of the groups have experimented with new ways of working. Placing a high value on the quality of their work lives as well as of their products, they have tried to develop nonhierarchical structures with an emphasis on collective decision making. Finally, they have been a vital and integral part of the larger women's movement. By providing an outlet for women's self-expression and a vehicle for communication within the movement, these institutions have been crucial to the development of feminist theory and consciousness.

Because women's cultural groups often operate on a local level—and on a shoestring budget—it is difficult to provide a comprehensive, accurate directory. The resources below should fill the gaps in the selective listings provided.

ART

Organizations:

Coalition of Women's Art Organizations
9112 Brierly Road
Chevy Chase, MD 20015

Women's Caucus for Art
59 Castle Howard Road
Princeton, NJ 08540

Resources:

Chrysalis. Order from: Chrysalis, 635 South Westlake Avenue, Los Angeles, CA 90057.

A quarterly of women's culture; includes poetry, art reproduction, fiction, feminist theory and listings of feminist works.

Guide to Women's Art Organizations: Groups, Activities, Networks, Publications, ed. by Cynthia Navaretta. New York: Midmarch Associates, 1979. Order from: Midmarch Associates, P.O. Box 3304, Grand Central Station, New York, NY 10017.

A most comprehensive directory of women's organizations in the visual arts, architecture, design, film and video, dance, music, theater, writing. The pamphlet also includes a bibliography and lists of funding organizations, art agencies and bookstores.

Heresies. Order from: Heresies, P.O. Box 766, Canal Street Station, New York, NY 10013.

Meg Christian, popular feminist singer and songwriter, is one of the founders of Olivia Records, an all-women recording company. © *Gail Bryan*

This quarterly is subtitled "a journal of feminist art and politics." Each issue is theme oriented; recent issues have discussed traditional arts and crafts, goddess religion, and lesbian art.

Women Artists News. Order from: WAN, P.O. Box 3304, Grand Central Station, New York, NY 10017.

A monthly which is somewhat New York-centered, but covers women's art news nationally.

FILM

Resources:

Positive Images: Nonsexist Films for Young People, compiled by Linda Artel and Susan Wengraf. San Francisco: Booklegger Press, 1976. Order from: Booklegger Press, 555 29th Street, San Francisco, CA 94131.

With an emphasis on their use with young adults, this directory lists films, video tapes, photographs, filmstrips and slide shows.

Women in Focus, compiled by Jeanne Betancourt. Dayton: Pflaum Publishing, 1974.

Geared for use in the classroom, this directory also includes a brief bibliography, program suggestions, and a theme index to films.

Women's Films in Print, compiled by Bonnie Dawson. San Francisco: Booklegger Press, 1975. Order from: Booklegger Press, 555 29th Street, San Francisco, CA 94131.

Probably the most extensive guide to films by women, this annotated directory lists eight hundred films.

Workprint. Order from: Filmwomen, P.O. Box 275, Cambridge, MA 02138.

Miriam Shapiro at work in her studio. Shapiro and other feminist artists have created an exciting new movement—both in their art and in their institutions. Shapiro, for example, uses many kinds of needlework, women's traditional art, in her work. She is also a member of the editorial collective of *Heresies*, a feminist art journal, and a founder of the Feminist Art Institute scheduled to open in New York City in the fall of 1979. © *Ellie Thompson, 1978*

MUSIC

Music Women. Order from: Sight and Sound Women, 20 West 22nd Street, New York, NY 10010.

The monthly newsletter of Sight and Sound Women.

Paid My Dues. Order from: Women's Soul Publishing, P.O. Box 11646, Milwaukee, WI 53211.

This quarterly publishes songs, articles about women musicians—living and dead—reviews, et al.

PUBLISHING AND LITERARY

The Feminist Writers Guild
P.O. Box 9396
Berkeley, CA 94709

Women's Institute for Freedom of the
  Press
3306 Ross Place N.W.
Washington, DC 20008

The Feminist Review. Order from: *New Women's Times,* 1357 Monroe Avenue, Rochester, NY 14618.

A recently initiated book review will appear monthly as a supplement to *New Women's Times.*

Guide to Women's Publishing, by Polly Joan and Andrea Chesman. Paradise, Calif.: Dustbooks, 1978. Order from: Dustbooks, P.O. Box 100, Paradise, CA 95969.

The first major directory of women's publishing, intended to be updated annually. The editors provide an interesting commentary on the state of feminist publishing in addition to the directory.

Media Report to Women. Order from: Women's Institute for Freedom of the Press (address above).

A monthly newsletter packed with information on women's media of all types. Recommended.

Motherroot Journal. Order from: Motherroot Publications, 214 Dewey Street, Pittsburgh, PA 15218.

Another new review journal for women's writing.

Women's Arts and Media Groups

ARTS

Washington Women's Art Center
1821 Q Street N.W.
Washington, DC 20009

Women in the Arts Foundation
435 Broome Street
New York, NY 10013

Women's Building
1727 North Spring Street
Los Angeles, CA 90012

Women's Interart Center
549 West 52nd Street
New York, NY 10019

FILM

Filmwomen
P.O. Box 275
Cambridge, MA 02138

Iris Films
P.O. Box 5353
Berkeley, CA 94705

New Day Films
P.O. Box 315
Franklin Lakes, NJ 07417

Women Make Movies
257 West 19th Street
New York, NY 10011

Women's Labor History Film Project
1735 New Hampshire Avenue N.W.
Washington, DC 20009

MUSIC

Feminist Radio Network
P.O. Box 5537
Washington, DC 20016

Olivia Records
2662 Harrison Street
Oakland, CA 94612

Sight and Sound Women
20 West 22nd Street
New York, NY 10010

PUBLISHERS

Alice James Books
138 Mt. Auburn Street
Cambridge, MA 02138

Daughters, Inc.
22 Charles Street
New York, NY 10014

Diana Press
4400 Market Street
Oakland, CA 94608

The Feminist Press
P.O. Box 334
Old Westbury, NY 11568

KNOW, Inc.
P.O. Box 86031
Pittsburgh, PA 15221

Lollipop Power
P.O. Box 1171
Chapel Hill, NC 27514

Shameless Hussy Press
P.O. Box 3092
Berkeley, CA 94703

Women's Press Collective
5251 Broadway
Oakland, CA 94618

WOMEN'S BOOKSTORES

FINDING BOOKS BY AND ABOUT WOMEN IN ONE'S LOCAL BOOKSTORE IS NOT always easy; this is especially true of books published by women's presses. So, over the years, bookstores specializing in feminist materials have cropped up across the country. Like other alternative institutions, some of them have not been financial successes and so were short-lived. Many feminist bookstores, however, have stayed in business past the five-year small business "make it or break it" point. Indeed, some of them have become well-known feminist cultural institutions offering autograph parties, poetry readings and study groups. The list below includes more than seventy stores in thirty-two states.

See also: Women's Arts and Media

♀ WOMEN'S BOOKSTORES ♀

Alaska
Ships, Shoes & Sealing Wax
4704 Kenai
Anchorage, AK 99504

Arizona
Antigone Books
415 North 4th Avenue
Tucson, AZ 85705 (602) 792-3715

Womanspace
2401 North 32nd Street
Phoenix, AZ 85008 (602) 956-0456

California
Fahrenheit 451
509 South Coast Highway
Laguna Beach, CA 92651 (714) 494-5151

Feminist Wicca
442 Lincoln Boulevard
Venice, CA 90291 (213) 399-3919

I.C.I./A Woman's Place
5251 Broadway at College
Oakland, CA 94618 (415) 654-9920

Interconnection
123 Pearl Alley
Santa Cruz, CA 95060 (408) 426-1317

Old Wives' Tales
532 Valencia Street
San Francisco, CA 94110 (415) 552-1015

Page One
26 North Lake Avenue
Pasadena, CA 91101 (213) 792-9011

Rising Woman Books
600 Wilson Drive
Santa Rosa, CA 95401 (707) 545-6590

Sacramento Women's Center
1230 H Street
Sacramento, CA 95814 (916) 457-2533

Sisterhood Bookstore
1351 Westwood Boulevard
Los Angeles, CA 90024 (213) 477-7300

Sojourner Bookstore
538 Redondo Avenue
Long Beach, CA 90814 (213) 433-5384

The Oracle
22640 Main Street
Hayward, CA 94541 (415) 886-1268

The Women's Store
2965 Beech Street
San Diego, CA 92102 (714) 233-4164

Womankind Bookstore
6551 Trigo Road
Isla Vista, CA 93017 (805) 685-3969

Colorado
Woman to Woman Bookcenter
2023 East Colfax
Denver, CO 80206 (303) 320-5972

Connecticut
Bloodroot Restaurant/Bookstore
85 Ferris Street
Bridgeport, CT 06605 (203) 576-9168

Sonya Wetstone Books & Cheese
529 Farmington Avenue
Hartford, CT 06105 (203) 232-3710

District of Columbia
Lammas Women's Shop
321 Seventh Street S.E.
Washington, DC 20003 (202) 546-7292

Florida
Amelia's
12 N.W. 8th Street
Gainesville, FL 32601 (904) 377-0234

Georgia
Charis: Books & More
419 Moreland Avenue N.E.
Atlanta, GA 30307 (404) 524-0304

Illinois
Jane Addams Bookstore
5 South Wabash Avenue
Chicago, IL 60603 (312) 782-0708

Small Changes Bookstore
409A North Main Street
Bloomington, IL 61701 (309) 829-6223

Sojourner Bookstore Center
203 East Locust
De Kalb, IL 60115 (815) 758-8178

Indiana
A Room of One's Own
101½ West Kirkwood
Bloomington, IN 47401 (812) 334-9733

Sisterspace
1414 Broadway
Fort Wayne, IN 46802 (219) 424-6317

The Woman's Touch, Inc.
6352 West 37th Street
Indianapolis, IN 46224 (317) 299-6336

Iowa
A Mind of Your Own
1171 25th Street
Des Moines, IA 50311 (515) 277-9091

Plains Woman Bookstore
529 South Gilbert
Iowa City, IA 52240 (319) 338-9842

Maryland
A Room of One's Own
12 Francis Street
Annapolis, MD 21401 (301) 267-6827

The 31st Street Bookstore
425 East 31st Street
Baltimore, MD 21218 (301) 243-3131

Massachusetts
Isis Unveiled
199 Commercial Street
Provincetown, MA 02657

New Words
186 Hampshire Street
Cambridge, MA 02139 (617) 876-5310

The Women's Bookstore
1087 Main Street
Worcester, MA 01603 (617) 791-5127

Womynfire Books
68 Masonic Street
Northampton, MA 01060 (413) 586-6445

Michigan
Her Shelf
2 Highland
Highland Park, MI 48203 (313) 869-4045

Womanself Bookstore
University Mall
220 MAC
East Lansing, MI 48823 (517) 337-2404

Womanspace
211½ North 4th Avenue
Ann Arbor, MI 48104 (313) 995-3400

Minnesota
Amazon Bookstore
2607 Hennepin Avenue South
Minneapolis, MN 55408 (612) 374-5507

Missouri
New Earth Bookstore
24 East 39th Street
Kansas City, MO 64111 (816) 931-5794

The Women's Eye
6344 South Rosebury
St. Louis, MO 63105 (314) 721-1616

Nebraska
The Book End
7641 Pacific Street
Omaha, NB 68114 (402) 391-1121

New Jersey
Herizon
92½ Elm Street
Morristown, NJ 07960 (201) 267-3858

New Hampshire
Women's Words
Fountain Square
Contoocook, NH 03229 (603) 456-3871

New Mexico
Full Circle Books
135 Harvard Street S.E.
Albuquerque, NM 87106 (505) 266-2333

New York
Alternatives Corner
374 Woodfield Road
West Hempstead, NY 11552 (516) 483-2050

Djuna Books
154 West 10th Street
New York, NY 10014 (212) 242-3642

Emma
2474 Main Street
Buffalo, NY 12414 (716) 836-8970

Kay's Book Studio
86 Front Street
Binghamton, NY 13902 (607) 722-4032

Shameless Hussy
9 Prospect Street
Nanuet, NY 10954 (914) 623-5819

Smedley's Bookshop
119 East Buffalo Street
Ithaca, NY 14850 (607) 273-2325

Womanbooks
201 West 92nd Street
New York, NY 10025 (212) 873-4121

Women's Works Bookstore
181 Seventh Avenue
Brooklyn, NY 11215 (212) 499-7763

North Carolina
The New Leaf
223 North Bloodworth Street
Raleigh, NC 27601 (919) 828-3135

Ohio
Coventry Books
1824 Coventry Road
Cleveland Heights, OH 44118 (216)
  932-8111

Fan the Flames
127 East Woodruff Avenue
Columbus, OH 43201 (614) 291-7756

Oregon
A Woman's Place Bookstore
1300 S.W. Washington
Portland, OR 97205 (503) 226-0848

Book and Tea Shop
1646 East 19th Avenue
Eugene, OR 97403 (503) 344-3422

Mother Kali's Books
541 Blair
Eugene, OR 97404 (503) 343-4864

Pennsylvania
Alternative Booksellers
10 North 4th Street
Reading, PA 19601 (215) 373-0442

Birmingham Booksellers
2222 East Carson Street
Pittsburgh, PA 15203 (412) 431-8666

Tennessee
Womankind Books
2015-B Belmont Boulevard
Nashville, TN 37212 (615) 292-1597

Texas
Common Woman Bookstore
1510 San Antonio Street, #4
Austin, TX 78704 (512) 472-2785

The Bookstore/Mary Ross Rhyne
1728 Bissonet
Houston, TX 77005 (713) 527-8522

Virginia
Labrys Books
8 North Allen
Richmond, VA 23220 (804) 355-2001

Washington
It's About Time
5241 University Way N.E.
Seattle, WA 98105 (206) 525-0999

Wisconsin
A Room of One's Own
317 West Johnson Street
Madison, WI 53703 (608) 257-7888

Sister Moon Bookstore/Gallery #1
1625 East Irving Place
Milwaukee, WI 53202 (414) 276-0909

Sister Moon Bookstore/Gallery #2
2128 East Locust
Milwaukee, WI 53202 (414) 962-3323

List compiled by and used with the permission of Womanbooks (see above, under New York, for address).

WOMEN'S CENTERS

WOMEN'S CENTERS ARE, IN MANY WAYS, THE BACKBONE OF THE CONTEMPORARY women's movement. Developed to serve needs on the local level, they often provide the first contact with organized feminist activity for women looking for involvement. Many are service oriented, providing everything from information and referral, to courses in car repair, to C-R groups; others may be simply a place for women to get together with other women—to talk, relax, console, plan, meet, laugh and cry in a supportive atmosphere.

The staff are usually volunteers from the constituency served by the centers; most are organized collectively with all staff participating in decision-making and sharing responsibilities from clean-up to fund-raising. Local YWCAs, which provide residences and programs for women, were forerunners of the modern women's centers. In fact, many Y's now house women's centers. The actual number of centers is unknown. Most centers face a day-to-day existence, relying on volunteer staff and on donations for space, equipment, and funds.

Estimates place the average life of a women's center at two years. In updating the Women's Action Alliance list of women's centers in the United States, we found that only half of a total of three hundred centers were still in operation after three years. Women's centers often live and grow and change into something else—a women's bookstore or restaurant, a social action group. Recently, many centers have become more specialized, offering assistance to battered women or rape victims. For all the centers that die each year, new ones spring up to take their place.

An important development for women's centers is the funding of the National Women's Centers Training Project by the Women's Educational Equity Act. The Project staff, currently working only with campus-based centers, hopes to branch out by offering the training to community-based women's centers as well.

To locate a center near you, see the list below or contact the following organizations for additional, up-to-date information.

See also: Women's Movement

Organizations:

National Women's Centers Training
Project
Women's Educational Equity Training
Project
Nelson House
University of Massachusetts
Amherst, MA 01003

Women's Action Alliance
370 Lexington Avenue
New York, NY 10017

YWCA
National Board
600 Lexington Avenue
New York, NY 10022

Resources:

Everywoman's Center: Evolution of an Alternative. Amherst: Everywoman's Center, 1975. Order from: Everywoman's Center, University of Massachusetts, Amherst, MA 01002.

This booklet offers insight into the development of a college-based women's center, including a chapter on staff, structure, and goals as well as chapters devoted to program development.

How to Organize a Multi-Service Women's Center. New York: Women's Action Alliance, 1976. Order from: Women's Action Alliance (address above).

A how-to guide including information on organizational structure, staffing, facilities, and operations; legalities, fund-raising and program development; includes case studies.

Union Center for Women: The Creation and Development of a Women's Center. Brooklyn: Union Center for Women, 1975. Order from: Union Center, 8101 Ridge Boulevard, Brooklyn, NY 11209.

This pamphlet provides helpful background information on the development of a neighborhood-focused women's center.

Developing Women's Programs. Amherst: National Women's Centers Training

Project, 1978. Order from: EDC/WEEAP, Distribution Center, 39 Chapel Street, Newton, MA 02160.

This pamphlet provides step-by-step guidelines for planning programs specifically geared to the needs of women, plus advice on assessing program needs, determining objectives, and selecting appropriate program approaches and activities.

Developing and Negotiating Budgets for Women's Programs. Amherst: National Women's Centers Training Project, 1978. Order from: EDC/WEEAP, Distribution Center, 39 Chapel Street, Newton, MA 02160.

A guide to various types of budgeting, ways of securing funds, and procedures to help plan budgeting cycles and to prepare actual budgets.

♀ WOMEN'S CENTERS ♀

Arizona
ASUA Women's Drop-In Center
S.U. 106
University of Arizona
Tucson, AZ 85721
602-884-3919

Flagstaff Women's Resource Center
3 North Leroux Street, Room 201
Flagstaff, AZ 86001
602-774-1008

Women's Center
333 East McDowell
Phoenix, AZ 85004
602-258-9227

California
Berkeley Women's Center
2112 Channing Way
Berkeley, CA 94704
415-548-4343

Center for Women's Studies & Services
908 F Street
San Diego, CA 92101
714-223-8984

Chicana Service Action Center
2244 Beverly Boulevard
Los Angeles, CA 90057
213-381-7261

ICI—A Woman's Place
5251 Broadway
Oakland, CA 94618
415-547-9920

Resource Center for Women
445 Sherman Avenue
Palo Alto, CA 94306
415-324-1710

Sacramento Women's Center & Bookstore
1230 H Street
Sacramento, CA 95814
916-442-4657

San Francisco Women's Center
3543 18th Street
San Francisco, CA 94110
415-431-1180

San Jose State University Women's Center
177 South 10th Street
San Jose, CA 95152
408-294-7265

San Luis Obispo Women's Resource
Center
738-D Higuera
San Luis Obispo, CA 93401
805-544-9313

South County Women's Center
25036 Carlos Bee Boulevard
Hayward, CA 94542
415-537-2112

U.C. Women's Center
University of California
Berkeley, CA 94720
415-642-4786

Women's Center
California State University
LH 209
Fullerton, CA 92634
714-870-3928

Women's Center
Compton Community College
1111 East Artesia Boulevard
Compton, CA 90221
213-635-8081

Women's Community
1727 North Spring Street
Los Angeles, CA 90012
  213-221-6162

Women's Resource Center
2 Dodd Hall
University of California
Los Angeles, CA 90024
  213-825-3945

Women's Resources and Research Center
TB116
University of California
Davis, CA 95616
  916-752-3372

Colorado
Boulder County Women's Resource Center
1406 Pine
Boulder, CO 80302
  303-447-9670

Research Center on Women
Loretto Heights College
3001 S. Federal Boulevard
Denver, CO 80236
  303-936-8441, ext. 253

Virginia Neal Blue Resource Center
Colorado Women's College
Montview and Quebec Streets
Denver, CO 80220
  303-399-8303

Connecticut
Hartford Women's Center
57 Pratt Street, Suite 301
Hartford, CT 06103
  203-525-2382

Information & Counseling Service for
  Women
301 Crown Street
New Haven, CT 06520
  203-436-8242

New Haven Women's Liberation Center
148 Orange Street
New Haven, CT 06510
  202-436-0645

Prudence Crandall Center for Women
37 Bassett Street
New Britain, CT 06051
  203-225-6357

UConn Women's Center
27 Whitney Road
Storrs, CT 06268
  203-486-4738

Women's Center
Asnuntuck Community College
111 Phoenix Avenue (Box 68)
Enfield, CT 06082
  203-745-1603, ext. 26

Women's Center
110 Broad Street
New London, CT 06320
  203-447-0366
  Rape Crisis: 203-886-2273 (24-hour
hotline)

Women's Center of Ridgefield
P.O. Box 112
Ridgefield, CT 06877
  203-438-9339

Women's Center of Southeastern
  Connecticut
120 Broad Street
Neighborhood Center
New London, CT 06320
  203-443-1425

Women's Place
73 Marshall Ridge Road
New Canaan, CT 06840
  203-655-4302

District of Columbia
Counseling and Career Center
Trinity College
Washington, DC 20017

Womanspace
Marvin Center #430
800 21st Street N.W.
Washington, DC 20052
  202-676-7554

Florida
Domestic Assault Shelter, c/o YWCA
901 South Olive Avenue
West Palm Beach, FL 33401
  305-833-2439

Women's Center
1200 West Platt Street
Tampa, FL 33606
  813-251-4089

Georgia
Feminist Action Alliance
P.O. Box 54717, Civic Center Station
Atlanta, GA 30308
  404-525-5138

Hawaii
University YWCA Women's Center
1820 University Avenue
Honolulu, HI 96822
  808-947-3351

Idaho
Women's Center
University of Idaho
Moscow, ID 83843
208-885-6616

Women's Resource Center
720 West Washington
Boise, ID 83669
208-243-3688

Illinois
Ecumenical Women's Center
1653 West School Street
Chicago, IL 60657
312-348-4970

Evanston Women's Liberation Center
2214 Ridge Avenue
Evanston, IL 60201
312-475-4480

Midwest Women's Center
53 West Jackson Boulevard, Room 623
Chicago, IL 60604
312-663-4163; 922-8530

South Suburban Area YWCA
45 Plaza
Park Forest, IL 60466
312-748-5660

University Feminist Organization
5655 South University Avenue
Chicago, IL 60637
312-684-3109

Women at Northwestern
619 Emerson Street
Evanston, IL 60201
312-492-3146

Women's Center
408 West Freeman
Carbondale, IL 62901
618-529-2324

Women's Information & Resource
  Exchange
1203 West Green
Urbana, IL 61801
217-344-7322

Indiana
Calumet Women United Against Rape
P.O. Box 2617
Gary, IN 46403

Everywoman's Center
6354 West 37th Street
Indianapolis, IN 46224
317-632-4637

Fort Wayne Women's Bureau
P.O. Box 554
Fort Wayne, IN 46807
219-424-7977

Woman Alive
229 Ogden Street
Hammond, IN 46325
219-838-7707

Iowa
Center for Women
3303 Rebecca
Sioux City, IA 51104
712-279-5406

Women's Resource and Action Center
130 North Madison Street
Iowa City, IA 52242
319-353-6265

Kansas
Kansas City Women's Liberation Union
3950 Rainbow
Kansas City, KS 66103
913-363-2864

Women's Center of Topeka
1268 Western
Topeka, KS 66604
913-357-7650

Women's Resource Center
Kansas State University Union
Manhattan, KS 66502
913-532-6541

Kentucky
Brescia Women's Center
120 West 7th Street
Owensboro, KY 42301
502-685-3132

Women's Center
Alternatives for Women
1628 South Limestone, Suite 301
Lexington, KY 40508
606-276-3542

Maryland
Baltimore Women's Resource Center
5210 York Road
Baltimore, MD 21212
301-323-2828

New Responses
6509 Westland Road
Bethesda, MD 20034
301-530-1584

Women's Center
Towson State University
Baltimore, MD 21204
301-321-2666

Women's Growth Center
339 East 25th Street
Baltimore, MD 21218
   301-366-4769

Women Together
5609 Cross Country Boulevard
Baltimore, MD 21209
   301-367-7262

Massachusetts
Boston University Women's Center
775 Commonwealth Avenue, PRO
Boston, MA 02215
   617-353-4240

Center for Women at Massasoit
Massasoit Community College
Brockton, MA 02402
   617-588-9100

Dorchester Children's Center
1882 Dorchester Avenue
Dorchester, MA 02124
   617-436-0541

Everywoman's Center
506 Goodell Hall
University of Massachusetts
Amherst, MA 01003
   413-545-0883

Origins
169 Boston Street
Salem, MA 01970
   617-745-5873

Somerville Women's Center
7 Davis Square
Somerville, MA 02144
   617-623-9340

Women's Center
Bristol Community College
64 Durfee Street
Fall River, MA 02720
   617-679-4483

Women's Center
15 Chestnut Street
New Bedford, MA 02747
   617-996-3341

Women's Counseling and Resource Center
1555 Massachusetts Avenue
Cambridge, MA 02139
   617-492-8568

Women's Educational Center
46 Pleasant Street
Cambridge, MA 02139
   617-354-8807

Women's Information/The Wire Service
117 Newbury Street
Boston, MA 02116
   617-247-4078

Women's Inner-City Educational Resource
   Service
134 Warren Street
Roxbury, MA 02119
   617-442-9150

Women's Resource Center
Andover Theological School
210 Herrick Road
Newton Center, MA 02159
   617-964-1100

Women's Services Center
33 Pearl Street
Pittsfield, MA 01201
   413-442-9458

YWCA Women's Resource Center
90 Irving Street
Framington, MA 01701
   617-873-9781

Michigan
Ann Arbor Women's Crisis Center
211½ North Fourth Avenue
Ann Arbor, MI 48104
   313-994-9100 (counseling);
   313-761-9475

Everywoman's Place
23 Strong Avenue
Muskegon, MI 49441
   616-726-4493

Women's Center
Wayne State University
167 MacKenzie
Detroit, MI 48202
   313-577-2332

Women's Resource Center
226 Bostwick
Grand Rapids, MI 49503
   616-456-8571

Women's Resource Center
Schoolcraft College
18600 Haggerty Road
Livonia, MI 48152
   313-591-6400

Minnesota
Minnesota Women's Center
306 Walter Library
University of Minnesota
Minneapolis, MN 55455
   612-373-3850

St. Cloud Area Women's Center
1900 Minnesota Boulevard
St. Cloud, MN 56301
  612-252-8831

Twin Cities Women
430 Oak Grove Street, B-10
Minneapolis, MN 55403
  612-871-2555

Women's Advocates
584 Grand Avenue
St. Paul, MN 55105
  612-227-8284

YWCA of the Minneapolis Area
1130 Nicollet Mall
Minneapolis, MN 55403
  612-332-0501

Missouri
Women's Center
University of Missouri
8001 Natural Bridge Road
St. Louis, MO 63121
  314-453-5380

Montana
Women's Place
1130 West Broadway
Missoula, MT 59801
  406-243-7606

Women's Resource Center
University Center
University of Montana
Missoula, MT 59801
  406-243-4153

Nebraska
Women's Study Group
Doane College
Crete, NB 68333
  402-826-2161

YWCA
1432 N Street
Lincoln, NB 68508
  402-432-2802

New Hampshire
Concord Women's Center
8 North Main Street
Concord, NH 03301
  603-643-5133
  603-224-4104

Women's Information Service
38 South Main Street
Hanover, NH 03755
  603-643-5133

Women's Resource Center of the YWCA
40 Merrimac Street
Portsmouth, NH 03801
  603-436-0162

New Jersey
Alternatives for Women NOW
517 Penn Street
Camden, NJ 08102
  609-964-8033

The Center for Women
YWCA of Burlington County
15 West Main Street
Moorestown, NJ 08057
  609-235-6697

The Woman's Place: Resource Center
1687 Lawrence Road
Lawrenceville, NJ 08648
  609-771-1424

The Women's Advisory Exchange
11 Green Hill Road
Madison, NJ 07940
  201-377-9031

The Women's Center of Morris
c/o Morristown Unitarian Fellowship
812 Normandy Heights Road
Morristown, NJ 07960
  201-267-0484

Women's Center
Jersey City State College
70 Audubon Avenue
Jersey City, NJ 07305
  201-547-3170/3189

Women's Center of Unitarian House for
  People
Whittredge Road
Summit, NJ 07901
  201-273-2383

Women's Resource & Survival Center
57 West Front Street
Keyport, NJ 07735
  201-264-4111

New Mexico
Women's Center
1824 Lomas N.E.
University of New Mexico
Albuquerque, NM 87131
  505-277-3716

New York
All the Queens Women
36-23 164th Street
Flushing, NY 11358
  212-359-9204

Barnard Women's Center
Barnard College
New York, NY 10027
   212-280-2067

Brookhaven Woman's Center
320 Main Street
Port Jefferson, NY 11777
   516-473-8663

Islip Women's Center
855 Montauk Highway
Oakdale, NY 11796
   516-589-7188

Nassau County Office of Women's Services
1425 Old Country Road
Plainview, NY 11803
   516-420-5101

Riverdale Neighborhood House
5521 Mosholu Avenue
Bronx, NY 10471
   212-549-8100

Syracuse University Women's Center
750 Ostrom Avenue
Syracuse, NY 13210
   315-423-4268

The Feminist Center for Human Growth
   and Development
303 Lexington Avenue
New York, NY 10016
   212-686-0869

The Feminist Union
Box 172
Vassar College
Poughkeepsie, NY 12601
   914-452-7000

The Women's Center of the Riverside
   Church
490 Riverside Drive
New York, NY 10027
   212-749-7000

The Women's Center of Yonkers
38 Palisade Avenue
Yonkers, NY 10701
   914-969-5800

Union Center for Women
8101 Ridge Boulevard
Brooklyn, NY 11209
   212-748-7708

Westchester County Women's Center
West 2nd Street & South 6th Avenue
Mount Vernon, NY 11101
   914-664-7988

Women's Center
Brooklyn YWCA
30 Third Avenue
Brooklyn, NY 11217
   212-875-1190

Women's Center
Hofstra University Student Center
Hempstead, NY 11551
   516-560-3580

Women's Center
YWCA
600 Lexington Avenue
New York, NY 10022
   212-753-4700, ext. 393

Women's Center and Rape Crisis Center
66 Chenango Street
Binghamton, NY 13901
   607-722-3679/4256

Women's Center for Education and Career
   Advancement
NCNW
198 Broadway
New York, NY 10028
   212-964-8934

Women's Information Center
601 Allen Street
Syracuse, NY 13210

Women's Liberation Center
243 West 20th Street
New York, NY 10011
   212-255-9802

North Carolina
A Woman's Place
110 Henderson Street
Chapel Hill, NC 27514
   919-967-8006

Council on Appalachian Women
P.O. Box 490
Mars Hill, NC 28754
   704-689-1331

Durham YWCA Women's Center
312 East Umstead Street
Durham, NC 27707
   919-688-4396

North Dakota
Office of Women's Programs
Box 326
University of North Dakota
Grand Forks, ND 58202
   701-777-4300

Antioch's Women's Center
Antioch College
Yellow Springs, OH 45387
    513-767-7331, ext. 311

Athens Women's Collective/Caucus
Baker Center
Ohio University
Athens, OH 45701

Dayton Women's Center
1309 North Main Street
Dayton, OH 45405
    513-223-3296

Oberlin Women's Service Center
92 Spring Street
Oberlin, OH 44074
    513-774-4377

WomenSpace
1258 Euclid Avenue, #200
Cleveland, OH 44115
    216-696-3100

Women's Center
Women's Affairs Council
206 T.U.C.
University of Cincinnati
Cincinnati, OH 45221
    513-475-3967

Women Together
P.O. Box 6331
Cleveland, OH 44101
    216-281-0600; Hotline: 961-4422

Oklahoma
Women's Center of Tulsa
1240 East Fifth Place, Rm. 200
Tulsa, OK 74135
    918-584-4444

Women's Resource Center
207½ East Gray
Norman, OK 73069
    405-364-9424

YWCA Women's Resource Center
3626 North Western
Oklahoma City, OK 73118
    405-528-5440

Oregon
Women's Resource Center of Lincoln
    County
9087 S.W. Hubert
Newport, OR 97365
    503-265-7751

Pennsylvania
Fishtown Women's Community Center
1340 Frankford Avenue
Philadelphia, PA 19125
    215-426-8610

Kensington Women's Resource Center
174 Allegheny Avenue
Philadelphia, PA 19133
    215-739-1430

Women Against Abuse
P.O. Box 12233
Philadelphia, PA 19144
    215-843-2438

Women's Center
YWCA
4th and Market Streets
Harrisburg, PA 17101
    717-233-4004

Women's Center & Shelter of Greater
    Pittsburgh
616 North Highland Avenue
Pittsburgh, PA 15206
    412-661-6066

Women's Information Service
Women's Action Coalition
P.O. Box 63
Media, PA 19063
    215-565-2960

Women's Switchboard of Philadelphia
27 Chestnut Street
Philadelphia, PA 19103
    215-563-8599

YWCA Women's Center
42 West Maiden Street
Washington, PA 15301
    412-222-3208

Rhode Island
Kingston Women's Liberation
Memorial Union
University of Rhode Island
Kingston, RI 02881
    401-792-2261

Women's Center
37 Congress Avenue
Providence, RI 02907
    401-781-4080

South Dakota
Brookings Women's Center
802 11th Avenue
Brookings, SD 57006
    605-688-4518

Tennessee
Knoxville Women's Center
406 Church Street
Knoxville, TN 37902
    615-546-1873

Women's Resources Center
499 South Patterson
Memphis, TN 38111
    901-458-1407

Texas
Austin Women's Center
711 San Antonio Street
Austin, TX 78701
    512-472-3775

Everywoman Center
Richland Community College
c/o Community Services
12800 Abrams
Dallas, TX 75243
    214-746-4447

Women's Center of Dallas
2001 McKinney Street, Suite 300
Dallas, TX 75201
    214-651-9795

Utah
Weber State College
Association for the Status of Women
3750 Harrison Boulevard
Ogden, UT 84408

Vermont
Women's Research Project
310 Main Street
P.O. Box 81
Bennington, VT 05201
    802-442-3180

Virginia
ACLU Southern Women's Rights Project
1001 East Main Street, Suite 512
Richmond, VA 23219
    804-643-6419

Williamsburg Area Women's Center
P.O. Box 126
Williamsburg, VA 23185
    804-229-9944

Women's Resource and Services Center
c/o YWCA
605 First Street, S.W.
Roanoke, VA 24011
    703-342-4076; 703-343-6016

Washington
Asian Counseling and Referral Service
655 South Jackson
Seattle, WA 98104
    206-623-6756

Crisis Clinic
1530 Eastlake, N.E.
Seattle, WA 98102
    206-329-1882

Lesbian Resource Center
YWCA
4221 University Way N.E.
Seattle, WA 98105
206-632-4747

Open Door Clinic
5012 Roosevelt Way N.E.
Seattle, WA 98105
    206-524-7404

University of Washington YWCA
4224 University Way N.E.
Seattle, WA 98105
206-632-4747

Women's Association of Self-Help
11100 N.E. 2nd
Bellevue, WA 98009
    206-454-9274

West Virginia
Women's Information Center
221 Willey Street
Morgantown, WV 26505

Wisconsin
Feminist Center
Student Union, Box 189
University of Wisconsin
Milwaukee, WI 53201
    414-963-7799

The Women's Center
419 North Grand Avenue
Waukesha, WI 53186
    414-547-4600

Women's Center
124 Blackhawk Commons
Oshkosh, WI 54901
    414-424-1491

Women's Coalition
2211 East Kenwood
Milwaukee, WI 53211
    414-964-6117

Women's Resource Center
2101A Main Street
Stevens Point, WI 54481
    715-346-4851

Wyoming
Women's Self Help Center
906 North Durbin
Casper, WY 82601
    307-235-2814

WOMEN'S EDUCATIONAL EQUITY ACT

IN 1973, BOTH THE HOUSE AND THE SENATE HELD HEARINGS ON PROPOSED women's educational equity legislation. Members of Congress left those hearings knowing "that educational programs in the United States . . . as presently conducted, are inequitable as such programs relate to women." The resulting Women's Educational Equity Act (WEEA) was passed with two major provisions: the appropriation of money for "programs and activities designed to achieve educational equity for all students" and the establishment of a council to oversee the administration of the act. Specifically, the Act allowed for appropriations of up to $30 million for each of three years. In 1976, the first year of operation, only $6.2 million was appropriated; grant applications received totaled $105 million—nearly eighteen times the amount available. The National Advisory Council on Women's Educational Programs, which was created by the Act, has issued guidelines for priority funding areas, made provision for general coordination of WEEA grants, and authorized studies of several crucial areas of women's education.

See also: Sex Discrimination in Education
            Title IX

Organizations:

National Advisory Council on Women's Educational Programs
1832 M Street N.W.
Washington, DC 20036

Resources:

Educational Equity: The Continuing Challenge; Fourth Annual Reports, 1978,
    prepared by the National Advisory Council on Women's Educational Programs,
    1979. Order from: Superintendent of Documents, Government Printing Office,
    Washington, DC 20402.
    The fourth annual report on activities related to the Women's Educational
Equity Act.

Women's Educational Equity Act of 1973. Washington: Project on the Status and
    Education of Women, 1974. Order from: Project on the Status and Education of
    Women, 1818 R Street N.W., Washington, DC 20009.
    This section-by-section summary fully explains the provisions of the Act.

WOMEN'S MOVEMENT

ACCORDING TO WEBSTER, FEMINISM IS "THE THEORY OF POLITICAL, ECONOMIC and social equality of the sexes" and "organized activity on behalf of women's rights and interests." If you asked feminists, you would get a different definition from each. There is no one accepted perspective or political stance among feminists, nor is there one organization which represents feminism and the women's movement as a whole. There are many different analyses, approaches, issues, and organizations. And, just as there is no easy definition of feminism, there is no easy explanation for the development of the women's movement.

In the last decade and a half of feminist activism, the women's movement has gone through enormous growth and growing pains. Publication of *The Feminine Mystique* in 1963 is used by many to date the beginnings of contemporary feminist activity. Betty Friedan's book had a consciousness-raising effect on many women, and started them thinking about their problems as more than just personal. It helped begin to break down the isolation so many women felt.

The climate of political activism in the 1960's—the civil rights movement, political activity on the campuses, the antiwar movement—had a tremendous effect on public consciousness. Women were active participants in every arena. More and more women realized as they worked for various social causes that they—as women—were being denied equal participation, not only in established institutions but in the very organizations that professed to work for justice, social change, and a new society. The dissatisfaction of women was growing in every quarter. In 1964, Ruby Doris Smith Robinson's paper on "The Position of Women in SNCC" (Student Non-Violent Coordinating Committee) created a stir of reactions—both hostile and sympathetic—in the civil rights movement. From the new left came Robin Morgan's "Goodbye to All That," urging women to leave behind the sexism of the male-dominated radical student, youth, antiwar, and ecology movements.

And many did. Women added a new dimension to the revolution in consciousness that was taking place. They began with themselves, meeting in consciousness-raising sessions to name the problem "that had no name." Soon, they moved on to action. Women began organizing to deal with their own problems: lobbying for equal legal status; publishing newsletters, position papers, manifestos; gathering in small groups and large conferences to discuss issues and ideology; and holding demonstrations. Events ranged from monumental mass actions like the August 1970 national strike in which women around the country demonstrated in the streets to "zap actions" like the disruption of the 1968 Miss America contest at which radical feminists crowned a live sheep to protest exploitation of women.

Many of the early groups were short-lived and local, focusing on specific actions; some developed alternative service projects such as women's health centers and rape-crisis counseling programs; still others turned their attention to national issues such as education, day care, abortion, and the Equal Rights Amendment. In 1966, the National Organization for Women, the single largest national organization demanding equal rights for women, was founded. While no one political ideology developed, groups tended to fall into one of three different theoretical perspectives. The viewpoints which we see today can generally be traced to these initial ideological developments; both the radical and reform strains of the movement have existed side by side.

Women's Rights groups, also called reformist or liberal, include such groups as NOW, Women's Equity Action League, the National Women's Political Caucus. Their basic premise is that women are not getting fair and equal treatment and that changes in laws and social policy are needed to give women equal status with men. Perhaps the founding goals of NOW state this perspective best: "To bring women into the mainstream of American society, now, full equality for women, in fully equal partnership with men."

Women's liberation groups, or radical feminist groups, included the Redstockings and New York Radical Feminists in the early days. Their analysis rests on the assumption that women's condition is a direct result of the patriarchal, or male-dominated, social system. To effect change a feminist revolution would be necessary.

A third current includes the socialist feminist groups. Socialist feminists are Marxists. Their analysis identifies the root of women's oppression in the economic system of capitalism. While fighting for reforms, socialist feminists believe that only under socialism will women find full equality. Like radical feminists, many of these women became disenchanted with the male-dominated new left groups to which they belonged. Some of them left to form independent socialist women's groups; others have worked to restore feminist demands to the programs of the socialist and left organizations.

The women's movement has become more issue-oriented in the last few years; many ideological differences have begun to blur. The early years were not without conflicts—sometimes bitter—over political ideology and actions, sexual orientation, racism, elitism and group structure. These internal splits did not stop the women's movement; instead, they fostered the growth of many different organizations, both local and national, to respond to the needs of various constituencies. The development of the diverse range of groups, representing many issues and interests, can be seen in the pages of this book. Together, all of these groups represent the women's movement of today.

During the past ten or more years the women's movement has grown up. While the media still prefers to treat it as a joke, increasingly, it is being taken seriously nationwide. Even the federal government formally recognized (some would say co-opted) the concerns of the women's movement. In 1977, the National Women's Conference, funded by federal money, was held in Houston. More than 20,000 people attended, including 1,430 delegates, 370 delegates-at-large and 186 alternates representing the fifty states; more than 2,000 invited guests, official observers and resource people; approximately 1,500 press representatives; and as many as 3,000 volunteers. The issues on the agenda included twenty-six topics, ranging from Arts and Humanities to Homemakers to Sexual Preference. The National Plan of Action was designed "to identify the barriers that prevent women from participating fully and equally in all aspects of national life and develop recommendations for means by which such barriers can be removed." While there are many questions about the lack of response from government agencies, policy makers and legislators mandated to carry out the recommendations, the efforts in Houston called national attention to the demands, scope, and diversity of the women's movement.

The women's movement is also having an effect on the "average American." The attitudes of Americans toward women have shown real change since the rebirth of feminist activism. Major public opinion polls indicate that the majority of Americans support efforts to improve the status of women (see chart below). Nearly 100,000 women, men, and children turned out in a demonstration of support for the Equal Rights Amendment in Washington, D.C. in July 1978.

Originally ridiculed by many as a fad, feminists have made it clear that the women's movement is here to stay.

Organizations:

See Directory of National Women's
  Organizations (p. 341)

Resources:

Capitalist Patriarchy and the Case for Socialist Feminism, by Zillah R. Eisenstein. New York: Monthly Review Press, 1979.
  A collection of writings on socialist feminist theory providing an analysis of history and women's roles, revolutionary models, and their implications for America.

Consciousness-Raising Guidelines. New York: Women's Action Alliance, 1974. Order from: WAA, 370 Lexington Avenue, New York, NY 10017.
  Contains supplemental guidelines for black women and young women.

The Dialectic of Sex: The Case for Feminist Revolution, by Shulamith Firestone. New York: William Morrow, 1970.
  This theoretical analysis of women's condition exemplifies the ideological basis of the radical feminist position.

Essays in Feminism, by Vivian Gornick. New York: Harper and Row, 1978.
  This collection of writings from one of the movement's major commentators provides valuable insight into the issues of the last ten years.

The Feminine Mystique, by Betty Friedan. New York: Norton, 1974.
  This book, originally published in 1963, stirred millions of women to question their lives and to look beyond their individual selves for answers.

Feminist Frameworks, by Alison M. Jaggar and Paula Rothenberg Struhl. New York: McGraw-Hill, 1978.
  An anthology of theoretical works presenting writings from all pespectives òf the women's movement.

Feminist Revolution, by the Redstockings. New York: Random House, 1978.
  This book provides invaluable insight into radical feminist perspectives on many issues and concerns, including consciousness-raising, work, love, sex, organizing and the women's movement.

Going Too Far: The Personal Chronicle of a Feminist, by Robin Morgan. New York: Random House, 1977.
  This collection chronicles Morgan's personal journey as a feminist as well as providing an account of the events, actions, conflicts, and joys of the contemporary movement.

Guidelines to Feminist Consciousness Raising, by Harriet Perl and Gay Abarbanell. Los Angeles: NOW Task Force on Consciousness Raising, 1976. Order from: Harriet Perl, 1121 Hi Point Street, Los Angeles, CA 90035.
  This booklet also contains CR guidelines for men's groups.

It Changed My Life, Writings on the Women's Movement, by Betty Friedan. New York: Random House, 1976.

Friedan discusses her last ten years as an activist, describing the impact of the women's movement both personally and politically.

Marxism & Feminism, by Charnie Guettel. Toronto: The Women's Press, 1974. Order from the Women's Press, Suite 305, 280 Bloor Street W., Toronto, Ontario, Canada.

A critical Marxist summary of the history of feminist thought: liberal, radical and socialist.

National Women's Agenda.

In 1975, the Women's Action Alliance surveyed national women's groups and women's caucuses of national organizations to determine their goals and priorities. This project was undertaken in response to the United Nations Declaration of International Women's Year and the Decade for Women. More than one hundred groups responded, and the result was the development of the National Women's Agenda, a statement of common purpose. In 1977, the National Women's Agenda Coalition formed "to achieve full equality for women of all ages by uniting the efforts of the organized women's community to realize the goals of the National Women's Agenda." The National Women's Agenda is available from the Women's Action Alliance, 370 Lexington Avenue, New York, NY 10017. The multi-issue coalition has thirty-two members.

American Association of University Women

American Civil Liberties Union Women's Rights Project

American Federation of Television and Radio Artists Women's Division

Association for Voluntary Association Women's Caucus

Catalyst

Church Women United

Federally Employed Women

Federation of Organizations for Professional Women

Gay Rights National Lobby Women's Caucus

Girls Club of America

Leadership Conference of Women Religious

National Abortion Rights Action League

National Association of Commissions for Women

National Association of Women Business Owners

National Committee on Household Employment

National Conference of Puerto Rican Women

National Council of Jewish Women

National Council of Negro Women

National Council on Alcoholism Office on Women

National Gay Task Force Women's Caucus

National Women's Political Caucus

Pioneer Women

Planned Parenthood Federation of America Women's Rights Project

Project on the Status and Education of Women of the Association of American Colleges

Rural American Women

Screen Actors Guild Women's Conference Committee

Unitarian Universalist Women's Federation

United Auto Workers Women's Department

Wider Opportunities for Women

Women's Institute for Freedom of the Press

Working Women

YWCA National Board

The New Feminist Movement, by Maren Lockwood Carden. New York: Russell Sage Foundation, 1974.
An instructive look at the women's movement, its many organizations, its development and the women involved.

Radical Feminism, ed. by Anne Koedt, Ellen Levine and Anita Rapone. New York: Quadrangle Books, 1973.
One of the best anthologies of contemporary feminist writings, containing classic essays from the early days of the movement.

Rebirth of Feminism, by Judith Hole and Ellen Levine. New York: Quadrangle Books, 1971.
A detailed and insightful look at the beginning years of the contemporary women's movement.

The Second Sex, by Simone de Beauvoir. New York: Bantam, 1970.
This monumental work by a French existentialist analyzing the social roles of women was first published in the United States in 1953 and has become a classic among feminist writings.

Sexual Politics, by Kate Millet. Garden City: Doubleday, 1970.
This book provides a critique of intellectual traditions and patriarchal culture in America.

Sisterhood is Powerful: An Anthology of Writings from the Women's Liberation Movement, ed. by Robin Morgan. New York: Random House, 1970.
This collection of early movement writings is essential reading for capturing the sense of the women's movement of the late 1960's.

The Spirit of Houston. Washington: National Commission on the Observance of International Women's Year, 1978. Order from: Superintendent of Documents, Government Printing Office, Washington, DC 20402.
The official report on the conference, with details of the event, the resolutions, the Plan of Action, participants and more.

Women in America: A Guide to Books, 1963–1975, by Barbara Haber. Boston: G. K. Hall, 1978.
A comprehensive annotated bibliography covering topics such as feminism, history, sex roles, and other issues concerning women.

Women's Consciousness, Man's World, by Sheila Rowbotham. Baltimore: Penguin Books, 1973.
This small volume examines women's condition in class society and integrates feminist analysis into a socialist construction for social change.

Women's Estate, by Juliet Mitchell. New York: Pantheon, 1971.
Mitchell puts forth a synthesis of structuralist theory and feminist consciousness to provide a framework for a socialist-feminist theory of women's oppression.

Women's Organizations and Leaders Directory, 1978–79, prepared by Women Today. Washington: Today Publications, forthcoming. Order from: Today Publications, National Press Building, Washington, DC 20045.
This directory, in its third edition, is an invaluable reference guide to women's organizations and leaders.

Women's Proper Place, by Sheila M. Rothman. New York: Basic Books, 1978.

An important work analyzing the impact of social history on women; it takes a critical look at the impact of the organized efforts of women's groups.

PERIODICALS

Chrysalis. Order from: Chrysalis, 635 S. Westlake Avenue, Los Angeles, CA 90057.

This magazine of women's culture includes feature articles on current affairs, arts, history and feminist theory, as well as interviews and resources.

Ms. Order from: Ms., 123 Garden Street, Marion, OH 43302.

The first commercial magazine to write from a feminist perspective, it features articles on women's issues, news about women's groups and actions, fiction, film and book reviews.

off our backs. Order from: off our backs, 1724 20th Street N.W., Washington, DC 20009.

In its ninth year, *off our backs* is one of the longest-running feminist newspapers.

Quest: A Feminist Quarterly. Order from: Quest, 1909 Q Street N.W., Washington, DC 20009.

This journal features articles of feminist theory and political analysis on themes such as Women in their Communities; The Body Politic; Work, Communications and Control; Organizations and Strategies; Change; Race, Class and Culture.

Spokeswoman. Order from: Spokeswoman, 53 W. Jackson, Chicago, IL 60604.

This monthly newsletter keeps its readers up to date on the issues affecting women, including news of important legislation, events and actions, both local and national; also includes book reviews and job advertisements.

Women: A Journal of Liberation. Order from: Women, 3028 Greenmount Avenue, Baltimore, MD 21218.

This quarterly magazine of feminist writing focuses each issue around a particular theme such as Power, Women Alone, Women Loving Women, Androgyny, and Liberation.

Women Organizing, A Socialist Feminist Bulletin. Order from: NAM Socialist Feminist Commission, 7125 McPherson Boulevard, Pittsburgh, PA 15208.

This publication reports on feminist organizing efforts around the country and includes articles on socialist feminist theory.

Women's Agenda. Order from: Women's Action Alliance, 370 Lexington Avenue, New York, NY 10017.

Published six times a year, this is the only magazine reporting on programs, issues, resources and events of women's groups throughout the country.

WIN News. Order from: Women's International Network, 187 Grant Street, Lexington, MA 02173.

A quarterly of international news for and about women, covering human rights, women and the United Nations, international affairs, women and development, etc.

PUBLIC OPINION AND THE WOMEN'S MOVEMENT
(Harris polls taken between June 27 and July 1, 1978)

"Many of those who favor women's rights favor the Equal Rights Amendment to the Constitution. This amendment would establish that women would have rights equal to men in all areas. Opponents argue that women are different from men and need to be protected by special laws which deal with women's status. Do you favor or oppose the Equal Rights Amendment?"

	July 1978	January 1978	1977	1976	1975
Favor	55%	51%	56%	66%	51%
Oppose	38%	34%	35%	23%	36%
Not sure	7%	15%	9%	11%	13%

"There has been much talk recently about changing women's status in society today. On the whole, do you favor or oppose most of the efforts to strengthen and change women's status in society today?

	1978	1977	1975	1971	1970
Favor	64%	64%	59%	48%	42%
Oppose	25%	27%	28%	36%	41%
Not sure	11%	9%	13%	16%	17%

WOMEN'S STUDIES

WOMEN'S STUDIES COULD BE CALLED THE INTELLECTUAL AND RESEARCH ARM of the women's movement. Through research, teaching, and writing, women's studies seeks to challenge every male-biased assumption ever made about women (and men) and to put women back into the study of history, literature, art, sociology—everything. Women's studies had its beginnings on college campuses in 1969. The 1970 *Guide to Current Female Studies* listed approximately one hundred women's studies courses; the second edition, published one year later, included more than six hundred. By 1978, 301 women's studies *programs* were in operation on college campuses in all but nine of the fifty states. The study of women was an idea whose time had come.

Women's studies programs have garnered growing interest and respect over the years, as well as increasing in size and number. Lone courses developed into full-fledged programs and many of those programs now offer a degree: eighty offer the B.A., twenty-one the M.A., and five the Ph.D. or equivalent. Although still located primarily on college campuses and constituted as a separate department, women's studies expects eventually to reintegrate, transforming all areas of education in the process—curriculum, research, writing, teaching, thinking. The point is not to create, for example, a separate curriculum for teaching women's history, but rather to completely revise history as currently taught to *include* the role of women. Nor is the intention to keep women's studies isolated on college campuses; the high school and elementary curriculum have already been affected. Ultimately, women's studies scholars hope to contribute to the transformation of society through their own avenues, research and education.

See also: Higher Education
          Nonsexist Education

Organizations:

The Feminist Press
P.O. Box 334
Old Westbury, NY 11568

National Women's Studies Association
University of Maryland
Foreign Language Building
College Park, MD 20742

Resources:

Female Studies I–X. Order Volumes I–V and VIII from: KNOW, P.O. Box 86031, Pittsburgh, PA 15221; order volumes VI, VII, IX and X from: The Feminist Press (address above).

The Female Studies series are volumes of course syllabi, essays and feminist teaching methods. Write the two publishers for complete information about the contents of each volume.

Seven Years Later: Women's Studies Programs in 1976, by Florence Howe. Washington: National Advisory Council on Women's Educational Programs, 1977. Order from: NACWEP, 1832 M Street N.W., Washington, DC 20036.

This study reports in detail on the history, curriculum, faculty, students, and campus-wide impact of fifteen women's studies programs.

Women's Studies Abstracts. Order from: Rush Publishing, P.O. Box 29, Rush, NY 14543.

This quarterly indexes nearly 250 journals, abstracting articles on women. The abstracts are arranged into seventeen subject categories with a separate section of book reviews. The only source of its kind.

Women's Studies Newsletter: Order from: The Feminist Press (address above).

This information-packed quarterly provides coverage of issues and events in women's studies, publishes bibliographies, news of resources and conferences. A complete list of women's studies programs is published annually. Recently, the *Newsletter* became the official organ of the National Women's Studies Association.

WORKING-CLASS WOMEN

THE MEDIA STEREOTYPE OF THE WORKING-CLASS WOMAN IS THAT OF A drudge, in hair rollers and housedress, reading confession magazines, watching TV and screaming at the kids. The media's depiction of all women is negative, but its presentation of the working-class woman is especially damaging. Only recently has Edith Bunker of "All in the Family" been portrayed as more than a "dingbat." The little research on working-class women that exists dates mostly from the 1950's and early 1960's and, unfortunately, tends to repeat the media myth. Social scientists, reflecting cultural biases, rarely look at working-class women separate from their husband and family group; often they ignore them altogether.

What exactly does "working class" mean? Don't we live in a classless society? Aren't most Americans middle class? Most Americans may think of themselves as middle class—with the subtle clarification "upper" or "lower"—but what is somewhat euphemistically called lower middle class is in fact the working class: men and women with high-school educations or less; with blue-collar, "pink-collar" and lower white-collar jobs; with relatively low incomes. While research on the working class usually focuses on urban white ethnics, the working class does, in fact, include all races, living in urban, suburban, and rural areas.

Who is the working-class woman? She represents the majority of women in this country and the majority of the female labor force, employed in low-income, sex-typed jobs such as clerical work, sales, and service work. She is a "pink-collar" worker: grocery clerk, beautician, waitress, department-store clerk, file clerk, typist.

The working-class woman is caught between cultural traditions, community standards, and a changing social and economic climate. Raised with expectations of marriage and motherhood as her primary role, she is not prepared for the reality of today—the necessity of a second income to support the family. As of 1976, 50 percent of all married women were working if the husband's income fell between $7,000 and $9,999. Of those women whose husband's income was under $7,000, 35 percent worked, and for those with husband's income over $10,000, 45 percent worked. Women are working out of economic necessity, whether married or single.

The working-class woman often finds herself in a low-paying, unsatisfying job in addition to working at home caring for her family. It is no wonder that being "just a housewife" may be a preferable alternative to her. She does not have the opportunities of advanced education, upward job mobility or adequate day care to aid her day-to-day existence. While the media have been ready to exclaim over the few success stories of women corporate executives, they have neglected to deal with the very real problems facing most women in America today.

Women's groups, however, are working on these problems. The National Congress of Neighborhood Women formed in 1975 to deal with issues of concern to working-class women. They have developed a neighborhood-based program providing educational opportunities to community women who would otherwise be unable to attend college or get a high-school diploma. The Women's Center for Educational and Career Advancement, a project of the National Council of Negro Women, has developed a program to help clerical workers take advantage of their companies' employee benefits such as tuition reimbursement. And women office workers and union women are organizing to improve wages, working conditions, and job opportunities.

The media are fond of criticizing the women's movement, calling it insensitive to the needs of working-class women and suggesting that it exists only to enhance the economic and professional status of upper-class women. Any thorough and thoughtful consideration of women's movement issues and activities would dispel such notions. Unfortunately the media have not often been so careful. And media presentations *have* had damaging effects. Both sides have been too ready to believe what they read in newspapers or see on TV. To deny that there have been disagreements and conflicts between middle-class feminists and working-class women would be to paint too rosy a picture. But the work of organizations such as the National Congress of Neighborhood Women is testament to the fact that both sides are seeing their common interests.

See also:　Earnings Gap
　　　　　　Homemakers
　　　　　　Labor Union Women
　　　　　　Sex-Typing of Occupations

Organizations:

Coalition of Grass Roots Women
1133 Broadway
New York, NY 10010

National Congress of Neighborhood Women
11-29 Catherine Street
Brooklyn, NY 11211

Resources:

Absent from the Majority: Working Class Women in America by Nancy Seifer. New York: National Project on Ethnic America, 1973. Order from: National Project on Ethnic America, The American Jewish Committee, 165 East 56th Street, New York, NY 10022.

In this pamphlet Seifer takes a look at the changes in the lives of working-class women.

Nobody Speaks for Me, by Nancy Seifer. New York: Simon and Schuster, 1976.

Seifer interviews ten working-class women, providing a remarkable portrait of complexity.

Pink Collar Worker, by Louise Kapp Howe, New York: Putnam, 1977.

A very readable and insightful account of the lives of pink-collar workers, including beauticians, sales workers, waitresses, office workers, and homemakers.

Where Feminism and Ethnicity Intersect, by Nancy Seifer. New York Institute on Pluralism and Group Identity, 1976. Order from: Institute on Pluralism and Group Identity, The American Jewish Committee, 165 East 56th Street, New York, NY 10022.

This paper examines both the women's movement and the white ethnic movement and their combined effects on working-class women.

Working Class Women and Grass Roots Politics, by Kathleen McCourt. Bloomington: Indiana University Press, 1977.

Based on research on women living on the southwest side of Chicago, this book examines the changes in the lives of working-class women and their attitudes toward those changes.

DIRECTORY OF NATIONAL WOMEN'S ORGANIZATIONS

This directory is an alphabetical listing of more than 250 national women's organizations and women's caucuses or divisions of national organizations. The only significant omission is professional associations; a lengthy directory of these groups is already available from the Federation of Organizations for Professional Women (see the Employment entry for specifics). Information on the organizations was gathered from questionnaires, brochures and telephone interviews. Whenever possible we have used the words of the organizations themselves, though we have edited for clarity. Projects and programs are listed under the name of the parent organization. SPRINT, a clearinghouse on women and sports, for example, is listed under its sponsor, Women's Equity Action League. Cross-references have been provided for every organization or program not listed under its own name. The name, address, phone number and a brief annotation are provided for government agencies in a separate section at the end.

ABUSED WOMEN'S AID IN CRISIS
G.P.O. Box 1699
New York, NY 10001
(212) 686-3628

GOALS: to provide assistance to battered women, including special services to Spanish-speaking women, the development of training and counseling programs, and the development of services to children and men.
PROGRAMS: telephone and on-site information and counseling; referrals to shelters and services for battered women; advocacy and support for clients; job counseling and training; volunteer training program; training and consulting for outside agencies; speakers' bureau, workshops, information packets, brochures, films, publications.

ADULT EDUCATION ASSOCIATION
CONTINUING EDUCATION FOR WOMEN SECTION
810 18th Street N.W.
Washington, DC 20006
(202) 347-9574

GOALS: to assist adult educators concerned with programming for women in the areas of research, counseling, teaching, outreach and administration; to promote assessment of the educational needs of women; to encourage flexible educational programming to meet women's needs.
PROGRAMS: workshops at annual conference; speakers' bureau, information service on continuing education for women, newsletter.

Advisory Committee on Women and Society, see: UNITED CHURCH OF CHRIST

ALL NATIONS WOMEN'S LEAGUE
41 Union Square
New York, NY 10003
(212) 989-3309

GOALS: to assist women of all nationalities to adjust to the American way of life; to advise them in the areas of employment, education, housing and immigration.

PROGRAMS: cultural events; arts and language classes; school for orphans in Colombia, South America; counseling; newsletter; affiliate branches in Argentina, Brazil, Colombia, Dominican Republic, Panama, Puerto Rico, Mexico, West Germany, South Korea.

ALLIANCE AGAINST SEXUAL COERCION
P. O. Box 1
Cambridge, MA 02139
(617) 661-4090

GOALS: to end sexual harassment of women at work; to offer assistance to women who are sexually harassed at their jobs; to provide information to concerned groups and individuals.

PROGRAMS: services to women workers who are victims of sexual harassment, including legal information and referrals, assistance in collecting unemployment insurance, referrals for vocational and educational counseling and other social services; outreach to women's and community groups and to agencies that serve women workers; survey of workplace harassment based on reports to rape crisis centers and women office workers groups; community education; newsletter (joint publication with Feminist Alliance Against Rape and National Communications Network for the Elimination of Violence Against Women).

ALLIANCE FOR VOLUNTEERISM
1214 16th Street N.W.
Washington, DC 20036
(202) 347-0340

GOALS: to strengthen the volunteer movement through cooperative action of national organizations that serve, support or use volunteers; to identify and define major issues facing volunteerism; to share services, facilities and ideas, and collaborate in developing model volunteer programs.

PROGRAMS: develops standards and guidelines for volunteer programs; training seminars to introduce these standards; services in program delivery and cooperative efforts to increase efficiency; exchange of resources and mailing lists; pilot projects to increase the number of women on boards and in other leadership positions in community organizations; training seminars for volunteer administrators in business and industry; research on minority participation in volunteer action and patterns of interagency collaboration; consultation and recommendations to government agencies on public policy development and support for volunteerism; awards for outstanding volunteer involvement and support.

AMERICAN ASSOCIATION FOR AFFIRMATIVE ACTION
% Betty Newcomb
Ball State University
Muncie, IN 47306
(317) 285-5162

GOALS: to establish a national office and encourage research to improve affirmative action programming for all minority groups.

PROGRAMS: study of qualifications and professional ethics for AA directors; speakers' bureau, training program for AA personnel; newsletter.

AMERICAN ASSOCIATION OF UNIVERSITY WOMEN
2401 Virginia Avenue N.W.
Washington, DC 20037
(202) 785-7700

GOALS: to involve women graduates of colleges and universities in fact finding, acquiring skills, continuous education; advocacy and participation in shaping policy on issues concerning the advancement of women, education, community, cultural interests, international relations and legislation.

PROGRAMS: Women as Agents of Change involves members in developing skills for effective action on program issues and legislation; Politics of Food program works to develop a national food policy; Redefining the Goals of Education monitors local schools to effect planning and policies; Legislative Program currently focuses on ratification of the ERA, elimination of sex discrimination, reproductive freedom, Title IX, and conservation; Education Fund finances fellowships for higher education for women.

AMERICAN ASSOCIATION OF WOMEN IN COMMUNITY AND JUNIOR COLLEGES
% Mildred Bulpitt
Phoenix College
1202 West Thomas Road
Phoenix, AZ 85013
(602) 264-2492

GOALS: to support program development tailored for women in two-year colleges; to disseminate information on women's programs and women's studies; to support and assist women in community and junior colleges in job development and to serve as a job clearinghouse for all women in the educational community.

PROGRAMS: produces educational materials for women's programs and courses; consults on program development; conducts state and regional workshops in leadership training and career planning; newsletter, publications, audiovisual resources.

AMERICAN CANCER SOCIETY
REACH FOR RECOVERY
National Headquarters
777 Third Avenue
New York, NY 10017
(212) 371-2900

GOALS: to provide a rehabilitation program for women who have had breast surgery; to help them meet their physical, psychological and cosmetic needs.

PROGRAMS: through programs in hospitals across the country, volunteers who have successfully adjusted to their own surgery visit with patients to help them in making adjustments to mastectomy; contact your local division or unit of the American Cancer Society for further information about programs in your area.

AMERICAN CIVIL LIBERTIES UNION
REPRODUCTIVE FREEDOM PROJECT
22 East 40th Street
New York, NY 10016
(212) 725-1222

GOALS: to challenge the Hyde Amendment; to safeguard women's right to abortion and personal choice.

PROGRAMS: publishes biannually all cases in the area of reproductive freedom, including birth control, sterilization and abortion; information and assistance on sterilization and birth-control litigation; brochures.

AMERICAN CIVIL LIBERTIES UNION
WOMEN'S RIGHTS PROJECT
22 East 40th Street
New York, NY 10016
(212) 725-1222

GOALS: to expand and enforce the rights of women through litigation; to ensure equality under the law; to provide service to ACLU state and local groups who are in pursuit of these goals; to provide training and information materials for nonlawyers.

PROGRAMS: litigation of sex discrimination cases; lobbying Congress on issues of concern to women; encouragement of legal, legislative and educational work on behalf of women's rights; publications, newsletter.

THE AMERICAN COLLEGE OF NURSE-MIDWIVES
1012 14th Street N.W.
Washington, DC 20005
(202) 347-5445

GOALS: to train registered nurses in the management and care of mothers and infants throughout the maternity cycle; to improve health-care services for mothers and infants; to promote and encourage midwifery in modern obstetrics.

PROGRAMS: Educational Program includes basic certificate in midwifery, refresher courses, internship, masters degree program; referrals for national nurse-midwifery services; certifies nurse-midwives through the National Certification Exam; publications; professional journal.

AMERICAN COUNCIL ON EDUCATION
OFFICE OF WOMEN IN HIGHER EDUCATION
1 Dupont Circle N.W.
Washington, DC 20036
(202) 833-4652

GOALS: to increase the number of women prominent in higher education; to promote the advancement of women in higher education administration.
PROGRAMS: guidance to colleges and universities on methods for promoting equality of opportunity for women; leadership to a variety of organizations seeking to promote equality for women and minorities; a National Identification Program for the Advancement of Women in Higher Education Administration to establish a personalized system for identifying and recommending the advancement of women administrators; publications.

AMERICAN FEDERATION OF TEACHERS
WOMEN'S RIGHTS COMMITTEE
1816 Chestnut Street
Philadelphia, PA 19103
(215) 567-1300

GOALS: to help eliminate sex discrimination in educational policy.
PROGRAMS: enforcing Title IX in federally funded educational institutions; providing information to members on issues like sick pay, disability, nonsexist academic curriculum; publications;

AMERICAN FEDERATION OF TELEVISION AND RADIO ARTISTS
NATIONAL WOMEN'S DIVISION
4953 South Aldrich
Minneapolis, MN 55409
(612) 825-4137

GOALS: to ensure equal rights and equal opportunities for all members of AFTRA; to call attention to images which debase, distort, or stereotype women; to promote ratification of the ERA.
PROGRAMS: statistical analysis of the representation of women on the air; newsletter.

AMERICAN FRIENDS SERVICE COMMITTEE
NATIONWIDE WOMEN'S PROGRAM
1501 Cherry Street
Philadelphia, PA 19102
(215) 241-7160

GOALS: to provide a feminist perspective, challenge sexist attitudes and practices, and support the development of women's programs in the AFSC; to provide resources for women struggling to change themselves and their lives; to build cooperation between women and other oppressed groups; to work together with women's organizations that share AFSC concerns.

PROGRAMS: nationwide feminist organizing network of AFSC women for the purpose of sharing ideas, resources and skills; resource and support center at AFSC national office to coordinate, encourage and assist feminist program development; participation in national policy-making bodies of AFSC; study groups, workshops and conferences on a range of feminist issues; technical assistance and training for organizing community campaigns and women's caucuses; pressure for affirmative action throughout organizations; advocacy for women political prisoners in the United States and other countries; local area projects include counseling for mothers in prison, workshops on menopause and middle age, projects in support of battered women and victims of rape and child molestation, campaigns against sterilization abuse; monitoring of Title IX enforcement; publications.

AMERICAN HEALTH FOUNDATION
WOMEN'S OCCUPATIONAL HEALTH RESOURCE CENTER
320 East 43rd Street
New York, NY 10017
(212) 953-1900

GOALS: to initiate and coordinate education, research and action on the occupational health and safety needs of women workers; to increase public awareness and make this issue a national policy and research priority; to link concerned organizations and individuals; to help develop equitable, effective and consistent safety and health policies for both women and men workers.

PROGRAMS: information and resource center including a library and research service to answer scientific, legal and educational questions related to occupational health; roundtable discussions between experts and lay people on women's occupational health issues; advocacy and action programs to reduce on-the-job health and safety hazards; network to link management, unions, women workers, scientists, policy makers, women's community and health organizations; technical bulletins; fact sheets on health hazards for women workers; surveys on health and safety hazards; newsletter.

AMERICAN JEWISH CONGRESS
NATIONAL WOMEN'S DIVISION
15 East 84th Street
New York, NY 10028
(212) 879-4500

GOALS: to promote women's equality, peace, justice and freedom; to promote Jewish survival.

PROGRAMS: supports ERA, divorce rights, abortion, birth control, equal treatment in housing, employment, education and credit rights; programs on political religious issues; hostel in Jerusalem; publications.

AMERICAN PARENTS COMMITTEE
1346 Connecticut Avenue N.W.
Washington, DC 20036
(202) 785-3169

GOALS: to press for legislation to improve national programs on behalf of children, particularly in the areas of foster care and adoption.
PROGRAMS: participation in drafting bills introduced in Congress to reform foster care and adoption systems; lobbying for this legislation and for expanded child welfare services; testimony on behalf of a coalition on children and youth working for a Comprehensive Health Assessment Program; newsletter; scoreboard of legislators' voting records on children's issues.

AMERICAN WOMAN'S ECONOMIC DEVELOPMENT CORPORATION
1270 Avenue of the Americas
New York, NY 10020
(212) 397-0880

GOALS: to offer management training and assistance to women entrepreneurs and women planning to start a business.
PROGRAMS: one-year training program consisting of sixteen seminars on various aspects of small business management, such as accounting, financial statements and financial planning, marketing and sales techniques, personnel management; expert assistance in preparing a business plan; staff and volunteer assistance during the start-up phase of a new business; individual consultations on specific business problems; network of business contacts.

THE AMERICAN WOMEN'S MUSEUM
1805 Burning Tree Drive
Chapel Hill, NC 27514
(919) 967-9938

GOALS: to encourage competent research on women's history; to develop teaching materials, research and exhibits on women; to develop a women's studies curriculum.
PROGRAMS: not yet established.

ASSOCIATION FOR INTERCOLLEGIATE ATHLETICS FOR WOMEN
1201 16th Street N.W.
Washington, DC 20036
(202) 833-5485

GOALS: to work for sports opportunities for women in collegiate women's sports.
PROGRAMS: coordinate national championships for collegiate women's sports; sponsor athletic events; work for equality of opportunity in women's sports,

including support of Title IX and ERA; membership open to educational institutions; newsletter.

ASSOCIATION FOR VOLUNTARY STERILIZATION
WOMEN'S CAUCUS
708 Third Avenue
New York, NY 10017
(212) 986-3880

GOALS: to make voluntary contraceptive sterilization available to anyone; to ensure the voluntary nature of the procedure; to promote voluntary sterilization as an accepted method of birth control.

PROGRAMS: donates funds for services and training for programs on voluntary sterilization worldwide; provides education and information to consumers and professional groups; referral service for individuals; survey project to determine availability of voluntary sterilization; speakers' bureau; publications; quarterly newsletter.

ASSOCIATION OF AMERICAN COLLEGES
PROJECT ON THE STATUS AND EDUCATION OF WOMEN
1818 R Street N.W.
Washington, DC 20009
(202) 387-1300

GOALS: to provide information about the status of women in education, particularly as employees or students at institutions of higher education.

PROGRAMS: clearinghouse of information about Title IX, affirmative action, and other federal requirements providing for equality of women in education; analyzes and monitors current campus policies, legal decisions and other developments related to educational equity in conformance with federal policy; coalition efforts with other concerned groups; liaison with government officials responsible for administering federal education policy; testimony at hearings on federal and local levels; speakers' bureau; publications.

ASSOCIATION OF JUNIOR LEAGUES
825 Third Avenue
New York, NY 10022
(212) 355-4380

GOALS: to promote volunteerism through the training and participation of volunteers in community service projects of local chapters.

PROGRAMS: Volunteer Career Development Program includes special programs for young people and older persons; community service projects of local chapters include child advocacy, historical preservation, rape crisis counseling, drug abuse counseling and promotion of the arts; newsletter.

BLACK CHILD DEVELOPMENT INSTITUTE
1463 Rhode Island Avenue N.W.
Washington, DC 20005
(202) 387-1281

GOALS: to serve as an advocate for the needs of black children and to implement community programs for them; to assist black parents in making policy decisions that will affect their children.

PROGRAMS: technical assistance to affiliates; implementation of Title XX of the Social Services Act; adoption program; curriculum training institute on black history; newsletter, publications.

BLACK WOMEN ORGANIZED FOR ACTION
P. O. Box 15072
San Francisco, CA 94115
(415) 387-4233

GOALS: to effect basic institutional changes that will expand opportunities for black women; to involve black women in political action and develop leadership skills.

PROGRAMS: legislative action, including testimony at hearings on women's issues from the black woman's perspective; participation in campaigns to elect black women to office; monitoring city councils, boards of supervisors, boards of education; talent bank for appointment or election to such bodies; educational programs on political techniques; information for members on education and employment opportunities; media campaign to present black perspectives on women's issues; conferences; credit union; student intern program and youth group; outreach to international women's organizations and co-sponsorship of African and other black women visitors from overseas; newsletter, brochure, publications.

BLACK WOMEN'S COMMUNITY DEVELOPMENT FOUNDATION
1028 Connecticut Avenue N.W.
Washington, DC 20036
(202) 466-6220

GOALS: to strengthen the role of black women in efforts to improve conditions and lower the barriers to full participation of black people in all aspects of American life; work with women in Africa and the Caribbean to help improve living conditions.

PROGRAMS: technical and financial assistance to selected programs with a substantial or sustained impact in black communities; educational projects to promote self-understanding, increase knowledge of current issues, and help young people gain maximum benefit from their education and make informed vocational choices; fellowships for research in black studies; underwriting of publications that contribute to the understanding of black heritage; student internship program; conferences, regional symposia, consultations with community leaders; career placement program serving young black people in the Washington, DC area; juvenile justice project providing a small residential facility in Washington for female juvenile offenders; rural community development project in Mali, West Africa, concentrating on nutrition, child and prenatal care, and improved marketing of agricultural products; outstanding achievement awards to women in black American communities; publications.

B'NAI B'RITH WOMEN
1640 Rhode Island Avenue N.W.
Washington, DC 20036
(202) 857-6600

GOALS: to promote Jewish culture and traditions; to support Israel; to provide community service projects.
PROGRAMS: Human Rights Project supports work on behalf of ERA, Soviet Jewry, Israel Children Home; Operation Stork works with National March of Dimes Foundation to aid teenage mothers and their newborn; Community Services aids veterans, blood banks, and supports genetic and Tay-Sachs counseling; aid to the elderly includes Meals on Wheels, collecting oral history, involvement in nursing homes; youth services include career counseling, on-campus Jewish education, audiovisual aids; publications, newsletter.

BUSINESS AND PROFESSIONAL WOMEN'S FOUNDATION
2012 Massachusetts Avenue N.W.
Washington, DC 20036
(202) 293-1200

GOALS: to promote career opportunities for women through research and education.
PROGRAMS: educational assistance through the Career Advancement Scholarship program for mature women; loans and scholarships for higher education and grants for research on women; management training seminars; library and reference service on subjects of concern to working women; funding source information for women's programs; publishes annotated bibliographies and research reviews.

CAMPAIGN TO END DISCRIMINATION
AGAINST PREGNANT WORKERS
1126 16th Street N.W.
Washington, DC 20036
(No phone)

GOALS: to end discrimination against pregnant workers.
PROGRAMS: lobbying for national and state legislation allowing pregnant women to receive disability payment; referrals for legal recourse.

CANTE OHITIKA WIN (BRAVE HEARTED WOMEN)
P.O. Box 474
Pine Ridge, SD 57770
(No phone)

GOALS: to provide a forum for the women of the Pine Ridge Reservation and to address the concerns of their people.

PROGRAMS: conducting meetings to involve more women in the organization; writing a book about women on the reservation; publication.

CATALYST
14 East 60th Street
New York, NY 10022
(212) 759-9700

GOALS: to help women choose, launch, and advance their careers; to provide career guidance to women; to assist employers with the recruitment, assimilation and upward mobility of women; to offer an informed perspective on women and employment to legislators, educators and the media.

PROGRAMS: nationwide network of Employment Resource Centers; library and information service; training program; Corporate Board Resource to assist corporations in finding women board members; career planning and educational opportunities publication series; "how-to" career development booklets; bibliographies. (For a list of local affiliates, see Career Development subject entry.)

CATHOLICS FOR A FREE CHOICE
201 Massachusetts Avenue N.E.
Washington, DC 20002
(202) 546-4523

GOALS: to support the concept of individual rights in making decisions about contraception and abortion; to support research and distribution of safe contraceptives.

PROGRAMS: works to safeguard women's right to legal abortion through lobbying on a national and state level; newsletter, publications.

CENTER FOR A WOMAN'S OWN NAME
261 Kimberley Road
Barrington, IL 60010
(312) 381-2113

GOALS: to promote the rights of women to choose their own name, regardless of marital status, and to participate fully in determining the surname of their children; to educate women about legal rights in this area and to press for reform through legislation, administrative action and judicial decision.

PROGRAMS: legal information service; litigation in precedent-setting names cases; information on current state laws, proposals for legislative reform and names litigation cases; lobbying, including testimony at legislative hearings and ongoing liaison with state officials; publications; bibliographies, posters, postcards.

CENTER FOR CONSTITUTIONAL RIGHTS
WOMEN'S RIGHTS PROGRAM
853 Broadway
New York, NY 10003
(212) 674-3303

GOALS: to use the law as a means for social progress and to protect the constitutional rights of all Americans; to train lawyers, law students and legal workers for this purpose.

PROGRAMS: public education and litigation concentrating on issues of abortion, rape, child molestation and battered women; major focus is the right of all women to legal, safe abortion, including litigation to challenge anti-abortion laws and restrictive Medicaid policies that would deny this to poor women; court action and community education campaign in coalition with other groups to combat pressures to cut off federal Medicaid funds for abortion and to pass state anti-abortion laws; survey on involuntary sterilization; training and court experience to prepare young attorneys to use the law for social change; information services; resource center; participation in panel discussions, lectures at law schools, colleges, community groups and lawyers' organizations on women's rights issues.

CENTER FOR CONSTITUTIONAL RIGHTS
WOMEN'S SELF-DEFENSE LAW PROJECT
853 Broadway
New York, NY 10003
(212) 674-3303

GOALS: to assist women victims of physical or sexual assault who face criminal charges for having defended themselves.

PROGRAMS: provides skill development assistance to attorneys and community people who represent women facing criminal charges for having defended themselves; offers case consultation, legal training, and public education; disseminates legal materials; publications.

CENTER FOR THE AMERICAN WOMAN AND POLITICS
Eagleton Institute
Rutgers University
New Brunswick, NJ 08903
(201) 828-2210

GOALS: to research, develop, and disseminate information on women's participation in American public life; to assist efforts aimed at increasing women's contributions to the political process.

PROGRAMS: collection of nationwide data on women in political office; studies on women in office; workshops on lobbying skills; small grants available to individuals researching women's participation in the political process; bibliography on women's participation in American politics, government and public life; publications.

CENTER FOR VOCATIONAL EDUCATION
Ohio State University
1960 Kenny Road
Columbus, OH 43210
(614) 486-3655

GOALS: to increase the ability of agencies, institutions and organizations to solve educational problems relating to career planning, preparation and progression.
PROGRAMS: Increasing Sex Fairness in Vocational Education program works in two areas: assessing factors influencing students in their decision to enroll in nontraditional vocational education programs and researching the underrepresentation of women in vocational education administration; has compiled literature reviews in both areas; prepared survey instrument to determine attitudes of high school students to nontraditional vocational education programs; prepared handbook of certification requirements needed by administrators of vocational education programs in each of the fifty states; information services; workshops; publications.

CENTER FOR WOMEN AND SPORT
White Building
Pennsylvania State University
University Park, PA 16802
(814) 865-7591

GOALS: to do research and disseminate information on all aspects of women and sports, including physiological, psychological, biochemical and sociological responses, and the impact of women's growing involvement in the world of sports.
PROGRAMS: basic research studies; seminars and conferences on women and sports.

Center for Women and Work, see: NATIONAL COMMISSION ON WORKING WOMEN

CENTER FOR WOMEN POLICY STUDIES
2000 P Street N.W.
Washington, DC 20036
(202) 872-1770

GOALS: to increase public awareness and effect changes in national policies on women's issues, especially in economic and legal areas; to conduct research and special investigative studies on problems related to the status of women in our society.
PROGRAMS: technical assistance, referral service and national clearinghouse of

information on sexual abuse and domestic violence are available to national and community organizations and projects, to criminal justice, health and social service agencies, and to policymakers; findings of an investigative study on rape distributed nationwide to increase sensitivity and improve response to rape victims by police, prosecutors, health and welfare practitioners and policy makers; consumer credit project to investigate differential treatment of women; consulting services in drafting guidelines for enforcement of the Equal Credit Opportunity Act; project to develop innovative approaches in rehabilitation of women offenders, including a survey of existing programs and a handbook containing model programs; training seminars to develop legal skills of women involved in equal rights litigation; expert witness testimony for Equal Employment Opportunity Commission in key national race and sex discrimination cases; testimony at Congressional hearings; technical journal on sexual assault and domestic violence; newsletter, bibliographies, publications, including *Yearbook in Women's Policy Studies*.

CENTER OF CONCERN
WOMEN'S PROJECT
3700 13th Street N.E.
Washington, DC 20017
(202) 635-2757

GOALS: to encourage women's involvement in all areas of public life with particular emphasis on women in development, employment and in the Roman Catholic Church.

PROGRAMS: prepares and circulates papers on topics including Women and World Economics, Alternative Approaches to Development, Women's Ordination and the Catholic Church; participates in workshops which focus on these issues; works with local International Women's Year groups; provides consultation for groups doing like-minded work; publications; newsletter.

Chicana Rights Project, see: MEXICAN-AMERICAN LEGAL DEFENSE AND EDUCATION FUND

CHILD WELFARE LEAGUE OF AMERICA
67 Irving Place
New York, NY 10003
(212) 254-7410

GOALS: to protect and promote the welfare of children and youth in the United States and Canada; to upgrade standards of care and improve services for deprived, dependent and neglected youngsters and their families; to promote public, governmental and professional understanding of their needs.

PROGRAMS: development of standards and guidelines for public and private agencies that offer child-welfare and related family-care services; accreditation of member agencies; consultations to affiliates and other agencies in the child-welfare field; research studies; regional conferences; reference library and information service; personnel referral service; community surveys of child-welfare needs and services; studies of agency problems to improve services; residential and nonresidential programs for young single parents, their infants and families, including medical care, education, counseling, health, family-life and parenting education; public education on child welfare issues; special projects, such as curriculum development to train foster parents and a special adoption center to promote placement of "hard to place" children; newsletter; directory; publications; professional journal.

CHILDREN'S DEFENSE FUND
1520 New Hampshire Avenue N.W.
Washington, DC 20036
(202) 483-1470

GOALS: to provide long-range and systematic advocacy for children; to work for the reform of harmful policies and laws affecting children.
PROGRAMS: research; public information; litigation; federal agency monitoring; technical assistance to local organizations in the areas of child education, health care, child care, institutional and foster care, and juvenile justice; publications.

THE CHILDREN'S FOUNDATION
1028 Connecticut Avenue N.W.
Washington, DC 20036
(202) 296-4450

GOALS: to achieve fully responsive food assistance programs at the national, state and local levels.
PROGRAMS: review and analysis of existing government and private programs; technical assistance to community groups working to improve or implement programs; advocacy for long- and short-range solutions to problems of hunger and malnutrition in America; family day-care organizing; publications.

CHILDREN'S RIGHTS
3443 17th Street N.W.
Washington, DC 20010
(202) 462-7573

GOALS: to educate the public on the problems and harmful effects of child abduction, concealment or restraint by one estranged or divorced parent from the other; to amend the federal kidnapping law to include such abductions as criminal violations and to enact a uniform child custody law.
PROGRAMS: monitors and lobbies Congress to include parental abduction and restraint of children under the federal kidnapping law; presses for more uniform state custody laws; sends alerts to Children's Rights chapters and other concerned citizens; provides information services; has chapters in sixty localities whose activities include community meetings, television appearances and newspaper articles to educate the public, hotlines and support groups, legislative action to reform state laws; newsletter; *Chapter Guide,* a public, comprehensive resource publication.

CHURCH WOMEN UNITED
475 Riverside Drive
New York, NY 10027
(212) 870-2347

GOALS: to encourage church women to work within the ecumenical movement for peace, social justice and equal rights; to serve as a channel for setting common goals and acting on common issues; to develop in women a confidence in their ability to participate fully and contribute to society.

PROGRAMS: recruitment of young women for training through the federal Job Corps program; lobbying, testimony at Congressional hearings, coalition work for the ERA; train women for citizen action; community education forums, pilot programs, task forces to improve urban living conditions, and open opportunities for women in transition; child development projects; inter-religious community centers to combat drug abuse; programs to improve or expand local health-care services; community reentry programs for women ex-offenders; self-help projects for Native American women; community development aid to women in war-devastated areas; peace-building activities; newsletter; study guides and workbooks on various issues; publications; films and filmstrips.

COALITION FOR CHILDREN AND YOUTH
815 15th Street N.W.
Washington, DC 20005
(202) 347-9380

GOALS: to provide a forum for exchange of ideas on programs affecting children and youth; to monitor relevant legislation and program implementation.

PROGRAMS: task forces on day care, foster care/adoption, health, parenting, juvenile justice; technical assistance; intern programs for college students; communications network; newsletter and directory.

COALITION FOR MEDICAL RIGHTS FOR WOMEN
3543 18th Street
San Francisco, CA 94114
(415) 621-8030

GOALS: to make the medical system more responsive to women's needs.

PROGRAMS: education of the public and the medical profession about the dangers of DES; pressures state health department and lobbies for legislation to protect against such health hazards and to provide for preventive treatment for mothers and children exposed to DES during pregnancy; works with state health authorities to prevent sterilization abuse; educational materials on DES, birth control, reproductive freedom, the Pap smear, sterilization abuse; referrals to local health-care providers, diagnostic labs and child-care facilities; newsletter.

COALITION OF GRASS ROOTS WOMEN
1133 Broadway
New York, NY 10010
(212) 243-7300

GOALS: to unite poor and working women, Black, Latin, Arab, American Indian women and lesbians into a strong political force; to provide their communities with needed services; to liberate women by bringing an end to poverty.

PROGRAMS: planning a women's conference in 1980; forming an Ad Hoc Committee for Unionization; organizing a speak-out for disenfranchised women; developing an immigration clinic in Manhattan which provides quality legal services, training of paraprofessionals, educational and organizational assistance to the immigrant community; linking women together locally, nationally, and internationally.

COALITION OF LABOR UNION WOMEN
15 Union Square
New York, NY 10003
(212) 777-5330

GOALS: to create a unified coalition of union women to determine common concerns and to develop action programs.

PROGRAMS: promotes unionization of unorganized women workers; supports affirmative action in the workplace, political and legislative actions on full employment, child care, improving employee benefits, health and safety coverage, educational opportunities, ratification of the ERA; publications; newsletter.

COALITION OF WOMEN'S ART ORGANIZATIONS
9112 Brierly Road
Chevy Chase, MD 20015
(301) 652-3811

GOALS: to achieve full equality for women in the arts by uniting the efforts of seventy-five organizations working toward this goal; to speak for women artists before legislators and government officials who make policy and funding decisions; to establish a nationwide network of communication among women in the arts.

PROGRAMS: testimony at Congressional committee hearings and local commissions on the status of women in the arts; ongoing efforts to increase involvement of women artists in government-funded programs and to increase number of public commissions awarded to women; participation in regional hearings on the White House Conference on the Arts; represented on the International Women's Year Continuing Committee; support for the Equal Rights Amendment.

COMISIÓN FEMENIL MEXICANA NACIONAL
379 South Loma Drive
Los Angeles, CA 90017
(213) 784-1515

GOALS: to upgrade the status of Chicanas; to develop Chicana awareness; to provide information on issues of concern to Chicanas and their communities.
PROGRAMS: class action suit against coerced sterilization; employment counseling and job training; bilingual-bicultural child development centers; scholarship fund; newsletter; bibliography.

Commission on Status and Role of Women, see: UNITED METHODIST CHURCH

COMMITTEE TO END STERILIZATION ABUSE
P.O. Box A-244
Cooper Station
New York, NY 10003
(212) 788-1775

GOALS: to end sterilization abuse in the United States and abroad; to help people find legal redress if their rights are abused.
PROGRAMS: resource/research files; monitors hospitals, population agencies, governmental agencies on their compliance with sterilization regulations; educational slide shows; publications.

COMMON CAUSE
2030 M Street N.W.
Washington, DC 20036
(202) 833-1200

GOALS: to lobby in the public interest; to make Congresspeople more accountable to their constituents.
PROGRAMS: lobbying for ratification of the ERA, public financing of elections, lobbying disclosure, legislative reform on the state level; newsletter; publications.

CONGRESSIONAL CLEARINGHOUSE ON WOMEN'S RIGHTS
Contact the clearinghouse through your Congressperson.

GOALS: to provide information on women's rights to members of Congress and their constituents.
PROGRAMS: supplies research to members of Congress in answer to constituents' questions; monitors legislation and federal regulations daily; maintains files on all documented issues; seminars; weekly newsletter.

CONSUMER CREDIT PROJECT
261 Kimberley Road
Barrington, IL 60010
(312) 381-2113

GOALS: to reduce discrimination against women in establishing credit and the reporting of credit information; to inform women about their rights under the Equal Credit Opportunity Act and to educate creditors about the law.

PROGRAMS: consumer assistance and counseling on credit rights and complaints of discrimination; consumer advocacy, including efforts to resolve complaints by advising creditors about practices that are in violation of the law; guidance to women for filing official complaints of illegal discrimination; clearinghouse of information; fact sheet, complaint form, publications.

COUNCIL OF ASIAN-AMERICAN WOMEN
3 Pell Street
New York, NY 10013
(212) 349-4417

GOALS: to research and document the changing roles of Asian-American women; to provide resource and referral services in the New York City area; to encourage communication among Asian-American women of different nationalities and members of other women's groups.

PROGRAMS: information gathering in Asian communities in the New York City area about education and employment of women; workshops on such subjects as inequities in the immigration law and small business opportunities; outreach into various New York City Asian communities through existing service network; newsletter.

Continuing Education for Women Section, see: ADULT EDUCATION ASSOCIATION

COUNCIL ON APPALACHIAN WOMEN
P.O. Box 490
Mars Hill, NC 28754
(704) 689-1331

GOALS: to provide an educational and support network for women in rural Appalachia.

PROGRAMS: clearinghouse and funding channel for local women's groups; advocate for women's programs on local, state and federal levels; research on rural women's history; newsletter.

COUNCIL ON INTERRACIAL BOOKS FOR CHILDREN
RACISM AND SEXISM RESOURCE CENTER FOR EDUCATORS
1841 Broadway
New York, NY 10023
(212) 757-5339

GOALS: to develop criteria for identifying racist and sexist stereotypes, distortions, omissions in classroom materials; to establish a resource center.
PROGRAMS: develops, publishes, distributes teaching materials; evaluates textbooks for race and sex bias; facilitates workshops on detecting race and sex bias in learning materials; develops audiovisual aids with teaching units on sexism and racism for elementary, secondary and college levels; teaches graduate courses on stereotype identification at Teachers College, Columbia University; Penn State University; City University of New York; catalog.

Council on Women and the Church, see: UNITED PRESBYTERIAN CHURCH

COYOTE
P.O. Box 26354
San Francisco, CA 94126
(415) 621-6111

GOALS: to defend the rights of prostitutes.
PROGRAMS: educating and lobbying for national decriminalization of prostitution; upgrading the status of prostitutes; social events; newsletters; films; research papers.

DAUGHTERS OF BILITIS
1151 Massachusetts Avenue
Cambridge, MA 02138
(617) 661-3633

GOALS: to provide programs responsive to the social, personal and vocational concerns of lesbians.
PROGRAMS: services vary according to chapter, but general activities include discussion groups, picnics, research projects, community organizing; newsletter; publications.

DAY CARE AND CHILD DEVELOPMENT COUNCIL OF AMERICA
805 15th Street N.W.
Washington, DC 20005
(202) 638-2316

GOALS: to promote comprehensive quality child-care services, supported by public funds under local community control; to mobilize public opinion and help formulate national policies on behalf of such a child-care system.
PROGRAMS: publishes and distributes resource materials offering guidance on child-care program planning and development, current information and trends in early childhood education and other areas of child development; assists local

groups in organizing child-care programs; provides technical assistance to communities developing coordinated systems of services for children; sponsors workshops, meetings, conferences to promote understanding of child development and to improve child-care programs; testifies before congressional committees; newsletter, action bulletins, publications.

DEMOCRATIC NATIONAL COMMITTEE
WOMEN'S DIVISION
1625 Massachusetts Avenue N.W.
Washington, DC 20036
(202) 797-5900

GOALS: to encourage maximum participation of women in the political process; to coordinate the efforts of women members of the DNC, others active in the Democratic Party, and Democratic women in public office on women's issues.

PROGRAMS: regional and state campaign seminars for women candidates; affirmative action workshops to promote selection of women delegates to party conferences and conventions; regional and state workshops to help women obtain jobs and political appointments; grass-roots lobbying and education on women's issues, with current action focused on ratification of ERA; newsletter; technical assistance publications.

DES ACTION NATIONAL
Long Island Jewish-Hillside Medical Center
New Hyde Park, NY 11040
(212) 343-9222

GOALS: to identify all persons—mothers, their daughters and sons—who were exposed during the mother's pregnancy to the cancer-linked synthetic hormone diethylstilbestrol (DES); to assist them in taking extra medical precautions against the health hazards associated with this drug; to develop special health-care services for those exposed to DES and compensation for medical costs; to encourage and support research on the effects of DES.

PROGRAMS: coalition of state DES Action groups; public education campaigns to alert and inform people about the dangers of DES, the importance of regular medical examinations for those who have been exposed, and available methods of treatment; counseling and referral for medical care; lobbying for federal and state laws to establish DES screening centers, registries, compensation for medical costs, and education of the public and health professionals; participation in a special DES Task Force established by the Department of Health, Education and Welfare reviewing all aspects of the DES issue and drafting recommendations for government action; model state programs, such as a consumer research project and outreach to DES-exposed persons; fact sheets; information kits; publications; newsletter.

DISABILITY RIGHTS CENTER
1346 Connecticut Avenue N.W.
Washington, DC 20036
(202) 223-3304

GOALS: to research and monitor the implementation of laws which regulate civil rights for the handicapped.

PROGRAMS: research study on federal employment of handicapped persons; consumer protection manuals on medical equipment and devices.

DISPLACED HOMEMAKERS NETWORK
% Business and Professional Women's Foundation
2012 Massachusetts Avenue N.W.
Washington, DC 20036
(202) 293-1200

GOALS: to provide information, advice and support to displaced homemaker centers across the country; to work for adequate federal funds for such programs; to make sure that this group of women receive effective help in preparing for and finding employment.

PROGRAMS: works with the Department of Labor to develop federally funded multipurpose programs that offer job training, placement and peer counseling for middle-aged women displaced from traditional homemaker roles by widowhood or divorce; newsletter; manual on how to organize local programs; tapes of sessions at first national training conference on displaced homemakers.

ENCORE, see: YOUNG WOMEN'S CHRISTIAN ASSOCIATION

EPISCOPAL WOMEN'S CAUCUS
935 East Avenue
Rochester, NY 14607
(716) 473-2977

GOALS: to encourage and affirm the ministry of ordained women; to broaden the dialogue on women's ministry within the church; to enhance the participation of women in the Episcopal Church.

PROGRAMS: works for employment of women in the Episcopal Church and the election and appointment of women to the political structure of the Church; participates in study and dialogue about human sexuality; joins other groups working for liberation of the oppressed within the United Sates; supports abused women, day care, rape victims, welfare recipients; quarterly newsletter.

Equal Rights Amendment Fund, see: NATIONAL WOMEN'S POLITICAL CAUCUS

ERAMERICA
1525 M Street N.W.
Washington, DC 20005
(202) 833-4354

GOALS: to mobilize support for ratification of the Equal Rights Amendment to the Constitution.

PROGRAMS: national campaign to organize and sustain efforts to ratify the ERA through a coalition of national and state organizations; clearinghouse of information about developments and political forces involved in the fight against ratification on the national and state scenes; research related to the ERA; bulletins, newsletter, informational brochure.

Federal Education Project, see: LAWYERS COMMITTEE FOR CIVIL RIGHTS UNDER LAW

FEDERALLY EMPLOYED WOMEN
485 National Press Building
Washington, DC 20045
(202) 638-4404

GOALS: to end job discrimination against women and minorities in the federal government; to increase opportunities for women and improve the merit system in government employment; to assist federal employees and applicants who encounter discrimination.

PROGRAMS: lobbying and monitoring enforcement of laws and civil service regulations that affect women in government employment; action in support of ERA ratification; regional conferences and training workshops for upward mobility; regional talent banks that offer listings of government job vacancies to advise government employees and others of current opportunities; Legal and Education Fund to provide legal assistance and educate federal employees on issues of discrimination; brochure; newsletter; publications.

FEDERATION OF FEMINIST WOMEN'S HEALTH CENTERS
1112 South Crenshaw Boulevard
Los Angeles, CA 90019
(213) 936-6293

GOALS: to provide high-quality medical care to all women at reasonable prices; to develop a supportive atmosphere for medical services.

PROGRAMS: self-help clinic; pregnancy screening; pregnancy counseling; referrals; abortion clinic; family planning service; newsletter, publications and audiovisual resources.

Affiliates: FWHC, 429 South Sycamore, Santa Ana, CA 92701
FWHC, 330 Flume Street, Chico, CA 95926
WOMANCARE, a FWHC, 424 Pennsylvania Avenue, San Diego, CA 92104

FWHC, 15251 West 8 Mile Road, Detroit, MI 48345
FWHC, 5801 4th Street NW, Atlanta, GA 30318
FWHC, 1017 Thomasville Road, Tallahassee, FL 32303

FEDERATION OF ORGANIZATIONS FOR PROFESSIONAL WOMEN
2000 P Street N.W.
Washington, DC 20036
(202) 466-3547

GOALS: to provide, through an association of more than ninety groups committed to attaining equal opportunities for women, a mechanism for increasing women's professional status and for improving public policy affecting women.

PROGRAMS: monitors impact of public policy on women and communicates the concern of its members to government officials through Washington-based coalitions like the National Coalition for Women and Girls in Education, the Ad Hoc Coalition for Women in Government, the Women's Health Roundtable, the National Women's Agenda Coalition; encourages the development of women's information networks; provides fund-raising assistance to affiliates; has sponsored Center for Research on Women in Higher Education and the Professions and the International Center for Research on Women; publications.

FEMINIST ALLIANCE AGAINST RAPE
P.O. Box 21033
Washington, DC 20009
(202) 543-1223

GOALS: to eliminate rape and other forms of violence toward women.
PROGRAMS: clearinghouse and referrals to organizations concerned with violence against women; newsletter.

THE FEMINIST PRESS
P.O. Box 334
Old Westbury, NY 11568
(516) 997-7660

GOALS: to eliminate sexual stereotypes in books and schools; to provide a new literature with a broader vision of human potential.
PROGRAMS: writes, edits, publishes and distributes educational materials; provides educational services for every level, K–12; maintains Clearinghouse on Women's Studies; newsletter and publications.

FEMINIST WRITERS GUILD
P.O. Box 9396
Berkeley, CA 94709
(No phone)

GOALS: to encourage the growth of community among feminist writers; to act as a service group and a political voice for feminist writers.

PROGRAMS: political, cultural, social activities organized at the local level; national writers' handbook (due 1979); referrals; newsletter.

FOUNDATION FOR MATRIARCHY
P.O. Box 271
Pratt Station
Brooklyn, NY 11205
(212) 625-5001

GOALS: to build an international matriarchal movement.
PROGRAMS: currently organizing matriarchy study groups and providing study guides; planning a Forum on the New Right; sponsored the Forum on the Future of the Women's Movement in New York City and Matriarchal Awareness Week at the University of Missouri; newsletter.

FUTURE HOMEMAKERS OF AMERICA
2010 Massachusetts Avenue N.W.
Washington, DC 20036
(202) 833-1925

GOALS: to encourage personal growth and prepare young people for family life, community involvement and employment through education in home economics; to provide opportunities for young people to assume responsibility and make decisions; to develop awareness of the multiple roles of men and women in today's society.
PROGRAMS: chapters in public and private schools offer opportunities for leadership development and activities such as encounter groups to help student members identify individual needs, interests and potentials, set goals and make plans; Healthy Babies: Chance or Choice, a peer education project on teenage parenting and birth defects, co-sponsored with the March of Dimes; research project to determine which forms of recognition for achievement are meaningful for today's youth; nationwide public education campaign to expand the image and change the definition of "homemaker" to encompass both men and women; workshops for teachers; newsletter, brochures, publications.

GAY RIGHTS NATIONAL LOBBY
WOMEN'S CAUCUS
110 Maryland Avenue N.E.
Washington, DC 20002
(202) 543-2447

GOALS: to pass federal civil rights legislation that would prohibit discrimination based on affectional or sexual preference in areas including but not limited to employment, housing, public accommodations and education.
PROGRAMS: lobbying Congress; publications.

GIRL SCOUTS OF THE UNITED STATES OF AMERICA
830 Third Avenue
New York, NY 10022
(212) 751-6000

GOALS: to develop and implement flexible, innovative programs which reflect the changing racial, ethnic and socioeconomic patterns of membership; develop ways to encourage creative thinking, open communication, and effective action within the organization and with other community groups.

PROGRAMS: development of publications and audiovisual materials for local Brownie and Girl Scout troops on growing up, women's changing role, ecology, community life, history, career education, scouting; development of training materials for Girl Scout volunteers and leaders; magazines for various levels of Scouts.

GIRLS CLUBS OF AMERICA
205 Lexington Avenue
New York, NY 10016
(212) 689-3700

GOALS: to advocate girls' rights; to help girls develop their fullest potential; to provide quality programs for girls.

PROGRAMS: Juvenile Justice Program: training and technical assistance to affiliates in advocacy for girls; delinquency prevention training and services in seven sites; career development and job training; tutorials and remedial education; health/sex/drug counseling; sports programs; community service and leadership training programs; preparation for parenthood workshops; art classes; programs for handicapped; publications; audiovisual aids.

GRAY PANTHERS
3700 Chestnut Street
Philadelphia, PA 19104
(215) 382-6644

GOALS: to eliminate ageism.

PROGRAMS: provides education and action on issues including nursing-home reform, national health service, geriatrics, media representation of the elderly, mandatory retirement; maintains a speakers' bureau; publishes newsletters, fact sheets, other publications.

HADASSAH
50 West 58th Street
New York, NY 10019
(212) 355-7900

GOALS: to provide American Jewish women with practical projects which preserve Jewish culture and identity; to give the American Jewish woman tools for self-instruction, guidance of her family, and participation in her community.

PROGRAMS: educational and medical facilities in Israel include Hadassah Medical

Center, community health clinics, high schools, vocational guidance institutes; in the United States Hadassah sponsors Zionist youth groups, community volunteer programs, and educational projects; publications and audiovisual aids.

HEALTHRIGHT
41 Union Square
New York, NY 10003
(212) 675-2651

GOALS: to provide health information for women; to publicly support women's health care.
PROGRAMS: advocacy for patients in cases of medical abuse; seminars such as "Know Your Body" and "The Health Care System"; speakers' bureau; newsletter and publications.

HOUSEWIVES FOR THE ERA
Route 3
Urbana, IL 61801
(No phone)

GOALS: ratification of the Equal Rights Amendment; full partnership for homemakers under the law.
PROGRAMS: provides information on the legal status of homemakers and their need for the Equal Rights Amendment; lobbying.

INSTITUTE FOR STUDIES IN EQUALITY
926 J Street
Sacramento, CA 95814
(916) 444-9196

GOALS: to serve as a national clearinghouse of information and research data about equality for women; to facilitate contact among concerned groups and individuals; to help society adapt to social change and to inform women about their rights and opportunities.
PROGRAMS: hotline providing current information on women's equality issues; data bank; program consultation and seminars on legal and social change for national organizations; equal rights task force to coordinate a nationwide network of concerned national leaders and citizens; referral service; speakers' bureau; syndicated newspaper column; film documentary on women's rights and needs; newsletter; brochure; publications.

INSTITUTE OF WOMEN TODAY
1340 East 72nd Street
Chicago, IL 60619
(312) 752-3337

GOALS: to bring church- and synagogue-related women into the women's movement to bring religious principles into the women's struggle for equality.

PROGRAMS: nationwide workshops in law, psychology, theology, and history to search out the religious and historical roots of women's liberation; research in women's studies; legal assistance to women in prisons; national faculty in law, psychology, theology and psychology; publications.

INSTITUTE ON WOMEN'S WRONGS
% Odyssey Institute
24 West 12th Street
New York, NY 10011
(212) 741-9570

GOALS: to provide psychiatric services to women.

PROGRAMS: therapy for incest victims; national campaign against child pornography; educational campaign on children and alcohol; workshops on women and psychiatry.

INTERCOLLEGIATE ASSOCIATION FOR WOMEN STUDENTS
% American Association of University Women
2401 Virginia Avenue, N.W.
Washington, DC 20037
(202) 785-7700

GOALS: to provide a voice for women students; to help women students maximize their cultural, intellectual, political and social potential.

PROGRAMS: supports legislation which enhances women's lives; works for passage of the ERA, enforcement of Title IX, quality child-care facilities, abortion rights, and the active involvement of women within the university and society; newsletter.

INTERNATIONAL CHILDBIRTH EDUCATION ASSOCIATION
P.O. Box 20852
Milwaukee, WI 53220
(612) 881-9194

GOALS: to promote family-centered maternity care; to encourage and educate expectant parents to understand and share all aspects of the childbearing experience; to promote childbirth options and freedom of choice based on alternative approaches and methods.

PROGRAMS: international conventions and regional conferences for professional and parent groups in the ICEA federation and for other concerned individuals; a nationwide network offering information and assistance to parents and professionals; state and local workshops to develop creative leadership in dealing with particular local situations and to encourage and assist hospitals in efforts to institute family-centered maternity care; public information programs, including speaking tours and traveling exhibits; research on current childbearing practices; newsletters, pamphlets, publications, audiovisual materials.

INTERNATIONAL ROSTER OF WOMEN SCHOLARS AND PROFESSIONALS

148 N Street
South Boston, MA 02127
(617) 269-5957

GOALS: to gather information about women with professional training and skills who desire to apply these skills to the solution of global problems; to help women gain access to research and policy-making bodies where such problems are investigated; to sponsor research to advance women's participation in all activities related to developing a more just and peaceful human society.
PROGRAMS: establishing a roster.

INTERNATIONAL WOMEN'S TRIBUNE CENTER

305 East 46th Street
New York, NY 10017
(212) 421-5633

GOALS: to act as point of entry for women from overseas; to develop and disseminate information about women and development; to provide a center for women working in this field.
PROGRAMS: connect resources of the United Nations, organizations and foundations to meet needs of women arriving from other countries; develop and distribute resource materials to help women involved in development activities around the world; workshops and seminars on program planning and design, materials development, communication and use of media; meetings of women involved in international development to provide exchange of ideas; project data bank; audiovisual aids; information kit; publications; newsletter.

LA LECHE LEAGUE INTERNATIONAL

9616 Minneapolis Avenue
Franklin Park, IL 60131
(312) 455-7730

GOALS: to educate women throughout the world about breastfeeding; to encourage mothers to nurse their infants and offer help to women who encounter problems in breastfeeding; to educate health-care professionals who work with new mothers.
PROGRAMS: personal instruction to women who want to nurse their infants; mother-to-mother help and encouragement through correspondence networks and telephone hotlines; educational meetings about the physical and psychological benefits of breastfeeding for mother and child; newsletter; journal; information packets; publications; audiovisual aids.

LAWYERS COMMITTEE FOR CIVIL RIGHTS UNDER LAW
FEDERAL EDUCATION PROJECT
733 15th Street N.W.
Washington, DC 20005
(202) 628-6700

GOALS: to enforce federal legislation concerning vocational education, specifically, the Vocational Education Amendments of 1976, Title IX of the Education Amendments of 1972, and Title VI of the Civil Rights Act of 1964.

PROGRAMS: approximately half of the Federal Education Project's work is in the area of vocational education; monitors compliance with all three laws at the federal level; monitors state one- and five-year plans required by the Vocational Amendments of 1976 to see that they comply with guidelines; consulting; publications.

LEADERSHIP CONFERENCE OF WOMEN RELIGIOUS OF THE USA
1302 18th Street N.W.
Washington, DC 20036
(202) 293-1483

GOALS: to assist women in religious orders who hold major administrative positions to develop creative, responsive leadership consonant with their mission in a changing world; to articulate a contemporary theology of religious life.

PROGRAMS: maintains task force on sex-role stereotyping in education; works to eliminate sexist language in liturgy and hymns; develops resources on the status and role of women; study of church symbols as they relate to women's concerns; national study of Roman Catholic women and the ministry; publications.

LEAGUE OF WOMEN VOTERS
1730 M Street N.W.
Washington, DC 20036
(202) 296-1770

GOALS: to achieve an open, accountable government through citizen participation in the political process.

PROGRAMS: lobbies, testifies, monitors, and publicizes issues of national concern, currently focusing on: equal rights for all; equal access to housing, employment, and education; wise use of natural resources; making government accountable, representative and responsive; and world peace; newsletter, publications.

LEAGUE OF WOMEN VOTERS
OVERSEAS EDUCATION FUND
2101 L Street N.W.
Washington, DC 20037
(202) 466-3430

GOALS: to encourage women in developing countries to participate more fully in their societies by helping them acquire vocational and leadership skills; to help women effect change in Third World countries through voluntary organizations; to improve health, nutrition and community development in these countries; to link women's groups overseas with women in the United States.

PROGRAMS: technical assistance; leadership, management and organizational training; skills training for low-income women; surveys of women's needs; resource centers; development of teaching methods and materials; educational exchange program for Asian and American women; publications, brochures.

LESBIAN MOTHERS NATIONAL DEFENSE FUND
2446 Lorentz Place North
Seattle, WA 98109
(202) 282-5798

GOALS: to help lesbian mothers win legal custody of their children.
PROGRAMS: provides emotional, financial and legal support; newsletter.

LINKS
1522 K Street N.W.
Washington, DC 20005
(202) 783-3888

GOALS: to pursue educational, cultural and civic activities through their 167 chapters.
PROGRAMS: provide financial support for the N.A.A.C.P., the United Negro College Fund and other organizations for civic achievement and voluntary public service; focus on community service through chapter programs in the arts, for youth, the environment, job counseling for women, minority business development, and more.

LUTHERAN CHURCH WOMEN
2900 Queen Lane
Philadelphia, PA 19129
(215) 438-2200

GOALS: to carry out the work of the Lutheran Church in America.
PROGRAMS: works for change in local juvenile justice systems; advocates support of legislation to improve quality of life; supports programs to strengthen the family; provides Bible study materials for new readers; volunteers in hospitals and community service organizations; participates in projects for Lutheran World Relief and Canadian Lutheran World Relief; pamphlets.

THE MARTHA MOVEMENT
1011 Arlington Boulevard
Arlington, VA 22209
(703) 323-5937

GOALS: to raise the status of and gain greater respect and recognition for homemaking; to identify and address the problems and needs of homemakers.

PROGRAMS: information and resources clearinghouse; support network for homemakers including a correspondence chain and nationwide toll-free hotline; seminars, research, position papers on problems affecting homemakers; pressure to include homemaker advocates on organization, company and foundation boards and at relevant professional conferences; local speakers' bureaus and resource talent banks; public information program including media appearances and syndicated radio show on homemaker issues; self-help activities and involvement in community projects that are "in the interests of homemakers"; newsletter; films; workbooks and tapes for use in marketable skills identification.

MATERNITY CENTER ASSOCIATION
48 East 92nd Street
New York, NY 10028
(212) 369-7300

GOALS: to work for the improvement of maternity care; to ensure that high-quality services are available before, during, and after birth.
PROGRAMS: develops programs on family-centered maternity care; supports and conducts research to improve the quality of maternity services; informs and educates the public and policy makers; offers classes on childbirth; sponsors conferences for child-care professionals; provides financial assistance to nurse-midwifery students; publications.

MEXICAN-AMERICAN LEGAL DEFENSE AND EDUCATION FUND CHICANA RIGHTS PROJECT
201 North St. Mary's Street
San Antonio, TX 78205
(512) 224-5476

GOALS: to research the civil rights and legal needs of Chicanas and to formulate litigation strategies to combat discrimination.
PROGRAMS: litigation focusing on sex discrimination in government employment programs, health care, day care, education, the penal system; publications.

MEXICAN-AMERICAN WOMEN'S NATIONAL ASSOCIATION
P.O. Box 23656
L'Enfant Plaza Station S.W.
Washington, DC 20024
(703) 521-0097

GOALS: to represent the cause and promote the status of Chicana women.
PROGRAMS: promoting professional, community and family leadership roles among Chicanas; improving Chicana communication nationwide; furthering parity between Chicanas and Chicanos; creating awareness of the Chicana viewpoint; newsletter.

MIDTOWN ADOLESCENT RESOURCE CENTER
℅ Odyssey House
309–311 East 6th Street
New York, NY 10003
(212) 741-9654

GOALS: to provide treatment resources for children used as prostitutes and for pornographic reasons; to provide information about sexual abuse of children and the services necessary to combat it; to serve as a model for future treatment centers; to campaign for legislative hearings on sexual exploitation of children; to identify those who profit by exploiting children.

PROGRAMS: the program plans of this newly formed center call for psychiatric and psychological counseling, dance, art, and poetry therapy to help the children express themselves and rebuild self-confidence; needs assessment of patients.

THE MIDWEST ACADEMY
600 West Fullerton Avenue
Chicago, IL 60614
(312) 953-6525

GOALS: to teach the skills necessary for building and maintaining social change organizations.

PROGRAMS: workshops and consulting for individuals and groups on how to organize for social change; program includes leadership development, planning and developing campaigns, research methods and fund-raising strategies; publications.

MINORITY WOMEN EMPLOYMENT PROGRAM
40 Marietta Street N.W.
Atlanta, GA 30303
(404) 681-0001

GOALS: to assist minority women in finding management, technical and professional jobs in the private sector.

PROGRAMS: career guidance before, during and after college; job counseling.

MS. FOUNDATION FOR WOMEN
370 Lexington Avenue
New York, NY 10017
(212) 689-3475

GOALS: to provide funding for women's projects in health, employment, violence against women and children, and for the advancement of nonsexist, multiracial education; seed money for grass-roots women's groups with minimal or no access to conventional funding sources.

PROGRAMS: grants to local groups and projects of national organizations, with emphasis on programs that serve as models for others; assistance in building coalitions and group networks and connecting women's activist organizations and others concerned with related problems; technical assistance on internal organization of projects; referrals; programs with other foundations to make feminist issues a higher priority; multimedia, nonsexist, multiracial educational and play materials called *Free to Be . . . You and Me.*

MS. FOUNDATION FOR WOMEN
PRO-CHOICE PROJECT FOR REPRODUCTIVE FREEDOM
370 Lexington Avenue
New York, NY 10017
(212) 689-3475

GOALS: to provide support and technical assistance to national, state, and local groups working to maintain every woman's right to choose abortion, regardless of economic status.
PROGRAMS: provides direct grants and technical assistance in such areas as organizing, coalition building, network development, publicity, education and fund-raising to groups working for reproductive freedom

NATIONAL ABORTION FEDERATION
110 East 59th Street
New York, NY 10022
(212) 688-8516

GOALS: to foster the provision of quality abortion services to all women; to provide a forum for abortion service providers, other organizations, and individuals committed to that goal.
PROGRAMS: promulgates professional standards and organizational ethics which guarantee the health, safety, and well-being of all patients; maintains clearing-house; provides technical assistance to affiliates; coordinates petition campaign for public support of abortion; publications.

NATIONAL ABORTION RIGHTS ACTION LEAGUE
825 15th Street N.W.
Washington, DC 20005
(202) 347-7774

GOALS: to preserve the 1973 Supreme Court decision guaranteeing the constitutional right to medically safe abortions.
PROGRAMS: building a pro-choice, grass-roots movement; lobbying Congress for public funding for abortions; raising funds to contribute to congressional races; endorsing pro-choice candidates; preparing materials for public education; training state and local groups to work with the media; monitoring congressional legislation; preparing information and memorandums for congressional offices on specific bills and amendments; following hearings on abortion and related subjects; speakers' bureau; newsletter; action alerts.

NATIONAL ACTION FORUM FOR OLDER WOMEN
School of Allied Health Professions
Health Science Center
State University of New York
Stony Brook, NY 11794
(516) 444-2989

GOALS: to increase public awareness of the status and needs of older women; to encourage development of resources and services to enhance the quality of life for women in their later years; to create a network to deal with special issues and problems.

PROGRAMS: resource exchange and information clearinghouse related to women in mid-life and late life; state steering committees working on model state plans to expand opportunities and services; legislative alerts on issues of concern; media watch to improve public image of older women; work with universities to include issues affecting women over forty in women's studies programs; newsletter and information kits.

NATIONAL ADVISORY COMMITTEE FOR WOMEN
200 Constitution Avenue, N.W., Room C5321
Washington, DC 20210
(202) 523-6707

GOALS: to monitor the progress of and advise the President on government action needed to implement the National Plan of Action of the First National Women's Conference (Houston, 1977); to gather and disseminate information about nationwide developments on women's issues.

PROGRAMS: review President Carter's report (issued after the National Women's Conference) on the current status of women in government and other areas of national life; review his legislative program as submitted to Congress; make recommendations to the President, following this review, for additional action on the federal level; provide clearinghouse of information about grass-roots activities to realize the aims defined in the Plan of Action; the Committee's term expires in the summer of 1980.

NATIONAL ALLIANCE FOR OPTIONAL PARENTHOOD
3 North Liberty Street
Baltimore, MD 21201
(301) 752-7456

GOALS: to make the child-free life-style a socially accepted and respected option.
PROGRAMS: public media campaign; library; seminars/courses on child-free living; research; support network; speakers' bureau; publications.

NATIONAL ALLIANCE OF BLACK FEMINISTS
202 South State Street
Chicago, IL 60604
(312) 939-0107

GOALS: to help promote the social, political, and economic welfare of black women through self-help on both a personal and a political level.

PROGRAMS: alternative school providing classes in assertiveness training, female sexuality, human sexuality, female/male relations, feminism, the black woman, and black feminism; retreats, C-R groups, and study groups for members; conferences and forums on topics of concern to black women; referrals (primarily for local Chicago area services) for legal, health, consumer, education, and employment information; an archive on black women; political actions on the ERA, reproductive freedom, and specific concerns such as the Joan Little case; publications.

NATIONAL ASSEMBLY OF WOMEN RELIGIOUS
1307 South Wabash
Chicago, IL 60605
(312) 663-1980

GOALS: to mobilize the Catholic women committed to a just society showing respect for all human life; to work for the liberation of people from all forms of oppression and to ensure effective participation in decisions which affect their lives.

PROGRAMS: committees and task forces that offer information and support for grass-roots action on current issues, such as discrimination in education, all forms of racism, economic exploitation of migrant workers and others, battered women, gay rights, the ordination of women, improved health care for neglected groups in society, ratification of the ERA, world hunger and peace; training workshops and seminars on health care, education for justice, community leadership, joint action of educators and social activists; seminars for consciousness raising and developing action strategies; newsletter; bulletins; publications; audiovisual resources.

NATIONAL ASSOCIATION FOR DIVORCED WOMEN
200 Park Avenue
New York, NY 10017
(212) 344-8407

GOALS: to provide information and guidance about the rights and opportunities of divorced women or women considering divorce; to offer benefits and services that meet the needs of divorced women and their families.

PROGRAMS: counseling on legal rights in separation and divorce; on money management, household budgeting, credit, and insurance; seminars on legal, financial and consumer subjects, child care, and other concerns of divorced women; information on education and employment, job hunting, career guidance and child care; listings of services and firms that prepare tax returns, loan and credit applications, and provide expert advice on insurance and investments; suggestions for building new social contacts; vacation and travel information, reduced rate tours and travel; newsletter; brochure.

NATIONAL ASSOCIATION FOR GIRLS AND WOMEN IN SPORT
1201 16th Street N.W.
Washington, DC 20036
(202) 833-5540

GOALS: to foster the development of girls' and women's sports programs in schools and colleges; to formulate principles and standards and provide a channel of communication for coaches, administrators and participants.

PROGRAMS: writes and interprets rules for girls' and women's sports in educational institutions; offers training, evaluation and rating of officials who govern intercollegiate sports for women; sponsors clinics and conferences in sports, coaching skills and administration; provides information about other workshops, conferences and events of interest, and about career opportunities for women in sports-related fields; promotes research on girls and women in sports; newsletter; publications.

NATIONAL ASSOCIATION FOR PARENTS AND PROFESSIONALS FOR SAFE ALTERNATIVES IN CHILDBIRTH
Marble Hill, MO 63767
(no phone)

GOALS: to explore and implement family-centered childbirth programs.

PROGRAMS: promotes education about natural childbirth and family-centered maternity care in hospitals; provides a forum for communication among parents, medical professionals and childbirth experts; assists in the establishment of home birth programs; conferences; provides referral service, research and speakers' bureau; publications, newsletter.

NATIONAL ASSOCIATION OF COLORED WOMEN'S CLUBS
5808 16th Street N.W.
Washington, DC 20011
(202) 726-2044

GOALS: to strengthen family life and educate parents so their children can grow into productive adults and useful citizens; to promote racial equality, freedom and justice.

PROGRAMS: local club-sponsored classes offering mothers instruction in homemaking, budgeting, child rearing; preschool programs; remedial tutoring for schoolchildren; association of girls clubs; scholarship fund for students attending Negro colleges; joint efforts with civil rights organizations in education, housing, employment; national legislative alerts to local clubs on civil rights issues; nongovernmental observer at the United Nations; newsletter, magazine, brochure.

NATIONAL ASSOCIATION OF COMMISSIONS FOR WOMEN
c/o Patricia Hill Burnett, President
Michigan Women's Commission
18261 Hamilton Road
Detroit, MI 48203
(313) 863-5566

GOALS: to promote full equality for women through legislation, lobbying, public education, recommendations to city, state and federal officials and agencies; securing ratification of the ERA.
SERVICES: resource center on women's issues; conferences; legislative action; coalition work; newsletter; publications. (For a list of member Commissions, see Commissions on the Status of Women subject entry.)

NATIONAL ASSOCIATION OF FEMINIST THERAPISTS
Boston Regional Association of Feminist Therapists
234 Putnam Avenue
Cambridge, MA 02139
(no phone)

GOALS: to establish a national network of feminist therapists; to provide support and peer supervision groups.
PROGRAMS: planning to establish a referral network of feminist therapists throughout the country.

NATIONAL ASSOCIATION OF NEGRO BUSINESS AND PROFESSIONAL
    WOMEN'S CLUBS
1806 New Hampshire Avenue N.W.
Washington, DC 20009
(202) 483-4880

GOALS: to assist black women in business and the professions.
PROGRAMS: provides workshops and programs on issues including revenue sharing, divorce, child custody, employment, filing a sex discrimination suit, older women, women in media, government, arts, day care; newsletter.

NATIONAL ASSOCIATION OF WOMEN BUSINESS OWNERS
2000 P Street N.W.
Washington, DC 20036
(202) 338-8966

GOALS: to build a network that encourages women to establish their own businesses; to advise and assist women entrepreneurs; to improve opportunities for women entrepreneurs and provide a collective voice for greater clout.
PROGRAMS: clearinghouse for information and referral to the talents, products, services and needs of businesswomen; workshops and seminars offering management training and technical assistance; group benefits, such as insurance, financing, purchasing, credit; lobbying and monitoring legislation in the interests of women in business; chapter programs deal with local problems and

needs; national and metropolitan area directories of businesses owned and operated by women; national indexing project to develop data bank about women in business; newsletter; brochures; organizing manual for chapters.

NATIONAL ASSOCIATION OF WOMEN IN CRIMINAL JUSTICE
906 Fifth Avenue
Pittsburgh, PA 15219
(412) 281-7380

GOALS: to improve the position of women in the criminal justice system as employee, offender or victim; to identify and increase educational and employment opportunities for women in criminal justice, and provide a communication network.
PROGRAMS: skills bank for women seeking educational or employment opportunities in the field; speakers' bureau; newsletter; membership directory; organizing manual for local associations.

NATIONAL BLACK FEMINIST ORGANIZATION
4812 46th Street N.W.
Washington, DC 20016
(202) 244-1010; (301) 598-5446

GOALS: to provide a voice for the concerns of black women.
PROGRAMS: members work through their chapters on a variety of issues, as advocates and educators; current issues of concern include rape and child abuse.

NATIONAL CENTER FOR LAW AND THE HANDICAPPED
1235 North Eddy Street
South Bend, IN 46617
(219) 288-4751

GOALS: to ensure equal protection under the law for handicapped people; to increase public and professional awareness of the rights of the disabled.
PROGRAMS: legal counsel for disabled individuals in selected court cases, usually in "friend of the court" role; legal consultations on rights of the handicapped with attorneys, organizations and individuals; drafting of model briefs; legal and social science research to encourage legal reform and promote rights of the disabled; workshops, seminars, conferences on education and employment opportunities, legal rights, medical care and treatment, transportation, accessibility for the disabled; intern program for law students; newsletter.

NATIONAL CENTER FOR THE PREVENTION AND CONTROL OF RAPE
National Institute of Mental Health
5600 Fishers Lane
Rockville, MD 20852
(301) 443-1910

GOALS: to develop, implement, and evaluate models of mental health and related services for rape victims, their families and offenders; to increase community awareness and promote better working relationships between agencies and groups dealing with the problem of rape.

PROGRAMS: provide grants for research and demonstration projects on causes of rape, laws dealing with rape, treatment of victims, and programs of prevention and control; clearinghouse of information for the public, professionals and researchers; compiles and distributes directories of services, bibliographies, reviews of printed and audiovisual materials, technical reports; training materials developed for personnel in rape treatment and prevention programs.

NATIONAL CENTER FOR VOLUNTARY ACTION
1214 16th Street N.W.
Washington, DC 20036
(202) 467-5560

GOALS: to stimulate and enhance the quality of volunteer action in solving social problems; to strengthen volunteering as a basic element of responsible citizenship in a free society.

PROGRAMS: supportive services to local Voluntary Action Centers that seek to increase citizen involvement in all areas of social action; technical assistance to local volunteer groups, including workshops in fund-raising and volunteer recruitment; model projects demonstrate new ways to involve volunteers; consultations and workshops for corporations interested in encouraging employee participation in community activity; monitoring legislation affecting volunteer organizations; national clearinghouse for information on volunteer programs of all kinds; magazine; publications.

NATIONAL CHICANA FOUNDATION
1005 South Alamo
San Antonio, TX 78210
(512) 226-7629

GOALS: to develop research and demonstration projects related to special problems and issues of concern to Mexican-American women; to develop program materials for women leaders in the Chicana community; to provide a vehicle through which Chicanas can funnel proposals for funding.

PROGRAMS: research project on female heads of households on welfare; testimony at hearings on welfare legislation; development of nonsexist, bilingual, multicultural curriculum for minority children in elemeny schools; publications.

NATIONAL COALITION AGAINST DOMESTIC VIOLENCE
% Cynthia Dames
Battered Women's Project
P.O. Box 1501
Santa Fe, NM 87501
(503) 281-2447

GOALS: to develop a support network of grass-roots women's groups to share information and resources; to encourage research and services; to increase public support and to gain political clout.

PROGRAMS: regional planning conference; organizing and lobbying for federal support of services for battered women.

NATIONAL COALITION FOR WOMEN AND GIRLS IN EDUCATION

% Leslie Gladstone
Women's Equity Action League
805 15th Street N.W.
Washington, DC 20005
(202) 638-4560

GOALS: to unite national organizations in joint actions to strengthen national policies and practices concerning women and girls in education.

PROGRAMS: Coalition has no fixed membership and no staff; each action or position differs according to priorities and concerns of participating organizations.

NATIONAL COALITION OF AMERICAN NUNS

1307 South Wabash
Chicago, IL 60605
(312) 643-0986

GOALS: to study, work and speak out on issues related to human rights and social justice.

PROGRAMS: services to women in prison; Jewish-Christian relations committee; advocacy of women's causes such as ERA; workshops, conferences, seminars on social justice issues; newsletter.

NATIONAL COMMISSION OF WORKING WOMEN
CENTER FOR WOMEN AND WORK

1211 Connecticut Avenue N.W.
Washington, DC 20036
(202) 466-6770

GOALS: to improve conditions of the vast majority of women in the work force who are concentrated in low-paying, low-status jobs; to press for equal pay for equal work, reduce barriers to upward mobility, and open opportunities for career development.

PROGRAMS: regional meetings with working women to encourage them to share concerns and form networks of action; guide to local and national agencies and organizations offering services to help women improve conditions and opportunities; drafts of model legislation; testimony at Congressional committee hearings; national exchange of ideas, information and research on working women provided through the Center for Women and Work; public information campaigns about women in the work force; news updates; program reports; fact sheet; brochure.

NATIONAL COMMITTEE ON HOUSEHOLD EMPLOYMENT
7705 Georgia Avenue N.W.
Washington, DC 20012
(202) 291-2422

GOALS: to upgrade private household employment through training and organizing; to press for better pay, working conditions and benefits for household workers; to improve their status and public image.

PROGRAMS: organizing on local level; promotes code of standards for employers and employees that includes information about legal minimum wage requirements, Social Security, workers' compensation, as well as recommended sick leave, paid holidays and vacations; training programs to improve skills of household workers; legislative action on behalf of expanded coverage and improved benefits under workers' compensation and unemployment insurance laws; Low Income Women's Action Plan with recommendations for meeting specific needs of all poor women submitted to federal officials and to feminist organizations; newsletter; publications.

NATIONAL COMMUNICATIONS NETWORK FOR THE ELIMINATION OF VIOLENCE AGAINST WOMEN
4520 44th Avenue South
Minneapolis, MN 55406
(612) 827-2841

GOALS: to generate a national network and to facilitate a dialogue among feminists working to eliminate violence against women.

PROGRAMS: gathers information about programs being developed throughout the country to help battered women, and reports on new projects and shelter facilities; keeps informed of, and reports about, current strategies to end abuse of women, including reform of state laws, court procedures, police practices, and legal defense committees to help women on trial in cases of self-defense against male violence; maintains contact with groups acting to end violence against women in other countries and reports on current developments; newsletter.

NATIONAL COMMUNITY ACTION TASK FORCE ON WOMEN IN POVERTY
% Bolliger
824 North Cooper
Peoria, IL 61606
(309) 673-5403

GOALS: to sensitize its parent organization, the Washington D.C. Community Services Administration, to the needs of poor women; to do coalition work with like-minded groups; to publicize the plight of poor women and of CSA's role in eradicating poverty; to organize women Community Action Program directors to educate their male counterparts on the issue of women in poverty.

PROGRAMS: due to lack of funds, the Task Force is limited to influencing the

CSA; particular concerns are job development, battered women, women and alcoholism; the Task Force also collects and disseminates information on women in poverty.

NATIONAL CONFERENCE OF PUERTO RICAN WOMEN
P.O. Box 4804
Washington, DC 20008
(no phone)

GOALS: to defend the rights, needs, and aspirations of Puerto Rican women as well as those of other women of Hispanic origin.

PROGRAMS: identification and development of leadership among constituents; building a national communications network and community-based Hispanic women's centers; community advocacy; chapter and national newsletters.

NATIONAL CONGRESS OF NEIGHBORHOOD WOMEN
11-29 Catherine Street
Brooklyn, NY 11211
(212) 388-6666

GOALS: to upgrade the status of working-class women; to achieve representation and recognition for poor and minority women.

PROGRAMS: establishing a community-based college program; building a coalition of affiliates around the country and offering technical assistance; providing shelter for battered women; organizing to revitalize and develop neighborhoods; conferences; speak-outs; legal services; newsletter.

NATIONAL COUNCIL FOR ALTERNATIVE WORK PATTERNS
1302 18th Street N.W.
Washington, DC 20036
(202) 466-4467

GOALS: to educate government, labor, management and other interested groups and individuals about alternative work patterns, such as flexible hours, part-time work and job sharing.

PROGRAMS: information clearinghouse and resource center; research on the social impact of alternative work patterns on communities and individual lives; conferences and seminars; legislative action to press for expanded part-time and flexitime opportunities in federal employment; speakers' bureau; directory of employers who have adopted flexible work schedules; newsletter; resource packet.

NATIONAL COUNCIL OF CAREER WOMEN
818 National Press Building
Washington, DC 20045
(202) 374-1401

GOALS: to promote careers and upward mobility for women.

PROGRAMS: conducts monthly meetings on topics of concern to career women, such as upward mobility, time management, salary negotiations, career fields, coping with dual careers; produces materials such as résumé guides and resource lists; plans to establish chapters across the country; newsletter.

NATIONAL COUNCIL OF JEWISH WOMEN
15 East 26th Street
New York, NY 10010
(212) 532-1740

GOALS: to advance human welfare and the democratic way of life through a coordinated program of education, services and social action.

PROGRAMS: volunteer services and fund-raising for day-care centers; nationwide survey on juvenile justice and development of community-based services outside the judicial system for runaways, truants and other status offenders; local health and welfare services such as counseling for women with special health problems or life crises, referral and direct service programs for the elderly, day programs and residences for the emotionally disturbed; community and legislative action on such issues as equal rights and opportunities for women, day care, youth employment, quality public education, support for Israel, human rights; periodical, newsletters, brochures, technical assistance manuals, films, program kits.

NATIONAL COUNCIL OF NEGRO WOMEN
815 Second Avenue
New York, NY 10017
(212) 687-5870
AND
1346 Connecticut Avenue N.W.
Washington, DC 20036
(202) 223-2363

GOALS: to link affiliated national organizations and mobilize women of diverse backgrounds on common efforts to meet the current economic, educational and social needs of minority and low-income women and their families; to develop the leadership potential of black and other minority women in American communities and in developing countries abroad.

PROGRAMS: network of local membership units; coalition work; leadership training; workshops and seminars; child development and day-care centers; immunization program for children; career development for high school students; Women's Center for Education and Career Advancement offering consultations and workshops on career development, career counseling, library and information services on employment opportunities, and an Associate Degree Program featuring a job-related curriculum; training of teenagers as community health aides; Health Careers Opportunity program to encourage minority students to seek careers in medicine and other professional health-care fields; rural self-help program to combat malnutrition; assistance to low-income families in home ownership; one-to-one volunteer program to help girl offenders; skills bank to share expertise in developing countries; archives of black women's history; fact sheet, newsletter, brochures, annual report.

NATIONAL COUNCIL OF WOMEN OF THE USA
345 East 46th Street
New York, NY 10017
(212) 697-1278

GOALS: to act as a catalytic agent for its member organizations; to improve the status of women; to examine different approaches and options for action on social issues faced by all women.

PROGRAMS: committees and task forces on various issues including education, careers, health, social development and the arts; seminars, lectures, cultural activities; international hospitality program; annual events, including a "Woman of Conscience" award to outstanding women in different fields; information on current national and international social issues; newsletter.

NATIONAL COUNCIL ON ALCOHOLISM
OFFICE ON WOMEN
733 Third Avenue
New York, NY 10017
(212) 986-4433

GOALS: to address the special needs and concerns of women affected by alcoholism; to encourage development of treatment programs, public policies and actions geared to these needs; to educate the public, health and helping professionals, employers and others about the problem of alcoholism among women; to identify related social, cultural and medical issues.

PROGRAMS: develops guidelines and standards for state task forces on Women and Alcoholism; promotes cooperative efforts between state task forces and other women's organizations; holds conferences and workshops on alcoholism and women; compiles and disseminates data on alcoholism and its impact on family violence, rape, and employment; serves as a resource and liaison to national health organizations and federal agencies in developing model treatment and prevention programs; information exchange and joint action with national women's groups on alcoholism education and awareness; course at Rutgers University Summer School of Alcohol Studies.

NATIONAL FEDERATION OF BUSINESS AND PROFESSIONAL WOMEN'S CLUBS
2012 Massachusetts Avenue N.W.
Washington, DC 20036
(202) 293-1100

GOALS: to elevate the standards of women in business and the professions, to promote the interests of business and professional women; to bring about a spirit of cooperation among business and professional women of the United States; to extend opportunities through education to business and professional women along the lines of industrial, scientific and vocational activity.

PROGRAMS: sponsors meetings and conferences on issues of interest to women, including topics related to effective political action and leadership; develops a legislative program with priority issues established at the annual membership conference; serves as a Washington representative on concerns of working women; produces materials for member clubs to assist them in their local programs.

NATIONAL FEDERATION OF REPUBLICAN WOMEN
310 First Street S.E.
Washington, DC 20003
(202) 484-6670

GOALS: to influence legislation, to educate voters about the Republican Party's philosophy, to elect party candidates.

PROGRAMS: supplying volunteers for Republican campaigns; sending interested women to campaign leadership school; newsletter.

NATIONAL FOUNDATION FOR THE IMPROVEMENT OF EDUCATION
RESOURCE CENTER ON SEX ROLES IN EDUCATION
1201 16th Street N.W
Washington, DC 20036
(202) 833-4402

GOALS: to achieve equity for women in educational programs and employment; to provide support services for individuals and groups working to reduce sex discrimination and sex-role stereotyping in education.

PROGRAMS: data bank of research on sexism in elementary and secondary schools; abstracting, storage, retrieval of literature relating to sex-role stereotyping and sex discrimination; technical assistance to individuals and groups working to combat sexism in schools; surveys of state departments of education and teacher training institutions to increase awareness of sexism; conferences; publications.

NATIONAL GAY TASK FORCE
80 Fifth Avenue
New York, NY 10011
(212) 741-5800

GOALS: to present alternatives to stereotypes of sex roles and of gay men and lesbians; to increase public awareness of gay men and lesbians.

PROGRAMS: campaigns for fair representation in the national media; speakers' bureau; coalition work; public education "We Are Your Children" campaign; action alerts; information packets; newsletter.

NATIONAL HOOK-UP OF BLACK WOMEN
2021 K Street N.W.
Washington, DC 20006
(202) 293-2323

GOALS: to provide a communications network for black women who are interested in improving the status of the black community in general and the black woman in particular.

PROGRAMS: supporting the efforts of the Congressional Black Caucus to use the legislative process to bring about full equality of opportunity; creating and implementing a Black Women's Agenda; making visible the significant contributions of black women to American society; working for passage of the ERA; providing a national support base for all black women elected, appointed or serving in organizations which promote full equality; speakers' bureau; talent bank for members; a directory of black women's organizations (forthcoming); publications; newsletter.

NATIONAL LESBIAN FEMINIST ORGANIZATION
P.O. Box 14643
Houston, TX 77021
(207) 799-8744

GOALS: to deal with the oppression of lesbians in all its manifestations; to improve the status and secure the rights of lesbians; to promote lesbian feminism.

PROGRAMS: not yet established.

NATIONAL MIDWIVES ASSOCIATION
P.O. Box 163
Princeton, NJ 08540
(609) 799-1942

GOALS: to provide a channel of communication and a central source of information for and about lay midwives (midwives who are not registered nurses but are trained in prenatal and maternal care and delivery); to gain legal and social recognition for midwifery; to offer training and opportunities for midwives.

PROGRAMS: provides training workshops and lectures, access to high-quality supplies, equipment and books for midwives; information clearinghouse on midwifery; legal and funding assistance in court cases against midwives; works with government agencies and others concerned with regulations, standards and licensing; works to gain accreditation and national licensing for midwives; newsletter; directories of midwifery services.

NATIONAL ORGANIZATION FOR WOMEN
ACTION CENTER
425 13th Street N.W.
Washington, DC 20004
(202) 347-2279

GOALS: to bring women into full participation in American society; to address and advocate women's issues at a national level and to work for their realization on a local level; to secure ratification of the ERA.

PROGRAMS: local and regional NOW groups organize in support of the ERA and women's rights in response to the needs and demands of their particular communities; twenty-one national committees implement its national resolutions on educational discrimination, early childhood development, women and religion, ageism and women, minority women, lesbian rights, media reform, mental health and women, violence against women, women and health, reproductive rights, economic planning, women and poverty, employment discrimination, labor unions/on-site organizing, full employment/minimum income, social security/pension discrimination, credit, pregnancy disability, displaced homemakers, homemaker rights; newsletter; regional and national conferences for members.

NATIONAL ORGANIZATION FOR WOMEN LEGAL DEFENSE AND EDUCATION FUND
36 West 44th Street
New York, NY 10036
(212) 354-1225

GOALS: to end discrimination and achieve equality for women by initiating and carrying out precedent-setting educational and legal projects designed to eliminate patterns of inequality and injustice based on sexism; to promote compliance with laws against sex discrimination.

PROGRAMS: nationwide monitoring network to press for enforcement of laws against sex discrimination; legal assistance and information; litigation in precedent-setting sex discrimination suits; public information campaigns; monitoring of federal judicial appointments; workshops and conferences; high-school essay contests on feminist subjects; research studies, educational materials, annual report, brochures, publications.

NATIONAL ORGANIZATION FOR WOMEN LEGAL DEFENSE AND EDUCATION FUND
PROJECT ON EQUAL EDUCATION RIGHTS
1029 Vermont Avenue N.W.
Washington, DC 20005
(202) 332-7337

GOALS: to encourage vigorous federal enforcement of the laws against sex discrimination in elementary and secondary education; to assist local efforts in this area.

PROGRAMS: monitors Title IX nationally; trains regional monitoring groups; provides information and guidance to local citizen groups working for educational equity; publications.

NATIONAL ORGANIZATION ON CONCERNS OF BLACK WOMEN
3958 Louise Street
Lynwood, CA 90262
(213) 564-4584; (213) 979-5193

GOALS: to work for the issues concerning black women in their communities.

PROGRAMS: active in a variety of issues such as education, child care and health; key issues of concern at present are unemployment in the black community and drug use, especially as it affects black youth; work to encourage community agencies to be responsive, and to identify the resources available and educate the local community about them.

NATIONAL ORGANIZATION TO INSURE SUPPORT ENFORCEMENT
12 West 72nd Street
New York, NY 10023
(212) 595-5299

GOALS: to persuade the insurance industry and/or government to make some form of divorce insurance available; to educate the public on law and litigation and the appropriate use of it; to find new ways to deliver inexpensive and speedy legal services.

PROGRAMS: Humanized Divorce Advisory Service helps divorcing couples negotiate support, custody and property settlements; consultation on family problems and their legal consequences.

NATIONAL RURAL CENTER
1828 L Street N.W.
Washington, DC 20036
(202) 331-0258

GOALS: to develop and advocate policy alternatives and to provide information that can help rural people achieve their full potential.

PROGRAMS: developing policy; evaluating and monitoring legislation and regulations that would affect rural areas and issues; providing information, library and reference services, technical assistance; a directory of rural organizations; publications.

THE NATIONAL SELF-HELP RESOURCE CENTER
2000 S Street N.W.
Washington, DC 20009
(202) 338-5704

GOALS: to aid the development of local community resource centers that provide information exchanges, community dialogues, and alliance building.

PROGRAMS: nationwide network for information exchange and technical assistance; resource collection; newsletter; workshops; publications.

NATIONAL SENIOR CITIZENS LAW CENTER
1200 15th Street N.W.
Washington, DC 20005
(202) 872-1404

GOALS: to help senior citizens live in dignity, free from poverty.
PROGRAMS: provides assistance to legal services, attorneys, state and local agencies whose attorneys work with the elderly poor; issues of concern include social security, public and private pensions, Medicare and Medicaid, nursing homes, guardianship and involuntary commitment, housing, veterans, older women; publications and newsletter.

NATIONAL SISTERS COMMUNICATIONS SERVICES
1962 South Shenandoah
Los Angeles, CA 90034
(213) 559-2944

GOALS: to help Roman Catholic sisters become more effective in their work by training them in communication strategies and skills; to provide communications resources and to develop a network of sister-communicators; to educate religious leaders to the value of communications skills.
PROGRAMS: intensive seminars in basic communications skills; employment clearinghouse for jobs in the ministry of communications (radio/TV/films, audiovisual instructional services, print media, public relations, communications education); involvement in ecumenical media projects; internships in communications positions; newsletters; job directories.

NATIONAL WOMAN'S PARTY
144 Constitution Avenue N.E.
Washington, DC 20002
(202) 546-1210

GOALS: ratification of the ERA, authored and introduced to Congress in 1923 by National Woman's Party Founder Alice Paul.
PROGRAMS: working in states for ratification of the ERA; publications.

NATIONAL WOMEN'S CENTERS TRAINING PROJECT
WOMEN'S EDUCATIONAL EQUITY TRAINING PROJECT OF EVERY-WOMAN'S CENTER
Nelson House
University of Massachusetts
Amherst, MA 01003
(413) 545-1558

GOALS: to define and address the needs of campus-based women's centers.
PROGRAMS: research to identify needs of campus-based women's centers; training program for women's centers to equip staff with effective program, organizational planning, and budgetary skills; training manuals.

National Women's Division, see: AMERICAN JEWISH CONGRESS; AMERICAN FEDERATION OF TELEVISION AND RADIO ARTISTS

NATIONAL WOMEN'S DRUG RESEARCH COORDINATING PROJECT
1015 East Huron Street
Ann Arbor, MI 48104
(313) 763-5538

GOALS: to collect and disseminate data about addicted women and about treatment programs that serve them.
PROGRAMS: research studies on the psychosocial differences among women addicts, women's drug programs in Detroit, organizational variables and their relation to service and treatment issues and models, medical needs of addicted women versus those of addicted men, hospital practices, the pregnant addict; newsletter.

NATIONAL WOMEN'S EDUCATION FUND
1410 Q Street N.W.
Washington, DC 20009
(202) 462-8606

GOALS: to increase the number and influence of women in public life by helping them develop political skills.
PROGRAMS: information on women in politics and assistance to women officeholders; campaign institutes; consulting to women's organizations for political programs; publications.

NATIONAL WOMEN'S HEALTH NETWORK
2025 I Street N.W.
Washington, DC 20006
(202) 223-6886

GOALS: to influence federal policy as it affects women, and monitor activities of agencies that carry out this policy.
PROGRAMS: clearinghouse of information on health topics most relevant to women; women's health resource guides; task forces that keep abreast of developments in women's health; monitoring of various federal health-related agencies, including meetings with officials; health hotline and referrals; calendar of conferences related to women's health; newsletter.

NATIONAL WOMEN'S POLITICAL CAUCUS
1411 K Street N.W.
Washington, DC 20005
(202) 347-4456

GOALS: to win full representation for women in government at all levels in both elective and appointive offices; to provide resources and practical skills for running successful election campaigns; to encourage national parties and candidates to speak out responsibly on issues of special interest to women.

PROGRAMS: national, state and local caucuses to build women's political clout on all levels of government; direct assistance to women candidates; lobbying for appointments of women to government office, including a Coalition for Women's Appointments in Washington; legislative program including formation of and participation in issue-oriented coalitions, testimony at hearings, alerts to nationwide network on women's issues before Congress, coordination of grass-roots lobbying and briefing of local caucus leaders; women's task forces in major political parties to press for support of women's issues; workshops and conferences; newspaper, brochures, quarterly reports, publications, position papers.

NATIONAL WOMEN'S POLITICAL CAUCUS
EQUAL RIGHTS AMENDMENT FUND
1411 K Street N.W.
Washington, DC 20005
(202) 347-4456

GOALS: to support pro-ERA candidates in campaigns for election to legislatures in states which have not ratified the Equal Rights Amendment; to lobby for ratification in these states.

PROGRAMS: contributes to campaigns of pro-ERA candidates in primary and general state elections; offers technical assistance to help run successful campaigns; mounts intensive statewide lobbying efforts for ratification of the ERA throughout legislative sessions.

NATIONAL WOMEN'S PROGRAM DEVELOPMENT
P.O. Box 9385
San Antonio, TX 78204
(512) 225-6647

GOALS: to organize and develop innovative programs that will help women to improve their family, economic, employment, educational and social lives.

PROGRAMS: The Low Income Women's Development Project seeks to develop a model welfare reform employment program; provides a month-long training course on career guidance in relation to life planning, skills assessment, self-evaluation, employment preparation and job-skills training.

NATIONAL WOMEN'S STUDIES ASSOCIATION
University of Maryland
Foreign Language Building
College Park, MD 20742
(301) 454-3757

GOALS: to promote women's studies at every educational level in academic and community settings throughout the country; to further social, political and professional support and development of such studies.

PROGRAMS: regional and national conferences and communications networks;

caucuses on women's studies areas such as Third World women, lesbianism, prekindergarten through high-school and community-college programs; task forces to develop programs and policies on curriculum and standards, employment, and the teaching of women's studies; research; funding and membership development; newsletter.

NATIONAL YOUTH ALTERNATIVE PROJECT
1346 Connecticut Avenue N.W.
Washington, DC 20036
(202) 785-0764

GOALS: to identify and promote the rights and concerns of youth by creating new youth services, expanding existing ones, and influencing public policy.

PROGRAMS: research project on runaway youth, technical assistance to the Department of Health, Education and Welfare's runaway youth program; conferences; monitoring youth employment and juvenile delinquency; seminars on fundraising and influencing public policy; publications.

Nationwide Women's Program, see: AMERICAN FRIENDS SERVICE COMMITTEE

NETWORK
1029 Vermont Avenue N.W.
Washington, DC 20005
(202) 347-6200

GOALS: to provide a religious lobby to insure national legislation responsive to the needs of the poor, the hungry, the unemployed, and the imprisoned.

PROGRAMS: concerns include ratification of the ERA, equitable food planning, full employment and welfare reform, alternatives to prison, decreased military spending; activities include legislative research for testimony and lobbying, coalition participation, intern program, workshops, clearinghouse, telephone alerts, publications.

NEW AMERICAN MOVEMENT
SOCIALIST FEMINIST COMMISSION
7125 McPherson Boulevard
Pittsburgh, PA 15208
(412) 363-0885

GOALS: to promote feminist theory and practices within NAM; to develop ties with women's, gay and lesbian groups; to produce literature on feminism and to move forward the theoretical and strategic debate concerning socialist feminism.

PROGRAMS: organizing efforts currently focus on issues of reproductive freedom and violence against women; publications.

NEW DIRECTIONS FOR WOMEN
346 South Scott
Tucson, AZ 85701
(602) 623-3677

GOALS: to help teenage women to develop skills preparing them for careers; to act as an advocacy agency in juvenile justice.

PROGRAMS: feminist counseling; assertiveness training; career awareness group; camping retreat program; development of sex-role stereotype awareness tools; high-school alternative diploma; conferences; workshops, publications.

NEW TRANSCENTURY FOUNDATION
SECRETARIAT FOR WOMEN IN DEVELOPMENT
1789 Columbia Road N.W.
Washington, DC 20009
(202) 462-6661

GOALS: to serve as a resource center on women and development, the Secretariat assists Third World women to integrate more fully into the development of their nations.

PROGRAMS: Publications Retrieval System for documents on Third World women and development; a funding resources bulletin, directory of projects, annotated bibliography on women in development; conferences; workshops; seminars.

NEW WAYS TO WORK
149 Ninth Street
San Francisco, CA 94103
(415) 552-2949

GOALS: to improve the quality of work life for all; to promote flexibility in employment and expanded opportunities for challenging jobs; to encourage development of innovative workplaces that meet the needs of workers and offer products and services which enhance the quality of community life.

PROGRAMS: seminars and workshops for individuals and organizations on new work concepts and employment options; individual counseling to help define work needs and assist in exploring suitable new job possibilities or improving current work situations; job listings available to registered clients; resource library with information on new work arrangements, community resources and local employment opportunities; publications.

Nonsexist Child Development Project, see: WOMEN'S ACTION ALLIANCE

Office of Women in Higher Education, see: AMERICAN COUNCIL ON EDUCATION

Office on Women, see: NATIONAL COUNCIL ON ALCOHOLISM

NORTH AMERICAN INDIAN WOMEN'S ASSOCIATION
% Hildreth Venegas
720 East Spruce Street
Sisseton, SD 57262
(No phone)

GOALS: to promote the betterment of home, family life, health, education and intertribal communications; to build an awareness of Indian culture.

PROGRAMS: current projects focusing on the year of the child include a study of boarding schools and the needs of Native American children, and a study of the needs of handicapped Native American children; chapters in more than twenty states.

OLDER WOMEN'S LEAGUE EDUCATIONAL FUND
3800 Harrison Street
Oakland, CA 94611
(415) 658-8700

GOALS: to focus public attention on concerns of middle-aged and older women; to reduce discrimination and increase understanding of their problems and needs among policy makers and specialists; to develop a network of women in this group to work on the issues that concern them.

PROGRAMS: provides information for and about older women; works to educate gerontologists, agencies and others concerned about their special problems; works with programs for the aging to inject a feminist viewpoint, to promote employment of older women in these programs, and to increase job opportunities; drafts model legislation; plans to form an advocacy arm to organize a nationwide action network and speak out in behalf of older women on public policy matters; publications, position papers.

OPTIONS FOR WOMEN
8419 Germantown Avenue
Philadelphia, PA 19118
(215) 242-4955

GOALS: to help women fulfill their employment potential through counseling and placement services; to help employers understand and comply with affirmative action requirements to recruit and upgrade women for higher-level jobs.

PROGRAMS: career development workshops; vocational and educational counseling and testing; guidance in résumé preparation and interview techniques; placement and recruitment services, particularly for professional and managerial positions; affirmative action consultations and management awareness seminars; presentations to top-level management groups on affirmative action questions; consultations to educational institutions; programs on career options for high school and college students; reports; brochure.

ORGANIZATION OF CHINESE-AMERICAN WOMEN
1443 Rhode Island Avenue N.W
Washington, DC 20005
(202) 232-3971

GOALS: to advance the cause of Chinese-American women; to promote equal participation in American life, and to integrate Chinese-American women into the mainstream of women's activities and programs.

PROGRAMS: monitors legislation which affects Asian-American women; maintains talent bank of members; establishes nationwide communications network; education, training and technical assistance; research; cultural events; publications.

ORGANIZATION OF PAN ASIAN-AMERICAN WOMEN
719 Fern Place N.W.
Washington, DC 20012
(No phone)

GOALS: to provide a voice for the concerns of Asian-American women; to develop leadership, a sense of sisterhood and a network of communication; to promote an accurate and realistic image of Asian women in America.

PROGRAMS: workshops and lectures on building a movement and on assertiveness training, featuring subjects such as organization and leadership styles and presentations by leaders of major national women's groups; brochure; publications.

ORGANIZATION OF WOMEN FOR LEGAL AWARENESS
94 Claremont Avenue
Maplewood, NJ 07040
(201) 762-5208

GOALS: to help women know and exercise their legal rights, especially in matters of separation and divorce, by increased understanding of the law and the legal process; to reform matrimonial law.

PROGRAMS: workshops and seminars; lecture series; self-help support groups; judicial reform activities, such as testimony at committee hearings, discussions with state bar association, investigation and filing of complaints; lobbying on state divorce legislation.

THE OTHER VICTIMS OF ALCOHOLISM
P.O. Box 921
Radio City Station
New York, NY 10019
(212) 247-8087

GOALS: to point up how alcoholism affects family, friends and others in the everyday lives of alcoholics and to combat the impact of alcoholism on our society.

PROGRAMS: national task force to establish network of concerned individuals and organizations; workshops, seminars, conferences to explore new programs and services for "the other victims" of alcoholism; newsletter, brochure, labor-management packet, posters, publications.

OUR PEOPLE'S TASK
114 Liberty Street
New York, NY 10006
(212) 691-7950 x966

GOALS: to provide a supplementary funding base for openly gay and lesbian candidates for political office; to support financially proposals which affect the gay community.
PROGRAMS: twenty-four-hour voter registration hotline; speakers' bureau; quarterly newsletter.

Overseas Education Fund, see: LEAGUE OF WOMEN VOTERS

PENSION RIGHTS CENTER
1346 Connecticut Avenue N.W.
Washington, DC 20036
(202) 296-3778

GOALS: to protect the rights of employees, retirees, and spouses.
PROGRAMS: fact sheets on women's pensions; seminars; conferences; information clearinghouse on pension rights; developing legislative strategies to support bills on women's pensions; newsletter.

PIONEER WOMEN
200 Madison Avenue
New York, NY 10016
(212) 725-8010

GOALS: an American Zionist organization, Pioneer Women works to elevate the quality of life in Israel; to train and equip the Israeli woman and her family to lead a full and productive life; to raise the status of women worldwide.
PROGRAMS: in Israel: assists Na'amat (a sister organization) in providing training, educational and social services for women and youth; assists the absorption of new immigrants; establishes child-care services, day-care centers, day/night homes; offers free legal counseling to women; builds community centers; educates young wives and mothers about health and family care.
in the United States: National American Affairs Department develops programs which encourage communal participation for enlightened social legislative action; participates in the affairs of the American Jewish community and local civic affairs; audiovisual aids; publications.

PLANNED PARENTHOOD FEDERATION OF AMERICA
810 Seventh Avenue
New York, NY 10019
(212) 541-7800

GOALS: to provide low-cost voluntary family planning services to all women who want them and need them regardless of age, race, marital or economic status.

PROGRAMS: voluntary health and education services on the benefits of birth planning; information on legislative developments which affect birth control; experts on family planning laws; coordination of family planning services and medical standards for 187 nationwide affiliates; technical assistance; research, program planning and policy formulation on United States family planning services and needs; educational materials, publications.

PRIESTS FOR EQUALITY
3311 Chauncy Place
Mount Rainier, MD 20822
(301) 699-0042

GOALS: to support women's equality in civil society and in the Roman Catholic Church; to influence the Church's position on women.

PROGRAMS: studies on women called to ordination and the readiness of Catholics to accept women in the ministry; active support for ratification of the ERA; liturgies of reconciliation between men and women; Operation Soapsuds to clean up sexist language in the church; conferences; newsletter.

Project on Equal Education Rights, see: NATIONAL ORGANIZATION FOR WOMEN LEGAL DEFENSE AND EDUCATION FUND

Project on the Status and Education of Women, see: ASSOCIATION OF AMERICAN COLLEGES

Racism and Sexism Resource Center for Educators, see: COUNCIL ON INTERRACIAL BOOKS FOR CHILDREN

RECRUITMENT AND TRAINING PROGRAM
162 Fifth Avenue
New York, NY 10010
(212) 691-0660

GOALS: to increase the number of minorities and women in the skilled trades and the professions.

PROGRAMS: recruitment, placement and work-related support services for skilled and semi-skilled trades and the professions; neighborhood outreach centers; teaching English as a second language; publications.

THE RELIGIOUS COALITION FOR ABORTION RIGHTS
100 Maryland Avenue N.E.
Washington, DC 20002
(202) 543-7032

GOALS: to encourage and coordinate support for legal abortion; to insure the individual's right to make decisions about abortion in accordance with her conscience and responsible medical practice; to oppose efforts to deny these rights on the basis of faith and moral conviction; to protect constitutional guarantees of privacy and religious freedom.
PROGRAMS: state affiliates to encourage action on a local level to counterbalance those taking a religious stand against abortion; education and action in support of pro-choice public policies; legislative alerts, publications.

RELIGIOUS COMMITTEE FOR THE ERA
475 Riverside Drive
New York, NY 10027
(212) 870-2494

GOALS: to secure ratification of the ERA.
PROGRAMS: educational projects among Catholic, Jewish and Protestant groups; to assist state coordinators in the drive for ratification.

Reproductive Freedom Project, see: AMERICAN CIVIL LIBERTIES UNION

Resource Center on Sex Roles in Education, see: NATIONAL FOUNDATION FOR THE IMPROVEMENT OF EDUCATION

ROSIE JIMENEZ FUND
711 San Antonio Street
Austin, TX 78701
(512) 654-8662

GOALS: to provide direct subsidies for poor women unable to obtain legal abortions due to the cut in Medicaid funding for abortions.
PROGRAMS: established in memory of an early victim of the elimination of Medicaid-funded abortions, the fund provides monies for abortions to participating clinics and medical facilities; individual women are referred to participating facilities; contact the Fund for further information and for assistance.

RURAL AMERICAN WOMEN
1522 K Street N.W.
Washington, DC 20005
(202) 785-4700

GOALS: to provide a forum and to serve as advocate for the concerns and needs of rural women.

PROGRAMS: research on the status of women in Appalachia; advocacy on issues and legislation affecting rural women, including displaced homemaker and battered women services, the ERA, improved educational opportunities, health care, child care, and legal services.

SAINT JOAN'S INTERNATIONAL ALLIANCE
435 West 119th Street
New York, NY 10027
(212) 663-3555

GOALS: to achieve equality for women in church, state and society.

PROGRAMS: organizes Catholic men and women with associate members in other faiths to achieve legal and de facto equality for women in all spheres; bulletin.

SCAPEGOAT
1540 Broadway
New York, NY 10036
(212) 757-6300

GOALS: to help prostitutes make decisions about how to change their lives; to assist women who want to leave prostitution by providing services for reentering the straight life; to set up a 24-hour hospitality house; to bridge the gap between the straight world and prostitutes.

PROGRAMS: offers prostitutes legal and medical help, sets up consciousness-raising groups, provides emergency housing for prostitutes and their children, handles referrals from the New York Police Department runaway squad, Family Court, parole agencies, city hospitals; assists each woman through the process of reentry.

SCREEN ACTORS GUILD WOMEN'S CONFERENCE COMMITTEE
7750 Sunset Boulevard
Hollywood, CA 90046
(213) 876-3030

GOALS: to broaden employment opportunities for women Guild members in films, television programs and commercials; to eliminate stereotyping and press for casting of women in a wider range of roles.

PROGRAMS: meetings with casting personnel of agencies, networks, and producers to change traditional views and limitations about casting women; information exchange among local branch committees on trends and techniques to achieve reforms; local self-help programs offer guidance on finding more work; monitoring of television programs and commercials to note casting patterns; action to combat sexual harassment on the job; lobbying on ERA and other women's issues in accordance with positions taken by the Guild Board of Directors.

Secretariat for Women in Development, see: NEW TRANSCENTURY FOUN-DATION

SEX INFORMATION AND EDUCATION COUNCIL OF THE U.S.
84 Fifth Avenue
New York, NY 10011
(212) 929-2300

GOALS: to provide information on all aspects of sexuality to professionals in health, education, religion, social work and other human services, as well as to individuals interested in increasing their knowledge and understanding of human sexuality; to assist agencies in program planning and problem areas related to sex education nd sexuality.

PROGRAMS: resource center and clearinghouse of materials and information about organizations in the field; referral service for professionals or individuals who need help; consultation service; research library; publications, bibliography, newsletter, information packets.

THE SIERRA CLUB
AD HOC TASK FORCE ON OUTREACH TO
WOMEN'S ORGANIZATIONS
530 Bush Street
San Francisco, CA 94108
(415) 981-8634

GOALS: to build more alliances with women's groups on issues of mutual concern such as toxic substances, workplace safety, air and water pollution.

PROGRAMS: monthly meetings in San Francisco Bay Area; Washington, DC, politcal coalition; speakers' bureau of women environmentalists.

Socialist Feminist Commission, see: NEW AMERICAN MOVEMENT

SPRINT, see: WOMEN'S EQUITY ACTION LEAGUE FUND

Task Force of Women in Judaism, see: UNION OF AMERICAN HEBREW CONGREGATIONS

TRANSIT, THE NATIONAL INSTITUTE FOR TRANSITION
22 Monument Square
Portland, ME 04111
(207) 773-7123

GOALS: to develop and distribute information relevant to life's transitions with specific regard for ex-offenders, older women, alcoholism, mid-life crisis, career and educational transitions.

PROGRAMS: conferences, symposia, workshops; consulting and public speaking; technical assistance in beginning second careers, ageing, women's issues, social issues, program development, fund-raising, staff development; bimonthly newsletter; quarterly journal.

UKRAINIAN NATIONAL WOMEN'S LEAGUE
108 Second Avenue
New York, NY 10003
(212) 533-4646

GOALS: to encourage new art forms among Ukrainian women; to channel members' energies to community service and volunteer work.
PROGRAMS: museum of folk art; community service projects; nursery schools; services to the elderly poor; bilingual publications.

UNION OF AMERICAN HEBREW CONGREGATIONS
TASK FORCE ON EQUALITY OF WOMEN IN JUDAISM OF THE NEW YORK FEDERATION OF SYNAGOGUES
838 Fifth Avenue
New York, NY 10021
(212) 249-0100

GOALS: liturgical, educational and interpersonal efforts to promote the equality of women within reform Judaism; to change sexist liturgical and prayerbook language; to insure that educational texts use nonsexist language and artwork; to develop curricula on women and Judaism; to integrate people who are alone into the congregation.
PROGRAMS: rewriting Passover Haggadah to include women and their concerns; designing course outlines on women and Judaism; conferences on role stereotyping and on working with Christian women's groups on women's religious issues and concerns; publications.

UNION WOMEN'S ALLIANCE TO GAIN EQUALITY
P.O. Box 462
Berkeley, CA 94701
(415) 655-2813

GOALS: to fight sex discrimination on the job, in the unions and society; to achieve equal rights, equal pay and equal opportunity for women workers.
PROGRAMS: chapters in different cities organize working women including housewives, the unemployed, the retired, those on welfare, as well as women with paying jobs; encourages women unionists to assume greater responsibility and leadership roles; exchanges information and experiences, successes and problems organizing women workers; provides education and guidance for effective organizing action; interprets the ERA and its implications for women workers; acts in behalf of special demands for women workers such as paid paternity leave, expanded maternity medical coverage, child-care facilities; newspaper; brochure; publications.

UNITARIAN UNIVERSALIST WOMEN'S FEDERATION
25 Beacon Street
Boston, MA 02108
(617) 742-2100

GOALS: to uphold and extend the philosophy of liberal religion and develop the potential of Unitarian Universalist women; to encourage involvement of women in denominational affairs and in action programs to benefit all women.

PROGRAMS: leadership training; consciousness-raising sessions; group discussions on issues like sex-role stereotyping, communication between generations, concerns of older women; community and legislative action in support of women's rights, including the ERA, reproductive freedom, educational and employment opportunities, quality child care; seed grants for regional conferences to develop the social involvement and personal potential of liberal church women; Clara Barton Camp for girls with diabetes; newsletter, publications, recordings, slide show about the girls' camp.

UNITED AUTO WORKERS WOMEN'S DEPARTMENT
8000 East Jefferson Avenue
Detroit, MI 48214
(313) 926-5237

GOALS: to increase participation of women members in the UAW at all levels and to promote awareness of job rights; to negotiate and monitor nondiscriminatory contracts and affirmative action; to develop educational programs and encourage union political action for equal rights.

PROGRAMS: assistance to local women's committees in planning programs and projects to stimulate union participation and community activity; workshops and conferences for regional women's committees; education and community action in cooperation with other UAW departments; lobbying, testimony at hearings, drafting of regulations and guidelines for equal rights laws.

UNITED CHURCH OF CHRIST
ADVISORY COMMITTEE ON WOMEN AND SOCIETY
297 Park Avenue South
New York, NY 10010
(212) 475-2121

GOALS: to use effectively human resources within the UCC, both paid and volunteer; to sound out women's positions in seminaries and theological education programs; to better understand family life, especially human sexuality; to support UCC Conference Task Forces and Women's Fellowships (more than thirty-nine diverse groups which suggest policy and action on women's issues).

PROGRAMS: committee has no programmatic funds, so works through other agencies of the UCC on issues like affirmative action, gay liberation, new attitudes toward male sexuality, lay leadership, human sexuality, ERA, health care, abortion, civil liberties for gays and bisexuals; quarterly newsletter.

UNITED METHODIST CHURCH
COMMISSION ON THE STATUS AND ROLE OF WOMEN
1200 Davis Street
Evanston, IL 60201
(312) 869-7330

GOALS: to ensure full participation of women in the United Methodist Church in policy-making, program development, lay leadership and employment as staff professionals.

PROGRAMS: task forces on theological education for women, varying life-styles, minority women, development of women's potential as lay leaders, employment on church staffs, information and research on discriminatory policies and practices; joint task force on sexism and racism; leadership development through talent banks and regional training events; consultation among ordained women to develop increased visibility, recognition and use of their talents in the church; communications network for regional women's units; district task forces on local church issues of concern to women.

UNITED METHODIST CHURCH
WOMEN'S DIVISION
BOARD OF GLOBAL MINISTRIES
475 Riverside Drive
New York, NY 10027
(212) 678-6084

GOALS: to strengthen the Women's Division as an autonomous, visible group in the mission program of the church; to help Methodist women become full participants in the worldwide struggle for justice through creative organized action; to eliminate racism in the Women's Division.
PROGRAMS: support of the ERA, abortion rights, human rights for people in all nations, and a just international economic order; media monitoring project on sex-role stereotypes; testimony at hearings on abortion and other issues; national assembly and seminars to develop program priorities; newsletter; publications; audiovisual materials; resource catalog.

UNITED NATIONS BRANCH FOR THE ADVANCEMENT OF WOMEN
United Nations, Room DC 1033
New York, NY 10017
(212) 754-8447

GOALS: to eliminate discrimination against women; to help women participate more fully in the social, economic, political and civil affairs of their nations.
PROGRAMS: implementing World Plan of Action through reporting system of U.N. member states who provide updates on targets, priorities, and progress; Voluntary Fund for the Decade for Women helps to support needy women in developing nations; quarterly bulletin; publications.

UNITED NATIONS DECADE FOR WOMEN 1976–1985
Center for Social Development and Humanitarian Affairs
United Nations
New York, NY 10017
(212) 754-8432

GOALS: to implement the International Women's Year World Plan of Action promoting full participation by women in the economic, social and political life of all nations; to involve governments, organizations and individuals in programs to achieve the aims defined in the Plan.

PROGRAMS: suggests programs to governments, international bodies, organizations and institutions to promote equal rights and opportunities for women; recommends information and education activities including use of the media, publications, seminars for policy makers and other leaders, elimination of sex-role stereotypes from educational materials and teaching sex equality in the schools; Research and Training Institute, a clearinghouse of information, conducts studies on the conditions of women and coordinates research and training efforts for the advancement of women; UN Voluntary Fund for projects to help women in the less developed nations; integration of women in development planning, expanded technical assistance to benefit women in under-developed countries, and regional conferences and seminars to promote such action; conferences and seminars on the changing roles of women and men in modern society; newsletter; reports; brochure; publications.

UNITED PRESBYTERIAN CHURCH
COUNCIL ON WOMEN AND THE CHURCH
475 Riverside Drive
New York, NY 10027
(212) 870-2019

GOALS: to identify women's issues and to help set policy on the status of women within the Church and society.

PROGRAMS: studies on rape and battered women; participation in coalitions supporting the ERA and abortion; task forces on racism and sexism; monitoring Church-wide policies on women; publications.

WAGES FOR HOUSEWORK
P.O. Box 830
Brooklyn, NY 11202
(No phone)

GOALS: to secure adequate and regular wages for all women who work in the home.

PROGRAMS: public education on the contributions of homemakers and the need to compensate them for their work; coalition work with other women's organizations; public speaking; publications.

WIDER OPPORTUNITIES FOR WOMEN
1649 K Street N.W.
Washington, DC 20006
(202) 638-4868

GOALS: to provide equal access to jobs, career guidance, education, and training through employment services and public education.

PROGRAMS: Work Center offering advisory, support and referral service; Work Options program for low-income, unskilled women and women offenders; Technical Assistance to employers; formation of a national network for women's employment advocacy programs; Washington-based monitoring and advocacy on employment-related issues; publications.

WOMEN AGAINST VIOLENCE AGAINST WOMEN
1727 North Spring Street
Los Angeles, CA 90012
(213) 223-8771

GOALS: to end the gratuitous use of images of physical and sexual violence against women by the mass media; to stop actual violence caused by media violence through public education, consciousness raising, and mass consumer action; to stop the glorification of victimization.

PROGRAMS: letter-writing campaigns; boycotting Warner/Elektra/Atlantic records because of particularly offensive record jackets; actions vary with the particular chapter—some have done in-store education, others have distributed leaflets; slide program on the use of images of violence and victimization as gimmicks and what women can do to change this; newsletters.

WOMEN AGAINST VIOLENCE IN PORNOGRAPHY AND MEDIA
P.O. Box 14614   AND   P.O. Box 3059
San Francisco, CA 94114   Grand Central Station
(415) 552-2709   New York, NY 10017

GOALS: to educate the public about the destructive consequences of violence and hatred of women expressed in pornography and other media; to oppose linking violence with sexual stimulation or pleasure; to create a public climate in which media violence toward women is not accepted or tolerated.

PROGRAMS: public information and education, including a slide show, antipornography display, library, literature packet and newsletter; communications network, including a hotline to report media portrayals of abuse of women; monitoring of trends in pornography; organizing women around the issue of pornography and abuse, including the first national feminist conference on pornography; meeting with owners of pornography stores and theaters, producers of record covers with images of violence, publishers of newspapers that devote considerable space to advertising pornographic movies, and officials who issue permits to shows and stores that sell pornography.

WOMEN EDUCATORS
P.O. Box 218
Red Bank, NJ 07701
(201) 671-1344

GOALS: to promote equality of opportunity for women in educational research at all levels; to eliminate sex bias in educational research.

PROGRAMS: develops guidelines to counteract prevalent bias in research methodology that distorts perception of women's abilities and to eliminate sexist language in research publications; develops instructional materials for teacher educators to increase awareness of sexist stereotypes in educational methods and research findings; surveys patterns in research and development for inequities encountered by women educators; newsletter with information on research-grant funds and job opportunities; lobbying for ERA.

WOMEN FOR ENVIRONMENTAL HEALTH
% Environmental Protection Agency
1525 18th Street
Washington, DC 20036
(202) 833-1484

GOALS: to help promote a healthy environment; to serve as a voice on issues which reaffirm women's concerns with environmental health.

PROGRAMS: Pesticide in Breast Milk Project (education and conference); project on women, work, and occupational health; lobbying for a Cosmetics Act requiring proper identification of products; promoting women in environmental protection; investigating PCB, the chemical contaminant implicated in birth defects; *Directory of Women Involved in Environmental Issues;* action alerts.

WOMEN FOR RACIAL AND ECONOMIC EQUALITY
266 West 23rd Street
New York, NY 10011
(212) 242-2366

GOALS: to end race and sex discrimination in hiring, pay and promotion practices; to support quality integrated public education and federally funded comprehensive child care and national health insurance; to promote disarmament, peace and solidarity with women in all countries.

PROGRAMS: legislative action, lobbying on equal employment, education, day care and health issues; community education and action campaigns; research projects; Women's Bill of Rights; brochures, newspaper.

WOMEN FOR SOBRIETY
P.O. Box 618
Quakertown, PA 18951
(215) 536-8026

GOALS: to establish self-help groups for women alcoholics and problem drinkers;

to establish a national support network of former alcoholics; to help addicted women create a positive self-image.

PROGRAMS: organizes local self-help groups for women confronting the problems of alcoholism; monthly newsletter; pamphlets; publications.

WOMEN IN COMMUNITY SERVICE
1730 Rhode Island Avenue N.W.
Washington, DC 20036
(202) 293-1343

GOALS: to help young women from poor, culturally disadvantaged families break out of poverty by enrolling in the Federal Job Corps program which offers basic remedial education, job skills training, and preparation for adult responsibilities; to offer encouragement and support services to young women after training, as well as to others who do not join the Job Corps.

PROGRAMS: recruitment and screening of young women from poor communities throughout the country for the Job Corps by trained volunteers from five national women's organizations in the WICS coalition; orientation sessions and field trips to prepare new enrollees for life at Job Corps centers; support services for Corps graduates include referrals to employment sources or additional training programs, job placement, help with budget planning, housing, health care, legal problems, and personal matters; referral services for other young women in poor communities to training or vocational rehabilitation programs and to social-service agencies.

WOMEN IN THE ARTS FOUNDATION
435 Broome Street
New York, NY 10013
(212) 966-5894

GOALS: to overcome discrimination against women artists and to work for just representation for women in the art world.

PROGRAMS: in-house gallery; actions against museums and galleries that discriminate against women artists; seminars; liaison with museums, galleries, and collectors; slide registry; publications.

WOMEN INVOLVED IN FARM ECONOMICS
P.O. Box 172
Crook, CO 80726
(No phone)

GOALS: to raise produce prices to protect family farmers.
PROGRAMS: local organizing; newsletter.

WOMEN LIBRARY WORKERS
P.O. Box 9052
Berkeley, CA 94709
(No phone)

GOALS: to change the existing power structure in library work and end discrimination against women in salaries, status, and employment opportunities; to unite professional librarians and support staff in opposition to discriminatory practices.

PROGRAMS: collective action by local chapters for equal opportunities in hiring and promotion, equal pay and benefits for women library workers on all job levels; local job counseling and résumé-writing workshops; conferences for chapter representatives to exchange ideas and plan action programs; information, assistance with strategy planning, and funding support provided for local action; work for changes in library school curricula to include recognition of women's contributions to the field; special programs at national and state library association conferences; work with the American Library Association Committee on the Status of Women in Librarianship; directory of feminist librarians; newsletter.

WOMEN OF ALL RED NATIONS
% Lorelei Means
General Delivery
Porcupine, SD 57779
(No phone)

% Indian Treaty Office
777 United Nations Plaza
New York, NY 10017
(212) 986-6000

% American Indian Treaty Council Information Center
870 Market Street
San Francisco, CA 94102
(415) 434-4917

GOALS: to further the work of the Native American movement and to provide a voice for Native American women.
PROGRAMS: establishing local chapters to work on issues of concern, including sterilization abuse and women's health, treaty and fishing rights, political prisoners, community education, family, legal and juvenile justice problems; publication.

WOMEN ON WORDS AND IMAGES
P.O. Box 2163
Princeton, NJ 08540
(609) 921-8653

GOALS: to develop guidelines for nonsexist educational and vocational materials.
PROGRAMS: research and consultation in the area of sex-role socialization; content analysis of various media; workshops; slides; publications.

WOMEN STRIKE FOR PEACE
145 South 13th Street
Philadelphia, PA 19107
(215) 923-0861

AND

120 Maryland Avenue N.E.
Washington, DC 20002
(202) 546-7397

GOALS: to end the armaments race and press for disarmament with effective international controls; to work for fulfillment of human needs and a peaceful, healthful future for the world's children.

PROGRAMS: billboard campaign in major cities to alert public about dangers of the nuclear arms race; special campaign against the neutron bomb, including petitions, demonstrations, and meetings of delegations with key government officials; legislative action, including monthly alerts to members on disarmament and other peace issues, human rights and civil liberties, international relations; public education and action campaign on the environmental and health hazards of radioactive fallout from materials used in increasing numbers of nuclear power facilities and from disposal of radioactive waste; newsletter; publications.

WOMEN'S ACTION ALLIANCE
370 Lexington Avenue
New York, NY 10017
(212) 532-8330

GOALS: to work for full equality for all persons regardless of sex; to educate the public on feminist issues; to assist, support, and sponsor feminist programs, issues, and actions.

PROGRAMS: Information Services provides information and referral on women's issues and programs; Technical Assistance for women's programs provides a proposal critiquing service, how-to workshops on fund-raising and communications, and referral to sources of program development and internal management; National Women's Agenda Project, developed and staffed by the Alliance, provides a vehicle for communication and action through a coalition of national women's organizations and women's caucuses of national organizations; Non-Sexist Child Development Project works to integrate nonsexist education into all early childhood programs and to provide the necessary resources; conferences and publications.

WOMEN'S ACTION ALLIANCE
NON-SEXIST CHILD DEVELOPMENT PROJECT
370 Lexington Avenue
New York, NY 10017
(212) 532-8330

GOALS: to integrate nonsexist education into all early childhood programs and to provide the necessary resources.

PROGRAMS: provides in-service teacher training and parent education programs, nonsexist curriculum and audiovisual aids, classroom materials and toys; conferences and publications.

WOMEN'S CAMPAIGN FUND
1521 New Hampshire Avenue N.W.
Washington, DC 20036
(202) 547-0444

GOALS: to provide bipartisan support to progressive and capable women running for political office.

PROGRAMS: helping progressive women leaders win elections; finding professional campaign advisers; fund-raising.

Women's Caucus, see: ASSOCIATION FOR VOLUNTARY STERILIZATION; GAY RIGHTS NATIONAL LOBBY

WOMEN'S CAUCUS FOR ART
59 Castle Howard Court
Princeton, NJ 08540
(609) 921-3480

GOALS: to improve the position of women in art professions.

PROGRAMS: national exhibitions; women's studies guides; research conferences; coalition work among women artists; job referral service; publications.

Women's Division, see: DEMOCRATIC NATIONAL COMMITTEE; UNITED METHODIST CHURCH

WOMEN'S ECUMENICAL CONSULTING GROUP
475 Riverside Drive
New York, NY 10027
(212) 870-2061

GOALS: sponsored and staffed by Church Women United and the Division of Church and Society of the National Council of Churches, this group is a vehicle for women from different denominations to come together to share resources, knowledge, and develop analyses and strategies which can be adopted at the denominational level.

PROGRAMS: initiates programs like the Religious Committee for the ERA and the Working Group on IWY, which are carried out by the appropriate church agency; prepares papers; brings together women from different religious and cultural traditions to discuss issues of mutual concern.

WOMEN'S EDUCATIONAL EQUITY COMMUNICATIONS NETWORK
Far West Laboratory
1855 Folsom Street
San Francisco, CA 94103
(415) 565-3032

GOALS: to provide greater access to information on research, activities, and grass-roots projects that explore the development of sex-role stereotypes and improve educational equity.

PROGRAMS: information service collects, stores, classifies, and provides research on educational equity; communications service facilitates contact between individuals, groups and agencies; publications.

WOMEN'S EQUITY ACTION LEAGUE
805 15th Street N.W.
Washington, DC 20005
(202) 638-4560

GOALS: to work for equal participation of women in society; to improve the social, economic, and legal status of women through education, legislation, and litigation.

PROGRAMS: develops public policy strategies in credit, insurance, education, health, social security; filing discrimination complaints against employers; advocates ratification of the ERA; alerts members to changes in laws which affect their lives; prepares kits for members' use in filing sex discrimination complaints; conducts research on enforcement of existing legislation related to education and economic status of women; newsletter.

WOMEN'S EQUITY ACTION LEAGUE FUND
805 15th Street N.W.
Washington, DC 20005
(202) 638-4560

GOALS: to secure the legal and economic rights of women, particularly in higher education.

PROGRAMS: offers support in paying legal costs for selected cases of sex discrimination brought against educational institutions; monitors enforcement of laws protecting the rights of women in education and employment; clearinghouse of information in these areas, including information kits about laws and regulations; research studies, primarily on patterns of discrimination and the status of women students, faculty members and administrators in higher education; publications.

WOMEN'S EQUITY ACTION LEAGUE FUND
SPRINT
805 15th Street N.W.
Washington, DC 20005
(202) 638-1961; (800) 424-5162

GOALS: to bring about sexual equality in sports.
PROGRAMS: clearinghouse for information on equality for women and girls in sports; coalition work; speakers' bureau; referrals; quarterly tabloid.

WOMEN'S HALL OF FAME
P.O. Box 335
Seneca Falls, NY 13148
(315) 568-8060

GOALS: to provide a permanent place of honor, a national museum, for America's women of outstanding achievement in all fields.
PROGRAMS: election of women past and present to the Hall of Fame by a panel of authorities representing different fields, specialties and geographical areas; nominations are submitted to the panel by the public, national organizations, newspaper and magazine editors.

WOMEN'S INFORMATION SERVICES NETWORK
P.O. Box 31625
San Francisco, CA 94131
(No phone)

GOALS: to facilitate information exchange among women's information services; to identify common needs and work together on projects which meet these needs.
PROGRAMS: compiling a directory of women's information services nationally; annual meeting.

WOMEN'S INSTITUTE FOR FREEDOM OF THE PRESS
3306 Ross Place N.W.
Washington, DC 20008
(202) 966-7783

GOALS: to conduct and publish research on how the nation's communications system could be expanded to enable people to speak for themselves rather than be portrayed to the public by others; to enable women to work together to contribute to the restructuring of the communications system, based on the principles of equality.
PROGRAMS: *Media Report to Women* (monthly periodical); a yearly annotated and cumulative index of *Media Reports; Directory of Feminist Media;* five-year, 1972–76, *Annotated Index to Media Reports; Women in Media: A Documentary Sourcebook.*

WOMEN'S INTERNATIONAL LEAGUE FOR PEACE AND FREEDOM
1213 Race Street
Philadelphia, PA 19107
(215) 563-7110

GOALS: to unite women in all countries who are opposed to war, exploitation and oppression; to work for universal disarmament and for the solution of conflicts through human solidarity, by worldwide conciliation and arbitration; and the establishment of social, political, and economic justice for all, regardless of race, sex, class or creed.

PROGRAMS: information on disarmament, economic priorities, and the dangers of nuclear energy; peace education curriculum; news bulletins and lobbying on peace and education issues; publications.

WOMEN'S LAW FUND
620 Keith Building
1621 Euclid Avenue
Cleveland, OH 44115
(216) 621-3443

GOALS: to support precedent-setting litigation in sex discrimination cases.
PROGRAMS: provides legal assistance for selected cases brought by women charging sex discrimination in employment, education (student and teacher rights), housing, voting rights, unemployment insurance, pregnancy disability and other health and welfare benefits; training program for Ohio University Law School students.

WOMEN'S LAW PROJECT
112 South 16th Street
Philadelphia, PA 19102
(215) 564-6280

GOALS: to end sex discrimination through litigation and public education.
PROGRAMS: legal services in cases involving sex discrimination; research and education of the public about women's rights and the law; publications.

Women's Occupational Health Resource Center, see: AMERICAN HEALTH FOUNDATION

WOMEN'S ORDINATION CONFERENCE
34 Monica Street
Rochester, NY 14619
(716) 436-6910

GOALS: to ordain women in the Catholic Church; to renew the priesthood.
PROGRAMS: Project Priesthood identifies women who want to be ordained; conferences; publications; newsletter.

WOMEN'S PRISON ASSOCIATION
110 Second Avenue
New York, NY 10003
(212) 674-1163

GOALS: to provide services for female offenders and ex-offenders.
PROGRAMS: Education and Awareness Project gives advice and information to

groups and individuals nationwide to develop programs to aid female offenders; publications.

Women's Project, see: CENTER OF CONCERN

WOMEN'S RABBINIC ALLIANCE
% Hebrew Union College
40 West 68th Street
New York, NY 10023
(212) 873-0200

GOALS: to provide women rabbinic students and rabbis with a support group, a political alliance, and a forum for exchange of ideas; to establish a formal liaison between Hebrew Union College and Reconstructionist Rabbinical College, both liberal rabbinical colleges.
PROGRAMS: monthly meetings, yearly retreat, information on issues which directly affect women rabbis; bibliographies.

WOMEN'S RESOURCE NETWORK
4025 Chestnut Street
Philadelphia, PA 19104
(215) 387-0420

GOALS: to reduce the incidence of wife abuse; to encourage the development of resources which support battered women.
PROGRAMS: training mental health personnel, law enforcement officers, and volunteers to work with abused women; counseling by phone, one on one, and in support groups; providing "expert witness" for abused women in difficulty with the law; counseling abusers; speakers' bureau; publications.

Women's Rights Committee, see: AMERICAN FEDERATION OF
    TEACHERS

Women's Rights Program, see: CENTER FOR CONSTITUTIONAL RIGHTS

Women's Rights Project, see: AMERICAN CVIL LIBERTIES UNION

WOMEN'S SPORTS FOUNDATION
195 Moulton Street
San Francisco, CA 94125
(415) 563-6266

GOALS: to encourage the participation of women in sports and the expansion of sports programs, facilities and training opportunities; to educate women and the general public about the value of sports for health and personal development.
PROGRAMS: organization of local Women's Sports Associations for women involved in local sports programs; workshops, seminars and clinics for coaches,

athletes and interested women to improve skills and techniques; motivational seminars on sports and fitness for businesswomen; information and resource center on sports programs, camps, scholarships, print and audiovisual materials; camp scholarships for promising young female athletes; magazine; publications.

WORKING WOMEN—NATIONAL ASSOCIATION OF OFFICE WORKERS
1258 Euclid Avenue
Cleveland, OH 44115
(216) 566-8511

GOALS: to gain equality in employment; to help organize new working women's groups throughout the country; to provide resources, training and technical assistance for leaders and staff of new groups; to focus national attention on the concerns of working women and influence public attitudes about these issues.

PROGRAMS: training for organizers and leaders of new working women's groups, offering on-site observation and learning of skills from established organizations; regional field organizers provide assistance to new groups; regional campaigns on enforcement of equal employment opportunity laws include monitoring of enforcement agencies, and campaigns to improve practices in major industries; local surveys of work forces and disclosure of results to antidiscrimination agencies; local campaigns targeting offending employers; promotion and coordination of local and national media coverage of working women's issues; technical assistance resource kits for starting new groups and mounting antidiscrimination campaigns; newsletter; documentary film on women office workers. (For a list of local affiliates, see Sex-Typing of Occupations subject entry.)

WORKING WOMEN UNITED INSTITUTE
593 Park Avenue
New York, NY 10021
(212) 838-4420

GOALS: to further the goals of equal employment opportunity, decent working conditions, and full involvement of women in decisions that affect their working lives; currently concerned with the issue of sexual harassment on the job.
PROGRAMS: legal project provides information on sexual harassment cases; information service provides information, referral, and speakers on sexual harassment; intervention project counsels victims of sexual harassment; publications, newsletter.

YOUNG WOMEN'S CHRISTIAN ASSOCIATION
NATIONAL BOARD
600 Lexington Avenue
New York, NY 10022
(212) 753-4700

GOALS: to help women and girls fulfill their individual potential and become citizens contributing to their communities; to help teenage women and Third World women become empowered to direct their own lives; to work toward the elimination of racism; to help women increase their decision-making capabilities.

PROGRAMS: Executive Management Development Program for women in the YWCA, including corporate management, executive and administrative training, advanced training in financial management, personnel administration and communications, on-site consultations, executive internships; national communications network to help women share in employment created by local public works projects; post-mastectomy rehabilitation project; pilot programs initiated by local groups; publications; newsletter.

YOUNG WOMEN'S CHRISTIAN ASSOCIATION
NATIONAL BOARD
ENCORE
600 Lexington Avenue
New York, NY 10022
(212) 753-4700

GOALS: to provide Encouragement, Normalcy, Counseling, Opportunities, Reaching out and Energies revived to post-mastectomy patients; more than 90,000 American women have had breast surgery; the National Board of the YWCA has trained more than 200 instructors nationwide to teach ENCORE at the local level in order to help women feel whole again.

PROGRAMS: ninety-minute weekly sessions divided into floor exercises, pool exercises and class discussion; the exercises strengthen chest muscles so that women can rebuild functionality and flexibility and the discussions give women an opportunity to express and to share their experiences.

THE YOUTH PROJECT
1555 Connecticut Avenue N.W.
Washington, DC 20036
(202) 483-0030

GOALS: to support and encourage the organization of grass-roots citizen action groups, governed and staffed by young people; to identify and develop young community leaders and equip them with skills and resources.

PROGRAMS: provides seed grants and technical assistance to women's, minority and low-income groups formed to deal with the local problems of working women, occupational safety, community economic development, environmental protection; acts as intermediary to channel grants from funding sources to community action programs developed by young people; sponsors training programs for young community leaders; regional offices in Washington, DC (East), Atlanta, GA (South), and San Francisco, CA (West) are contact points for local groups seeking funds or technical assistance; publications.

ZONTA INTERNATIONAL
59 East Van Buren Street
Chicago, IL 60605
(312) 939-3850

GOALS: to encourage high ethical standards in business and the professions; to improve the legal, political, economic, and professional status of women; to work for peace through a world fellowship of executive women in business and the professions.

PROGRAMS: Amelia Earhart Fellowship Awards to women for advanced study in aerospace sciences and engineering; Colombia Urban Slum Project provides health and education services to those living in slums of Colombian cities; consultative status with the United Nations; community service projects by member clubs; publications for members.

GOVERNMENT OFFICES

ALCOHOL, DRUG ABUSE, MENTAL HEALTH AGENCY
WOMEN'S COUNCIL
9000 Rockville Pike
Building 36
Bethesda, MD 20014
(301) 496-5670

Represents interests of women workers in the Agency as well as working on alcohol, drug abuse, and mental health issues involving women.

AGENCY FOR INTERNATIONAL DEVELOPMENT
OFFICE OF WOMEN IN DEVELOPMENT
State Department
Washington, DC 20523
(202) 632-3992

Research and publications on women and development.

DAY CARE SERVICES DIVISION
OFFICE OF CHILD DEVELOPMENT
P.O. Box 1182
Washington, DC 20013
(202) 755-7420

Supports and develops standards for day-care services.

EQUAL EMPLOYMENT OPPORTUNITY COMMISSION
2401 E Street N.W.
Washington, DC 20506
(202) 634-6700

Enforces Title VII and the Equal Pay Act.

FEDERAL PARENT LOCATOR SERVICE
  OFFICE OF CHILD SUPPORT ENFORCEMENT
  Department of Health, Education and Welfare
  Washington, DC 20201
  (202) 245-8717

Provides assistance to states in enforcing child support rulings.

FEDERAL WOMEN'S PROGRAM
  CIVIL SERVICE COMMISSION
  1900 E Street N.W., Room 7540
  Washington, DC 20415
  (202) 632-7082

Represents women employees of the federal government as well as women's issues within each department.

NATIONAL ADVISORY COUNCIL ON WOMEN'S EDUCATIONAL
    PROGRAMS
  1832 M Street N.W.
  Washington, DC 20036
  (202) 653-5848

Oversees Women's Educational Equity Act.

NATIONAL INSTITUTE ON DRUG ABUSE
  PROGRAM FOR WOMEN'S CONCERNS
  5600 Fisher's Lane
  Rockville, MD 20852
  (301) 443-3693

Identification of and research into women's drug problems.

NATIONAL CLEARINGHOUSE FOR ALCOHOL INFORMATION
  WOMEN'S PROGRAM
  P.O. Box 2345
  Rockville, MD 20852
  (301) 282-4450

Develops and distributes materials on the woman alcoholic in an effort to increase public awareness.

OFFICE FOR CIVIL RIGHTS
  Department of Health, Education and Welfare
  Washington, DC 20201
  (202) 245-6404

Enforces Title IX.

OFFICE OF FEDERAL CONTRACT COMPLIANCE
Employment Standards Administration
Department of Labor
Washington, DC 20210
(202) 523-9475

Enforces affirmative action requirements of Executive Order 11246/11375.

OFFICE FOR HANDICAPPED INDIVIDUALS
Department of Health, Education and Welfare
Washington, DC 20201
(202) 245-1961

Provides information and services to the handicapped.

OFFICE OF MINORITY BUSINESS ENTERPRISE
Department of Commerce
Washington, DC 20230
(202) 377-5713

Coordinates government and private programs for minorities in business.

OFFICE OF WOMEN IN BUSINESS
Small Business Administration
Washington, DC 20416
(202) 653-6407

Coordinates government programs for women business owners.

WOMEN'S BUREAU
Office of the Secretary
Department of Labor
Washington, DC 20210
(202) 523-6653

Major source of statistics and information on women workers.

Index